VARIETIES OF MONETARY REFORMS:
Lessons and Experiences on the Road to Monetary Union

VARIETIES OF MONETARY REFORMS:
Lessons and Experiences on the
Road to Monetary Union

Edited by

Pierre L. Siklos
Wilfrid Laurier University
Waterloo, Ontario

Kluwer Academic Publishers
Boston/Dordrecht/London

Distributors for North America:
Kluwer Academic Publishers
101 Philip Drive
Assinippi Park
Norwell, Massachusetts 02061 USA

Distributors for all other countries:
Kluwer Academic Publishers Group
Distribution Centre
Post Office Box 322
3300 AH Dordrecht, THE NETHERLANDS

Library of Congress Cataloging-in-Publication Data

Varieties of monetary reforms: lessons and experiences on the road to monetary union/ edited by Pierre L. Siklos.

    p. cm.
    Includes bibliographical references and index.
    ISBN 0-7923-9474-7

       1. Monetary policy--Europe--Case studies--Congresses. 2. Monetary policy--United States--Congresses. 3. Monetary unions--Europe--Congresses. 4. Banks and banking, Central--Europe--Congresses. 5. Federal reserve banks--Congresses. 6. Foreign exchange rates--Congresses. I. Siklos, Pierre L., 1955- .
HG930.5.V37   1994
332.4'6--dc20   94-13036
                                   CIP

CONTENTS

CHAPTER	PART I - SURVEYS	PAGE
1	"Varieties of Monetary Reforms" *Pierre L. Siklos*	1
2	"Optimal Currency Areas: A Fresh Look at the Traditional Criteria" *Paul R. Masson, Mark P. Taylor*	23

PART II - EXCHANGE RATE MANAGEMENT

3	"Exchange Rate Pegging as a Disinflation Strategy: Evidence from the European Monetary System" *Richard C.K. Burdekin, Jilleen R. Westbrook, Thomas D. Willett*	45
4	"How Much to Commit to an Exchange Rate Rule: Balancing Credibility and Flexibility" *Alex Cukierman, Miguel A. Kiguel, Nissan Liviatan*	73

PART III - CENTRAL BANK INDEPENDENCE

5	"Central Bank Dependence and Inflation Performance: An Exploratory Data Analysis" *Forrest H. Capie, Terrence C. Mills, Geoffrey E. Wood*	95
6	"Political Effects on Central Bank Behaviour: Some International Evidence" *David R. Johnson, Pierre L. Siklos*	133
7	"Reputation, Central Bank Independence and the ECB" *Michele Fratianni, Haizhou Huang*	165
8	"An Institutional Analysis of the Proposed European Central Bank with Comparisons to the U.S. Federal Reserve System" *Nathaniel Beck*	193

CONTENTS

PART IV - COUNTRY STUDIES

9   "Monetary Union and Monetary Policy: A
       Review of the German Monetary Union"   219
       Jürgen von Hagen

10   "Designing a Central Bank in a Federal
       System: The Deutsche Bundesbank, 1957-
       1992"   247
       Susanne Lohmann

11   "Rules, Discretion, and Central Bank
       Independence: The German Experience,
       1880-1989"   279
       Bernhard Eschweiler, Michael D. Bordo

12   "The Origins of the Monetary Union in the
       United States"
       Arthur J. Rolnick, Bruce D. Smith, Warren 323
       E. Weber

13   "On the Coyne-Rasminsky Directive and
       Responsibility for Monetary Policy in
       Canada"   351
       Thomas K. Rymes

14   "Crippled Monetary Policy in Transforming
       Economies: Why   Central   Bank
       Independence Does Not Restore Control"   367
       István Ábel, John P. Bonin, Pierre L. Siklos

       INDEX   556

CONTRIBUTORS (in alphabetical order)

István Abel
Budapest Bank Rt.
Budapest V., Alkotmány u.3.
Postacim: 1852,
Hungary

Nathaniel Beck
Department of Political Science
University of California, San Diego
La Jolla, California
USA   92093

John P. Bonin
Department of Economics
Wesleyan University
Middletown, CT
USA   06459

Michael D. Bordo
Department of Economics
Rutgers University
New Brunswick, NJ
USA   08903

Richard C. K. Burdekin
Claremont McKenna College
850 Columbia Avenue
Claremont, California
USA   91711

Forrest H. Capie
City University Business School
Department of Banking and Finance
Frobisher Crescent, Barbican Centre
London, United Kingdom   EC2Y 8HB

Alex Cukierman
Department of Economics
Tel Aviv University
Ramat Aviv, P.O.B. 39040
69978 Tel Aviv, Isreal

Bernhard Eschweiler
Head of Economic Reserach
J.P. Morgan GmbH
Mainzerlandstr. 46, 6000 Frankfurt,
Germany

Michele Fratianni
Indiana University
Graduate School of Business
Bloomington, IN
USA   47405

Haizhou Huang
Indiana University,
Graduate School of Business
Bloomington, IN
USA   47405

David R. Johnson
Department of Economics
Wilfrid Laurier University
Waterloo, Ontario
Canada   N2L 3C5

Miguel A. Kiguel
The World Bank
1818 H Street N.W.
Washington, D.C.
USA   20433

Nissan Liviatan
The World Bank
1818 H Street N.W.
Washington, D.C.
USA   20483

Susanne Lohmann
Department of Political Science
University of California, Los Angeles
Los Angeles, California
USA   94305-5015

Paul R. Masson
Research Department
International Monetary Fund
Washington, D.C.
USA   20431

Terrence C. Mills
Dean of the School of Economic Studies
The University of Hull
Hull,
United Kingdom   HU6 7RX

Arthur J. Rolnick
Research Department
Federal Reserve Bank of Minneapolis
250 Marquette Avenue
Minneapolis, Minnesota
USA   55401-0291

Thomas K. Rymes
Department of Economics
Carleton University
1125 Colonel By Drive
Ottawa, Ontario
Canada   K1S 5B6

Pierre L. Siklos
Department of Economics
Wilfrid Laurier University
Waterloo, Ontario
Canada   N2L 3C5

Bruce D. Smith
Department of Economics
Cornell University
Ithaca, New York
USA   14850

Mark P. Taylor
Research Department
International Monetary Fund
Washington, D.C.
USA   20431

Jürgen von Hagen
Lehrstuhl für VWL VI
University of Mannheim
Seminargebäude A5 D-6800,
Mannheim 1   Germany

Warren W. Weber
Research Department
Federal Reserve Bank of Minneapolis
250 Marquette Avenue
Minneapolis, Minnesota
USA   55401-0291

Jilleen R. Westbrook
Department of Economics
Temple University
Philadelphia, Pennsylvania
USA   19122

Thomas D. Willett
Horton Professor of Economics
Claremont Graduate School
and Claremont-McKenna College
500 E. 9th Street
Claremont, California
USA   91711

Geoffrey E. Wood
City University Business School
Department of Banking and Finance
Frobisher Crescent
Barbican Centre
London
United Kingdon   EC2Y 8HB

REFEREES

Peter Bernholz	University of Basel
Michael D. Bordo	Rutgers University
John F. Boschen	The College of William and Mary
Richard C. K. Burdekin	Claremont Graduate School
Pierre Fortin	Université du Québec á Montréal
Rik W. Hafer	Southern Illinois University at Edwardsville
Edouard Hochreiter	Austrian National Bank
Carl-Ludwig Holtfrerich	Freie Universität Berlin
David R. Johnson	Wilfrid Laurier University
Miguel A. Kiguel	World Bank
Leroy D. Laney	First Hawaiian Bank
Susanne Lohmann	University of California, Los Angeles
Thomas K. Rymes	Carleton University
Pierre Siklos	Wilfrid Laurier University
Jürgen von Hagen	University of Mannheim
Carl E. Walsh	University of California, Santa Cruz
Steven B. Webb	World Bank
Thomas D. WIllett	Claremont Graduate School
Mark E. Wohar	University of Nebraska at Omaha

PREFACE

The idea to edit a volume on monetary reforms began when I was a visiting scholar at the University of California, San Diego in 1991. Kluwer's editor at the time, Mr. David McConnell, suggested that the imminent arrival of Europe 1992 as well as negotiations over what would be called the Maastricht Treaty might make it interesting to compile a book about central bank independence. I was reluctant to edit a book on such a topic because so many had already dealt with the issue from several perspectives but also because I felt that such an approach would disguise the fact that experiences with monetary reforms were varied and not restricted solely to questions about central bank independence the subject of so much discussion stemming from plans for a European Central Bank. As a result, I suggested that a book dealing with varieties of monetary reforms would bring a fresh perspective amid the plethora of separate volumes about monetary union, exchange rate arrangements and optimum currency areas. Hence the title for this volume. I was also determined, however, to attract case studies to buttress some of the theoretical and applied arguments also presented in this volume. The reason is that case studies offer the opportunity to consider the historical and institutional aspects of the menu of monetary reforms available to policy makers. Second, individual country studies reveal that policy constraints also differ across countries and hence help explain the variety of monetary reforms. I only hope that the right "mix" of papers was generated.

Many of the papers in this volume were presented at two Conferences during the course of 1992. A special Economic Inquiry session was organized at the Western Economic Association International (WEIA) Conference in San Francisco in July 1992. A second Conference on the Political Economy of Global Monetary Stabilization at the Claremont Graduate School in October 1992. I owe special thanks to Tom Willett and the staff at the Claremont Graduate School who were responsible for organizing the wonderful Claremont Conference. Tom also had a hand in organizing the WEIA session. I am also grateful to the discussants at the two conferences as well as the referees who were kind enough to provide me with comments which ultimately improved every paper contained in this volume.

The time necessary to edit the volume and comment on every paper would not have been possible without grants from the Research Office of Wilfrid Laurier University as well as the Vice-President Academic's Academic Development Fund which provided me with the release time during the Fall of 1992 to complete much of the editing for this volume and to write my own contributions to the volume. Cindi Wieg as well as Elsie Grogan and the word processing staff ensured that communications with all the authors went on smoothly and efficiently as well as helping process my own manuscripts.

Finally, of course, I owe a great deal of thanks to all the authors and co-authors who agreed to contribute to the volume and who completed their tasks more or less on time. The collection of authors in this volume includes many distinguished academics and they all contributed to enlighten me about monetary reforms. I only hope the reader comes away feeling the same way.

Pierre L. Siklos
Waterloo, Ontario
April 1994

VARIETIES OF MONETARY REFORMS:
Lessons and Experiences on the Road to Monetary Union

CHAPTER 1

VARIETIES OF MONETARY REFORMS[1]

Pierre L. Siklos

1. INTRODUCTION

Inspiration for the title of this volume can be traced to the country studies published in 1970 under the title Varieties of Monetary Experience, edited by David Meiselman. In that collection of essays the focus was strictly about the role of monetary aggregates on various aspects of business cycle behaviour but, primarily, their influence on the price level. Few now dispute the notion that "money matters". Instead, those in the profession who study monetary policy have concentrated on issues surrounding the **design** of monetary policy. It has thus been accepted, for good or ill, that intervention by the monetary authorities and politicians will take place and that, if some socially appropriate objective is to be pursued, zero inflation is one such goal which comes to mind, institutions should be so designed as to maximize the likelihood that the stated goals can be attained. Thus the title of this volume suggests that a debate still exists about varieties of monetary reforms and their comparative advantage under different situations.

2. TYPES OF MONETARY REFORMS

The last few years seem to have inspired economists to refine old proposals for macroeconomic reforms or to develop new ones. Many of these have been focused on reforms aimed at controlling inflation via changes in the relationship between central banks and politicians though, of course, fiscal reforms have not been

[1] Support from Wilfrid Laurier University in the form of a Book preparation grant, a course remission grant, and the Academic Development Fund is gratefully acknowledged. Comments on a previous draft by Richard Burdekin and Tom Willett were very helpful.

entirely ignored.[2] These have culminated with the various proposals for the European dream of monetary union which was given further impetus, despite some setbacks, by the Maastricht Treaty of 1991 and the advent of the single European market on January 1, 1993.

An entirely different set of reforms, toward achieving market liberalization, have been proposed in the wake of the demise of the former Communist bloc. The relevant proposals are more microeconomic in nature[3] though their macroeconomic consequences are significant.

The objectives of this introduction is to briefly outline what has been learned over the last few years in three areas of economic reforms with monetary consequences. These are, not in any order of importance, the selection of an exchange rate regime, central bank independence, and optimal currency areas or currency unions.

The list of issues considered probably does not need much justification. The choice of an exchange rate regime has consequences for domestic inflation and domestic policy independence in the pursuit of chosen macroeconomic objectives. Indeed, under a monetarist interpretation, a fixed exchange rate regime is akin to a monetary union. Central bank independence potentially also has inflationary consequences as well as externalities for overall domestic economic policies. Thus, if central banks have a common objective the end result is practically as economically effective as a monetary union.[4] Finally, currency unions present an extreme version of a fixed exchange regime depending on the mechanics and structure of such a union. Therefore, exploration of each of the three questions considered so far provide lessons on the road to a possible European monetary union.

---

[2]   Thus, any successful stabilization following a hyperinflation must be accompanied by an end to unsustainable fiscal deficits. For a survey of hyperinflation, see Siklos (1990)and Végh (1992). For a review of pre-twentieth century evidence, see Burdekin and Langdana (1992, chapter 3).

[3]   See, for example, the collection of articles in European Economy (1991). It should be pointed out that reforms aimed at freeing markets were also much discussed during the 1980s especially when economic conditions in Latin and South American countries generated much interest. See Dornbusch and Edwards (1991), for example, though the literature here is vast.

[4]   Though without an effective monetary union members may find it easier to opt out from time to time as domestic considerations require. The behaviour of several countries during the post-World War I version of the Gold Standard is a case in point.

It is important to recognize, however, that there are unmistakable political ramifications for each of the issues just listed, the most important being the loss of sovereignty under a monetary union. For this reason any purely economic analysis must be complemented with knowledge accumulated from the political economy literature.

Finally, as has been demonstrated all too often, the lessons of history are easily dismissed, ignored, or incorrectly learned. Thus, in what follows I also rely on historical precedents or experiences with monetary reforms.[5]

3.   CHOOSING AN EXCHANGE RATE REGIME

In the Mundell (1963)-Flemming (1962) approach, a purely flexible exchange rate can isolate the domestic economy from foreign monetary shocks. By contrast, a strictly fixed exchange rate regime implies that the inflation rate of the country (or countries) to which the exchange rate is fixed will be imported. In practice, of course, actual exchange rate regimes have lied somewhere between the two extremes.[6]

However, if one distinguishes between aggregate demand and supply shocks, the former induced by government policies while the latter is a reflection of the real side of economic activity, an entirely different picture emerges. Eichengreen (1992a, 1992b; see also references within) finds instead that monetary policy can be more effective under a fixed exchange rate system provided it is consistent with such a rate. As a result, the debate about the relative merits of fixed versus flexible exchange rates continues unabated.[7]

The world has experienced a variety of exchange rate regimes from the Bretton Woods system[8], designed as a type of fixed exchange rate regime with a narrow band within which exchange rates could fluctuate, to a period of managed

---

[5] I draw here first upon the excellent survey by Bordo (1986) though much new relevant material has appeared since the publication of his article.

[6] The adoption of a currency union would, as in the case of an eventual adoption of the ECU or European Currency unit, represent a strict fixed exchange rate regime. We consider this possibility in section 5 below.

[7] For simplicity, the discussion distinguishes between the two extreme exchange rate regimes even though much research has lately focused on the intermediate case of exchange rate target zone (see Svensson 1992 for a survey).

[8] See Bordo (1992) for an historical overview of Bretton Woods and Swoboda (1991) for an assessment.

floating following the demise of Bretton Woods in 1971. Meanwhile, several European countries participate in a hitherto fixed exchange rate regime called EMS or European Monetary System. The variety of exchange rate regimes through time, as well as within a particular episode of monetary history, suggests recurrence of fixed and flexible exchange rate regimes.[9] An exchange rate regime is tried and, when deemed unsuccessful, the regime is transformed into some alternative. But, how is success measured and to whom is it successful? If success is measured by the volatility[10] of selected economic variables then the evidence is mixed. Barone-Adesi and Yeung (1990) find that flexible exchange rates mean less output volatility in industrialized countries. Baxter and Stockman (1989) find, however, few systematic differences between fixed and flexible exchange rates for a variety of aggregates including output and trade flows.[11]

If, instead, success is measured in terms of mean levels of economic variables then the matter is more controversial. Several authors, notably Swoboda (1991) and Dornbusch (1992), point out that a currency is a strong symbol of nationhood. Perusal of European newspapers in 1992, for example, makes it quite clear how, politicians at least, are attached to their home currencies. In addition to attachment to a particular currency there is, from time to time, strong attachment to the value of a currency, again largely for political reasons. This was true in the U.S., Japan (Frankel (1990), Volcker and Gyohten (1992)), as well as in Canada during 1988 and 1986 when the dollar hit record lows against the U.S. dollar. Perhaps it is puzzling then that many European politicians insist on a monetary union to the exclusion of the alternative of permitting flexible exchange rates between member countries. For while real variables such as output were relatively more stable and grew more rapidly during the adjustable peg of Bretton Woods, an exchange rate regime broadly comparable to the EMS, monetary policies of the members did not show strong tendencies to converge (Bordo 1992). Thus, as Feldstein (1992) and Bean (1992) contend, we return to the view that the issue is predominantly a political one.

---

[9] Indeed, Giovannini (1991) suggests that there is a good reason for an almost cyclical like behaviour in the choice of exchange rate regimes.

[10] There exist a variety of ways in which volatility can be measured but, at present, the model based measure called ARCH, which stands for autoregressive conditional heteroskedasticity, or some of its variants, appear most popular. See, for example, Bollerslev, Chon, and Kroner (1992) for a survey of this literature. Rather than assume that volatility is some average of the standard deviation of a time series, ARCH arises out of the behaviour of the errors generated by a particular econometric model.

[11] Both studies do conclude, however, that exchange rate volatility is greater under flexible than under fixed exchange rates.

Thus, a common currency is a reflection of the desire for a common political goal.[12]

These views are to be contrasted with others which emphasize the need for a common currency to enforce a common discipline enforced by the country with the best record in the area of monetary policy. Related to this position is the notion that while a common currency as an exchange rate instrument is desirable it needs to be phased in until convergence is achieved. Indeed, the Maastricht Treaty has detailed provisions for achieving convergence, that is, uniformity in inflation, interest rates and budget deficits (de Grauwe 1992).[13] Why such conditions are important is unclear, except as a means of ensuring commitment to a common monetary policy or to placate a "dominant" partner in a monetary union. The historical record of Bretton Woods suggests that relatively better convergence was achieved during this period than at practically any time during 20th century monetary history (Bordo 1992), and Swoboda 1991). This despite greater differences in institutions and economic structures than is the case today. The premise that both the uncertainty of any formal monetary union as well as the current structure of the European Monetary System could produce more economic instability and, consequently, a greater likelihood of exchange rate realignments in the future (Froot and Rogoff 1991) predated the withdrawal of Italy and the U.K. from the Exchange Rate Mechanism (ERM) in September 1992. But, as noted above, the choice of one arrangement over another may simply reflect the dominant political considerations of the time. Policymakers attempt to devise a regime which will produce some desirable objective but build in a sufficient number of escape clauses that may make the system not only complex but eventually one doomed to failure.[14]

The foregoing considerations lead us to the crux of the matter, namely that an important element in the choice of an exchange rate regime involves a desire by some group or groups to achieve credibility of purpose. Credibility can be defined in many ways but the most general definition perhaps comes from Cukierman (1986, p. 6) who refers to credibility as

---

[12] Siklos (1993) suggests that a similar argument may hold for the Soviet Union of the 1920s.

[13] For example, member states will be permitted a maximum of 1.5% above the mean three lowest inflation rates countries; long-term government bond yields to be 2% above the mean three lowest rates; government budget deficit must be maintained at levels up to 3% of GDP, while gross public sector debt cannot exceed 60% of GDP; finally, no exchange rate realignment for at least two years.

[14] This kind of behaviour is not new as Bordo and Kydland's (1992) model of the Gold Standard period reveals.

"... the extent to which the public believes that a shift in policy has taken place when, indeed, such a shift has actually occurred."

Unfortunately, as Dornbusch (1988) argued, economists have no adequate theory of credibility. This problem is particularly noticeable in the literature on hyperinflations whose end is often signalled by a return to fixed exchange rates as part of a package of monetary and fiscal reforms (see Siklos (1990) and Végh (1992) for surveys). The need for credibility, as defined above, is great under these circumstances but there is disagreement in the literature about which ingredients, or combination of ingredients, are necessary to end high inflation. At one end of the spectrum is Sargent (1986, ch. 4) who believes that central bank autonomy and a sustainable budget constraint are necessary and sufficient conditions. Alternatively, there is the broader historical perspective which suggests that Sargent's conditions are necessary but not sufficient ones [Siklos (1993a), and Webb (1989), for example].

Returning to the issue of exchange rate regimes, the problem of credibility is at the center of the continuing debate about the credibility of the European Monetary System which pegs European exchange rates in fairly narrow bands (Weber (1991), and references therein). Thus, in the parlance of economic analysts, it became clear by the Spring of 1992 that the fundamental inconsistency between German fiscal and monetary policies and those of the U.K. and Italy in particular could not continue unless either Germany would sacrifice its domestic commitment to high interest rates or else the U.K., in particular, had to accept higher interest rates in the midst of a recession. In practice, domestic policy concerns appeared to dominate over pre-announced commitments to the ERM which is reminiscent of the pressures on the U.S. which hastened the end of Bretton Woods (Volcker and Gyohten 1992).

The credibility question is at also the heart of all three varieties of monetary reforms covered in this volume. But nowhere is this more highlighted than in the problems and questions surrounding the question of central bank independence, to which I now turn.

4.   CENTRAL BANK INDEPENDENCE

The inflation of the 1970s and early 1980s, together with the experiences of financial liberalization world-wide, have combined to bring out the pivotal role of central banks in the economy and, perhaps more importantly, their relationship with elected governments. Paralleling these developments has been the renaissance of the literature on political business cycles which lay moribund for several years in the wake of the rational expectations revolution. The latter seemed to put to rest the possibility that a regularly exploitable Philipps curve type trade-off could exist. However, it is now apparent by both the weight of theoretical arguments and the empirical evidence that economically motivated central governments can occasionally succeed in influencing economic outcomes to better their chances for reelection.

Theoretical advances include the argument that since there is an information asymmetry between voters and policymakers, the former group has difficulty distinguishing between, say, temporary from permanent effects of government spending on debt (Cukierman-Meltzer 1986, Rogoff-Siebert 1988, Rogoff 1987). In consequence, elections matter even if voters behave rationally.[15] A competing explanation suggests that politicians and their parties are ideologically motivated with distinct preferences about inflation versus unemployment goals. Proponents of rational partisan cycles argue that politically-influenced business cycles arise because while voters know (or believe they know) where politicians stand in terms of their preferences for certain types of economic policies there is uncertainty over election outcomes (see Alesina and Sachs 1988, and Havrilesky 1990).

The list of recent empirical studies in this literature has grown so quickly and has become so large that a list of references would be inadequate. However, Alesina (1988) provides a general survey centered on U.S. studies. More recent U.S. studies are cited in Siklos (1992). Cargill and Hutchinson (1991) provide a list of references for works which have used data other than from the U.S.

Typically neglected in this literature has been the role of the central bank. This is partly due to the focus of such studies on the belief that politicians are able to manipulate the instruments of macroeconomic policy to improve their electoral prospects or in response to the preferences of their own party. Nevertheless, while politicians may control the instruments of fiscal policy it is the central bank which is responsible for monetary policy.[16] Since central banks differ widely across countries in the degree of statutory independence (Fair (1980), and Cukierman (1992)) the role played by a central bank independence has once again become paramount.

With few exceptions (see Johnson and Siklos (1992), for a survey), the literature consists of indexes of central bank independence generated via a weighting scheme which assigns points according to the degree to which provisions in central

---

[15] Some authors have instead proposed that policy makers are satisficers so that they attempt to influence economic outcomes only when they are unfavourable. These are the so-called satisficing models of political business cycles (Davidson, Fratianni and von Hagen 1992, and references therein).

[16] There is, of course, linkage between fiscal and monetary policies. Nevertheless, the two can be sufficiently distinct to call into the question the assumption that the role of the central bank can be completely ignored. Hamburger and Zwick (1981), Parkin (1986), Havrilesky (1988), and Burdekin and Wohar (1990) all make this point with empirical evidence.

bank legislation provide independence of action to central bank authorities.[17]

Table 1 provides a selective list of six such central bank independence index style rankings. The only agreement in these rankings is for Germany, the U.S., Switzerland, and Japan. Otherwise, the same legislation gives rise to considerable variation in the rankings of other industrialized countries. It is also noteworthy that several countries appear to have equally independent central banks despite large differences in their legislation. For example, Japan and Canada are ranked as equally independent in the Burdekin-Willett ranking despite considerable differences in the legislation governing the two countries' central banks. While Cukierman, Webb and Neyapti (1992) rank each central bank differently it is not known whether the differences are meaningful in some statistical sense. Apart from this problem, there are two other glaring discrepancies in the rankings. Japan ranks high (independent) on some lists but is statutorily dependent. Austria, constitutionally one of the most independent of central banks, typically ranks low (dependent), except in the Cukierman, Webb, and Neyapti (1992) and Burdekin and Willett (1991) rankings (see also Cukierman 1992).

At best, the rankings are interesting and suggestive. At worst, they may overstate the degree of independence because the literature seems to imply that formal independence translates into substantive independence which, of course, need not be the case, as Mayer (1976) and Cargill (1989, 1992) have pointed out. Indirect support at a more formal econometric level for the rankings produced via qualitative comparisons of central banks does, however, exist (Demopoulos, et. al. (1987), and Burdekin and Wohar (1990)). Existing studies also appear to place a significant portion of the weight of actual inflation on central bank performance. Yet inflation is driven by fiscal policy as well as aggregate supply shocks over which central banks have little control. However, while it may be argued that more independent central banks also face less fiscal pressure (i.e., are less likely to monetize the debt (Parkin (1986) and Burdekin and Laney (1988)) the ability and ease with which governments can borrow from abroad reduces the importance of this constraint on the fiscal side in government-central bank relations. In addition, examination of central bank legislation suggests that the maintenance of economic growth or the reduction of unemployment is at least as important, if not more important, a task for central banks to accomplish as is the maintenance of price stability. This aspect of the question is not entirely ignored in the relevant literature. Finally, there is the question of the exchange rate regime countries operate under. If inflation is the variable supposedly under the control of the central bank then the concept of independence loses a considerable amount of significance when exchange rates are fixed. The top-left panel of Figure 1 plots average inflation rate for 17 OECD

---

[17] There exists, however, a literature in which single equation reaction functions for central banks are estimated. See, for example, Banaian, Laney and Willett (1983) or Burdekin and Laney (1988).

Table 1

Indexes of Central Bank Independence

Country	Cukierman et al. 0 = Least Ind. 1 = Most Ind.	Grilli et al. Econ. Independence 7 = Most Ind. 0 = Least Ind.	Parkin and Bade 4 = Most Ind. 1 = Least Ind.	Epstein and Schor 3 = Most Ind. 1 = Least Ind.	Burdekin and Willett 3 = Most Ind. 1 = Least Ind.
Switzerland	.64	7	4	NR	3
Germany	.66	7	4	3	3
Austria	.57	6	NR	NR	2
U.S.	.51	7	3	2	2
Denmark	.47	5	2	NR	NR
Canada	.46	7	2	1	1
Ireland	.45	4	NR	NR	NR
Netherlands	.42	4	2	1	1
U.K.	.32	5	2	1.5	1
Australia	.30	6	1	NR	1
France	.28	5	2	1	1
New Zealand	.26	3	1	NR	1
Sweden	.26	NR	2	NR	1
Italy	.25	1	½	1	1
Belgium	.19	6	2	1	1
Japan	.18	5	3	1	1
Norway	.14	NR	NR	NR	NR

Rankings are Cukierman, Webb and Neyapti (1992), Grilli, Masciandaro and Tabellini (1990), Parkin (1986), Epstein and Schor (1986), and Burdekin and Willett (1991). NR means not ranked.

countries during the fixed exchange rate period (generally 1960 to 1971) against the index of independence proposed by Cukierman, Webb, and Neyapti (1992; see also Cukierman 1992).[18] The scatter plot shows no obvious link between independence and inflation.[19] The top-right panel shows the same relationship for the flexible exchange rate period. Here there is a more discernible relationship such that more independent central banks (a higher value for the index) are associated with lower inflation rates.

---

[18] Their index is chosen because it is the only one which has a ranking for the 17 countries considered as well as because it assigns a distinct value for the index for each central bank in the sample.

[19] A simple regression for the two series confirms this result. After writing this paper I became aware of Eichengreen (1992b) who conducts a similar analysis in this context.

Figure 1
Inflation, Unemployment, Central Bank Independence
and the Exchange Rate Regime

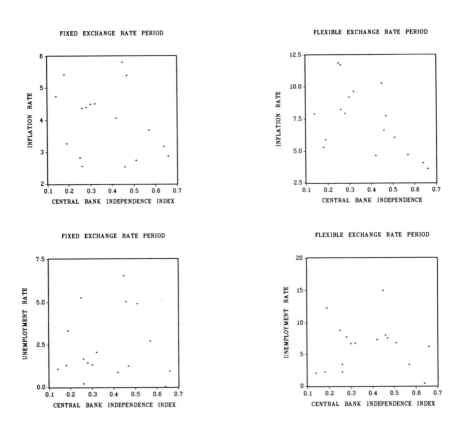

Source: Quarterly data were used and are from Johnson and Siklos (1992) and are
            for the period 1960-1990. Index of central bank independence is that of
            Cukierman, Webb, and Neyapti (1992). Johnson and Siklos (in this
            volume) provide the details about dating each exchange rate regime as
            well as the definitions for inflation and unemployment.

However, the relationship is weak (but statistically significant).[20] Thus, even during a period when central banks supposedly are able to conduct an independent monetary policy, statutory independence, while no doubt a helpful condition for attaining low inflation, does not constitute a sufficient correlation. If, instead, we plot the unemployment rate against a measure of central bank independence the latter has even less predictive power as an explanatory variable for either exchange rate regime.[21]

Notice, however, that both inflation and unemployment rates are substantially higher, on average, during the flexible period than under the fixed exchange rate portion of the sample. While a variety of factors explain this result the persistently high values for both series has raised the issue of credibility at a time when policy-makers are touting low inflation - high growth objectives. At a general level, many authors (Dornbusch (1992), Woolley (1991)) have noted the need for credibility to be built upon an institutional foundation, requiring domestic political structures and conditions to ensure that a particular policy be carried out and that it be believed by the public.

At the political level, regular elections can possibly serve as a sufficient enforcement mechanism to generate credible outcomes (see, for example, Alesina 1988) though the weight of the evidence on political business cycles suggests that this is a highly unlikely outcome. At the economic level, the problem of credibility must be squared against the now well-known problem of time inconsistency. Put simply, policy-makers are tempted to manipulate, say, the short-term economic trade-off between inflation and unemployment in the full knowledge that monetary policy is neutral in the long-run (Barro and Gordon (1983a, 1983b), Kydland and Prescott (1977), and Blackburn and Christensen (1989) for a survey). Implicit in this view is the idea that the central bank is politically motivated. Recently, however, attention has focused on how to design monetary policy such that independence is guaranteed through a "conservative" central banker, that is, someone who would respond to higher expected inflation by raising short-term interest rates, or is rewarded somehow when achieving specific inflation targets as in New Zealand, but where sufficient flexibility is built-in to enable central bank independence to be suspended for certain contingencies such as oil price or other aggregate supply type shocks (Lohmann (1992) and Walsh (1992)).[22]

---

[20] The relevant regression produces a statistically significant coefficient for the index. The fit as measured by the adjusted R^2 is only 0.23.

[21] The relationship is statistically insignificant for both exchange rate regimes.

[22] Put differently, the fundamental problem is the design of a central bank with enough discretion to prevent elected governments from entirely abdicating their responsibilities for the ultmate effects of economic policies. Since this is a condition

Regardless of the type of contract there is also the issue of the structure and responsibility of a central bank. Clearly, if all central banks have similar contracts for their Presidents or Governors and countries are agreed that low or even zero inflation are desirable objectives, then why not have just one central bank? Apart, of course, from the political considerations, aired persistently throughout the ratification process of the Maastricht Treaty, economists have proposed currency or unions as a third variety of monetary reform which I now consider.

5.   CURRENCY UNIONS

Under this heading are generally two types of arrangements. Individual countries within the currency union can retain their respective currencies while adopting a fixed exchange rate with a central or dominant currency (such as the Bundesbank in Europe). The exchange rate could be guaranteed by a currency board (see Schwartz (1992) for a survey) which would issue domestic currency convertible into the currency at the center of the fixed exchange rate arrangement at a fixed rate. Reserves would fully back the domestic currency and there would be no room for individual currencies under such an arrangement to engage in discretionary policies. Alternatively, countries can join together into currency unions by adopting a single currency, as in the proposals embedded in the Maastricht Treaty of European monetary union (EMU).[23]

No matter what route is taken toward greater monetary integration economists have, over many years now, analyzed the preconditions necessary for the successful adoption of currency unions. Beginning with Mundell's (1960) seminal work, this area of research has given rise to a literature on so-called optimum

---

which is likely to be difficult to attain, to say the least, why not simply abolish central banks and permit free banking? This is a serious option entertained by money economists but a discussion of the arguments for or against such a view would take us too far afield.

[23]   Also commonly known as EMU or European Monetary Union. Under the Treaty Stage One, as it is called, European Community (EC) members agree to convergence criteria intended to reduce fiscal and inflationary discrepancies of member states. Stage Two is set to begin in 1994 with the Establishment of the European Monetary Institute (EMI). The purpose of the EMI is to facilitate the introduction of the European Currency Unit (ECU), monitor the EMS, and facilitate coordination of member states monetary policies. Stage Three marks the beginning of the ECU as the single currency and the establishment of the European Central Bank (ECB). This stage is set for the end of the century. See The European 16-19 July 1992 for the relevant text of the Maastricht Treaty.

currency areas. Since Masson and Taylor, in this volume, survey all the relevant issues there is no need to dwell on the essential points (see also Wihlborg and Willett 1992) except to point out some historical precedents not described in their article.[24]

A Currency union existed in the Austro-Hungarian monarchy of the 19th and early 20th centuries. Only the Austrian crown circulated[25] and, with the central bank and the political authority both in Vienna, the monetary system was operated for the benefit of Austria. The lack of concern over balancing the fiscal and monetary needs of the member states is but one of the factors, along with of course World War I, which helps explain the eventual dismemberment of the monarchy and the resulting monetary chaos vividly described most recently by Dornbusch (1992; see also Siklos (1992) for the Hungarian experience). Since it is arguably the case that modern-day European countries face significant differences in their economic state, together with the often expressed concern that a European Central Bank (ECB) would essentially operate for the benefit of the Bundesbank, read Germany, historical precedents are not without some lessons. This perhaps suggests why so much discussion is taking place not only about where the ECB should be located but also whether EMU should be a "two-speed" process with only those economies which have converged by some date forming a monetary union with the remainder joining at some later stage.

Monetary union on a smaller scale than the Austro-Hungarian example also took place in 19th century Germany (Holtfrerich 1991). A customs union among the German states (or Zollverein) in 1834 predates monetary union achieved in the period 1871-76. As Holtfrerich explains, standardization of the coinage (following a treaty in 1837) also predates monetary union. However, coins were minted in many different states. The modern-day equivalent would be the currency board suggestion outlined earlier which would permit several currencies rigidly fixed to one currency. The final lesson from the German experience is that the more rules there are spelling out the operation of a currency union, especially as regards monetary policy, the greater the guarantee that some commonly desired goals, such as price stability, will be attained. In a sense then the convergence requirements as well as the draft statutes of the ECB fulfill these functions. What remains unclear, however, about the lessons from the German experience is the degree of economic integration achieved by the formerly independent German states during this period prior to monetary unification. By contrast, the dispersion in economic conditions across the EC states is well known. Forecasts and estimates given in Table 2 reveal that by 1993 inflation, budget deficit, and interest rate convergence was expected in a majority of current and future (expected) member states with only a few of those failing to meet the current criteria by the end of 1992 unlikely to do so even by the time Stage Three of EMU begins.

---

[24] See Graboyes (1990a) for a list and description of historical experiences with monetary unions.

[25] Although roubles and German marks also circulated in Poland.

While the data in Table 2 are impressive, German reunification and the Bundesbank's monetary policy rendered these predictions far to optimistic. In any event, a more problematical issue is the lack of convergence in income levels -- even though convergence in income growth is fairly well advanced, at least for the eight countries chosen. Presumably, however, it is convergence in the former which is the desirable goal otherwise there is no incentive for the relatively poorer members to sacrifice independence in monetary policies by joining in EMU (Casella (1992) provides a theoretical justification for this view). Hence, the demands by the poorest EC members for a fund which amounts to transfer payments from the richest to the poorest members. This problem is one which supporters of EMU have trouble accepting and is a distinguishing characteristic of federal structures such as the U.S. or Canada (see Sachs and Sala-i-Martin 1991).[26] and the lessons from Federal structures need to be understood in the context of EMU. In other words, unless there is some mechanism for transfers from rich to poor and the accompanying political structure to accomplish such an objective it is difficult to see, based on the historical experience of Germany and others, how EMU can succeed at the macroeconomic level (see also Froot and Rogoff (1991) and Bayoumi and Eichengreen (1992)). Of course, it has been assumed that convergence is a desirable goal by itself. As Figure 1 reveals, however, the fixed exchange rate period, also known as the Bretton Woods period, produced superior macroeconomic performance at least for the countries sampled despite vast differences in the economic structures of these countries (see also Swoboda (1991) on this point). However, Bretton Woods was not a system in which exchange rates were irrevocably fixed, as required by EMU, which of necessity raises the issue of convergence (see also Giovannini 1991).

---

[26] Also see the arguments by M. Feldstein in The Economist (June 13, 1992) and the reply by four European economists in the July 4, 1992 issue of The Economist.

Figure 2
Convergence in Levels and Growth in Eight EC States*

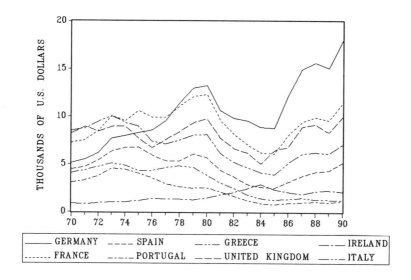

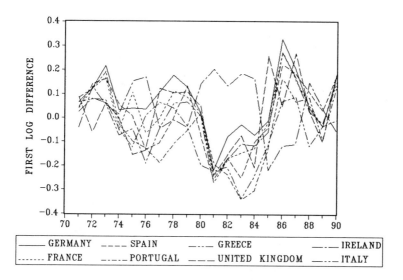

*   The top panel shows real per capita GDP converted into U.S. dollars. The bottom
     panel shows the rate of change in the levels. The data are from International
     Financial Statistics (Washington: International Monetary Fund).

Table 2

EMU Convergence Criteria: Some Estimates

Country	Convergence Criteria			
	Inflation[1]	Deficit	Debt	Interest Rate[1]
Maastricht Treaty	(*) 3.9	(*) 3.0	(*)60	(*)11.0
Belgium	2.4	5.2-fail[3]	106.1-fail[3]	8.64
Denmark	2.1	.2[3]	(*) 71.3-fail	9.47
France	2.4	1.4[2]	26.7[2]	8.60
Germany	4.1-fail	2.6[2]	26[2]	7.96
Greece	15.8-fail	13.8-fail[2]	(*) 114.8-fail	28.71-fail
Ireland	3.0	2.4[1]	(*) 100-fail	9.11
Italy	5.2-fail	10.2-fail[2]	(*)108.5-fail	10.10[2]
Luxembourg	3.1	-5.1[3,4]	3.2[3]	7.90
Netherlands	3.7	2.8[2]	62.3-fail[2]	8.10
Portugal	8.90-fail	(*)5.7-fail[1]	(*) 69.5-fail	15.38-fail
Spain	5.9-fail	2.2[4]	(*) 46	12.17-fail
Austria	4.1-fail	1.9	55.0	8.3
Finland	2.6	8.9-fail	37.0	12.4-fail
Norway	2.3	2.9	47.0	9.8
Sweden	2.3	8.9-fail	55.0	9.4
Switzerland	4.1-fail	1.8	55.0	9.4
United Kingdom	3.7	-.1[3]	(*) 35.9	9.15

Source: All data are from International Monetary Fund, *International Financial Statistics*(IFS). All data are annual and were latest available according to the October 1993 issue of IFS. Data marked (*) are from *World Economic Outlook* (May 1993), International Monetary Fund.Inflation is calculated as the annual proportional change in the Consumer Price Index (line 64). These may not be, strictly speaking, compararable across countries as required in the Maastricht Treaty. Deficit is line 80 in IFS, debt is calculated as lines 88+89. The deficit and debt levels are then divided by GDP estimates (line 99). The long-term interest rate is from line 61. Again, the data may not match actual (but incomplete) definitions to be used in the application of the Treaty.

Notes: 1. 1992, 2. 1991, 3. 1990, 4. A negative number means a surplus; *fail* means failure to pass Maastricht convergence criteria.

REFERENCES

Alesina, A., "Macroeconomics and Politics", in S. Fischer (ed.) *Macroeconomics Annual 1988* (Cambridge, Mass.: The MIT Press, 1988), pp. 13-51.

Alesina, A. and J. Sachs (1988), "Political Parties and the Business Cycle in the United States, 1948-1984", *Journal of Money, Credit and Banking* 20 (February): 63-82.

Alesina, A. and N. Roubini (1990), "Political Cycles: Evidence from OECD Countries", manuscript.

Bade, R. and M. Parkin (1985), "Central Bank Laws and Monetary Policy", unpublished.

Banaian, K., L. Laney, and T.D. Willett (1983), "Central Bank Independence: An International Comparison", Federal Reserve Bank of Dallas *Economic Review*, 1-13.

Barone-Adesi, G. and B. Yeung (1990), "Price Flexibility and Output Volatility: The Case for Flexible Exchange Rates", *Journal of International Money and Finance*, 9: 276-98.

Barro, R.J. and D.B. Gordon (1983a), "A Positive Theory of Monetary Policy in a Natural Rate Model", *Journal of Political Economy*, 91 (August): 589-610.

Barro, R.J. and D.B. Gordon (1983b), "Rules and Discretion and Regulation in a Model of Monetary Policy", *Journal of Monetary Economics*, 12 (January): 101-22.

Baxter, M. and Alan Stockman (1988), "Business Cycles and the Exchange Rate System: Some International Evidence", *Journal of Monetary Economics*, 23: 377-400.

Bayoumi, T. and B. Eichengreen (1992), "Shocking Aspects of European Monetary Unification", NBER working paper no. 3949 (January).

Bean, C.R. (1992), "Economic and Monetary Union in Europe", *Journal of Economic Perspectives*, 6 (Fall), 31-52.

Bernanke, B. and F.S. Mishkin (1992), "Central Bank Behavior and the Strategy of Monetary Policy: Observations from Six Industrialized Countries", NBER Macroeconomics Annual 1992 (forthcoming).

Blackburn, K. and M. Christensen (1989), "Monetary Policy and Policy Credibility", *Journal of Economic Literature*, 27 (March): 1-45.

Bollerslev, T., R.Y. Chon, and K.F. Kroner (1992), "ARCH Modeling in Finance: A Review of the Theory and Empirical Evidence," *Journal of Econometrics*, 52: 5-59.

Bordo, M.D. (1992), "The Bretton Woods International Monetary System: An Historical Overview" in M.D. Bordo and B. Eichengreen (Eds.), *A Retrospective on the Bretton Woods System* (Chicago: University of Chicago Press), pp. 3-98.

Bordo, M.D. (1986), "Explorations in Monetary History: A Survey of the Literature", *Explorations in Economic History*, 23: 339-415.

Bordo, M.D. and F.E. Kydland (1992), "The Gold Standard as a Rule"; Federal Reserve Bank of Cleveland working paper no. 9205 (March).

Burdekin, R.C.K. and F. Kangdama (1992), *Budget Deficits and Economic Performance* (Longon: Routledge).

Burdekin, R.C.K. and T.D. Willett (1991), "Central Bank Reform: The Federal Reserve in International Perspective", *Public Budgeting and Financial Management*, 3 (no. 3): 619-650.

Burdekin, R.C.D. and T.D. Willett (1990), "Central Bank Reform: The Federal Reserve in International Perspective", Claremont-McKenna College.

Burdekin, R.C.D. and M.E. Wohar (1990), "Monetary Institutions, Budget Deficits and Inflation: Empirical Results for Eight Countries", *European Journal of Political Economy*, 6: 531-51.

Burdekin, R.C.K., and L. Laney (1988), "Fiscal Policy and Central Bank Institutional Constraint", *Kyklos*, 4, 647-62.

Burdekin, R.C.K. (1988), "Interaction Between Central Bank Behaviour and Fiscal Policy: The U.S. Case", *Applied Economics*, 20 (January): 97-112.

Cargill, T.F. (1992), "The Bank of Japan and Federal Reserve: An Essay on Central Bank Independence", mimeo, University of Nevada, Reno.

Cargill, T.F., "Central Bank Independence and Regulatory Responsibilities: The Bank of Japan and the Federal Reserve", Solomon Brothers Center for the Study of Financial Institutions Monograph 1989-2.

Cargill, T.F. and M.M. Hutchinson (1991), "Political Business Cycles with Endogenous Election Timing: Evidence from Japan", *Review of Economics and Statistics*, 73 (Nov.): 733-39.

Casella, A. (1992), "Participation in a Currency Union", *American Economic Review*, 82 (September): 847-63.

Cukierman, A. (1992), *Central Bank Strategy, Credibility and Independence: Theory and Evidence* (Cambridge, Mass.: The MIT Press).

Cukierman, A. (1986), "Central Bank Behavior and Credibility: Some Recent Theoretical Developments", Federal Reserve Bank of St. Louis *Review* 68 (May): 5-17.

Cukierman, A., S.B. Webb, and B. Neyapti (1992), "Measuring the Independence of Central Banks and Its Effects on Policy Outcomes", *World Bank Economic Review*, 6 (no. 3): 353-98.

Cukierman, A. and A.H. Meltzer (1986), "A Theory of Ambiguity, Credibility and Inflation Under Discretion, and Asymmetric Information", *Econometrica* 53 (September): 1099-1128.

Davidson, L.S., M. Fratianni and J. von Hagen (1992), "Testing the Satisficing Version of the Political Business Cycle 1905-84", *Public Choice*, 73: 21-35.

Demopoulos, G.D., G.M. Katsimbris, and S.M. Miller (1987), "Monetary Policy and Central Bank Financing of Government Budget Deficits: A Cross-Country Comparison", *European Economic Review*, 31 (July): 1023-50.

de Grauwe (1992), "Inflation Convergence During the Transition to EMU", CEPR Discussion paper no. 658 (June).

Dornbusch, R. (1992), "Monetary Problems of Post-Communism: Lesson from the End of the Austro-Hungarian Empire", mimeo, MIT.

Dornbusch, Rudiger (1988), "Notes on Credibility and Stabilization" NBER no. 2790, December.

Dornbush, R. and S. Edwards (Eds.) (1991), *The Macroeconomics of Populism in Latin America* (Chicago: University of Chicago Press).

Eichengreen, B. (1992a), "Three Perspectives on the Bretton Woods System", in M.D. Bordo and B. Eichengreen (Eds.), *A Retrospective on the Bretton Woods System* (Chicago: University of Chicago Press), pp. 621-58.

Eichengreen, B. (1992b), "Should The Maastricht Treaty Be Saved?", working paper 1.10, Political Economy of European Integration Group.

Epstein, G.A. and J.B. Schor (1986), "The Political Economy of Central Banking", Harvard Institute of Economic Research, Discussion Paper 1281.

European Economy (1991), The Path of Reform in Central and Eastern Europe, Special Edition No. 2.

Fair, D.E. (1980), "Relations Between Government and Central Bank: A Survey of Twenty Countries", in *Appendices, Committee to Review the Function of Financial Institutions* (London: Her Majesty's Stationery Office).

Frankel, J.A. (1990), "The Making of Exchange Rate Policy in the 1980s", NBER working paper no. 3539 (December).

Frankel, J.A. and M. Goldstein (1991), "Monetary Policy in an Emerging European Economic and Monetary Union: Key Issues", *IMF Staff Papers*, 38 (June): 356-73.

Froot, K.A. and K. Rogoff (1991), "The EMS, The EMU, and the Transition to a Common Currency", NBER working paper no. 3684 (April), forthcoming in *NBER Macroeconomics Annual* 1991.

Giovannini, A. (1991), "The Currency Reform as the Last Stage of Economic and Monetary Union: Some Policy Questions", NBER working paper no. 3917 (November).

Goodhart, C. (1992), "The Draft Statute of the European System of Central Banks: A Commentary", LSE Financial Markets Group Special Paper no. 37.

Goodhart, C. (1989), "The Conduct of Monetary Policy", *Economic Journal*, 99 (June): 293-346.

Graboyes, R.F. (1990), "The EMU: Forerunners and Durability", *Economic Review*, Federal Reserve Bank of Richmond, 76 (July/August): 8-17.

Grilli, V., D. Masciandaro and G. Tabellini (1990), "Political and Monetary Institutions and Public Financial Policies in the Industrial Countries", *Economic Policy* (13): 342-392.

Hamburger, M.J. and B. Zwich (1981), "Deficits, Money and Inflation", *Journal of Monetary Economics* 7: 141-150.

Havrilisky, T. (1988), "Monetary Policy Signaling from the Administration to the Federal Reserve", *Journal of Money, Credit and Banking* 20 (February): 83-101.

Hibbs, D. (1977), "Political Parties and Macroeconomic Policy", *The American Political Science Review*, 71 (December): 1467-1487.

Holtfrerich, C.L. (1991), "The Monetary Unification Process in 19th-century Germany: Relevance and Lessons for Europe Today", in M. DeCecco and A. Giovannini (Eds.), *A European Central Bank? Perspectives on Monetary Unification after Ten Years of the EMS* (Cambridge: Cambridge University Press), pp. 216-43.

Johnson, D.R. and P.L. Siklos (1992), "Empirical Evidence on the Independence of Central Banks", mimeo, Wilfrid Laurier University.

Kydland, F.E. and E.C. Prescott (1977), "Rules Rather Discretion: The Inconsistency of Optimal Plans", *Journal of Political Economy*, 85 (June): 473-91.

Mayer, T. (1976), "Structure and Operations of the Federal Reserve System", in *Compendium of Papers Prepared for the Financial Institutions and the Nation's Economy Study*, Committee on Banking, Currency and Housing, 94th Congress, Second Session (Washington, D.C.-GPO).

Lohmann, S. (1992), "Optimal Commitment in Monetary Policy: Credibility versus Flexibility", *American Economic Review*, 82 (March): 273-86.

Mundell, R.A. (1961), "A Theory of Optimum Currency Areas", *American Economic Review*, 51 (September): 657-65.

Nordhaus, W. (1975), "The Political Business Cycle", *Review of Economic Studies*, 42: 169-90.

Parkin, M. (1986), "Domestic Monetary Institutions and Deficits", in J.M. Buchanan, C.K. Rowley and R. Tolkson (Eds.) *Deficits* (London: Basil Blackwell).

Rogoff, K. (1987), "Reputational Constraints on Monetary Policy", in K. Brunner and A.H. Meltzer (Eds.) *Carnegie - Rochester Conference Series on Public Policy*, vol. 24 (Amsterdam: North-Holland).

Rogoff, K. and A. Siebert (1988), "Equilibrium Political Business Cycles", *Review of Economic Studies*, 55 (January): 1-16.

Sachs, J. and X. Sala-i-Martin (1991), "Fiscal Policies and Optimum Currency Areas: Evidence form Europe and the United States", mimeo, Harvard University.

Sargent, T.J. (1986), *Rational Expectations and Inflation* (New York: Harper and Row).

Schwartz, A.J. (1992), "Currency Boards: Their Past, Present, and Possible Future Role", prepared for Carnegie-Rochester Conference Series on Public Policy.

Siklos, P.L. (1993), "Can There be a Currency Union Without Political Union? The Early Soviet Experience", unpublished Manuscript, Wilfrid Laurier University.

Siklos, P.L. (1993a), "Interpreting a Change in Monetary Regimes: A Reappraisal of the Hungarian Hyperinflation and Stabilization of the 1920s", in M.D. Bordo and F. Capie (Eds.) *Monetary Regimes Transformations* (Cambridge: Cambridge University Press), pp. 274-311.

Siklos, P.L. (1992), "Politics and U.S. Business Cycles: A Century of Evidence", *European Journal of Political Economy* (forthcoming).

Siklos, P.L. (1991), *War Finance, Hyperinflation and Stabilization in Hungary 1938-1948* (London and New York: Macmillan and St. Martin's Press).

Siklos, P.L. (1990), "Hyperinflations: Their Origins, Development, and Termination", *Journal of Economic Surveys*, 4: 225-48.

Svensson, L.O. (1992), "An Interpretation of Recent Research on Exchange Rate Target Zones", *Journal of Economic Perspectives*, 6 (Fall): 119-44.

Swoboda, A.K. (1991), "The Road to European Monetary Union: Lessons from the Bretton Woods Regime", Per Jacobsson Lecture (June 9).

Végh, C.A. (1992), "Stopping High Inflation: An Analytical Overview", *IMF Staff Papers*, 39 (September): pp. 626-95.

Volcker, P., and T. Gyohten (1992), *Changing Fortunes* (New York: Times Books).

Walsh, C.E. (1992), "Optimal Contracts for Central Bankers", mimeo, University of California, Santa Cruz.

Webb, S.B. (1989), *Hyperinflation and Stabilization in the Weimer Republic* (New York: Oxford University Press).

Weber, A. (1991), "EMS Credibility", *Economic Policy* (April): 58-102.

Wihlborg, C. and T. Willett (1992), "Optimum Currency Areas Revisited", in C. Wihlborg, M. Fratianni, and T.D. Willett (Eds.) *Financial Regulation and Monetary Arrangements After 1992* (Amsterdam: Elsevier).

Woolley, J.T. (1991), "1992, Capital, and the EMS: Policy Credibility and Political Institutions", mimeo, University of California, Santa Barbara.

CHAPTER 2

OPTIMAL CURRENCY AREAS: A FRESH LOOK AT THE TRADITIONAL CRITERIA[1]

Paul R. Masson
Mark P. Taylor

1. INTRODUCTION

In this paper we reconsider the traditional criteria which are usually advanced as the prerequisites of successful monetary unions or, indeed, as the defining characteristics of "optimum currency areas." Monetary, or exchange-rate unions, can be defined as areas within which exchange rates bear a permanently fixed relationship to each other. In the absence of capital controls, there can exist only one monetary policy in such areas.[2] In the limit, such areas of exchange stability might also involve the replacement of the currencies of member countries by a common currency, that is, the formation of a common currency area or currency union. The implications for monetary policy independence are however the same for monetary and currency unions, so the two will be treated together in what follows.[3] In this paper, some

[1] We are grateful to a number of our colleagues for comments, and especially to Charles Adams, Tamim Bayoumi, Morris Goldstein, Jocelyn Horne, Peter Isard, George Kopits, Donald J. Mathieson, Patrice Muller, Kent Osband, Pierre Siklos, Horst Ungerer, and Jürgen von Hagen. The views expressed in this paper are those of the authors and do not necessarily represent those of the International Monetary Fund.

[2] Corden (1972, p. 3) calls areas with ostensibly fixed exchange rates but without integration of economic policies, or a common pool of foreign exchange reserves, or a single central bank, "pseudo-exchange-rate unions," because they cannot ensure the permanence of the relationship among currencies.

[3] Allen (1976, p. 4), for instance, states: " ... in any monetary union either there must be a single currency, or, if there are several currencies, these currencies must be fully convertible, one into the other at immutably fixed exchange rates, creating effectively a single currency."

empirical evidence relevant to these criteria is presented for Canada, the United States, and for other currency unions where requisite data are available; the same measures are also calculated for European countries which are members of the European Monetary System (EMS).[4] Attempts to simulate macroeconomic models in order to analyze the nature of shocks facing economies are also surveyed.

The traditional criteria for a successful monetary union include factor mobility (Mundell, 1961)--labor, financial capital, and physical capital--the level of intra-union trade (McKinnon, 1963), the degree of industrial and portfolio diversification (Kenen, 1969), and the degree of wage and price flexibility.

2.   FACTOR MOBILITY

The superiority of monetary exchange over barter is enhanced by widening the domain over which any single currency can be utilized. Nevertheless, as Mundell (1961) pointed out in a pathbreaking article, there are reasons related to macroeconomic shocks that constrain the size of an optimal currency area. In particular, Mundell argued that unless factors of production--labor and capital--can freely move between regions, shifts in demand facing one region relative to another may lead to unemployment in the absence of flexibility of the nominal exchange rate.[5] If wages and prices are sticky, real exchange rate depreciation can only be accomplished through nominal exchange rate changes. However, depreciation would be ruled out if the two regions were part of a currency union. Therefore, the criterion that Mundell proposed for an "optimum currency area" was a country or region in which factor mobility was high.

2.1   Labor mobility

It is hard to obtain direct information on labor mobility. Barriers to migration may include formal immigration restrictions, social services or pensions that are not immediately available to migrants, and language or cultural differences. If employment were the only motive for migration, then mobility should narrow differences among unemployment rates.[6] Figure 1 presents data for the dispersion of unemployment rates across nine U.S. census regions and ten Canadian provinces. Despite absence of formal barriers to mobility, the dispersion of unemployment rates

---

[4] We include the U.K. and Italy in this grouping, given that their departure from the System is so recent.

[5] Clearly, wage and price flexibility makes exchange rate flexibility unnecessary. See Section V below.

[6] Eichengreen (1990a).

is large in Canada--over 3 percentage points, or about 1/3 of the mean unemployment rate.[7] In contrast, dispersion has averaged a little over 1 percent in the United States, or 1/5 of mean unemployment. Furthermore, deviations from the average by individual states or provinces exhibit persistence. In the United States, the Pacific Northwest region is consistently above the national average, while the West North Central region is consistently below.[8] In Canada, the Maritime provinces (Newfoundland, Nova Scotia, New Brunswick and Prince Edward Island) exhibit persistently higher unemployment, and Ontario, Manitoba, and Saskatchewan, generally lower unemployment. However, it is also the case that different regions have experienced a boom and a subsequent bust, leading their unemployment rates to dip below, and then rise substantially above, the national average.[9] Correspondingly, this would suggest that flows of population to and from these areas have on occasion been high.

In Europe, national unemployment rates exhibit greater dispersion than in either the United States or Canada, at least since 1979 (Figure 1).[10] The greater dispersion in the EC may to some extent be attributed to the fact that migration among EC countries is clearly less substantial than within either the United States or Canada. A study cited by Eichengreen (1990b, p. 9) concluded that mobility in the United States was roughly two to three times as high as mobility within European states, as measured by the proportion of the population that changed region of residence;[11] migration between European states is no doubt much lower still. Relatively low mobility of labor is thus a potential handicap for the EC as it progresses toward monetary union.

---

[7] To some extent this has reflected unemployment insurance provisions that have been more generous in the less prosperous provinces.

[8] The Pacific Northwest region consists of Alaska, Idaho, Montana, Oregon, Washington, and Wyoming. The West North Central region consists of Iowa, Kansas, Minnesota, Missouri, Nebraska, North Dakota, and South Dakota.

[9] Most notably, in the United States the West South Central region which consists of Arkansas, Louisiana, Oklahoma, and Texas, and (in Canada) Alberta, related to oil price increases.

[10] Estimates of dispersion of unemployment rates for German Länder however are similar to those for the 12 EC countries. See EC Commission (1990, p. 151)

[11]See also EC Commission (1990, p. 151).

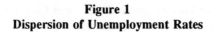

Figure 1
Dispersion of Unemployment Rates

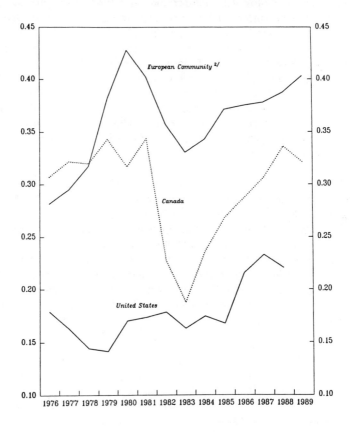

1.   Coefficient of variation, i.e. standard deviations of unemployment rates, scaled by the mean (components are weighted by population).

2.   12 current members, excluding Luxembourg, for which data were not available.

2.2   Capital mobility

When considering capital mobility, a distinction should be made between financial capital and physical capital. While expected rates of return on financial assets, such as bonds, tend to be equalized across countries, the same may not be true of expected returns on physical capital.[12] If a claim on physical capital in one country or region is not a perfect substitute for such claims in another country or region, then arbitrage need not ensure that their expected returns are the same. In fact, lack of such arbitrage may explain the observed close correlation of savings and investment in individual countries (Dooley, Frankel, and Mathieson, 1987).

For industrial countries without exchange controls, mobility of <u>financial</u> capital is generally thought to be very high. Countries participating in the Exchange Rate Mechanism of the EMS, for instance, abolished any remaining exchange controls by July 1990, the date fixed by the Delors Report for passage to Stage 1 of economic and monetary union (see Section VI below). High mobility of financial capital allows, in principle, for financing differences between national saving and investment. But if adjustment requires private sector investment, the issue of mobility of <u>physical</u> capital comes into play once again.

Mobility of physical capital is typically higher <u>within</u> than between countries, for a number of reasons: absence of exchange rate risk, uniformity of tax codes, similarity of regulations, common national characteristics (language, political goals, etc.). The well-known result of Feldstein and Horioka (1980)--which has been confirmed by others using alternative data sets and techniques--points to the high correlation between national saving and investment ratios as evidence of relatively low international capital mobility.[13] In contrast, Bayoumi and Rose (1991) find <u>no</u> correlation between regional saving and investment for Britain, suggesting perfect capital mobility. Identifying the separate effect of a common currency on capital mobility is difficult. However, some evidence is provided by saving/investment correlations of countries within the EMS, which are substantially lower than those of non-EMS countries; this suggests that exchange rate stability tends to enhance capital mobility (Bhandari and Mayer, 1990). Moreover, the liberalization of trade in goods and financial services associated with the EC 1992 program should work to increase capital mobility further.

---

[12] This is not to deny that equity prices (i.e., claims to physical capital) may vary in response to changes in the profitability of the capital stock; however, various lags and installation costs will make physical investment slow to adjust.

[13] Other reasons may explain this correlation, for instance deliberate government policy to limit current account imbalances, and shocks that have common effects on saving and investment.

Capital accumulation may in principle substitute for labor mobility in accommodating some demand shifts and income shocks. However, given the lags involved in the installation of plant and equipment, capital mobility is likely to be helpful mainly for narrowing persistent regional disparities rather than for offsetting short-term shocks. A case in point is Germany, where one of the objectives of currency union was to encourage the capital flows needed to modernize the east German economy, and thereby stem massive migration to the west of the country.

Even within countries, movements of physical capital are often insufficient to ensure development of depressed areas, as witnessed by the persistence of low relative per capita income in the south of Italy, the north of England, the maritime provinces of Canada, and West Virginia in the United States (see the discussion of convergence in Section V below). In a situation of regional specialization in goods which are no longer in high demand, there may not be incentives for productive investment. In these circumstances, labor and capital may both move out.[14] It is therefore doubtful that formation of a currency union can, in and of itself, lead to a sufficient mobility of physical capital either to cushion shocks completely or to lead to quick elimination of underdevelopment.

3.   OPENNESS AND REGIONAL INTERDEPENDENCE

Since one benefit of extending the use of a common currency is the reduction in transactions costs, the greater is the volume of inter-regional trade within a common currency area, the greater is the cost saving, other things equal, from the currency union. McKinnon (1963) also showed that the usefulness of exchange rate flexibility to achieve external balance, without inducing large internal price level changes, is greater when an economy is relatively closed. In order to maintain external balance in the face of a fall in the real demand for the country's exports, resources in a fully employed economy must be shifted toward production of traded goods and away from nontraded goods sectors. The smaller the nontraded goods sector the larger the exchange rate change needed to transfer a given amount of resources, and the larger the movement in internal prices that would result. Given the objective of price stability, therefore, very open economies (in the sense of having a relatively large tradeables sector) are good candidates for fixed exchange rates against their trading partners. This includes possibly joining with them in a currency union, provided that the policies of their neighbors are consistent with price stability.

A comparison of the degree of openness between countries inside and outside existing currency unions is hampered by a relative paucity of data on trade flows within currency unions. One can nevertheless examine the trade patterns of groups

---

[14] Fiscal incentives may however be put in place to encourage investment and/or discourage outward migration.

of countries, and calculate the proportion of their trade that is internal to the group. Some illustrative data are presented in Table 1. It can be seen that the twelve EC countries, taken as a group, have a high proportion of internal, relative to external trade--as do the ten present participants of the Exchange Rate Mechanism of the EMS. Moreover, while all individual EC economies have a high degree of openness, the European Community as a whole is relatively closed to the rest of the world--with about the same ratio of external trade to GDP as the United States or Japan. On this criterion, the EC would seem to have the makings of natural common currency area.

Other European countries (for instance members of EFTA) also have close trading ties with EC countries, suggesting that even a wider currency area might be desirable. The importance of trade with EC countries no doubt is a primary reason for the explicit policy of "shadowing" of the deutsche mark by Austria, and of recent decisions by Norway, Sweden, and Finland to peg their currencies to the ECU. In the future, trade flows between Eastern European countries and the EC may also expand, raising the possibility of closer monetary integration.

Within the United States and Canada, states and provinces no doubt have a large amount of trade among themselves. One effect of currency union is to encourage integration. Looking at the two countries together, the United States and Canada also have a large proportion of bilateral trade, and this proportion may well increase as the Free Trade Agreement between the two countries comes into full force. However, the importance of the United States to Canada is much greater than the reverse. A North American free trade area that included these two countries plus Mexico would, on the basis of existing trade patterns, be more open than Europe.

Turning to the CFA franc zone, the extent of intra-union trade depends heavily on whether and how trade of the African countries with France is treated in the calculations (Table 1). If only trade among African countries is considered, intra-union trade turns out to be relatively low. A larger proportion of trade is "internal" when trade with France is included in the numerator (but French overall exports and imports are not included in the denominator). The explanation lies in the fact that France is a much more important trading partner for each of the African countries than those countries are for France. As noted in Table 1, once African countries and France are treated as a group, the share of internal trade is much reduced. Another currency union, that among Eastern Caribbean countries, also exhibits only a small amount of intra-regional trade; exports, which consist mainly of primary commodities, are directed primarily to the rest of the world.[15]

---

[15] The East Caribbean Currency Area includes Antigua, Dominica, Grenada, Montserrat, St. Kitts, and St. Lucia.

Table 1
Selected Country Groupings: Intra-Area Trade
as a Share of Total Trade

(Average 1982-85)

	Percent of Exports	Percent of Imports	Percent of Total Trade
European Community			
EC 12 1/	54.3	51.4	52.8
ERM 10 2/	52.7	50.6	51.6
North America			
Canada and the U.S.	37.4	34.5	35.7
Canada, the U.S. and Mexico	39.0	35.5	37.0
CFA Franc Zone			
African countries only 3/	6.6	10.7	8.6
African countries including trade with France	27.9	38.6	37.8
CFA Franc Zone plus France	2.1	2.4	2.3

Notes:

1/   Belgium, Denmark, France, Germany, Greece, Ireland, Italy, Luxembourg, Netherlands, Portugal, Spain, and the United Kingdom. Data for Belgium and Luxembourg are consolidated.

2/   EC 12 minus Greece and Portugal.

3/   Benin, Burkina Faso, Cote d'Ivoire, Mali, Niger, Senegal, Togo, Cameroon, Central African Republic, Chad, Congo, Gabon, and Equatorial Guinea.

Clearly, in the cases of the CFA franc zone and the East Caribbean currency union, the size of intra-regional trade has not been the main motivation for currency union. More important has been the objective of enhanced monetary stability through a supra-national monetary institution.[16] This issue is discussed further below in Section IV.

---

[16]   Since 1983, the institutions of the East Caribbean currency union have included a common central bank.

4.   INDUSTRIAL AND PORTFOLIO DIVERSIFICATION

The likelihood that an adverse shock would have a major impact on an economy will depend to some extent on how diversified is the economy's production structure.[17] If a country exports a wide variety of goods, and if shocks are primarily either to supply (i.e., technology) or to consumers' preferences (affecting relative demands for different goods), then the effect of any shock on output in the whole economy will be less (even in absolute terms) than the effect on individual industries. Other things equal, a diversified economy, therefore, has less need to retain exchange rate flexibility in order to mitigate the effects of shocks.[18] Countries whose production is not diversified, but instead is concentrated in a few goods, include a number of primary commodity exporters. Though industrial countries typically export a wider range of goods, there are some countries among them that are highly dependent on primary commodities: Australia for mineral resources and cereals, and Portugal, Greece, and New Zealand for agricultural products. Thus, Blundell-Wignall and Gregory (1990) argue, in the context of large and persistent commodity price fluctuations of the past two decades, that macroeconomic stabilization--in particular, the objective of price stability--calls for exchange rate flexibility for Australia. Increases in world commodity prices raise domestic output prices, to a greater extent, the greater is the share of commodities in output; this pressure can be mitigated by exchange rate appreciation. However, the appreciation will tend to crowd out other tradables production, in particular, manufactures, so that such sectoral considerations, to the extent they are judged important, may weigh against an appreciation. In addition, exchange rate flexibility in the face of a negative commodity price shock may, through exchange rate depreciation, increase the consumer price index by an amount proportional to the share of importables in consumption, and thereby exacerbate inflationary pressures. There thus are some qualifications to the argument for exchange rate flexibility, even in this case; its relative advantages would depend on both the nature of shocks and the precise objectives of policy.

Canada and the United Kingdom are substantial exporters of energy, but in fact their net exports of energy goods are modest as a proportion of total exports (Table 2). A broad impression of the diversification of domestic production can be obtained from industry output shares for a number of industrial countries (Table 3). For the major industrial countries and for the other European countries for which data were available, the manufacturing sector constitutes between 1/5 and 1/3 of

---

[17]   Kenen (1969).

[18]   However, avoiding unemployment would depend on the existence of inter-sectoral factor mobility, so that sectors facing adverse demand shocks contract, and sectors with increased demand expand.

production.[19] Reliance on production of primary commodities (roughly agriculture, energy, and mining) is relatively small, except for Greece (where it is 22 percent of GDP), and, to a lesser extent, the Netherlands, Portugal and Canada between 12 and 14 percent of GDP). For the most part, the EC includes countries with a well diversified structure of production. An interesting question is whether this diversification will continue with the abandonment of remaining trade barriers, making EC economies even more similar, or whether instead increased specialization will result, making the countries more dissimilar. Which of the two occurs will depend in large part on whether increased trade takes the form of inter- or intra-industry trade. In the latter case, specialization may occur, but with countries remaining diversified, so that shocks to the demand for a particular industry's product should not affect countries asymmetrically. The EC Commission (1990, p. 142) estimates that between 57 percent and 83 percent of intra-EC trade excluding Portugal and Greece was intra-industry. On the other hand, a comparison of regional output variability (within a given European country) with variability across European countries suggests that economic integration does not make the occurrence of asymmetric shocks less likely, and that divergence across countries may actually increase as a result of EMU (De Grauwe and Vanhaverbeke, 1991).

Another aspect to the issue is portfolio diversification. Adverse shocks to incomes in particular regions can be cushioned by holdings of assets which are claims to outside income streams. In principle, such diversification could provide insurance against purely regional shocks, and could make consumption independent of those shocks (Cochrane, 1988). Unfortunately, little is known about how widespread such portfolio diversification is in practice. There are likely to be great differences in the abilities of individuals and particular firms to hold diversified portfolios, due for instance to capital market imperfections (preventing borrowing against future income) or transactions costs.

5.   WAGE AND PRICE FLEXIBILITY

Implicit in the early literature on "optimum currency areas," which considered the value of exchange rate adjustments for achieving internal and external balance, was the assumption that wages and domestic output prices were fixed, at least in the short run. It is now usual practice to regard wages and prices as "sticky" rather than fixed and to expect this stickiness to recede in the long run.

---

[19] Of course, within the manufacturing sector, countries differ greatly in the range of goods produced, and also whether the goods produced are exported.

Table 2
Selected Industrial Countries: Shares of
Exports by Commodity Categories

Country	Agricultural Products[1]	Energy[2]	Other
Canada	19	9	72
United States	16	3	82
Japan	1	--[3]	99
France	17	2	81
Germany	6	1	93
Italy	7	2	91
United Kingdom	8	7	85
Australia	34	18	48
New Zealand	61	1	38

Sources: World Bank Trade System and Fund Staff estimates. Based on data for 1988.

[1]   Food, beverages, and Tobacco; Agricultural Non-Food (SITC 0,1,2,4, less SITC 27,28,233,244,266, and 267).
[2]   Mineral Fuels, etc. (SITC 3).
[3]   Less than 1 percent.

Short-run stickiness may differ across countries. In some countries the response of wages and prices to nominal exchange rate changes could be large enough to limit the usefulness of nominal exchange rate changes as an instrument of adjustment. It is important to distinguish between two types of wage and price flexibility: real and nominal. Changes in a nominal price like the nominal exchange rate are a substitute for domestic price or wage changes, and may facilitate real adjustment. In the limiting case of real wage rigidity (for instance, due to complete indexation of wages), employment and net exports would however be unaffected by nominal exchange rate changes, because rigidity of the real wage is tantamount to rigidity of the real exchange rate.

In the other limiting case of perfect flexibility of real wages, the freedom to modify the nominal exchange rate can be helpful if nominal wages are sticky but redundant if nominal wages or prices are themselves flexible enough to do the job of altering real exchange rates.

On the spectrum stretching from perfect rigidity to perfect flexibility, evidence presented in Bruno and Sachs (1985) suggests that Europe is closer than the

Table 3
Selected Industrial Countries: Shares of Production
by Category in 1986[1]
(in percent)

	Agriculture[2]	Construction	Energy and Mining[3]	Manufacturing	Services[4]
Canada	4.0	7.6	9.0	23.4	56.0
United States	2.3	5.5	5.8	22.2	64.2
Japan	3.1	8.1	4.2	31.4	53.3
France	4.7	6.6	3.8	27.8	57.0
Germany	2.1	6.1	4.2	38.3	49.4
Italy	5.0	6.7	5.7	27.2	55.5
U. K.	2.1	6.7	7.8	27.6	55.9
Belgium	2.5	5.8	4.1	25.4	62.2
Denmark	6.6	8.3	3.0	24.6	57.5
Greece	17.3	7.4	5.1	21.1	49.1
Netherlands	5.2	6.3	9.1	23.4	56.0
Portugal	8.6	6.4	3.6	33.8	47.5
Spain	6.1	7.5	3.4	31.2	51.8

Source: OECD National Accounts

[1]   GDP at current prices. Shares are scaled to sum to 100.
[2]   Including hunting, fishing, and forestry.
[3]   Mining and quarrying (including petroleum and natural gas production), plus electricity generation and gas and water distribution.
[4]   Excluding government services.

United States to the real wage rigidity end, while the reverse obtains for nominal wage rigidity.[20] This implies both that nominal exchange rate changes would be a

[20]   Studies of relative price flexibility that compare data for individual countries with those for Europe include Vaubel (1976), Poloz (1990), and Eichengreen (1990b). Though Vaubel concludes that the EC is in greater need of real exchange rate adjustment then Germany, Italy, or the United States taken individually, the latter two studies are inconclusive as to whether the United States and Canada exhibit more relative price flexibility than Europe. The comparison is complicated by the fact that countries/regions differ in the extent to which price levels include traded goods (whose price may vary little relative to external prices) as opposed to nontraded goods (for which no arbitrage that would tend to equalize prices exists).

more effective tool in North America, and that the existence of higher real wage rigidity in Europe places a premium on other instruments to counter real shocks and well as on measures to improve labor market flexibility.

6. AN OVERVIEW OF THE TRADITIONAL CRITERIA AND THE RESPONSE TO SHOCKS

It is clear from the above discussion that there is no single over-riding criterion that could be used to assess the desirability or viability of a currency union. Some of the traditional flexibility criteria are favorable to existing and/or prospective currency unions, while others are adverse. Increasing analytical attention has therefore turned to analyses of shocks affecting economies since shock-absorption combines the net influence of several of the traditional criteria.[21],[22]

One central aspect of the question is whether shocks are symmetric or asymmetric (i.e., hit countries differently). Similar industrial structures may imply that real shocks facing industrial countries are symmetric. Another aspect is whether shocks are temporary or permanent. Temporary shocks may in principle be cushioned by financing, while permanent shocks require adjustment. A third issue is the origin of shocks: whether they are primarily nominal (i.e., to the price level) or real, domestic or foreign. Nominal exchange rate flexibility is likely to do the best job in insulating the domestic economy from foreign, nominal disturbances. Fourth, there is the question of whether financial market shocks occur primarily in demands for money, or across domestic interest-bearing assets, or for foreign assets.[23] For example, if shocks occur in foreign exchange markets and are unrelated to economic fundamentals, then fixing the exchange rate may be the best solution.

Cohen and Wyplosz (1989) analyze shocks to real GDP, to the GDP deflator, to real wages, and to the current account ratio, for both France and Germany. They decompose these shocks into permanent and temporary components, and also examine

---

[21] A critique of the single-criterion approach is given in Argy and De Grauwe (1990).

[22] Attempts to provide a general theoretical framework are made by Ishiyama (1975), Tower and Willett (1976), and Argy (1990). Boyer (1978), Henderson (1979), Flood and Marion (1982), and Aizenman and Frenkel (1985) all examine the question of the optimal degree of exchange rate flexibility in response to shocks, using simple theoretical models. However, they do not attempt to quantify the relative variances, nor do they consider the benefits of a currency union in lowering transactions costs.

[23] See Henderson (1979), Alexander and Henderson (1989).

their degree of symmetry. They find that symmetric shocks to the two economies dominate the asymmetric ones; however, the same is not true when "Europe" (i.e., France and Germany taken together) is compared to the United States. Also, they find that symmetric shocks to France and Germany tend to be permanent, not temporary. Cohen and Wyplosz (1989) conclude from these results that monetary integration between France and Germany may be more viable than between Europe and the United States.

A recent study (Bayoumi, 1991) examines the nature of shocks hitting ERM countries since 1982 (arguably, the year when realignments became less frequent and the commitment to exchange rate fixity was reinforced--Giavazzi and Spaventa, 1990), and compares responses to shocks of ERM countries to those of selected non-ERM countries. The main conclusions are as follows: (1) constraining the flexibility of exchange rates tends to produce a more drawn out response to shocks; (2) price responses (in either direction) to shocks tend to be larger for ERM countries (aside from Germany) than for non-ERM countries; (3) a comparison of the 1970s with the period since 1982 suggests that the formation of the ERM has made the responses of participating economies to shocks more similar; (4) in contrast, the ERM does not seem to have increased the correlation across countries of the shocks themselves; and (5) already in the 1970s, shocks hitting ERM countries tended to be more symmetric than the shocks hitting non-ERM countries.

A complementary method for assessing the response to shocks within a currency union is to do stochastic simulations of an empirically based macroeconomic model. Repeated drawings are made from the estimated joint probability distribution of the shocks, the model is solved under different assumptions concerning the policy regime in place, and variances of variables of interest--for instance output and inflation--are calculated. This methodology was employed by Frenkel, Goldstein, and Masson (1989), using the International Monetary Fund's MULTIMOD model. They considered the use of both monetary and fiscal policy instruments to hit various intermediate targets. Shocks were applied to all the behavioral equations of the model, consistent with their historical distribution.[24] The results of that exercise suggested that fixing exchange rates among the United States, Japan, and Germany would lead to larger variances for key macroeconomic variables than maintaining flexible exchange rates accompanied by either monetary targeting or nominal GNP targeting. Again, these findings are consistent with the conclusion that the three largest economies may not constitute an optimal currency area.

---

[24] Except for shocks to the interest rate parity condition, which were set to zero in the fixed exchange rate regime.

A similar methodology was used by the EC Commission to analyze fixed exchange rates within the EMS.[25] Figure 2, which summarizes their results, is taken from that study. It suggests that a move from free floating of European currencies to the EMS system of infrequent and partial realignments increased average output variability in member countries, while reducing inflation variability.[26] The reduction in inflation variability is due to a reduction in asymmetric exchange rate shocks and to an enhancement of price discipline in EMS countries other than Germany. Output variability increases outside of Germany because of the need to devote monetary policy in these countries to limiting currency movements against the deutsche mark (EC Commission, 1990; p. 154). A further move toward monetary union with irrevocably fixed exchange rates is argued to reduce both output and inflation variability. This would result from the disciplinary effects of narrower exchange rate margins and from the implementation of a cooperative symmetric monetary policy. The EC Commission study highlights the following potential positive effects of currency union: (1) intra-EMS exchange rate shocks (i.e., shocks to interest rate parity) disappear; (2) the elimination of expected devaluations dampens inflationary pressures;[27] and (3) by enforcing coordination of monetary policies (making them identical, as a result of sharing the same currency), monetary union would reduce costs related to the attempt to use the exchange rate within the EC in a beggar-thy-neighbor fashion.[28] The negative effects of currency union are those associated with the loss of exchange rate flexibility, as discussed above.

The EC Commission study was criticized by Minford and Rastogi (1990), who concluded on the basis of simulations of the Liverpool World Model that EMU was unambiguously bad for the United Kingdom, and also bad for the other three major EC countries if the U.K. joined. Furthermore, Hughes Hallett, Minford and Rastogi (1991) analyzed the EMS using stochastic simulations, and found that the EMS was destabilizing, both for member countries as well as non-members such as

---

[25] EC Commission (1990), Chapter 6 and Annex E. The simulations were also performed using the Fund's MULTIMOD model (see Masson, Symansky, and Meredith, 1990), by the staff of the EC Commission. The model does not include all the EMS members separately; results apply to Germany, France, Italy, the United Kingdom, and the Smaller Industrial Country Region. Implicitly, then, all EC member countries are assumed to participate in EMU.

[26] Variability is an appropriate criterion if shocks do not affect long-run values of variables, so that the purpose of economic policy is to smooth the transition back to an unchanged long-run equilibrium. It is implicitly assumed that in the long run, growth rates of monetary aggregates, and hence inflation rates, are unaffected.

[27] This effect depends on some "forward-looking" behavior in wage setting.

[28] See, for instance, Oudiz and Sachs (1984).

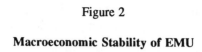

Figure 2

Macroeconomic Stability of EMU

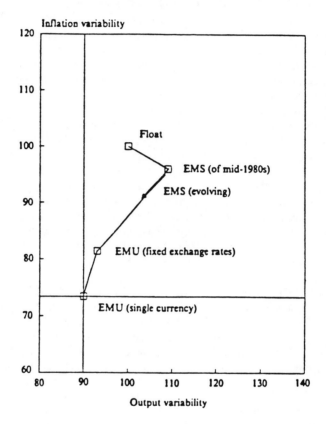

Indices EC average, free float = 100

This graph plots the combinations of variability of output (GDP) and inflation for the Community average in index form as resulting from the stochastic simulations. The position of each of the four regimes ("free float", "EMS", "asymmetric EMU" and EMU) corresponds to an intersection between a regime-dependent output-inflation trade-off curve and a shifting preference curve.

Source: Stochastic simulations with the Multimod model of the IMF under the responsibility of the Commission services. GDP is measured as a percentage deviation from its baseline value, inflation is measured in percentage point differences with respect to baseline inflation rates. The indices used in the graph are obtained by averaging, first, the squares of the deviations for 43 simulations over the period 1990-99 and by taking the square root. Dividing by the root mean-squared deviations for the free float regime and multiplication by 100 then gives the indices.

FROM EC COMMISSION (1990), P. 154

Canada and the United States.

In attempt to understand the reasons for differences in results between the EC Commission and Minford and associates, Masson and Symansky (1992) redid simulations of MULTIMOD with different assumptions concerning the nature of the shocks (in particular, of risk premium shocks to exchange rates) and concerning rules for realignments in the EMS. They concluded that fairly arbitrary choices concerning modelling realignments and estimating the size of risk premiums explained the differences in results. They also raised the issue of how to evaluate the gains (or losses) from monetary union: for instance, is the variability of the EC's inflation rate from period-to-period the correct criterion, or are we still interested in the variability of each country's inflation rate? Which criterion is used makes an important difference for the evaluation of gains or losses.

Despite the attractions of the simulation methodology, therefore, it is important also to recognize its limitations. First, the reduction in transactions costs resulting from introduction of a common currency is not captured in such macroeconomic models.[29] Second, a comparison of different policy regimes, assuming that the structure of the rest of the economy is unaffected, may give misleading results. For instance, the degree of labor mobility or wage/price flexibility may respond endogenously to the elimination of exchange rate fluctuations.[30] Third, there are other issues, concerning the credibility of the commitment to price stability and the need to discipline fiscal policy, that go beyond the scope of most empirical macro models. Finally, as discussed above, fairly arbitrary choices in constructing the simulations can be crucial to the results.

7.   CONCLUSION

Some useful insights emerge from the traditional criteria for optimal currency and from an analysis of shocks facing regional and national economies. The benefits of a currency union among a group of countries are likely to be enhanced if they have a large amount of intra-union trade. The costs of abandoning the exchange rate instrument are likely to be smaller: if labor mobility is high among member countries; if there is considerable nominal and price flexibility; if each constituent national economy has a diversified industrial structure; and if shocks are predominantly common rather than country specific.

---

[29] A more microeconomic approach was used to analyze the benefits of creating the single European market: see "The Economics of 1992," European Economy, No. 35 (March 1988).

[30] A preliminary attempt to endogenize the degree of labor mobility in a theoretical model is made by Bertola (1989).

Application of these criteria to prospective common currency areas reveals factors working both for and against success. In the EC, for example, the large volume of internal trade, the fairly high degree of diversification of most member country economies, and the relatively symmetric nature of shocks--are all advantages. On the negative side, labor mobility seems to be lower in the EC than in North America. The same kind of analysis likewise suggests that Europe is a lot closer to an optimal currency area than would be a larger area consisting of, say, Europe, North America, and Japan.

These conclusions need to be tempered by recognizing several limitations of the analysis: (1) because the criteria are overlapping, there is no unique decision variable; (2) because currency unions also cause other changes in the economic structure, which are typically not captured in economic models, calculated effects should be regarded as only approximately of the true effects; and (3) because the formation of a currency union has political as well as economic dimensions, it interacts with other policies--particularly fiscal policy--in complex ways.

REFERENCES

Aizenman, Joshua, and Jacob A. Frenkel, "Optimal Wage Indexation, Foreign Exchange Intervention, and Monetary Policy,"*American Economic Review*, Vol. 75 (June 1985), pp. 402-23.

Alexander, William E., and Dale W. Henderson, "Liberalization of Financial Markets and the Volatility of Exchange Rates," in Robert M. Stern (ed.), *Trade and Investment Relations Among the United States, Canada, and Japan* (Chicago: University of Chicago Press, 1989), pp. 365-78.

Allen, Polly Reynolds, "Organization and Administration of a Monetary Union," Princeton Studies in International Finance No. 38, Princeton University (June 1976).

Argy, Victor, "Choice of Exchange Rate Regime for a Smaller Economy: A Survey of Some Key Issues," in Argy and De Grauwe, eds. (1990), pp. 6-81.

_____, and Paul De Grauwe, "Introduction," in Argy and De Grauwe, eds. (1990), pp. 1-5.

_____, and Paul De Grauwe, eds., *Choosing an Exchange Rate Regime: The Challenge for Smaller Industrial Countries* (Washington, D.C.: International Monetary Fund, 1990).

Bayoumi, Tamim, "The Effects of the ERM on Participating Economies," IMF Working Paper WP/91/86 (September 1991).

_____, and Andrew K. Rose, "Domestic and Intra-National Capital Flows," mimeo, 1991.

Bertola, Giuseppe, "Factor Mobility, Uncertainty and Exchange Rate Regimes," in de Cecco and Giovannini, eds. (1989), pp. 95-118.

Bhandari, Jagdeep, and Thomas Mayer, "A Note on Saving-Investment Correlations in the EMS," International Monetary Fund (Washington), Working Paper No. WP/90/97 (October 1990).

Blundell-Wignall, Adrian, and Robert G. Gregory, "Exchange Rate Policy in Advanced Commodity-Exporting Countries: Australia and New Zealand," in Argy and De Grauwe, eds. (1990), pp. 224-71.

Boyer, Russell, "Optimal Foreign Exchange Market Intervention," *Journal of Political Economy*, Vol. 86 (December 1978), pp. 1045-55.

Bruno, Michael, and Jeffrey Sachs, *Economics of Worldwide Stagflation*, Cambridge, Mass., National Bureau of Economic Research (1985).

Bryant, Ralph A., David A. Currie, Jacob A. Frankel, Paul R. Masson, and Richard Portes, eds. *Macroeconomic Policies in an Interdependent World* (Washington, D.C.: International Monetary Fund, 1989).

Cochrane, John H., "Test of Consumption Insurance," NBER Working Paper No. 2642 (July 1988).

Cohen, Daniel, and Charles Wyplosz, "The European Monetary Union: An Agnostic Evaluation," in Bryant and others, eds. (1989), pp. 311-37.

Corden, W. M., "Monetary Integration," Essays in International Finance No. 93, Princeton University (April 1972).

De Grauwe, Paul and Wim Vanhaverbeke, "Is Europe and Optimum Currency Area? Evidence from Regional Data," *Centre for Economic Policy Research Discussion Paper*, No. 555 (May 1991).

de Cecco, Marcello, and Alberto Giovannini, eds., *A European Central Bank? Perspectives on Monetary Unification after Ten Years of the EMS* (Cambridge: Cambridge University Press, 1989).

Dooley, Michael, Jeffrey Frankel, and Donald J. Mathieson, "International Capital Mobility: What Do Saving-Investment Correlations Tell Us?" International Monetary Fund (Washington), *Staff Papers*, Vol. 34 (September 1987), pp. 503-30.

EC Commission, "One Market, One Money: An Evaluation of the Potential Benefits and Costs of Forming an Economic and Monetary Union," *European Economy*, No. 44, Brussels, Commission of the European Communities (October 1990).

Eichengreen, Barry (1990a), "One Money for Europe? Lessons from the U.S. Currency Union," *Economic Policy*, No. 10 (April 1990), pp. 117-87.

_____ (1990b), "Is Europe and Optimum Currency Area?" University of California at Berkeley, Department of Economics, Working Paper No. 90-151 (October 1990).

Feldstein, Martin, and Charles Horioka, "Domestic Saving and International Capital Flows," *Economic Journal*, Vol. 90 (June 1980), pp. 314-29.

Flood, Robert P., and Nancy Marion, "The Transmission of Disturbances under Alternative Exchange-Rate Regimes with Optimal Indexing," *Quarterly Journal of Economics*, Vol. 97 (February 1982), pp. 43-66.

Frenkel, Jacob A., Morris Goldstein, and Paul Masson, "Simulating the Effects of Some Simple Coordinated Versus Uncoordinated Policy Rules," in Bryant and others, eds. (1989), pp. 203-39.

_____, and Assaf Razin, "The Mundell-Fleming Model A Quarter Century Later: A Unified Exposition," International Monetary Fund *Staff Papers*, Vol. 34 (December 1987), pp. 203-39.

Giavazzi, Francesco, and Luigi Spaventa, "The New EMS," CEPR Discussion Paper No. 369 (January 1990).

Henderson, Dale, "Financial Policies in Open Economies," *American Economic Review*, Vol. 69 (May 1979), pp. 232-39.

Hughes Hallett, Andrew, Patrick Minford, and Anupam Rastogi, "The European Monetary System - Problems and Evolution," in John Driffill and Massimo Beber, eds., *A Currency for Europe* (London: Lothian Foundation Press, 1991), pp. 79-99.

Ishiyama, Yoshide, "The Theory of Optimum Currency Areas: A Survey," International Monetary Fund *Staff Papers*, Vol. 22 (July 1975), pp. 344-83.

Kenen, Peter, "The Theory of Optimum Currency Areas: An Eclectic View," in Robert Mundell and Alexander Swoboda, eds., *Monetary Problems in the International Economy* (Chicago: University of Chicago Press, 1969).

Masson, Paul R., and Steven Symansky, "Evaluating the EMS and EMU Using Stochastic Simulations: Some Issues," in Ray Barrell and John Whitley, eds., *Macroeconomic Policy Coordination in Europe: The ERM and Monetary Union* (London: Sage Publications, 1992), pp. 12-34.

Masson, Paul R., Steven Symansky, and Guy Meredith, *MULTIMOD Mark II: A Revised and Extended Model*, IMF Occasional Paper No. 71 (July 1990).

McKinnon, Ronald I., "Optimum Currency Areas," *American Economic Review*, Vol. 53 (September 1963), pp. 717-25.

Minford, Patrick, and Anupam Rastogi, "The Price of EMU," in *Britain and EMU*, Centre for Economic Performance (London: London School of Economics, 1990), pp. 47-67.

Mundell, Robert A., "A Theory of Optimum Currency Areas," *American Economic Review*, Vol. 51 (September 1961), pp. 657-65.

Oudiz, Gilles, and Jeffrey Sachs, "Macroeconomic Policy Coordination among the Industrial Economies," *Brookings Papers on Economic Activity*, 1: (1984), pp. 1-76.

Poloz, Stephen S., "Real Exchange Rate Adjustment Between Regions in a Common Currency Area," mimeo, Bank of Canada, Ottawa (February 1990).

Tower, Edward, and Thomas D. Willett, "The Theory of Optimum Currency Areas and Exchange-Rate Flexibility," Special Papers in International Economics No. 11, Princeton University (May 1976).

Vaubel, Roland, "Real Exchange-Rate Changes in the European Community: The Empirical Evidence and Its Implications for European Currency Unification," *Weltwirtschaftliches Archiv*, Bd. 112 (1976), pp. 429-70.

CHAPTER 3

EXCHANGE RATE PEGGING AS A DISINFLATION STRATEGY: EVIDENCE FROM THE EUROPEAN MONETARY SYSTEM[1]

Richard C. K. Burdekin
Jilleen R. Westbrook
Thomas D. Willett

1.   INTRODUCTION

One of the few predictions that can be confidently made in international monetary economics is that the debate over alternative exchange rate regimes will have a long life. The attention this issue receives rises and falls over time and the center of gravity of professional opinion shifts back and forth from the pro fixity to pro flexibility side of the spectrum. In recent years, the support for exchange rate pegging has been on the upswing. In fact, current discussions of exchange rate arrangements for Western Europe are reminiscent of the immediate post-war era, when -- nearly forty years ago -- Milton Friedman (1953, p. 203) complained that a flexible exchange rate system

> has been ruled out in recent years without extensive explicit consideration, partly because of a questionable interpretation of limited historical evidence; partly, I believe, because it was condemned alike by traditionalists, whose ideal was a gold standard that either ran itself or was run by international central bankers but in either case determined internal policy, and by the dominant strain of reformers, who distrusted the price system in all its manifestations -- a curious coalition of the most unreconstructed believers in the price system, in all its other roles, and its most extreme opponents.

[1] Earlier versions of this paper were presented at the Claremont Workshop on "The Political Economy of Global Monetary Stabilization," October 9-10, 1992 and at the meetings of the European Community Studies Association in Washington, D.C., May 27, 1993. The authors thank David Andrews, Pierre Siklos and Mark Wohar for helpful comments.

Despite the crises of the Exchange Rate Mechanism (ERM) of the European Monetary System (EMS) in September, 1992 and July/August, 1993, the finance ministers of the EMS countries have continued to reaffirm their pursuit of a return to a pegged rate system. Pegged rates have been prominent in the stabilization packages adopted by many of the developing economies of Latin America and newly market-orientated economies of Central and Eastern Europe. Indeed, debate on the type of exchange rate arrangements that should be adopted by the nascent Commonwealth of Independent States has often taken the adoption of a pegged system as given -- and discussion has centered on whether the individual republics should jointly align their exchange rates on EMS-type lines or instead simply peg to a common external currency (Bofinger, 1991; Bofinger and Gros, 1992). (For a contrary view see Willett, Al-Marhubi and Dahel, 1993.)

Perhaps the most popular reason presented in policy circles for pegged exchange rates at the current time is the discipline that fixed exchange rates are assumed to impose. In particular, by fixing a nation's exchange rate to that of a low inflation anchor country, domestic monetary authorities may be more disciplined. If domestic policy makers attempt to create a money supply surprise, reserves will flow out of the country. Either the exchange rate must change or (unless sterilized) the reserve flow will reduce the domestic money supply automatically. In addition to the discipline effects acquired through a fixed exchange rate, there is the theoretical possibility that this regime will enhance the credibility of the high inflation country, thereby reducing the output costs associated with disinflating.

This paper critically evaluates the recent arguments for fixed exchange rates, focusing particularly upon the credibility, or reputational, argument for fixity. We argue that the theoretical basis for a belief that pegging one's exchange rate will immediately enhance credibility is weak, but that there is good reason to believe that exchange rate pegging, backed by consistent macroeconomic policies, will gradually enhance a monetary authority's reputation. The credibility of a pegged exchange rate will also be greater the higher are the political costs of exchange rate adjustments.

We divide the analysis of the credibility issue into three theoretical sections as follows: 1) a discussion of how the credibility argument evolved from the rules vs. discretion literature but also needs to be related to the theory of optimal currency areas, 2) an analysis of the theoretical underpinnings of the potential credibility gains from exchange rate pegging, and 3) a critical evaluation of the simple view of credibility gains from exchange rate pegging. We then offer new empirical evidence on the EMS, and find that there is little support for the view that the adoption of EMS arrangements fostered substantial immediate credibility gains. We believe that this should not be surprising when one remembers the crucial distinction between adjustably pegged and genuinely fixed exchange rates. Credibility as an inflation fighter needs to be earned over time. Successful defense of pegged rates can have an important influence on the speed of this process, but we find that the conventional credibility argument in favor of pegged exchange rates has been overstated. Our results support Woolley's (1992, p. 167) argument that "domestic political commitments made the EMS credible in the early 1980s, not the other way round."

2.   ORIGINS OF THE CREDIBILITY ARGUMENTS FOR PEGGED EXCHANGE RATES

By the late 1970s, there was considerable support for the adoption of monetary policy rules, owing, in large part, to the fact that activist monetary policy had been associated with stagflation in many industrialized countries. During that time period there were frequent calls for a return to the gold standard as a strong policy rule. While no post-war government has actually pegged their currency to gold, many governments peg their national currency to another foreign currency -- thereby tying their rate of money issue, not to gold, but to the rate of money issue in the foreign country. Such policies often appear to have been directed at "importing" the credibility of the monetary authority in a nation that has a reputation for providing relatively low inflation rates.

The historical argument for using an exchange rate anchor as part of an anti-inflation policy was based upon the idea that the exchange rate acts a constraint that may be more binding than money supply targeting (see the analysis and references in Willett and Mullen, 1982). Wage demands would be more constrained with an exchange rate peg, and therefore inflationary inertia might be reduced under a pegging arrangement. The rational expectations addition to this argument asserted that there was not only a discipline effect but also a credibility effect. Weber (1991), for example, argues that exchange rate pegging influences the success of an anti-inflation policy in two distinct ways: first, through borrowed credibility that reduces the costs of disinflation, and, second, through discipline that may have raised the costs of engineering higher inflation rates -- as such expansionary policies would hurt the export sector and/or compel the government to abandon the peg and perhaps incur political, as well as economic, costs in doing so.

Many countries have used exchange rate anchors to attempt to fight inflation when inflation rates become very high. Latin American countries like Argentina, Bolivia and Mexico have pegged to the dollar with varying degrees of success over the last decade (see Bruno, 1991, and Claassen, 1991). The discipline imposed on these countries as they defend the pegging arrangement often causes unemployment, however, and wages do not appear to have fallen rapidly enough to insulate the real economy from the effects of the disinflation. If the credibility of a high inflation country's monetary authorities could be enhanced merely by pegging, then the unemployment costs associated with the disinflation would be reduced. The remarkable conclusion from imposing rational expectations on the traditional open economy model was the possibility, at least in theory, of a costless disinflation provided that the government could convince the market that it would follow through with the announced plan.

A country making a decision about its international monetary arrangements must, however, weigh the costs and benefits from exchange rate pegging given its particular economic conditions and those of its partner country. For example, an important criteria for success is relatively free capital and labor mobility between two countries. The optimum currency area literature also points out that nations with very different monetary policy goals and nations subject to different monetary shocks would not make good candidates for a currency area (Tower and Willett, 1976; Wihlborg and Willett, 1991). Nevertheless, the possibility that this type of regime could lower inflationary expectations gave highly inflationary countries another theoretical reason for choosing to peg their exchange rates. Thus, within the context of this literature and the rules versus discretion literature, a new set of optimal currency area criteria developed. These criteria dealt with political concerns rather than being concerned only with structural factors and patterns of shocks (for a full analysis, see Wihlborg and Willett, 1991).

3.   THE THEORETICAL CASE FOR CREDIBILITY GAINS UNDER PEGGED RATES

Several game theoretic models support the notion of a credibility gain with exchange rate pegging. Giavazzi and Pagano's (1988) influential paper argued that in an open-economy, game-theoretic framework exchange rate pegging could enhance the credibility of high inflation countries' monetary authorities if the authorities cared about competitiveness and real exchange rate changes. In this framework the players' inflationary expectations should be lower under fixed rates since surprise inflations are now less attractive to the central bankers. Higher rates of inflation lead to a real exchange rate appreciation under fixed rates, and associated loss of competitiveness. Since agents are assumed to know the preferences of the authorities, their inflationary expectations will adjust downward with a fixed exchange rate regime if pegging alters the incentive/constraint structure of the monetary authorities in this way.

On the other hand, Artus (1991) shows how the effects of exchange rate regime changes may derive from contractual rigidities in labor markets. The exchange rate regime affects how expectations are formulated, and hence how wage contracts are set, yet the agents' actions also take into account the actual behavior of the authorities and do not depend entirely on announcement effects. Artus' results are driven by the existence of a wage-price spiral that is worsened by the expectation of exchange rate depreciation. In his model, labor sets its wage contracts at the beginning of the period and cannot change them until the next bargaining period. Workers desire a specific real wage and therefore demand higher wage increases to offset any perceived deterioration in their purchasing power.[2] This mechanism may ultimately give rise to mutually-reinforcing cycles of currency depreciation, wage-

---

[2] For a similar argument, see Carter and Maddock (1987).

push, and monetary accommodation of the type known to have been operative in many previous inflationary episodes, including the German hyperinflation (Robinson, 1938; Burdekin and Burkett, 1993). (For a critical examination of this vicious circle analysis, see Willett and Wolf, 1983). In this context, credibility gains from exchange rate pegging would emerge only to the extent that the probability of a depreciation declines.

In contrast to Giavazzi and Pagano (1988) -- who rely upon specific assumptions about the asymmetry of the arrangements and the nature of the monetary authority's preferences -- the most satisfactory explanation of the gains from exchange rate pegging focuses on the high political costs from breaking the exchange rate arrangement. These costs are particularly evident, and the temptation to inflate further diminished, when the exchange rate arrangement is tied to other goals between countries (see Melitz, 1988, and von Hagen, 1990). For example, in Europe the EMS is tied to the greater concept of Economic and Monetary Union. Thus a credibility boost might be attained by pegging one's currency to a low inflation country, since excessive inflation will ultimately force devaluations that are politically costly.

Quite aside from any shifts in inflationary expectations, Wihlborg and Willett (1991; 1993) propose that the structure of the economy itself will shift following a change in the exchange rate regime. The authors argue that the Phillips curve will steepen with flexible rates, since depreciations immediately impact the price level. Therefore, although real exchange rate appreciations under pegged rates may constrain the monetary authority, so too may flexible rates since there is less of an incentive to use monetary shocks to expand the economy when the Phillips curve is steep. Their formulation of the Phillips curve points out that we do not fully understand how the exchange rate regime will influence inflation, since there are structural changes occurring with a regime shift that are completely separate from the changes that occur with expectations adjustment.

Finally, Lächler (1988) offers a dynamic model of the economy in which there is some price sluggishness but in which perfect capital mobility forces the uncovered interest parity condition to hold. The leadership in countries with long histories of highly inflationary policies will have a difficult time convincing the public that they have really changed their priorities and plan to stick to a low inflation policy. In an environment in which the authority has a "bad reputation," an exchange rate target (as opposed to a money supply target) may lead to a long-run failure of the anti-inflation plan. If an exchange rate target is undertaken in Lächler's model, the nominal and real interest rates decline, raising aggregate demand and domestic prices. This initial expansion undermines the policy, since it sends a signal to agents that the economy is expanding, not contracting.

Studies of the dynamics of the issue suggest that if a country uses an exchange rate target for stabilization, real exchange rate appreciations will lead to balance of payments problems in the long run. That is, owing to the inflationary inertia embedded in the economy by previous expansionary policies, the real exchange rate must rise as it did in Israel, Poland, Yugoslavia, and indeed all other countries that have followed such an exchange rate based approach. Even if the impact of this inflationary inertia on the real exchange rate can be accurately calculated and allowed for in the initial parity setting, what of the other real shocks and shifts in the pattern of trade that may arise in the future? These concerns, of course, apply with even more force to the emerging market-orientated economies of Central and Eastern Europe than to the EMS countries. In such cases, Crow (1990, p. 12), points out that

> the real exchange rate will likely have to move as part of the general process of relative price adjustment. Without some flexibility in the nominal exchange rate, it may well not be possible to get anything approximating the necessary exchange rate shifts in real terms except at great economic costs in terms of foregone output and increased unemployment.

Eventually, these pressures are likely to force the authorities to devalue the currency. For example, Yugoslavia abandoned its previously announced fixed exchange rate on January 1, 1991, and in May 1991 Poland devalued the zloty by about 17% and switched from a dollar peg to a currency basket.[3] Such devaluations may be interpreted by agents as signalling a lack of commitment to the disinflation effort. There is also a danger that devaluations may lead to higher wage claims and an inflationary spiral. Thus, even though in the short-run the unemployment problems associated with disinflation may be mitigated, in the long-run the policy could well lead to future devaluations and renewed inflationary problems (see also Solimano, 1990; Kiguel and Liviatan, 1991).[4]

4.   PROBLEMS WITH THE CONVENTIONAL VIEW ON CREDIBILITY GAINS

The influential and intuitively appealing view that exchange-rate pegging enhances the credibility of a stabilization policy as modelled by Giavazzi and Pagano is ultimately not very convincing. A policy is only fully credible, or believable, if it

---

[3] Even in the generally successful Israeli stabilization, similar problems with excessive real exchange rate appreciation arose until exchange rate restraint was relaxed in 1989 (Bruno, 1992).

[4] Williamson (1991, p.137) has also concluded that "the exchange rate is too brittle to serve as a satisfactory nominal anchor for more than the first few months, or at most for the first year or two, after a stabilization program is implemented." Williamson, in fact, argues that nominal income may be the best longer run target variable in such cases.

is a "best reply strategy" of the central banker involved in the game. Any change in credibility must be due to a change in the full price of inflating, whether because of a change in the basic structure of the economy under a fixed exchange rate regime, or because of fewer political pressures to push the unemployment rate lower. Simply pegging the exchange rate does not address the fundamental pressures to inflate, nor is it clear how to credibly peg if credibility is lacking in the first place.

Wihlborg and Willett (1993) argue that "there is an inherent contradiction in the concept of fully credible fixed exchange rates. Some possibility of changing rates in the long-run will always remain, even if fixed rates may be credible in the short-run or medium-run." A more general criticism of the credibility literature is that, in the context of repeated games, the discount rate must be sufficiently low in order to avoid high inflation. It is not clear, however, that this discount rate will remain constant under the transition to a fixed exchange rate regime. Most likely the discount factor is a function of optimum currency area conditions and is time-varying. For example, in the face of a real shock to the domestic economy, that causes a high level of unemployment, the discount rate will likely increase. If this is the case, no unique equilibrium can be attained in the game-theoretic framework.

In reality, large discrete shifts in the credibility of central bankers are rare given that the true underlying incentive structure of the authorities is not known to the public (nor is the true model of the economy for that matter). The public only has the behavior of the monetary authorities with which to deduce the underlying preferences. Money reaction functions tend to be quite unstable over time, and therefore any shift in the behavior of central bankers must be assessed over a longer term period in order to be believable. It is possible that in a world in which information is imperfect, pegging may act as a signal to the market that a regime change has taken place, but time will be needed in order for the market to assess the situation. Signaling will likely not change expectations immediately, rather leaders must build a reputation in order to signal true preferences to the market. Therefore, credibility is most likely to be earned over a period of time.

Analysis of this issue raises many questions. Indeed, if the exchange rate is an asset price, reflecting the fundamentals, then pegging the exchange rate in an attempt to bring the fundamentals into alignment will only be credible if the fundamentals move quickly to the new level through other policy changes. Ironically, if the fundamentals are brought into alignment, there would be no need to formally peg, since market pressure on the exchange rate would not exist. Large budget deficits and high unemployment rates may make the short-run benefits of breaking the exchange rate arrangement very attractive, and thus completely undermine any credibility effects.

The most convincing argument in support of the idea of credibility gains from exchange rate pegging is the argument involving the political costs of devaluations. If the political costs of devaluation are high, a pegged exchange rate regime might truly discipline the monetary authority. We probably will not see instantaneous credibility effects, but they will occur over time, particularly if the political commitment to the regime is growing. For example, as the idea of "One Europe" became increasingly popular in the 1980s, the political costs of devaluations probably rose. A devaluation in the post-1987 period would have signaled a lack of commitment to the Common Market and a failure of the domestic policy makers (Weber, 1991). Furthermore, such concerns appear to have had a major influence on President Mitterand's decision to reverse course and adopt hard money policies in France in 1983 (Goodman, 1992; Woolley, 1992). Just as the cost of devaluing the currency or dropping out of the EMS rose it also became easier for politicians to sell tight macroeconomic policies to the domestic electorate.

Full credibility was never achieved in the EMS, although the absence of any exchange rate realignments in the post-1987 period of stability that prevailed through mid-1992 was associated with a substantial narrowing of interest rate differentials (Giovannini, 1990; Frankel and Phillips, 1991; Froot and Rogoff, 1991; Weber, 1991; Fratianni and von Hagen, 1992). The withdrawal of Italy and the United Kingdom in September 1992 -- followed by the devaluations of the Spanish peseta, the Portuguese escudo and the Irish pound, and the crisis that culminated in the widening of the exchange rate bands to 15% in August 1993 -- perhaps imply that this lack of full credibility was justified.

There is also the question of whether an announced commitment to EMS membership will itself be seen as credible in the eyes of the public. The credibility of an announced EMS commitment may, for example, be threatened if EMS membership will have injurious effects on a country in the face of particular shocks. In a sense, full credibility is not obtained because it is too costly to stay the course of a highly restrictive, "Bundesbank mimicking" policy over the long-run. Some analysts have argued that this is justification for removing the "back door," and moving to a common currency for the core countries as soon as possible, thus eliminating the potential for re-alignments and perhaps forcing the fundamentals into convergence.

Recently, the movement towards a common currency has received a number of serious setbacks. The first blow was the Danish voters' initial rejection of the Maastricht agreement that provides for the establishment of a common currency before the end of the century. This was followed by the turmoil of September 1992, and the very narrow acceptance of the treaty by the French voters at that time. The relatively weak economies of some of the member countries, and tension over the high interest rates maintained by Germany through the summer of 1993, have left the fate of the ERM itself in doubt, and the resolve of many of the participants seems to have weakened. As the movement toward currency unification slows, it is perhaps more important than ever to assess the extent to which present EMS arrangements have added to the credibility of the member countries.

The remaining portion of this chapter provides some new quantitative analysis on the effects of EMS membership on risk premia and interest rate differentials. Our analysis examines not only whether risk premia and interest rate behavior may have changed with EMS membership but also whether there is any evidence that the participating countries have gained credibility over time. Quantification of these credibility gains would be an important part of any cost-benefit analysis of the merits of the present EMS arrangements.

5.   AN EMPIRICAL MODEL OF EXCHANGE RATE EXPECTATIONS

With perfect capital mobility, risk neutrality and rational expectations, uncovered interest parity should hold within the bounds of transactions costs:

$$(1) \quad r_t - r_t^* = \Delta s_t^e = f_t - s_t = Fp_t$$

where

r_t is the nominal rate of interest at home,

r_t^* is the nominal rate of interest abroad,

Δs_t^e is the expected change in the spot exchange rate (defined in units of home currency per unit of foreign currency),

f_t is the forward exchange rate,

s_t is the current spot exchange rate, and

Fp_t is the forward premium (or discount).

If these conditions hold, expectations about changes in the spot rate would be directly measurable either through interest differentials or the forward premium or discount. Under pegged exchange rates, a substantial interest rate differential would suggest a lack of credibility of the exchange rate arrangements.

However, a large body of research in this area has shown that, although covered interest parity typically holds -- so that interest differentials and forward premia can effectively be used interchangeably -- uncovered interest parity frequently does not hold. The forward rate is often a biased estimator of the future spot rate and there has been considerable scope for profits in European currency speculation. For example, Giovannini (1990) finds that if an investor were to have "shorted the Deutschmark" throughout much of the 1980s and taken a long position in either Italian lira or French francs, enormous profits would have been made.

Research has pointed to the existence of a time-varying risk premium as one explanation for the persistence in the ex-ante profits in foreign exchange markets.[5] Some researchers have attempted to measure this risk premium, but with less than satisfying results. The risk premium is unobservable and cannot be disentangled from the rational expectations forecast error. We can separate the risk premium into its stationary and time-varying components as shown below:

$$(2) \quad s_t^e = a + m_t + {}_{t-1}f_t$$

where

a is the stationary component of the risk premium,
m_t is the time varying component, and
${}_{t-1}f_t$ is the last-period expectation of today's forward rate.

Since rational expectations do not imply perfect foresight, individuals will make mistakes and thus a forecast error must be added to the model. Thus m_t and the error will be bundled together in the empirical work.[6] The less one can correct for risk premia, the less good are interest rate differentials and forward rates as proxies for exchange rate expectations.

Analysts have typically jointly tested the theory of rational expectations and the theory that exchange rate pegging enhances credibility. The usual method has been to include a dummy variable in empirical equations for the year when the exchange rate regime switched from flexible to fixed, thus exploiting the implications of the Lucas critique. A rejection of the hypothesis that exchange rate pegging lowers inflation expectations could merely be a rejection of the model used in proxying expectations.

Moreover, most prior studies have examined the possible effects of the EMS on inflation - output trade-offs; yet, if any price or wage rigidity is present, the response to credibility effects would necessarily be damped. This may help explain the findings in many of these studies that the EMS was not important for enhancing credibility (Christensen, 1987a,b and 1990; Collins, 1988; Giavazzi and Giovannini, 1988; De Grauwe, 1989; Egebo and Englander, 1992; and Fratianni and von Hagen,

---

[5] Market irrationality is another possible explanation, but it is less appealing to most mainstream economists than the possibility of risk-averse behaviour.

[6] Engle (1982) and Baillie and Bollerslev (1990) model the risk premium with an autoregressive conditional heteroskedasticity (ARCH) technique. Frankel and MacArthur (1988) separate and more completely identify the components of the risk premium.

1992). This paper focuses solely on exchange market data. Consequently, we will not explicitly test whether exchange rate pegging lowers the costs of disinflating, but rather we test whether the exchange rate arrangement is affected by political events that support a tight money policy. Our study seeks to determine whether the policy actions undertaken in order to support the EMS enhanced the credibility of the arrangement itself, and in so doing enhanced the overall credibility of the monetary authorities.

6.   **TESTING FOR CREDIBILITY EFFECTS AMONGST EMS COUNTRIES**

Within the EMS the policy goal of members was to bring inflation rates into line with those of Germany. As the arrangement evolved, fewer re-alignments occurred and governments took measures domestically to defend the peg and avoid devaluations. If the policy actions undertaken addressed the fundamental inflationary pressures in the domestic economies, the credibility of the overall anti-inflation stance should have been enhanced, thus augmenting the credibility of the peg.

Previous studies of credibility in the EMS have made use of the simplifying assumption of perfect, risk-neutral capital mobility. We extend this literature by allowing for the presence of a time-varying risk-premium through estimating the equations with an ARCH model. We proxy changes in the expected spot rate ($E[s_t - s_{t-1}]$) with the forward premium/discount plus a risk-premium. Subtracting last period's spot rate (s_{t-1}) from both sides of the equation, we have:

$$(3) \quad E[s_t - s_{t-1}] = [a - s_{t-1}] + [m_t - s_{t-1}] + [_{t-1}f_t - s_{t-1}]$$

We can re-write equation (3) in order to see the relationship between the forward premium/discount (Fp) and changes in the expected spot rate:

$$(4) \quad Fp_t = E[s_t - s_{t-1}] - \delta - \mu_t$$

where δ is $[a - s_{t-1}]$, and

μ_t is $[m_t - s_{t-1}]$.

The above equation represents a theoretical relationship between the forward rate and the spot rate. This relationship can be used in order to choose a proxy for expectations about the spot rate. As theory suggests that political decisions and devaluations might affect expectations about the exchange rate, we estimate the following error correction model to control for the heteroskedasticity in the data:

$$(5) \quad Fp_t = b_0 + b_1\mu_t + b_2Fp_{t-1} + b_3EMSdum + b_4Political$$

$$+ b_5Realign + e_t$$

where

EMSdum is a dummy variable set equal to 1 from March 1979,

Political and Realign refer to the set of political decisions and exchange rate re-alignments detailed below,

$$\mu_t^2 = Alpha(0) + Alpha(1)e_{t-1}^2 + Beta(1)\mu_{t-1}^2, \text{ and}$$

$$e_t \sim N(0, \mu_t).$$

The ARCH technique allows a linear regression model to have residuals with changing variance. The generalized version of the original ARCH model (GARCH) provides for the existence of a moving average term and "weighting factors" in the variance of the error term. These weighting factors can include any number of variables hypothesized to affect the variance. By including a lagged dependent variable, we capture any persistence in the error term arising from 1) monthly sampling of a three month forward premia, or 2) any auto-correlation due to the persistence of shocks. GARCH is utilized for estimating the equation.[7]

We create political and re-alignment variables using the information from Weber's (1991, pp. 65-67) Table 1 (See Appendix 1). The re-alignment variable is 0 except when a re-alignment occurs. It then takes on the value of the re-alignment against the Deutschmark (DM). For example, in June of 1982 the DM re-valued by 4.25% and the French franc (FF) de-valued by 5.75% for a total devaluation of 10%. The political variable is continuous and "switches" to a higher value with each new political event that might enhance credibility. For example, the variable is 0 for France until October 5, 1981, when France instituted a temporary price and profit freeze. It is then 1. It becomes 2 in June of 1982 with the new budget plans and 3 in March of 1983 when the stringent austerity program was instituted. It increases in this way, becoming 11 when capital controls were removed in July of 1990.

The formulation of the political variable weights equally each political event and does not account for actions that might have hurt credibility. This biases the tests against our hypothesis that credibility was raised over time by domestic political actions. Some political events may not have influenced expectations to a large degree

---

[7] GARCH estimates are produced using the TSP software package. The algorithm used in the ARCH procedure is BHHH, which solves for the coefficient estimates iteratively.

or may have hurt credibility. Indeed, the single political variable conflates stronger policy actions such as fiscal austerity packages with other weaker signals whose effects may be less clear cut. In Westbrook (1993), the relative importance of the different types of policy actions is examined by breaking policy decisions into categories. Events which signal intent are distinguished from cases where actions were undertaken. Further, weak actions are distinguished from strong actions. This investigation suggests that fiscal policy adjustments are, in fact, the most important factor in enhancing credibility.

The pattern of results reported here was not significantly altered when tests were undertaken to examine the effects of adding a time trend to the model. The inclusion of a time trend tests for the degree to which the changes in expectations can be attributed to expectations simply adjusting continuously over the time period for which the authorities maintained the peg as opposed to adjusting in response to specific policy actions. As such, this empirical issue mirrors the distinction between credibility enhancement as fundamentals adjust and the gains in reputation that occur from sticking to stated policies.[8]

Summary statistics are presented in Table 1. The estimation results, allowing for one lagged dependent variable, are in Table 2. The countries studied are Belgium, Denmark, France, Italy, the Netherlands, and the United Kingdom. While the lagged dependent variable is also statistically significant, the most striking feature of the results is the consistent significance of the political variable across the EMS countries that participated in the ERM from its inception in 1979.[9] There is evidence of a time-varying risk-premium for all countries. The United Kingdom does not appear to have gained credibility as the political events unfolded. This probably follows from the fact that the United Kingdom did not join the ERM until 1990, and hence was not pegging over the vast majority of the 1971-1991 sample period.

The GARCH(1,1) model is not fully satisfactory in this context because it shows signs of a non-stationary conditional variance, which is indicative of an Integrated ARCH process (IGARCH). IGARCH occurs when the coefficients on the autoregressive and the moving average components (Alpha(1) and Beta(1)) of the

---

[8] The formulation employed here does not account for events that might have reduced credibility over the time period studied. However, the paucity of strong government actions that might have hurt credibility suggests that the exclusion of credibility-reducing events in this study should not produce any substantial bias (see Westbrook, 1993 for further analysis). Further, the bias that is created should lead to a failure to reject the null hypothesis.

[9] Augmented Dickey Fuller tests were used in testing for the stationarity of the forward premia. The results universally rejected the null hypothesis of a unit root for the forward premia data.

variance equation equal one (see Bollerslev, Chou and Kroner, 1992). Lamoreaux and Lastrapes (1990) argue that when empirical estimates show evidence of an IGARCH process, the most likely cause is mis-specification of the variance equation. When IGARCH occurs the estimates in the mean equation remain asymptotically unbiased, however (Bollerslev, Chou and Kroner, 1992). Accordingly, the estimates reported in Table 2 are not invalidated.

The above results provide support for the hypothesis that pegging adds to credibility when the political costs of devaluing are high. Notice that the EMS dummy is not statistically significant for any of the EMS countries except for the Netherlands. This finding suggests that there was generally no discrete jump in credibility associated with initial participation in the EMS, and that the foreign exchange markets adjusted only gradually as subsequent political events appeared to confirm the EMS countries' commitment to the "DM standard." The evidence of the Netherlands being an exception here is itself consistent with Weber's (1991) conclusion that the Netherlands was the only EMS country to have used a hard-peg strategy in line with Germany. Weber suggests, meanwhile, that the rest of the core EMS countries used a soft-peg strategy by pegging to the French franc.

In order to check for the robustness of the estimation results, a covered interest parity model is imposed upon the data, and interest rate differentials are used as a proxy for changes in the expected spot rate. The same political and re-alignment variables are used. The results are reported in Table 3. The data begins in 1978, so the use of the EMS dummy is likely not helpful in checking for a regime change but it is included for completeness. Another limitation is that the required data on euro-currency interest rate differentials are available only for France, Italy and the Netherlands. In this case, the political variables are once again found to be statistically significant for France and Italy -- thus providing support for the qualitative discussion in Goodman (1992) and Woolley (1992).[10] These results help provide insight into the impact of political events on expectation formation in Europe. The political events seem to have enhanced credibility and contributed to a decline in interest rate differentials. Yet, evidence from the coefficient estimates in the forward premium equation shows that full credibility was lacking.

---

[10] In the case of the Netherlands, the EMS dummy remains significant as before but the political dummy is now insignificant.

Table 1

Summary Statistics: 3 Month Annualized Euro-Interest Rates, monthly data (1978:01-1990:12), and 3 Month Forward Premium/Discount, monthly data (1971:01-1991:11).

INTEREST RATE DIFFERENTIALS (DOMESTIC RATE MINUS GERMAN RATE) BROKEN DOWN BY PERIOD

Sample period 1978:01 - 1984:01

EMS members	mean	st. dev	Non-EMS member	mean	st. dev.
France	7.13	4.25	U.K.	5.57	2.53
Germany	0.00	0.00			
Italy	13.20	3.02			
Netherlands	1.02	1.65			

Sample period 1984:02 - 1987:01

EMS members	mean	st. dev	Non-EMS member	mean	st. dev.
France	5.65	2.07	U.K.	5.87	1.38
Germany	0.00	0.00			
Italy	8.78	1.90			
Netherlands	0.95	0.39			

Sample period 1987:02 - 1990:12

EMS members	mean	st. dev	Non-EMS members	mean	st. dev
France	3.04	1.26	U.K.	6.22	0.88
Germany	0.00	0.00			
Italy	5.64	1.05			
Netherlands	0.43	0.58			

FORWARD PREMIUM/DISCOUNT
COMPLETE SAMPLE

	mean	st. dev
1971:01 - 1991:11		
France	-4.97	3.60
Netherlands	-0.86	1.49
U.K.	-5.56	2.42
1978:01 - 1991:08		
Belgium	-3.99	2.42
Denmark	-5.92	3.66

Table 1 (cont'd)

1974:01 - 1991:11

Italy   -9.56   4.95

BROKEN DOWN BY PERIOD

Sample period 1978:01 - 1984:01

	mean	st. dev
Belgium	- 5.44	2.30
Denmark	- 8.36	3.80
France	- 5.71	4.01
Italy	-12.02	4.90
Netherlands	- 1.00	1.83
U.K.	- 5.62	2.81

Sample period 1984:02 - 1987:01

	mean	st. dev
Belgium	-4.52	1.36
Denmark	-4.75	1.03
France	-5.64	2.00
Italy	-8.84	1.90
Netherlands	-0.86	0.40
U.K.	-5.74	1.35

Sample period 1987:02 - 1991:11

	mean	st. dev
Belgium	-1.70	1.04
Denmark	-3.46	2.37
France	-2.52	1.60
Italy	-4.90	2.01
Netherlands	-0.45	0.47
U.K.	-5.26	1.74

Note: Italian data are from DRI and cover only 1981:01 - 1990:06. All other data are from the International Financial Statistics tape. Netherlands data are quarterly, the rest are monthly.

7.   CONCLUSIONS AND IMPLICATIONS

Our results suggest that EMS membership has had a significant effect upon the risk premia and interest rate differentials amongst the participating countries. Thus, we offer some support for the premise that commitment to the EMS exchange rate arrangements permitted the member countries to build up some credibility as the political costs of breaking the arrangement grew over time. However, our results strongly reject the simplistic view that the mere announcement that a country will participate in the EMS fosters immediate credibility gains (Giavazzi and Pagano, 1988). Any benefits accruing from using Germany as a low inflation, "anchor" country seem to have accrued only gradually over a period of years -- and the exchange rate regime may not have mattered as much as did the actual anti-inflationary policy actions that were undertaken in the member countries. Our findings suggest that EMS countries may have an incentive to persevere with the ERM even if the ultimate goal of a common currency should become unattainable. Certainly, there is no evidence of any inflationary effects associated with the operation of the pegged system. On the other hand, it is not clear that the EMS experience really provides any evidence in favor of pegged exchange rates per se. Rather, it appears that it is the revealed willingness of member countries to adopt painful austerity in order to match Germany's anti-inflationary policies that were key to the disinflation achieved during the 1980s. Commitment to the German standard perhaps became a way of signalling a change in the relative weights attached to inflation and unemployment in traditionally higher-inflation countries such as France and Italy.

The implications for other countries that are presently adopting pegged exchange rates do not appear to be particularly favorable, at least in the short run. Doubts that the market may have had about the sustainability of the new pegged rates adopted in countries such as Poland appear to have been confirmed by the devaluations that took place in 1991. On the other hand, there is reason to hope that, over time, a more general commitment to anti-inflationary policies will enable the governments of such countries to reap the same sort of credibility gains earned by a number of the EMS countries.

However, an exchange rate peg is only one element in a government's economic policies.[11] It was the observed sustained commitment to prudent macro-

---

[11] We have argued elsewhere (Burdekin, Westbrook and Willett, forthcoming) that countries with independent central banks have consistently enjoyed lower inflation rates than countries whose central banks are under direct government control. It may not be coincidental that the two countries most strongly associated with the "hard currency policy" in the EMS, namely Germany and the Netherlands, also have the most autonomous central banks within the System (see also Burdekin, Wihlborg and Willett, 1992).

Table 2

ARCH ESTIMATES

ARCH or GARCH Estimation. Dependent Variable: Forward Premium/ Discount.
Monthly Federal Reserve data, 1971:01-1991:11.

NON-EMS COUNTRY:

UNITED KINGDOM

Constant	Fp(-1)	EMSdum	Political
-.464	.902	-.058	.053
(.154)**	(.023)**	(.120)	(.069)

Alpha(0)	Alpha(1)
.649	.468
(.059)**	(.103)**

$R^2 = .820$,   DW = 1.61,   NOB = 250

EMS COUNTRIES:

BELGIUM

Constant	Fp(-1)	EMSdum	Political	Realign
-1.359	.770	-.157	.192	23.349
(.689)*	(.035)**	(.690)	(.027)**	(12.166)

Alpha(0)	Alpha(1)	Beta(1)
.0021	.335	.717
(.0031)	(.069)**	(.032)**

$R^2 = .784$,   DW = 1.90,   NOB = 163

DENMARK

Constant	Fp(-1)	EMSdum	Political	Realign
-2.422	.804	.895	.166	22.246
(.862)**	(.051)**	(.610)	(.064)*	(8.211)**

Alpha(0)	Alpha(1)	Beta(1)
.052	.261	.723
(.037)	(.085)**	(.074)**

$R^2 = .805$,   DW = 1.475,   NOB = 163

Table 2 (cont'd)

FRANCE

Constant	Fp(-1)	EMSdum	Political	Realign
-1.038	.851	-.007	.093	3.681
(.143)**	(.023)**	(.114)	(.015)**	(10.074)

Alpha(0)	Alpha(1)	Beta(1)
.008	.525	.635
(.009)	(.095)**	(.036)**

$R^2 = .774$,   DW = 1.84,   NOB = 250

ITALY

Constant	Fp(-1)	EMSdum	Political	Realign
-2.125	.833	-.119	.193	-9.627
(.337)**	(.039)**	(.343)	(.045)**	(3.972)*

Alpha(0)	Alpha(1)	Beta(1)
.0054	.349	.721
(.012)	(.056)**	(.032)**

$R^2 = .785$,   DW = 1.66,   NOB = 214

NETHERLANDS

Constant	Fp(-1)	EMSdum	Political	Realign
.164	.844	-.363	.041	-11.497
(.062)**	(.027)**	(.071)**	(.011)**	(40.175)

Alpha(0)	Alpha(1)	Beta(1)
.0017	.570	.598
(.0011)	(.089)**	(.048)**

$R^2 = .668$,   DW = 1.75,   NOB = 250

Note: ** denotes significance at the 5% level
         * denotes significance at the 10% level
         Standard errors are in parentheses
         DW is the value of the Durbin-Watson statistic
         NOB is the number of observations

economic policies that appears to have been the major source of EMS credibility gains. The question of whether the credibility increase exceeded the gains that could have been attained under flexible exchange rates remains an important issue for future research.

Table 3

UNCOVERED INTEREST PARITY ESTIMATES

Dependent Variable: Euro-Interest Rate Differentials with Germany, Domestic Rate minus German Rate. Monthly data, 1978:01-1990:12.

NON-EMS COUNTRY:

UNITED KINGDOM

Constant	r-r*(-1)	EMSdum	Political
1.349	.879	-.714	.015
(.346)**	(.035)**	(.248)**	(.058)

$R^2 = .833$,   Dh = 3.856,   NOB = 155

EMS COUNTRIES:

FRANCE

Constant		r-r*(-1)	EMSdum	Political Realign
.599	.839	.809	-.109	16.640
(.614)	(.049)**	(.585)	(.049)*	(12.844)

$R^2 = .734$,   Dh = -.345,   NOB = 155

ITALY (DRI data 1981:02 - 1990:06)

Constant	r-r*(-1)	Political	Realign
1.992	.888	-.194	9.486
(.669)**	(.040)**	(.066)**	(6.077)

$R^2 = .930$,   Dh = 3.76,   NOB = 113

Table 3 (cont'd)

NETHERLANDS (Quarterly data 1978:01 - 1990:04)

Constant	r-r*(-1)	EMSdum	Political	Realign
3.239	.531	-2.929	-.041	7.822
(.601)**	(.099)**	(.605)**	(.088)	(23.643)

R^2 = .602,   Dh = 1.041,   NOB = 50

Note: Dh is the value of Durbin's h-statistic

REFERENCES

Abel, István and Bonin, John P. "The 'Big Bang' Versus 'Slow But Steady': A Comparison of the Hungarian and the Polish Transformations." Discussion Paper No. 626, Centre for Economic Policy Research, London, January 1992.

Artus, P. "The European Monetary System, Exchange Rate Expectations and the Reputation of the Authorities," in Carlo Carraro, Didier Laussel, Mark Salmon, and Antoine Sonbeyran (eds.), *International Economic Policy Co-Ordination*, Basil Blackwell, Oxford, 1991, pp. 9-34.

Baillie, Richard T. and Bollerslev, Tim. "A Multivariate Generalized ARCH Approach to Modeling Risk Premia in Forward Foreign Exchange Rate Markets." *Journal of International Money and Finance* 9 (September 1990): 309-324.

Bofinger, Peter. "Options for a New Monetary Framework for the Area of the Soviet Union." Discussion Paper No. 604, Centre for Economic Policy Research, London, November 1991.

Bofinger, Peter and Daniel Gros. "A Multilateral Payments Union for the Commonwealth of Independent States: Why and How?" Discussion Paper No. 654, Centre for Economic Policy Research, London, May 1992.

Bollerslev, Tim; Chou, Ray Y. and Kroner, Kenneth F. "ARCH Modeling in Finance: A Review of the Theory and Empirical Evidence." *Journal of Econometrics* 52 (April-May 1992): 5-59.

Bruno, M. "High Inflation and the Nominal Anchors of an Open Economy." *Essays in International Finance*, No. 183, Princeton University, June 1991.

Bruno, M. "From Sharp Stabilization to Growth: On the Political Economy of Israel's Transition." *European Economic Review* 36 (April 1992): 310-319.

Burdekin, Richard C.K. and Burkett, Paul. "Hyperinflation, the Exchange Rate, and Endogenous Money: Post-World War I Germany Revisited." Paper presented at the meetings of the North American Economics and Finance Association in Anaheim, California, January 5-7, 1993.

Burdekin, Richard C.K.; Westbrook, Jilleen R. and Willett, Thomas D. "The Political Economy of Discretionary Monetary Policy: A Public Choice Analysis of Proposals for Reform," in Richard H. Timberlake and Kevin Dowd (eds.), *Money and the Nation State*, The Independent Institute, forthcoming.

Burdekin, Richard C.K.; Wihlborg, Clas and Willett, Thomas D. "A Monetary Constitution Case for an Independent European Central Bank." *World Economy* 15 (March 1992): 231-249.

Carter, Michael and Maddock, Rodney. "Inflation: The Invisible Foot of Macroeconomics." *Economic Record* 63 (June 1987): 120-128.

Christensen, Michael. "Disinflation, Credibility and Price Inertia: A Danish Exposition." *Applied Economics* 19 (October 1987a): 1353-1366.

Christensen, Michael. "On Interest Rate Determination, Testing for Policy Credibility and the Relevance of the Lucas Critique - Some Danish Experiences." *European Journal of Political Economy* 3 (1987b): 369-388.

Christensen, Michael. "Policy Credibility and the Lucas Critique - Some New Tests with an Application to Denmark," in P. Artus and Y. Barroux (eds.), *Monetary Policy: A Theoretical and Econometric Approach*, Kluwer Academic Publishers, Dordrecht, The Netherlands, 1990, pp. 79-95.

Claassen, Emil-Maria. *Exchange Rate Policies in Developing and Post-Socialist Countries*, Institute for Contemporary Studies Press, San Francisco, California, 1991.

Collins, Susan M. "Inflation and the European Monetary System," in Francesco Giavazzi, Stefano Micossi and Marcus Miller (eds.), *The European Monetary System*, Cambridge University Press, New York, 1988, pp. 112-136.

Crow, John W. "Monetary Policy and the Control of Inflation," in *Central Banking Issues in Emerging Market-Oriented Economies*, A Symposium Sponsored by the Federal Reserve Bank of Kansas City, Kansas City, Missouri, 1990, pp. 9-21.

De Grauwe, Paul. "Disinflation in the EMS and in the non-EMS Countries. What Have We Learned?" *Empirica* 16 (1989): 161-176.

Egebo, Thomas and Englander, A. Steven. "Institutional Commitments and Policy Credibility: A Critical Survey and Evidence from the ERM." *OECD Economic Studies* No. 18 (Spring 1992): 45-84.

Engle, Robert F. "Autoregressive Conditional Heteroscedasticity With Estimates of the Variance of United Kingdom Inflation." *Econometrica* 50 (July 1982): 987-1007.

Frankel, Jeffrey A. and MacArthur, Alan T. "Political vs. Currency Premia in International Real Interest Rate Differentials: A Study of Forward Rates for 24 Countries." *European Economic Review* 32 (June 1988): 1083-1114.

Frankel, Jeffrey and Phillips, Steven. "The European Monetary System: Credible at Last?" Working Paper No. 3819, National Bureau of Economic Research, August 1991.

Fratianni, Michele and von Hagen, Jürgen. *The European Monetary System and European Monetary Union*, Westview Press, Boulder, Colorado, 1992.

Friedman, Milton. "The Case for Flexible Exchange Rates" in his *Essays in Positive Economics*, University of Chicago Press, Chicago, Illinois, 1953, pp. 157-203.

Froot, Kenneth A. and Rogoff, Kenneth. "The EMS, the EMU, and the Transition to a Common Currency," in Olivier Jean Blanchard and Stanley Fischer (eds.), *NBER Macroeconomics Annual 1991*, MIT Press, Cambridge, Massachusetts, 1991, pp. 269-317.

Giavazzi, Francesco and Giovannini, Alberto. "The Role of the Exchange-Rate Regime in Disinflation: Empirical Evidence on the European Monetary System," in Francesco Giavazzi, Stefano Micossi and Marcus Miller (eds), *The European Monetary System*, Cambridge University Press, New York, 1988, pp. 85-107.

Giavazzi, Francesco and Pagano, Marco. "The Advantage of Tying One's Hands: EMS Discipline and Central Bank Credibility." *European Economic Review* 32 (June 1988): 1055-1082.

Giovannini, Alberto. "European Monetary Reform: Progress and Prospects." *Brookings Papers on Economic Activity*, 1990, No. 2: 217-291.

Goodman, John B. *Monetary Sovereignty: The Politics of Central Banking in Western Europe*, Cornell University Press, Ithaca, New York, 1992.

Kiguel, Miguel A. and Liviatan, Nissan. "Stopping Inflation: The Experience of Latin America and Israel and the Implications for Central and Eastern Europe," in Vittorio Corbo, Fabrizio Coricelli and Jan Bossak (eds.), *Reforming Central and Eastern European Economies: Initial Results and Challenges*, World Bank, Washington, D.C., 1991, pp. 83-100.

Lächler, Ulrich. "Credibility and the Dynamics of Disinflation in Open Economies: A Note on the Southern Cone Experiments." *Journal of Development Economics* 28 (May 1988): 285-307.

Lamoreaux, Christopher G. and Lastrapes, William D. "Persistence in Variance, Structural Change, and the GARCH Model." *Journal of Business and Economic Statistics* 8 (April 1990): 225-234.

Melitz, Jacques. "Monetary Discipline and Cooperation in the European Monetary System: A Synthesis," in Francesco Giavazzi, Stefano Micossi and Marcus Miller (eds.), *The European Monetary System*, Cambridge University Press, New York, 1988, pp. 51-79.

Parks, Michael. "Russia Frees Ruble to Float as Part of Market Reforms." *Los Angeles Times*, July 2, 1992: A9.

Robinson, Joan. "Review of *The Economics of Inflation*, by C. Bresciani-Turroni." *Economic Journal* 48 (September 1938): 507-513.

Solimano, Andres. "Inflation and the Costs of Stabilization: Historical and Recent Experiences and Policy Lessons." *World Bank Research Observer* 5 (July 1990): 167-186.

Tower, Edward and Willett, Thomas D. *The Theory of Optimum Currency Areas and Exchange Rate Flexibility*, Special Papers in International Economics, No. 11, Princeton University, May 1976.

von Hagen, Jürgen. "Policy-Delegation and Fixed Exchange Rates." Mimeo, Indiana University, February 1990.

Weber, Axel. "Reputation and Credibility in the European Monetary System." *Economic Policy* No. 12 (April 1991): 57-102.

Westbrook, Jilleen R. "The Effects of Exchange Rate Pegging on the Credibility of Stabilization Programs: An Empirical Investigation of the European Monetary System." Unpublished Ph.D. Dissertation, Claremont Graduate School, May 1993.

Wihlborg, Clas and Willett, Thomas D. "Optimal Currency Areas Revisited on the Transition Path to a Currency Union," in Clas Wihlborg, Michele Fratianni and Thomas D. Willett (eds.), *Financial Regulation and Monetary Arrangements after 1992*, North-Holland, Amsterdam, 1991, pp. 279-297.

Wihlborg, Clas and Willett, Thomas D. "The Instability of Half-Way Measures in the Transition to a Common Currency," in Herbert Grubel (ed.), *EC 1992 - Perspectives from the Outside*, Macmillan, London (forthcoming, 1993).

Willett, Thomas D. and Mullen, John. "The Effects of Alternative International Monetary Systems on Macroeconomic Discipline and Inflationary Biases," in Raymond E. Lombra and Willard E. Witte (eds.), *Political Economy of International and Domestic Monetary Relations*, Iowa State University Press, Ames, Iowa, 1982, pp. 143-156.

Willett, Thomas D. and Wolf, Matthias. "The Vicious Circle Debate: Some Conceptual Distinctions." *Kyklos* 36 (1983): 231-248.

Willett, Thomas D.; Al Marhubi, Fahim and Dahel, Riad." Currency Policies for Eastern Europe and the Commonwealth Countries: An Optimum Currency Areas Approach." Paper presented at the meetings of the Atlantic Economic Society in Anaheim, California, January 5-7, 1993.

Williamson, John. "Comments on 'Stopping Inflation: The Experience of Latin America and Israel and the Implications for Central and Eastern Europe' by Miguel A. Kiguel and Nissan Liviatan," in Vittorio Corbo, Fabrizio Coricelli and Jan Bossak (eds.), *Reforming Central and Eastern European Economies: Initial Results and Challenges*, World Bank, Washington, D.C., 1991, pp. 135-137.

Woolley, John T. "Policy Credibility and European Monetary Institutions," in Alberta M. Sbragia (ed.), *Euro-Politics: Institutions and Policymaking in the "New" European Community*, Brookings Institution, Washington, D.C., 1992, pp. 157-190.

Appendix 1

Weber's Classification of EMS Realignments and
Selected Policy Changes Signalling a Move Towards More Deflationary
Policies in EMS Member Countries

1979 March 13   EMS: exchange rate mechanism (ERM) starts to operate;
                      initial currency weights in ECU currency basket: DM 32%,
                      FF 19%, UKL 15%, LIT 10.2%, Bf 8.5%, Dkr 2.7%, Dra
                      1.3%, IRL 1.2%.
      Sep. 4   EMS: realignment (DM +2%, Dkr -2.9%).
      Nov. 30 EMS: realignment (Dkr -4.8%).
              Denmark: short-term price and wage freeze.

1981 March 9   Belgian-Luxembourg   Economic   Union   (BLEU):
                      convention for BLEU (fixed parity without bands) renewed
                      for 10 years.
      March 22   EMS: realignment (LIT -6%)
              Italy: government spending cut plans
      July   Italy: Banca d'Italia freed from the obligation to purchase unsold
              public debt at the Treasury auctions, which gave the government
              preferential access to monetizing fiscal deficits.
      July   Netherlands: the Nederlandsche Bank abandons control of domestic
              liquidity and gears its monetary policy towards the external
              constraint, in particular the DM exchange rate.
      Oct. 5 EMS: realignment (DM +5.5%, FF -3%, LIT -3%, Hfl +3.5%).
              France: temporary price and profit freeze.

1982 Feb. 22 EMS: realignment (Bf -8.5%, Dkr -3%).
              Belgium: general price freeze until end of March, selective freeze
              thereafter; freeze of wage indexation (until May); also longer-run
              measures to impede complete wage indexation.

      June 14 EMS: realignment (DM +4.25%, FF -5.75%, LIT -2.75%, Hfl +
              4.25%)
              France: temporary freeze of prices, wages, rents and dividends until
              October; reduction in 1983 budget deficit plans.
      June 23 Italy: announcement of budgetary austerity measures.

      Oct. 16 Denmark: comprehensive stabilization package: automatic wage
              indexation suspended; wage freeze until March 1983; tight fiscal
              policy; progressive dismantling of capital controls.
      Dec. 30 Belgium: selective price freeze extended until end of 1983; wage
              restraint (flat rate indexation) until end of 1984.

1983   March 21   EMS: realignment (DM +5.5%, FF -2.5%, LIT - 2.5%, Hfl
                        + 3.5%, BF + 1.5%, Dkr, +2.5%, IRL -2.5%).
        March 28   France: stringent austerity programme aiming at bringing
                        down inflation via monetary restraint, restoring external
                        balance via foreign exchange controls and reducing the
                        public budget deficit by cutting expenditures and raising
                        taxes.
        April 12   Denmark: government announces further liberalization of
                        capital movements to take place on May 1.
        April   Denmark: government guidelines for an upper-limit of 2% for the
                annual wage increase in the new two-year wage agreement.
        Dec.   EEC: target dates for the expiry of capital restrictions set for France
                (end of 1986) Italy and Ireland (end of 1987) in order to allow for
                a gradual relaxation of the controls.

1984   Sept. 17 EMS: revision of currency weights in ECU currency basket (DM
                32%, FF 19%, UKL 15%, LIT 10.2%, Hfl 10.1%, Bf 8.5%, Dkr
                2.7%, DRA 1.3%, IRL 1.2%).

1985   Jan. 1 France: start of a two-year transition of monetary policy operating
                procedures from quantitative credit controls to a more market based
                system of reserve requirements.
        March 12   EMS: Council of Central Bank Governors decides on a
                        package to strengthen role of the ECU in the EMS.
        April   Denmark: government enforces a 2% legal upper limit for the
                annual wage increase in the new two-year wage agreement.
        July 22 EMS: realignment (DM +2%, FF+2%, LIT -6%, Hfl +2%, Bf +2%,
                Dkr +2%, IRL +2%)
        July   Italy: announcement of revenue raising measures to contain the
                increase in the budget deficit.
                Italy: modification of wage indexation mechanism, scala mobile.

1986   Feb.   EEC: European Single Act sets 31. December 1992 as target date
                for completion of internal market with free movement of goods,
                persons, services and capital.
        Apr. 7 EMS: realignment (DM +3%, FF-3%, Hfl +3%, Bf +1%, Dkr
                +1%).
                France: steps to slow nominal wage growth; plans to reduce
                government budget deficit; relaxation of exchange controls.
        June   Denmark: wage indexation law (suspended 1982) is abolished.
        Aug. 4 EMS: realignment (IRL -8%)

1987   Jan. 12 EMS: realignment (DM +3%, Hfl +3%, Bf +2%, Dkr, +2%)
        Sept. 12 EMS: Basle-Nyborg Agreement of the Committee of Central Bank
                Governors to strengthen the exchange rate mechanism of the EMS;

measures include a wider use of fluctuation bands, an extension of
the very short-run financing facilities and the use of ECU for
inframarginal intervention.

1989   Apr. 17 EMS: Delors Committee Report proposes a three stage transition to
                Economic and Monetary Union:
                stage 1: extension of ERM to all EMS member countries, reduction
                of fluctuation bands to narrow range, infrequent realignments
                subject to mutual agreement, full capital mobility;
                stage 2: creation of new Community institution, increasing co-
                ordination of national monetary policies;
                stage 3a: irrevocably fixed exchange rates without bands, new
                Community institutions (Eurofed) functioning:
                stage 3b: single currency monetary union at a later date.
        June 19 EMS: Spain enters the exchange rate mechanism of the EMS with
                a wide fluctuation margin of 6%.
        June 27 EMS: European Council decision to enter the first stage of EMU
                from Delors Committee Report on 1 July 1990.
        Sept. 21 EMS: revision of currency weights in ECU currency basket (DM
                30.1%, FF 19%, UKL 13%, LIT 10.15%, Hfl 9.4%, Bf 7.9%, PES
                5.3%, Dkr 2.45%, IRL 1.1%, DRA .8%, ESC .8%)

1990   Jan   EMS: realignment (LIT -3.7%), narrowing of band to 2.25%.
        June   Belgium: central bank declares German mark exchange rate as its
                main official policy target.
        July 1 EMS: complete removal of all capital controls except for Ireland,
                Spain, Portugal, and Greece (deadline 1992).
                Germany: monetary union between East and West Germany.
        Oct. 3 Germany: six East German federal states join the Federal Republic
                of Germany.
        Oct. 8 EMS: UK enters the exchange rate mechanism of the EMS with a
                wide fluctuation margin of 6%.

Source: Weber (1991, Table 1, pp. 65-67).

CHAPTER 4

HOW MUCH TO COMMIT TO AN EXCHANGE RATE RULE: BALANCING CREDIBILITY AND FLEXIBILITY

Alex Cukierman
Miguel A. Kiguel
Nissan Liviatan

1. INTRODUCTION

A fixed exchange rate can be supported by various degrees of commitment. The gold standard represents the strongest possible commitment, in the sense that domestic money must be fully backed by gold, governments have no leeway in setting the money supply, and changes in the parity are extremely rare events. A currency board is a slightly weaker commitment, as domestic currency may be only partly backed by foreign assets. Similarly, the fixed exchange rates regime under the Bretton Woods system was even weaker, as central banks were not required to back the issuance of money with foreign assets, and devaluations were accepted as part of the rules of the game (especially to deal with external imbalances).

Fixed exchange rates have become a central component in many disinflation programs. The successful stabilization programs of Israel (1985) and Mexico (1987) started with a fixed exchange rate, and so did the less successful Austral plan in Argentina (1985) and the Cruzado plan in Brazil (1986). The Chilean stabilization process of 1974-82 relied on a fixed exchange rate at a late stage for around three years. Likewise Denmark and Ireland and other European countries fixed their exchange rates within the EMS.[1]

An important difference among these programs is the strength of the commitment to the fixed exchange rate. The weakest commitment states that the exchange rate will be fixed (in order to provide a nominal anchor for the stabilization program), but with the implicit understanding that the rule will be changed if inflation

---

[1] The first four programs are described in Bruno, Fischer Helpman and Liviatan (1991). Giavazzi and Pagano (1991) examine the Danish and Irish stabilization programs.

persists (e.g. in the Cruzado plan). A stronger commitment is effected when the fixed exchange rate is supported with a promise not to print money to finance the budget deficit, as for example in the Israeli program or the Austral Plan. A third group of countries went further by supporting the fixed exchange rate with a legal obligation to back all or part of the issuance of money with foreign assets, as in the programs aimed at stopping the Europeans hyperinflations in the 1920s, or in the 1991 Convertibility plan in Argentina.[2]

Full dollarization, understood as complete substitution of the U.S. dollar for the domestic currency as the only legal tender, is a special case of a fixed exchange rate. While this regime has been proposed as a way to bring down inflation, it has not yet been implemented in Latin America for this purpose. A distinctive feature of this arrangement is that the government gives up the privilege to collect seigniorage.[3] We want to make clear at this point that full dollarization can be abandoned, in the same way that countries in the past renege from strong commitments, such as during the gold standard. During that era, countries either suspended convertibility of the domestic currency or alternatively devalue the currency when facing severe external shocks. In both cases the decisions implied reneging on a commitment that was probably equivalent to what full dollarization would be nowadays.

By making a stronger commitment, a policymaker "ties his hands" to a certain degree and hence he is more likely to successfully affect inflationary expectations. The reason is that the political costs of reneging from a given exchange rate regime are generally larger the tighter the commitment implicit in that regime. As a consequence the announcement of a fixed exchange rate has a stronger impact on expectations when it is associated with monetary institutions that imply a stronger commitment. But, even strong commitments can be broken.

This paper examines the considerations that policymakers typically take into account before choosing a commitment level. We view the strength of the commitment as being inversely related to the potential costs of reneging on it. An implication of this approach is that one explanation for not observing high inflation countries rushing to full dollarization as a way to bring down inflation is that policymakers are not sufficiently confident that they can sustain the regime for a prolonged time, especially because such economies are prone to large, adverse external shocks. It is this concern that induces their policymakers to maintain national currencies.

---

    [2]   Canavese (1992) provides and excellent description of the convertibility program.

    [3]   Panama is the only fully dollarized economy in Latin America, but its original adoption was not related to an attempt to stop high inflation.

The need to raise seigniorage is less important in our view. The economies that are now considering full dollarization are those that are seriously trying to stabilize, and hence are willing to eliminate the budget deficit. In addition, if they succeed in stabilizing, the revenue from seigniorage is likely to be small (low inflation economies generally collect around one percent of GDP from seigniorage). In Argentina or Brazil, this amount represents around 3 percent of revenues of the consolidated public sector. It is thus doubtful that a serious stabilizer will not dollarize because he is worried about losing this relatively meager revenue.

There are a number of reasons that can force governments to finally devalue. In almost every case devaluations are induced by balance of payments problems. In some cases the external difficulties arise from inconsistencies in the design of the program, e.g. the exchange rate is maintained fixed while at the same there are significant budget deficits financed by money creation. In other cases, however, adverse external shocks or unfavorable domestic political developments are the main causes for reneging on an announcement. As a result, in an uncertain world, the ability to precommit is greatly affected by the nature and distribution of shocks.

A second type of problem is that the public is typically uncertain about the extent to which the policymaker in office views his announcement as a serious commitment. Policies to stabilize prices are put in place by governments who are ready to pay the related costs, as well as by those who most likely will abandon them as soon as signs of hardship show up. It is thus difficult to anticipate, at the beginning, what will be the response of a policymaker. As a result, most stabilization programs face adverse expectations in the sense that even a policymaker who largely intends to be live up to his policy preannouncements is not fully believed.

The purpose of this paper is to identify the factors which determine the strength of commitment that policymakers choose to back up a fixed exchange rate system. In practice the commitment level is achieved by choosing a particular set of monetary and exchange rate arrangements. Section 2 develops a Barro-Gordon type model in which the policymaker has to decide how much to commit under uncertainty. An important assumption is that the stronger the commitment to the fixed exchange rate the greater the political cost of reneging on it. Thus, prior to deciding on the choice of exchange rate arrangements the policymaker has to weigh the benefits, to the disinflation program, from making a strong commitment against the potential costs of being forced to renege on it. Some of the more technical details are presented in appendices. Section 3 illustrates the results of the model with examples from Latin American countries. We conclude in section 4 with a comparison of the results of our approach with related work.

2.   THE MODEL

The model highlights the trade off between credibility and flexibility.[4] We assume that the policymaker has some degree of freedom in determining the strength of his commitment to a fixed exchange rate policy. An assertion such as "the exchange rate is pegged to the dollar for the time being but the policy will be reexamined shortly" is a weak commitment. A fixed exchange rate which is a cornerstone of a major stabilization program (as in the Austral plan in Argentina) is a stronger commitment.

We shall model the uncertainty about the seriousness of the policy announcement by assuming that there are two types of policymakers - a dependable one (D) who is subject to a reneging cost and an alternative policymaker (W) who is not bound by his policy announcement. D incurs a cost of reneging which W does not. The public has a prior probability (α) that the policymaker is D. This prior is used in forming expectations.

The objective functions of D and W are given by a modified version of the Barro-Gordon model.

$$J_D = x(\pi - \pi^e) - h\frac{\pi^2}{2} - bc \tag{1a}$$

$$J_W = x(\pi - \pi^e) - \frac{h\pi^2}{2} \tag{1b}$$

$$x \geq 0, \quad 0 \leq c \leq 1, \quad h, \ b > 0.$$

$\pi - \pi^e$ denotes the surprise-devaluation, i.e. the devaluation in excess of what was expected. By creating a surprise devaluation the policymaker can create a temporary real devaluation, or a reduction in real wages, which will improve the trade balance. However, devaluation (inflation) as such is undesirable, as is reflected by the term $(-\frac{h}{2}\pi^2)$.

If D announces a fixed exchange rate he also chooses the degree of commitment c. The cost of deviating from the rule is bc, where b is a fixed parameter that determines the size of the cost incurred by D when he reneges on a commitment of degree c. One reason for the existence of this cost is that a broken commitment undermines the subsequent dependability of the policymaker (both in economic as well as in political terms). This is something that D cares about but W does not. Breaking a commitment shows that the policymaker is unable to live by the rules

---

[4] Related discussions appear in Flood and Isard (1989), and Lohmann (1992).

which he himself set. However, abiding to the rules is an essential input into the reduction of long term inflationary expectations (this goes beyond π^e in our model). We interpret c as the proportion of agents who take the exchange rate announcement seriously. We assume that the policymaker can influence this proportion by the strength of his assertion. However, the larger is c the larger will be the cost of reneging. W does not incur any cost of reneging.

The parameter x measures the relative importance that the policymaker attaches to output gains from surprise inflation as compared with his aversion to inflation (devaluation) as in the Barro-Gordon model. We consider x as a being subject to shocks which may be due either to external developments (a balance of payment crises may raise the preference for output gains) or to unexpected changes in the balance of power between groups which favor a reduction in unemployment and those who attach greater importance to price stability.

The interaction between the policymaker in office and the public can be thought of as a four-stage game which relates to a fixed exchange rate regime. First the policymaker chooses his degree of commitment (c) to the regime. In the second stage the preference parameter (x) realizes. In the third stage, after the realization of x, the public forms its expectation of the rate of devaluation π^e. In the fourth, and final, stage the policymaker picks the actual rate of devaluation (π). If D does not renege $\pi_D=0$, and if he does $\pi_D>0$ as will be seen later. The following figure summarizes the timing of events.

1	2	3	4
Policymaker chooses c	x realizes	public forms expectations π^e	Policymaker picks π

Note that the only thing which the public does not know in stage 3 is the identity of the policymaker. The announcement of c in the first stage does not reveal the type because W, for whom the announcement is costless, will always mimics D's announcement (but not necessarily his acts).

To ensure the time consistency of the solution for D we start from the final stage and work backward in the dynamic-programming fashion. According to (1) D will renege on the fixed exchange rate if his benefit from maintaining $\pi=0$ is less than the benefit of adjusting π optimally in view of the realization of x. In the case of reneging both W and D will find it optimal to set

$$\pi_w = \frac{x}{h}. \tag{2}$$

According to (1) D will renege if

$$x(\frac{x}{h}-\pi e)-\frac{x^2}{2}h - bc > -\pi^e x \tag{3}$$

which implies that reneging will take place when

$$x > (2hbc)^{\frac{1}{2}} \equiv x_c \tag{3'}$$

Hence

$$\pi_D(x) = \begin{cases} 0 & if \quad x \leq x_c \\ \dfrac{x}{h} & if \quad x > x_c \end{cases}. \tag{4}$$

For any agent who takes the announcement of the fixed exchange rate seriously the expected π is $\alpha\pi_D + (1-\alpha)\pi_W$. We assume that for any other agent $\pi^e = \pi_W$. Since the proportion of the former group is c, the (average) expected π in the population is

$$\pi^e_{(x)} = c[\alpha\pi_D + (1-\alpha)\pi_w] + (1-c)\pi_w = c\alpha\pi_D(x) + (1-c\alpha)x. \tag{5}$$

Hence

$$\pi^e(x) = \begin{cases} (1-\alpha c)\dfrac{x}{h} & if \ x \leq x_c \\ \dfrac{x}{h} & if \ x > x_c \end{cases}. \tag{6}$$

D's objective in stage 1 is as follows:

if $x \leq x_c$

$$J_D(x) = x\left[0-(1-\alpha c)\frac{x}{h}\right] - \frac{0.h}{2} = -(1-\alpha c)\frac{x^2}{h} \tag{7}$$

and if $x > x_c$

$$J_D(x) = x\left(\frac{x}{h}-\frac{x}{h}\right)-\frac{h}{2}\left(\frac{x}{h}\right)^2 - bc = -\left(\frac{1}{2h}x^2-bc\right) \tag{8}$$

Hence

$$Q(c) \equiv EJ_D(x) = \int_0^{x_c} -(1-c\alpha)\frac{x^2}{h}dF(x) - \int_{x_c}^{\infty}\left(\frac{x^2}{2}h + bc\right)dF(x) \tag{9}$$

where F is the distribution function of x and (from (3')) $x_c = (2hbc)^{\frac{1}{2}}$.

We assume, for simplicity the uniform distribution with density K in the interval [0,a], i.e. $0 \le x \le a$.[5] The objective function can then be written as

$$Q(c) = -K\left[\left(\frac{1-\alpha c}{h}\right)\int_0^{x_c} x^2 dx + \int_{x_c}^{a}\left(\frac{1}{2h}x^2 + bc\right)dx\right] \tag{10}$$

After some algebra this reduces to

$$aQ(c) = -\left(\frac{\frac{1}{2}-\alpha c}{3h}\right)x_c^3 - \frac{a^3}{6h} + bcx_c - bca. \tag{11}$$

A straightforward calculation (see appendix) shows that the second order derivative of Q with respect to c is always positive. Hence the optimal value of c occurs at the boundary of its range, and must, therefore, be at either c = 0 or c = 1. This special feature is not an essential part of the problem. It is a consequence of the particular density function chosen. But since, the main qualitative results of our discussion carry over to more general cases we illustrate them, for simplicity, by means of the uniform distribution.

The maximal commitment c=1 arises when Q(1) > Q(0). This implies (see appendix) that there is a commitment when the following inequality holds

$$\Delta \equiv a \ [Q(1) - Q(0)] = \left(\frac{\alpha-\frac{1}{2}}{3h}\right)x_c^3 + b(x_c-a))0^{1/2}. \tag{12}$$

It follows from this inequality that a commitment is more likely to result, when credibility (α) is higher and when the range of x (i.e. a) is smaller (since $x_c < a$ there will be no commitment with $\alpha < \frac{1}{2}$). This likelihood will also rise with h provided

---

[5]Note that aK=1. It is also assumed that at c=1 $x_c<a$, i.e. there are values of x for which D will renege.

$\alpha > \frac{1}{2}$ (this is a sufficient but not necessary condition). The effect of a larger b is ambiguous.[6]

Let us turn now to the intuition behind these results.

Consider first the effect of α on commitment. Viewed from stage 1 (before the realization of x) the expected value of π^e (x), when D is in office is

$$E_x \pi^e(x) = \begin{cases} \dfrac{Ex}{h} - \alpha \dfrac{b}{a} & \text{when } c = 1 \\[3mm] \dfrac{Ex}{h} & \text{when } c = 0 \end{cases} \tag{13}$$

where Ex is the expected value of x (also equal to $\frac{a}{b^2}$). Hence by making a commitment (setting c=1) expectations are reduced by $\alpha \frac{a}{a}$. Thus the larger is α the larger the average reduction in inflationary expectations that is achieved through the commitment to a fixed exchange rate regime.

A similar calculation with respect to π_D (the average realized rate of devaluation when D is in office), yields

$$E_x \pi_D(x) = \begin{cases} \dfrac{Ex}{h} - \dfrac{b}{a} & \text{when } c = 1 \\[3mm] \dfrac{Ex}{h} & \text{when } c = 0 \end{cases} . \tag{14}$$

Note that (Unlike to $E_x \pi^e(x)$ in equation (13) this term is independent of α. Hence, the larger is x the lower is α the lower is the average negative surprise inflation in the presence of a commitment (c=1) when D is in office. From (13) and (14) this surprise inflation is given by

$$E_x \pi_D(x) - E_x \pi^e(x) = -(1-\alpha)\dfrac{\alpha x_c^2}{2ah}. \tag{15}$$

Hence the larger is α the larger the beneficial effect of a commitment on unexpected inflation. On the cost side, the commitment (with c=1) implies an expected value of costs (viewed from stage 1), through bc, equal to $bc(a - x_{cl})$ which is independent of α. Thus raising c from 0 to 1 leads to a larger reduction in $E\pi^e(x)$ when α is larger but this consideration does not affect costs. This explains why a higher reputation is conducive to a stronger commitment.

---

[6]A larger b enables a stronger commitment, with c=1. However, it also increases the risk of paying a high reneging cost in case of an unfavorable shock.

It can be seen from (12) that an increase in 'a' reduces the likelihood of a commitment. This is so because a larger 'a' i.e. a wider range of variation for x, implies a higher expected cost associated with reneging. Note that an increase in 'a' is a simultaneous increase both in expected x and its standard deviation leaving the coefficient of variation constant. Consequently, another way of expressing the foregoing result is by saying that an increase in Ex, holding the coefficient of variation constant, will reduce the tendency to make a commitment on fixing the exchange rate.

The intuition underlying the result that a larger h raises the likelihood of a commitment is straightforward. A larger h means that the policymaker is relatively more concerned about the costs of inflation. Since actual inflation is lower in the presence of a commitment than in its absence (see equation (14)), the commitment is more valuable the larger is h.

Before discussing the implications of the model in more detail, it is important to point out some of its limitations for empirical analysis and ways in which it can be extended. First, the fixed cost of reneging (c) is intended to capture the inability of D of revealing himself as the dependable policymaker or alternatively the costs of not being able to stick to announcements. The nature of these costs is not explicit in a one period model of the type used in the paper, but it is easy to interpret them once we extend the model to two periods. If D reneges in the first period he is not revealed as being the dependable policymaker, and/or one who sticks to his announcements. As a result, he cannot reap the benefits of a good reputation in the second period. In much of the discussion that follows we assume that the results of the model can be extended to a multiperiod framework. Second, while the policymaker is free to choose any value of c between 0 and 1, when we conduct the analysis using the uniform distribution we find out that the policymaker will choose either full, or not commitment at all. While this is a restrictive result, we show in appendix 3 that for a general distribution function it is possible that the policymaker chooses an internal solution.[7] Thus in general, the policymaker has more options regarding the degree of commitment than what is implied by the uniform distribution case. Third, in the model we assume that the public has a prior probability (α) that the policymaker in office is D. While α is exogenous in the model, it could be endogenized by including prior actions on the fiscal deficit. In practice, policymakers do not signal only on one front. Instead they try to enhance their reputation by making policy decisions in various areas.

---

[7] The full implications of this case need to be study in more detail, something that we plan to do in future work.

3.   **PRACTICAL IMPLICATIONS OF THE THEORY**

        This section illustrates the practical implications of the model presented above with specific examples drawn from the experiences of Latin American countries during stabilization attempts. In particular, we provide examples that indicate the different degrees of commitment in various stabilization programs, and show how these commitments are related to some of the variables suggested in the model. We also examine some of the reasons that led policymakers to renege on announcements, and explore the consequent costs.

3.1   **Degree of Commitment**

        Policymakers have a range of options regarding the type of exchange rate rule that they announce to support stabilization programs. In some cases they announce a fully fixed exchange rate, while in others they opt for a preannounced crawling peg. This paper focusses on cases in which the policymaker announces a fixed exchange rate. The announcement can be backed in different ways. In some cases this involves not printing money to finance the budget deficit (while the option of providing credit to the private sector is maintained), in others to issue money only to buy foreign exchange. Finally, the commitment to the exchange rate rule can be supported with full convertibility or with restrictions on the capital or current account, in which case a parallel foreign exchange market usually develops. It is easier for policymakers to stick to their exchange rate commitment by introducing such restrictions. However, when they follow such a course of action they damage their reputation, and reduce the chances that their policies will succeed in the long run.

        The strength of commitment depends on the combination of these three elements. The stronger commitment corresponds to cases where the exchange rate is fixed, the monetary base is <u>fully</u> backed by foreign exchange and there is <u>full</u> convertibility of the domestic currency. Additional features that one might want to consider for evaluating the seriousness of the commitment to a fixed exchange rate regime are the degree of independence of the central bank in setting the exchange rate and/or monetary targets, and the conditions under which a devaluation can take place.[8]

        Empirically, the convertibility plan launched in Argentina in March 1991 represents one of the strongest commitments made so far in Latin America. The central components of the plan were a fixed exchange rate to the US dollar, established by law with a ceiling at 10,000 Australes per U.S. Dollar, and an obligation to print money only to purchase foreign exchange. There was full

---

        [8] There is some evidence suggesting that, other things the same, inflation is lower in countries whose central banks preannounce monetary targets (Cukierman (1992) chapter 20, section 5).

convertibility of the domestic currency as all restrictions on external payments were eliminated. Legally, the monetary base had to be 100% backed by foreign assets, although part of this (around 10%) could be public debt denominated in foreign currency valuated at market prices. A key element in enhancing the strength of the arrangement was the inability of the central bank to devalue, since this action required Congressional approval.

Examples of weaker commitments are fixed exchange rates of the type used in the Krieger Vassena stabilization program in Argentina in 1967, and in Chile starting in June 1979, when the administration fixed the Peso at $39 per U.S. dollar.[9] In both cases, there was a strong commitment to the fixed exchange rate, in the sense that the exchange rate was a symbol of overall nominal stability. In addition, there were essentially no restrictions on the current and the capital account (evidence of this was a very small or non-existent parallel foreign exchange market). On the other hand, in these two instances the central bank maintained control of exchange rate policy, and there was no legal requirement to back domestic currency with foreign assets.

The fixed exchange rate announced in the Austral plan and in the 1985 Israeli program were examples of even weaker commitments. The authorities announced a fixed exchange rate and promised not to print money to finance the deficit. However, it was not clear how long the exchange rate would remain fixed, and the limitations on printing money were not supported by strong legislation.

Finally, the announcements of a fixed exchange rate in the Cruzado plan in Brazil and in the various programs that followed it, as well as those that followed the Austral plan in Argentina represent cases of very weak commitment. Policymakers did not tie their hands in any way, and it was clear from the outset that their main objective was to halt an inflationary acceleration rather than to bring about permanent price stability.

In Europe, during the end of the eighties some members of the EMS like Italy and France became strong supporters of a European monetary union. Since the same countries previously had a clear preference for national monetary flexibility their support of a monetary union constitutes a marked shift towards a preference for a stronger commitment to fixed exchange rates.[10]

---

[9] De Pablo (1972) examines the Krieger Vassena program while the Chilean experience in analyzed in Corbo (1985) and Edwards and Edwards (1987) among others.

[10]Chapter 6 of Cukierman (1992) shows that from the point of view of an individual country replacement of the EMS by a monetary union constitutes a stronger commitment.

3.2   What Explains the Degree of Commitment?

The model developed in the previous section indicates that the degree of commitment preferred by policymakers depends on the direct costs of reneging (b), the distribution of the shock x as characterized by its upper bound, 'a', the aversion to inflation (h), and the prior that the public has regarding whether the government is dependable or weak (α). A casual look at stabilization experiences in Latin America indicates that these are useful parameters for explaining the flexibility of exchange rate policy.

The discussion of the previous subsection implies that the Argentine stabilization attempts can be ranked in terms of their degree of commitment to a fixed exchange rate in the following manner: First, the Convertibility Program (1991); second, the Krieger Vassena plan (1967); third, the Austral plan (1985), and fourth, those that follow the latter. What explains those different commitment levels?

When the Convertibility plan was launched the overall situation was ripe for a strong stabilization program. The fiscal position had improved in 1990, when the government maintained a modest primary surplus and a much lower overall budget deficit than in previous years. Without question, in early 1991 the country enjoyed the strongest fiscal balance of the preceding 20 years.[11] Since the possibility of maintaining a sound fiscal position was also better than in previous years it was probably easier to convince the public that the policymaker would stick to his commitment.

A second important consideration was the public's demand for price stability as a result of the tremendous costs associated with the previous hyperinflation. The fact that agents were more willing to make concessions strengthened the position of the government and in this sense it made it more likely to be of the dependable type; in terms of the model, it could be argued that both α and h had increased. The government certainly had increased its reputation prior to March 1991, as it had already taken numerous structural measures aimed at demonstrating a break from the past. Particularly important in this respect were the privatization of public sector enterprises, policies to reduce the size of the public sector and to reduce government intervention in the markets. Finally, the potential costs of an adverse external shock were dampened by the fact that the country was running a record high trade surplus. This provided a large enough cushion to withstand a deterioration in the terms of trade or a temporary increase in imports characteristic of exchange rate based stabilizations (in other words, 'a' was considered to be small by policymakers).

---

[11] Of course, the fiscal situation was not strong enough as to erase any doubts of a reversal. Nevertheless, on an ex-ante basis the program had a reasonable chance of success.

If one compares the initial conditions with those in the Austral plan, it is clear that the situation was more fragile in the latter case, and hence the probability of reversal was larger. Although the budget deficit was reduced from 16 to 5 percent of GDP, the deficit was larger than prior to the convertibility plan, while much of the reduction in the deficit was based on temporary measures. This indicates that there were probably more doubts as to whether the policymaker was of the dependable type (α was probably much smaller than in the convertibility program).

In between these two programs lies the Krieger-Vassena plan, which was unquestionably the most serious stabilization attempt prior to the convertibility plan. The commitment to the fixed exchange rate was strong in the sense that when they fixed it at 350 pesos to the dollar (after an initial 40% devaluation) it was viewed as a symbol that would measure the success or failure of the program (much in the same way as in the 1991 convertibility plan). A relevant question is why didn't the authorities tie their hands further by adopting full convertibility? After all, the fiscal balance was probably as strong as it ever had been, while the economy was enjoying a relatively comfortable external position.

There are two possible explanations for stopping short of full convertibility in the Krieger-Vassena program. The first one is that it was implemented during the Bretton Woods era in which full convertibility was considered as unnecessarily restrictive. A commitment of this type was simply not considered within the feasible set of policy options. Second, the overall economic situation, especially the initial rate of inflation, was much more manageable in the 60s than more recently. This means that b, the fixed cost associated with reneging from a commitment was smaller, while h, the aversion to inflation was higher. So even for the same α and 'a' it was still rational to commit strongly through a fixed exchange rate.

A related issue is why was the commitment weak in the programs that followed the Austral plan? The typical program implemented between 1986 and 1989 (including the Bunge and Born plan to stop hyperinflation) was based on a fixed exchange rate, supported by price and wage controls, but a relatively small fiscal effort (usually temporary increases in revenues). The state of the underlying fundamentals made such a weak commitment reasonable. The large budget deficits could be reduced only temporarily through increases in public sector prices and the levying of emergency taxes. In addition, the country had a weak external position with limited access to external financing. Finally, there was a large quasi-fiscal deficit, much of it driven by high interest rates, which was almost automatically monetized. Since, under those circumstances even small shocks could destabilize the program, policymakers avoided strong commitments.

Finally, an interesting question is why didn't Peru, a country that like Argentina experienced a hyperinflation and which has gone through a similar stabilization process, adopt a convertibility program. The stabilization program in Peru was launched in August 1990 in response to a drastic and long hyperinflation. This was an orthodox money based program, similar to the one that successfully stopped hyperinflation in Bolivia in 1985. The results in Peru have been mixed. Hyperinflation stopped but inflation has remained stubborn at around 5 percent per month. Although the government has been successful in securing a balanced budget on a cash basis the stabilization effort still faces large risks. That could explain why the exchange rate commitment has been weak so far. The model predicts that the larger the probability of adverse shocks (the larger is a), the less likely it is that the policymaker will make a strong commitment to a fixed exchange rate. While the stabilization program has been moderately successful, it certainly continues to be extremely fragile. On the fiscal side, government revenues are very low (around 8 percent of GDP), a level which is not enough to sustain the necessary level of current and capital expenditures. In addition, the external situation continues to be fragile. While Peru has restored the dialogue and/or entered into negotiations with the multilateral organizations and the commercial banks, it is still far from receiving voluntary lending from the private sector. These two weakness of the program probably generate enough uncertainty so as to prevent the government from feeling sufficiently secure to make a strong commitment such as full convertibility.

The fact that so far Peruvian authorities have relied primarily on tight money and have avoided entirely using the exchange rate as a nominal anchor is in itself an indication that they consider the potential costs of reneging on an exchange rate announcement as high -- even for a relatively weak commitment. Hence they probably consider that before entering this phase the external and fiscal conditions need to be in much better shape. In terms of the model α is low and 'a' high. Both features tend to discourage the use of the exchange rate as a nominal anchor.

3.3   When to Renege on a Commitment?

One feature common to many exchange rate based programs is that policymakers tend to stick to the fixed exchange rate even past the point at which it becomes clear that a devaluation is necessary. It seems that the perceived cost of

deviating from the rule creates an incentive to stick with the policy even if this implies a bigger cost at a later stage.

One example of this type is the period of a fixed exchange rate in Chile in the late seventies and early eighties. In 1978 the Chilean authorities started to preannounce the exchange rate and gradually reduced the announced rate of devaluation as part of their strategy to reduce inflation. In June 1979, in response to the slow pace of inflation reduction (which was still running above 35 percent per year), the authorities fixed the exchange rate at $39 per US dollar. This was presented as a strong commitment to the stabilization program, with the idea that the exchange rate would remain fixed for the foreseeable future. While inflation slowed down in response to the new policy, it remained well above international levels and resulted in a strong real appreciation. In 1981, there were clear signs of looming problems.

The current account deficit had increased to around 17 percent of GDP, well above sustainable levels, while real interest rates reached 58 percent, mainly because the private sector was already anticipating a devaluation.

The devaluation finally came in June 1982, in response to a severe deterioration in the balance of payments prompted in part by a sharp fall in the price of a copper, and a tightening in foreign lending. It now seems clear that earlier action on the exchange rate would have reduced the large costs associated with the drastic real appreciation and the ensuing depreciation (which are discussed in section III.iv). However, the authorities chose to wait and instead only devalued when forced to do so by the size of the external shocks.

The Chilean experience fits very nicely with the predictions of the model. When they made the initial commitment in 1979, they probably considered the parameter b to be large, and they chose to make the strong commitment because the prior was that they were perceived as a strong government (α was estimated to be high). However, once they established the strong commitment it was extremely difficult to deviate from it, probably because the anticipated cost of this action was very large. They would only deviate from it once it became clear that there was no other reasonable option. As a result they over-extended the period of the fixed exchange rate and made things worse in the longer term.

It is interesting to note that we also observe an over-extension of the period of fixed exchange rates even in programs where the commitment is weak. A clear example of this type is the Brazilian Cruzado plan of February 1986, where a program based on a fixed exchange rate and a wage and price freeze was implemented to stop high rates of inflation (in excess of 20 percent per month). The Cruzado plan quickly ran into difficulties, as reflected in a sharp depreciation of the Cruzado in the parallel market, the existence of widespread shortages of goods which led to the emergence of black markets, and a deterioration in the trade balance. In spite of these symptoms the government maintained its policies, and only changed them after the November election took place. Once again, the explanation for not

taking earlier action on the exchange rate was that there was a cost (c), in this case political, on reneging on the announcement.[12]

---

[12] The stabilization program implemented in Uruguay in 1967 provides another example of a case where the fixed exchange rate was maintained longer than was reasonable because of the political cost of reneging on a preannouncement. The authorities ultimately devalued but only after the 1971 election. As in the recent Cruzado program, the parallel rate had depreciated significantly well before the devaluation, and the symptoms of overvaluation were felt economy-wide. This episode is analyzed in Viana (1989) among others.

3.4   **The Costs of, and the Reasons for Deviating From a Fixed Exchange Rate Rule**

It is difficult to identify and measure precisely the costs of reneging once an announcement is made. What the model of the previous section indicates is that these costs increase with the strength of the commitment. We will now illustrate the nature and magnitude of the costs involved in departing from an announced rule.

The Chilean devaluation of June 1982 illustrates some of the costs that can be associated with over-extending the period of the fixed exchange rate and then effecting a late maxi-devaluation. By and large, the main costs were a steep recession (output fell by 14 percent in 1982), a financial crisis, and a sharp increase in the fiscal deficit as a result of subsidies provided to firms and the financial system to offset the effects of the devaluation.

The 1982 recession was the largest one in Chile since the depression of the thirties. Although part of it can be explained by the adverse external shocks of 1981-82, domestic factors were probably equally (if not more) important in this case.[13] There was a tightening of domestic policies starting in the second half of 1981, which were adopted with the intention of reducing domestic prices and improving the balance of payments. A second cost was the large financial crisis caused by the extremely high (ex-post) real interest rates during the years that preceded the devaluation. A third important cost resulted from the government provision of a host of (post devaluation) subsidies to compensate agents that had contracted loans in foreign currency. While this was extremely costly to the public sector, one could argue that it was not entirely unreasonable since those loans were originally taken on the basis of a given rule (that the government would stick to the fixed exchange rate rule). Once the government reneged on its rule and devalued, domestic borrowers suffered a large capital loss.[14] Since the government could not distinguish between agents that had borrowed fully believing the announcement and those which did not, an argument was created for compensating all borrowers. In any case, the costs of these policies were extremely onerous to the public sector.

In Chile, these losses were absorbed by the central bank, and appear in the quasi-fiscal deficit. Marshall and Schmidt-Hebbel (1991) present estimates of these

---

[13]   Minister Luders argued at the time that approximately two thirds of the recession was caused by domestic policies.

[14]   On the other hand one could argue that domestic agents could have anticipated that the government would not stick to the fixed exchange rate since the external imbalance was unsustainable. If this was the case, the government should have compensated less for the effect of the devaluation.

deficits for the 1982-85 period. These losses averaged 10 percent of GDP during those years. A decomposition of these losses indicate that the main factors were loan subsidies to bankrupt financial institutions, and losses arising from exchange rate guarantees.

The sheer size of the costs of sticking for too long to the fixed exchange rate in Chile indicates that indeed they are positively correlated with the strength of the commitment. Interestingly, while Chile suffered large output and fiscal losses, the stubbornness with which the government adhered to the exchange rate rule had one benefit: the crisis did not lead to a resurgence of high inflation later on, in fact inflation has remained moderate (at around 20 percent per year) ever since.

The Argentine devaluation of 1970, which marks the end of the stabilization attempt started under Krieger Vassena is a second example of reneging on a strong commitment. The devaluation (25 percent) was a clear indication that the low rates of inflation that the program was aiming at were probably out of reach. As in Chile, by the time the devaluation was effected (June 1970) it was already clear that the program was not sustainable. Krieger Vassena was forced to resign in 1969 as a result of labor unrest, primarily in Cordoba, an industrial city. His successor, Dagnino Pastore, initially adhered to the exchange rate policy but eventually was forced to devalue. This was a critical turning point in economic policy, as it marked the beginning of a long period of lax fiscal management and high inflation. The short term effects of the devaluation were an increase in inflation from 7 percent in 1969 to 35 percent in 1971. But more important than this short term costs (which clearly meant a reversal for the original program) was the fact that agents were left with the perception that price stability was a difficult goal to reach. The fact that an authoritarian government was forced to back up from a strong commitment reduced the chances that the ensuing administrations would attempt such a daring policy.

Finally, it is useful to try to evaluate the costs of reneging from a weak commitment. Are they indeed smaller? If we consider the period of the 1985-1989 period in Argentina and 1986-90 in Brazil, what we observe is a series of stabilization programs in both countries (the first ones being the Austral plan in Argentina and the Cruzado plan in Brazil) where the fixed exchange was perceived as a temporary device to generate transitory price stability.[15] The large reliance on income policies in these programs, especially in the follow-ups to the original plans, was an indication of their weakness. The analysis in Kiguel and Liviatan (1991) indicates that in contrast to Chile, the failure of the successive plans did not produce large costs in terms of output losses (certainly nothing like in Chile). On the other hand, the continuous failure to bring down inflation for long periods increased nominal instability, eventually leading to a full blown hyperinflation in Argentina and a short one in Brazil. All in all, one ends up with the impression that indeed reneging on

---

[15] Kiguel and Liviatan (1991) provide a fuller discussion of these programs.

weaker commitments have smaller real costs.

4.   CONCLUDING REMARKS

        The central message of this paper is that the cost of reneging is a key reason
that holds policymakers back from making strong commitments on their exchange rate
policy. The stronger the commitment to an exchange rate rule, the more difficult it
is to deviate from it. The ability to stick to preannounced rules depends not only on
the intentions of the policymakers but also on the type and size of shocks which
affect the economy. When the economy is hit by a large shock it may be optimal to
deviate from the rule even for a policymaker that is serious about the rule.

        Exchange rate rules have been particularly important in disinflation programs.
In those cases the announcement of a fixed exchange is intended to reverse
inflationary expectations and convince the public that prices are going to stabilize.
The policymaker (especially if he is serious about bringing down inflation) attempts
to stick to the rule for as long as possible in order to convince the public about his
determination to disinflate. However, in doing that he losses the ability to use the
exchange rate to offset external shocks. As a consequence the use of exchange rate
rules as instruments of stabilization also involves costs.

        Full dollarization, an option that has been considered as a possible device for
stabilizing high inflation, is one of the strongest forms of commitment. By accepting
full dollarization, and hence giving up the domestic currency, the policymaker forgoes
two benefits: first, the capacity to obtain seigniorage, and second, the ability to
devalue. Much of the existing literature emphasizes the first one, we will argue that
the second one is at least as important, if not more.

        Fischer (1982) argues that seigniorage is an important source of public
revenues in developing countries. In Argentina, for example, seigniorage has been
fluctuating between 3 and 6 percent of GDP during the seventies and eighties. Is
revenue from seigniorage a strong enough reason to stop short of dollarization if a
policymaker is willing to stabilize? Probably not. If a policymaker is truly committed
to stabilization -- in the sense of bringing down inflation to one digit -- then he must
also be ready to take the fiscal measures to ensure the sustainability of the program.
Given that seigniorage in low inflation economies net around 1 percent of GDP, if
full dollarization is one of the few ways to ensure long term price stability then it is
difficult to argue that this revenue is the main consideration for not dollarizing. A
determined government should be willing and able to increase revenues or reduce
expenditures by this relatively small amount.

        The model developed in this paper provides an alternative explanation for
stopping short of such a strong commitment. Policymakers are concerned that even
strong commitments may have to be broken sometimes (when shocks are sufficiently

large), and that there are costs associated with such a course of action. The debt crisis, the accompanying higher interest rates and the deterioration in the terms of trade periodically experienced by some Latin American countries is the type of shock that can lead to reneging on a commitment. In the 1982 crisis in Chile, these shocks were handled through a devaluation of the domestic currency, and even in that case there was a severe recession. An open question is how the Chilean government would have handled that crisis if it had chosen full dollarization and what would have been the costs in that case? A stronger commitment such as dollarization would have triggered two opposing effects. On one hand, by reducing inflationary expectations further, it would have prevented some of the real appreciation, thus reducing some of the cost of sticking to the commitment. On the other hand, the Chilean government would probably have adhered to the commitment for a longer time in the face of the adverse external shocks. This would have increased costs. Thus the overall effect of the stronger commitment on costs is ambiguous. But it is likely that in its presence devaluation would have been postponed even further. Nonetheless, one cannot rule out the possibility that the authorities would ultimately have reneged even under full dollarization.

Many economists believe that revenue from seigniorage is the main argument for maintaining a national currency. Others claim that issues related to national pride are also important (and they probably are). In our view, an equally (if not more) important motive for stopping short of full dollarization are the difficulties and costs of reneging on such a commitment when the country faces large adverse shocks, whose adverse effects can be alleviated, at least temporarily, by a devaluation.

REFERENCES

Bruno, M., S. Fischer, E. Helpman and N. Liviatan (1991). *Lessons from Stabilization and Its Aftermath*, Cambridge: MIT Press.

Canavese, Alfredo (1992). "Hyperinflation and Convertibility Based Stabilization in Argentina," mimeo, Instituto Di Tella, Buenos Aires.

Corbo, V. (1985). "Reforms and Macroeconomic Adjustments in Chile during 1974-83," *World Development*, Vol. 13 No.8, pp. 893-916.

Cukierman, Alex (1992). *Central Bank Strategy, Credibility and Independence: Theory and Evidence*, Cambridge, MA., The MIT Press, Forthcoming.

De Pablo, Juan Carlos. (1972). *Politica Anti-inflacionaria en la Argentina 1967-1970*. Buenos Aires: Amorrortu Editores.

Edwards, Sebastian and Alejandra Cox Edwards. (1987). *Monetarism and Liberalization: The Chilean Experiment*, Cambridge, Massachusetts: Ballinger Publishing Company.

Fischer, S. (1982). "Seigniorage and the Case for a National Money," *Journal of Political Economy*, Vol 90, pp.295-313, April.

Flood, Robert P. and Peter Isard (1989). "Monetary Policy Strategies" *IMF Staff Papers*, Vol. 36. pp. 612-632, September.

Giavazzi, Francesco and Marco Pagano (1990). "Can Severe Fiscal Contractions be Expansionary?: Tales of Two Small European Countries," in *NBER Macroeconomics Annual*, Olivier Blanchard and Stanley Fischer editors,

Kiguel, Miguel and Nissan Liviatan (1991). "The Inflation Stabilization Cycles in Argentina and Brazil," in *Lessons from Stabilization and Its Aftermath*, editors M. Bruno, S. Fischer, E. Helpman and N. Liviatan, Cambridge, MIT Press.

Lohmann, Susanne (1992) "Optional Commitment in Monetary Policy: Credibility Versus Flexibility", *American Economic Review*, Vol. 82, 273-286, March.

Marshall, Jorge and Klaus Schmidt-Hebbel (1991). "Macroeconomics of Public Sector Deficits: The Case of Chile," mimeo, The World Bank.

Viana, Luis (1989) "The Stabilization Plan of 1968," mimeo, CERES Uruguay.

Appendix

1. Derivation of a condition for the emergence of a commitment. The expected value of D's objective function in stage 1 (equation [10]) is given   by

$$Q = E_x J^D = \int_0^{x_c} -(1-\alpha c)\frac{x^2}{h} \, \$ \,(x)dx - \int_{x_c}^a \left[\frac{1}{2h}x^2 + bc\right] \$ \,(x)dx \quad \text{(A-1)}$$

Using the uniform distribution over the range [0,a] with density $\$ \,(x) = K$, so that ak=1, we can write (A-1) as (equation [11])

$$aQ(c) = -\frac{(\frac{1}{2}-\alpha c)}{3h}x_c^3 - \frac{1}{6h}a^3 + bcx_c - bca \quad \text{(A-2)}$$

Since $x_c = (2hbc)^{\frac{1}{2}}$ we have $aQ(0) = -\frac{a^3}{6h}$. Hence

$$a(Q(1) - Q(0)) = \left[\frac{\alpha-\frac{1}{2}}{3h}\right]x_{c1}^3 + bx_{c1} - ba \quad \text{(A-3)}$$

where $x_c = (2bh)^{\frac{1}{2}}$ is the value of x_c at c=1.

2. Demonstration that the optimal c is always at a corner. Differentiating (A-2) with respect to c we obtain

$$\frac{\partial aQ(c)}{\partial c} = -(\frac{1}{2}-\alpha c)x_c^2\frac{\partial x_c}{\partial c} + \frac{\alpha}{3h}x_c^3 + bx_c$$

$$+ bc\frac{\partial x_c}{\partial c} - ba \quad \text{(A-4)}$$

Note that $\frac{\partial x_c}{\partial c} = hbx_c^{-1}$. Substituting in (A-4) and rearranging we obtain

$$\frac{\partial aQ(c)}{\partial c} = \alpha cbx_c + \frac{\alpha}{3h}x_c^3 + b(x_c-a) \quad \text{(A-5)}$$

$$\frac{\partial aQ(c)}{\partial c} = \alpha cbx_c + \frac{\alpha}{3h}x_c^3 + b(x_c - a) \tag{A-5}$$

Since x_c is an increasing function of c this expression increases in c. Hence the second partial derivative with respect to c is positive for all c>0. This implies corner solutions at c=0 or c=1. Thus (A-3) is the only relevant criterion for determining c.

3.   Extension to the case of a general density function and the existence of an internal solution

From equation (9) with h = b = 1 we have

$$Q(c) = \int_0^{x_c} -(1-\alpha c) \, x^2 dF(x) - \int_{x_c}^{\infty} (\frac{x^2}{2} + c) \, dF(x) \tag{A-6}$$

where $x_c = (2c)^{\frac{1}{2}}$. The first order condition for optimality is

$$Q'(c) = \int_0^{x_c} \alpha x^2 \, dF(x) - (1-\alpha c)(2c)^{\frac{1}{2}} f(x_c) - \int_{x_c}^{\infty} dF(x) + (2c)^{\frac{1}{2}} f(x_c) = 0$$

where $f = \frac{dF(x)}{dx}$ is the density function. This can be simplified to

$$Q'(c) = \alpha \int_0^{x_c} x^2 dF(x) - \int_{x_c}^{\infty} dF(x) + (2c)^{\frac{1}{2}} cf(x_c)\alpha = 0 \; . \tag{A-7}$$

It can be seen that all the expressions in Q'(c) are increasing in c except for $f(x_c)$ which may be decreasing. Since in general f' can be changed arbitrarily for a given f and a given x_c there generally exist distributions that yield an internal solution (o < c < 1) for c. Such solutions always occur on a downward sloping portion of the density function, i.e., where f' < o and Q"(c) < o.

Since Q^l is increasing in α, it follows from the second order condition that an increase in α raises c (as in the text). Note also that a shift in the probability mass to the right of x_c reduces $Q^l(c)$ which means that it decreases the optimal c. This is the equivalent result to that of an increase in 'a' in the uniform distribution as discussed in the text.

CHAPTER 5

CENTRAL BANK DEPENDENCE AND INFLATION PERFORMANCE: AN EXPLORATORY DATA ANALYSIS[1]

Forrest H. Capie
Terrence C. Mills
Geoffrey E. Wood

1.   INTRODUCTION

Most studies of the conduct of monetary policy have been concerned with describing, analysing or prescribing techniques of monetary control. In recent years, however, a new strand of literature has abstracted from these issues and, focusing on the problem of time consistency, has analysed how an equilibrium monetary policy is determined through the strategic interactions of the monetary authority and the public.

The general conclusion of this literature (exemplified by Barro and Gordon, 1983a, 1983b) is that control of monetary policy by government inevitably brings too high inflation, and that this can be ended only by giving control of monetary policy to an agency outside the political process - an independent central bank. This conclusion has, in turn, led to a body of empirical work which has apparently confirmed such a conclusion.

Although there are a substantial number of papers which support that conclusion, the weight of evidence is not as great as it might first appear, for a good part of the work has been carried out on the same, or substantially overlapping, data sets. While there are good reasons for this, it is nevertheless an impediment to relying completely on these results. The aim of this paper is to explore how robust these results are when a much longer and wider set of data is examined.

After a brief review of the analytical models, the conclusions of which suggest "central bank independence" is the only route to price stability, the remainder of the paper is in four sections. The next section reviews, again very briefly, the empirical

[1] We should like to thank Michael Bordo and Pierre Siklos for helpful comments.

work which supports this conclusion. The third section describes the data set of the paper and the criteria by which we have classified central banks as dependent or independent, while the fourth discusses the statistical techniques used to examine it; the nature of the data require slightly unusual techniques. The results of the application of these techniques are then set out. The paper then concludes with a brief discussion of the implications of these findings.

The pioneering models are those of Kydland and Prescott (1977) and Barro and Gordon (1983a). In a time consistent equilibrium, the public expects the policy maker to deliver the equilibrium policy, and the best the policy maker can do (from the point of view of his own self interest) is to validate this expectation. The policy that results is one which produces higher inflation than the public desires; for the authorities prefer positive inflation. (Unexpected inflation is usually given as their preference, but if the motive is the collection of higher tax revenue, this restriction is unnecessary.)

Reputational considerations can modify this conclusion, as can assumptions either about the public's knowledge of the policy makers preferences or about whether the public is modelled as a strategic player or as a set of atomistic agents. Grossman (1991, pages 335-340) provides a brief and clear survey of these matters and, as that survey shows, there is an abundance of possible inflationary equilibria. Nevertheless, the empirical work that has ensued universally shows the inflation rate to be higher when monetary policy is run, directly or by proxy, by government than when it is run by a central bank independent of political influence. It is useful next to review that body of work.

2.   PREVIOUS EMPIRICAL STUDIES

A pioneering study is Bade and Parkin (1987; although an earlier version dates from 1978). They examine twelve countries during the years 1973 to 1986. The starting point of the data set is important, for it is the beginning of the post-war period of floating exchange rates. Only during the floating rate period did national policy makers have unfettered freedom to reveal their inflationary preferences, and that is why most studies are of this period.

Bade and Parkin distinguish two types of government influence on central banks, these being "financial type" and "policy type". The former relates to government influence in selecting board members; in setting their salaries; in determining the bank's budget; and in determining who gets the profits. "Policy type" refers to government influence in board meetings, and whether it has the final say on monetary policy. Bade & Parkin found that "policy type" influence was crucial: central banks free of it delivered significantly lower inflation than did those susceptible to such influence.

Another approach to the measurement of independence was that by Masciandaro & Tabellini (1988). In their study of five Pacific basin countries (Australia, Canada, Japan, New Zealand and the U.S.), they focus on government influence on the appointment of the board and subsequently on the board's decisions. The primary concern of this study was on the relationship between central bank dependency and fiscal deficits, but that between dependency and inflation was also examined. The conclusion supported that of Bade and Parkin; so too did Alesina (1988, 1989) and Alesina & Summers (1991). All in all, then, the empirical work displays a remarkable consensus.

It is worth remarking also that the empirical work has in common a feature additional to its conclusions. This is that the meaning of independence is left largely unexplored. In an illuminating early discussion, Friedman (1962) suggests that what is usually meant is that an independent central bank has a relation with government similar to that of the judiciary. It could carry out a law or laws passed by the government, but the government could not influence its operations without changing the law. This may be what is meant by independence in these studies.

But in only a few cases is the mandate of central banks explicit and clear; why independent central banks generally deliver lower inflation than dependent ones in the studies referred to above is therefore not obvious. Why do they act in the "public interest" and, if doing so, why do they not deliver stable prices? These are surely important questions, but to pursue it would take us well beyond the exploration of the data which this study comprises.

3.   THE DATA

Our data comprise annual inflation rates for fourteen countries, drawn primarily from Mitchell (1981, 1982, 1983): the earliest starting date is 1871, the latest 1916, with all series ending in 1988.

This period encompasses a variety of exchange rate regimes and a variety of inflationary experiences, including hyper-inflations. These latter episodes, which would, in any case, require detailed within-year inflation data, are not explicitly considered. As discussed in Capie (1986) and Capie and Wood (1991), these episodes have inevitably resulted from a breakdown of the governments tax gathering capacity in the face of civil unrest: in the extreme, civil war or revolution. Examples in the period covered in this paper (there are others from earlier years: see Capie, 1986) are Russia after 1917, Hungary in 1919, Poland in the early 1920s, Germany in the same period (when there were attempted communist coups and a Bolshevik government in Bavaria); and, after the Second World War, China and Greece, both with civil war. In all these cases, resort to the inflation tax was a last desperate gamble, after many other legislative restraints had already been overthrown. They do not, therefore, provide suitable data to test the effects of the niceties of central bank-government relations. Nor do we explore the possible significance of whether countries are industrialised or not. This interesting distinction has been examined in Cukierman (1992); unfortunately, too few non-industrialised countries have the long runs of data we exploit in this paper.

The variety of exchange rate regimes may seem at first glance to be a considerable handicap. But, in fact, exchange rate fixity was never the norm. Before 1914, not every country was on the gold standard and, it is fair to say, few seemed to regard it as being as immutable as Britain did. For the core countries of the world economy (France, Germany, the USA and the UK) it was essentially a rule which guided monetary policy; for the remainder it was more akin to a pegged exchange rate regime such as that of Bretton Woods. (Further discussion of this can be found in Bernholz, 1986). Adherence to the gold standard sometimes proved impossible and, whilst there was considerable success, there were no guarantees, for there were often times when the pressures on countries proved too great, particularly in times of war or serious financial crisis. Such a case was Britain in 1797 when she had to suspend convertibility during the Napoleonic Wars.

Gold convertibility was eventually restored in 1821 but had to be suspended again in 1914: such experience was quite common. But even in the heyday of the classical gold standard - 1880 to 1913 - there were countries who found it impossible to behave in a way that allowed them to join the gold standard or, for those who did manage it, to adhere to the standard. Spain was in the former category. Although she never formally joined the standard, staying with bimetallism, Spain behaved as if constrained by gold standard rules. But in 1882 convertibility was suspended and thereafter she made a bold attempt at what today would be called convergence to the path of her European neighbours, although without complete success.

Italy abandoned convertibility into gold in 1866, and then immediately considered returning but could not. It was 1884 before convertibility was restored. Public finances, however, deteriorated again and in 1894 the standard was abandoned for a second time.

It was in Latin America that there was least success with the standard. In 1883 Argentina formally rejoined the gold standard after an absence, only to return to inconvertibility the following year, although in 1890 she once again rejoined. (Argentina also led the way off the new standard in the 1920s, abandoning that in 1929.) Similarly Chile, who had been on gold since 1870, suspended convertibility in 1878 following a financial crisis. They then restored the standard in 1895 at a depreciated parity and then abandoned again in 1898.

Even where the standard was not abandoned there were instances where it may easily have been. The most notable was the United States. The United States had been on the gold standard de jure since 1879 (de facto a bit longer). But in the 1890s serious consideration was given to restoring the use of silver: indeed, the famous election campaign of 1896 was fought on the issue of silver. There was no guarantee that the U.S. would adhere to monometallism, as was evidenced by the seriousness with which the issue was taken.

In the interwar years international monetary affairs were in some disarray. Exchange rates floated for the first few years after the war, until in 1925 Britain went back to a version of the gold standard - the gold exchange standard. Other countries followed in 1926 and 1927, but by 1929 the system was already breaking up. (The Governor of the Bank of England considered devaluation in 1927.) Britain abandoned gold for good in 1931, moving to a managed float, and was followed by all other countries in the next few years. The Americans held on until 1933 and the French, together with a dwindling gold bloc, until 1936. Thus there were, for most of the international economy, more years of floating rates between the two world wars than years of fixed rates with, moreover, the period of fixed rates carrying little conviction.

Even in the Bretton Woods system, there was some degree of monetary independence: Britain, for example, went through several cycles of greater monetary ease than was compatible with the exchange rate, followed by devaluation and a period of stringency (see Williamson and Wood, 1976).

In summary, then, throughout the period of the data of this study, most countries had some degree of monetary independence. Further, as Grossman (1991) has pointed out, the conditions which lead to the prediction of higher inflation resulting from politically controlled monetary policy should apply to any period, not just to recent years; for governments wanted revenue even when not dependent on a popular mandate. It is plainly worthwhile finding what, if anything, the historical data suggest.

The countries investigated are listed in Table 1, along with a classification of the status of their central bank. Twelve of the countries have been classified into periods in which they had independent or dependent central banks (or none was established) while two, Belgium and Italy, have been left unclassified.

The data on which our classification is based comprise the Appendix. The method of classification uses the criteria of the papers by Bade and Parkin (1987) and by Masciandaro and Tabellini (1988) and, in addition, takes into account the ownership of the bank, and whether it has the sole right to issue notes and coins.

We would stress that the classification shown in Table 1 is, like the rest of this paper, exploratory. It provides a part of the framework within which we examine the data. The results of that examination in turn shed light on the classification.

Table 1

Central Bank Classifications

U.K.	independent up to 1945, then dependent
U.S.	independent
Belgium	unclassified
Argentina	established in 1935, independent up to 1945, then dependent
Brazil	established in 1965 as dependent
Austria	dependent
Canada	established in 1935, dependent up to 1937, independent up to 1959, then dependent
France	dependent
Germany	dependent up to 1946, then independent
Italy	unclassified
Japan	dependent
New Zealand	established in 1933, independent up to 1935, then dependent
Spain	dependent
Sweden	dependent

Note: These classifications are based on the references and data contained in Appendix 1.

4.   EXPLORATORY DATA ANALYSIS OF INFLATION RATES

When examining the relationship between central bank dependency and the rate of inflation, it is tempting to compute the sample mean and the sample variance to provide measures of these features of the data. It is well known, however, that the mean is only appropriate when the sample distribution is approximately symmetric, while the sample variance requires the distribution to be approximately normal. The two statistics are also heavily influenced by the presence of extreme observations, or outliers. When the sample distribution is asymmetric and when outliers are present, it is important to consider alternative measures of location and variability that are more 'robust' to such departures from approximate normality. Inflation rates are typical of asymmetric economic time series having outliers; this is confirmed by computing Lagrange Multiplier statistics, which test departures from normality (see Jarque and Bera, 1980).

Figure 1
Examples of Inflation Histograms

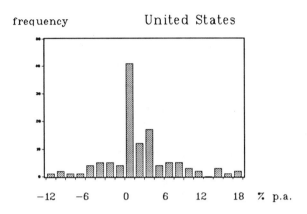

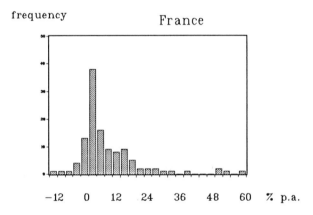

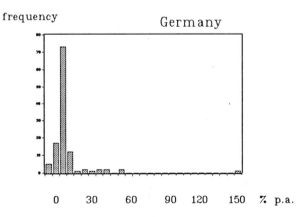

These are reported in Table 2, denoted JB and distributed as c with two degrees of freedom, along with conventional statistics of the first four moments of the sample data, and show that only for two series, New Zealand and Canada, can the normality assumption not be rejected: all other series yield significant test statistics, some of which are extremely large. Moreover, these rejections of normality are usually a consequence of there being both excess skewness and kurtosis: these patterns are perhaps more clearly seen in the histograms for selected countries presented as Figure 1.

A simple yet robust measure of location that has been used extensively by Tukey (1977) and his coworkers is the median, which has been found to be a good measure of location in these circumstances, particularly with small sample sizes. When assessing variability, we often make comparisons between two or more data sets by constructing confidence intervals around the location measure. If the sample mean, x, is used, then an approximate 95% confidence interval, based on an underlying normality assumption, is given by

$$x + 1.96 \ s/\sqrt{n}$$

where n is the sample size and s is the sample standard deviation. When the sample is non-normal and we are using the median, m, as a measure of location, an analogous interval is given by

$$m + 1.58 \ \text{H-spr}/\sqrt{n}$$

Table 2

Sample Statistics

	First Obs	$\bar{x}$	s	sk	$kurt$	$JB \sim x\frac{2}{2}$
U.K.	1871	3.22	6.43	0.62	4.90	25.19
U.S.	1871	2.04	17.83	0.62	4.42	17.50
Belgium	1871	2.53	6.11	0.62	4.87	23.82
Argentina	1915	140.46	411.42	5.74	40.76	4803
Brazil	1913	40.72	89.18	5.31	36.37	3883
Austria	1916	49.21	297.44	8.19	68.74	13961
Canada	1911	3.49	5.36	-0.01	4.14	4.24
France	1871	6.98	11.96	2.15	8.39	233.1
Germany	1871	5.49	16.21	6.03	49.10	11166
Italy	1887	8.32	15.50	3.04	14.86	755.0
Japan	1903	13.09	57.26	7.94	68.91	16469
New Zealand	1915	5.44	5.77	0.17	2.87	0.43
Spain	1915	7.10	7.59	0.82	3.85	10.44
Sweden	1871	2.49	5.22	-0.28	5.29	27.22

where the H-spread (H-spr) is the difference between the 'hinges', those values which split into half the two halves of the data initially split by the median (and hence are similar to quartiles). The statistical reasoning underlying this interval, in particular the scaling factor 1.58, is developed in McGill, Tukey and Larsen (1978) and Velleman and Hoaglin (1981), and the endpoints are referred to by these authors as 'notches': Mills (1990, chapter 3) provides a text book discussion of these concepts of exploratory data analysis (often refered to as EDA) within the context of analysing economic time series.

Table 3

Notched Intervals

U.K. (independent)	(-0.28, 0.58, 1.44)
U.K. (dependent)	(3.57, 4.85, 7.12)
U.S. (independent)	(0.54, 1.12, 1.70)
Belgium (unclassified)	(1.20, 2.22, 3.24)
Austria (dependent)	(3.07, 4.00, 4.93)
Canada (nonexist, independent)	(-0.04, 0.97, 1.98)
Canada (dependent)	(2.88, 3.88, 4.88)
France (dependent)	(1.63, 3.06, 4.49)
Germany (dependent)	(1.22, 1.94, 2.66)
Germany (independent)	(1.88, 2.71, 3.54)
Italy (unclassified)	(2.74, 4.35, 5.96)
Japan (dependent)	(2.82, 3.99, 5.15)
New Zealand (nonexist, independent)	(-0.22, 1.12, 2.46)
New Zealand (dependent)	(4.57, 5.67, 6.77)
Spain (dependent)	(4.63, 6.26, 7.39)
Sweden (dependent)	(1.61, 2.31, 3.01)
Argentina (nonexistent)	(-4.9, 1.8, 8.5)
Argentina (independent)	(1.8, 4.5, 7.2)
Argentina (dependent)	(15.8, 51.5, 87.2)
Brazil (nonexistent)	(7.3, 10.2, 13.1)
Brazil (dependent)	(15.0, 41.4, 67.8)

Table 3 presents schematic representations of these robust confidence intervals, or notch intervals, for each country classified by central bank behaviour, i.e. as listed in Table 1. Samples whose intervals do not overlap can be said to be significantly different at roughly the 5% level (although this is an individual 5% level, no allowance being made for the number of comparisons considered).

From this set of intervals there does seem to be some evidence that countries with an independent (on our classification) central bank, or without one at all, enjoy levels and variability of inflation rather less than those countries with a dependent central bank. This is perhaps better seen by considering the scatterplot of median inflation against the H-spread measure of inflation variability for the non-South American countries presented as Figure 2.

Two distinct clusters of points are revealed: one containing all the independent central bank samples plus the period when Germany had a dependent central bank, and one containing the remaining dependent central bank samples. Indeed, a simple discriminatory rule is revealed from this scatterplot: if (median+H-spread<6), the central bank is independent. As a by-product, we see that the rule classifies both Belgium and Italy as having dependent central banks.

Also shown in Figure 2 is the same scatterplot, but this time using the mean and standard deviation as measures of location and variability. Certain similarities are apparent, but the observations now fall into two different clusters: the 'low inflation' cluster containing the independent central banks plus Sweden and Belgium, and the 'high inflation' cluster containing all the other dependent central banks plus Italy. Note that discrimination is achieved by just looking at mean inflation: by using standard deviations, the variability of inflation has little discriminatory power.

Given our preference for using robust measures, Figures 3 to 6 repeat the median-H-spread scatterplots for different time periods: pre-1914, inter-war, 1947 to 1971 (the Bretton Woods era), and post-1971. Pre-1914 was a period of low and stable inflation rates, but the tendency for countries with dependent central banks to have higher and more variable rates of inflation is readily apparent. During the inter-war period the range of inflation was much wider, but again those countries with independent central banks (along with Sweden) experienced lower and more stable rates. The Bretton Woods era shows a marked convergence in inflation experience, although the U.S. and Germany have the best performance, while the post-Bretton Woods period exhibits the greatest fluctuations in inflation. Nevertheless, the two countries with independent central banks during this last period, the U.S. and Germany, along with Austria and Belgium, again achieve low and stable inflation.

We have so far concentrated on 'cross-sectional' analysis of central bank inflation performance, but we can also investigate the inflation behaviour of the countries in our sample set individually through time. Not surprisingly given the evidence of Table 2, most of the inflation series are contaminated at frequent intervals by outliers, either appearing singly as 'spikes' or in groups as 'bursts' of aberrant inflation behaviour.

From our discussion in Section 4 above, we wish to be able to concentrate on the long-run inflation experience of countries having dependent or independent central banks: short-run aberrant inflation behaviour needs to be ignored. To do this requires smoothing the data to extract the underlying, long-run, pattern from the short-run 'noise'. There are many methods of doing this, ranging from fitting a

Figure 2
"Median-HSpread" Scatterplot

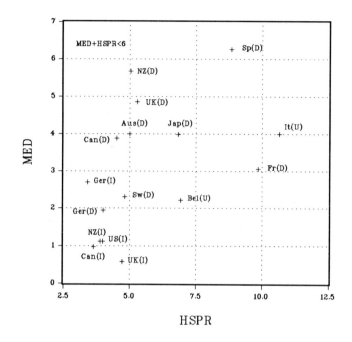

Figure 2 (cont'd)
"Mean-Standard Deviation" Scatterplot

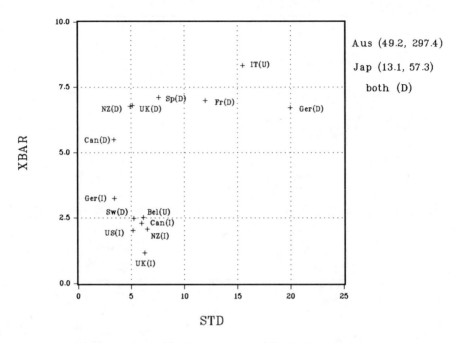

(D): Dependent; (I): Independent; (U): Unclassified

Figure 3
"Median-HSpread" Scatterplot: Pre-1914

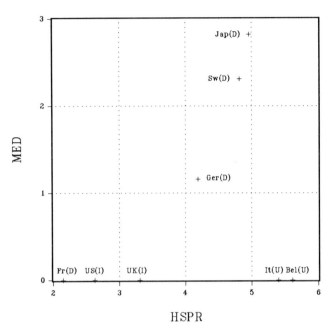

HSPR

(D): Dependent; (I): Independent; (U): Unclassified

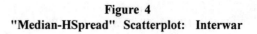

Figure 4
"Median-HSpread" Scatterplot: Interwar

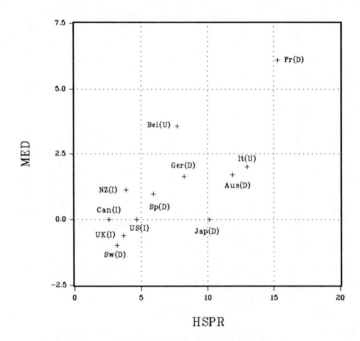

HSPR

(D): Dependent; I: Independent; (U): Unclassified

Figure 5
"Median-HSpread" Scatterplot: 1947 - 1971

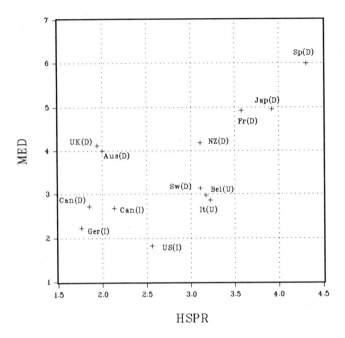

HSPR

(D): Dependent; (I): Independent; (U): Unclassified

Figure 6
"Median-HSpread" Scatterplot: 1972 - 1988

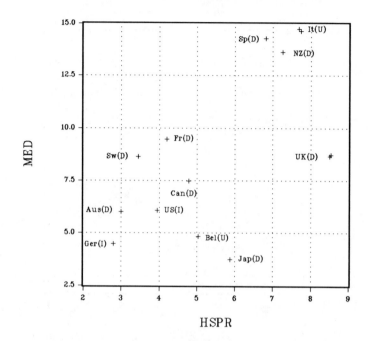

(D): Dependent; (I): Independent: (U): Unclassified

constant mean or deterministic trend, to estimating a stochastic trend component via signal extraction.

These latter, more sophisticated, models correspondingly require more formal assumptions to be made about the error processes driving the unobserved components that are to be estimated, particularly about their distributions and parameter constancy.

Given our exploratory theme, we wish to discover these long-run patterns while making as few assumptions about data structure as possible, using techniques with properties that change only gradually across a wide range of noise distributions. It has been found that nonlinear data smoothers provide a practical method of finding general smooth patterns for time series data confounded with long-tailed noise, exactly the position with the inflation data being analysed here.

The nonlinear smoother that we employ is that originally proposed by Tukey (1977), known as 3RSSH, twice, and is based on using repeated running medians of order 3, with additional embellishments to smooth end values (this being required because values before and after the sample, which are needed to compute medians, are missing) and to eradicate certain undesirable features of median smoothers: for example, running medians of order 3 have a tendency to chop off 'peaks' and 'valleys' in the data, leaving flat 'mesas' and 'dales' two observations wide. These flat segments can be smoothed by an operation known as 'splitting'. The properties of this 'compound' smoother are analysed in Velleman (1980) and Gebski and McNeil (1984), while Velleman and Hoaglin (1980) and Mills (1990, chapter 4) provide textbook discussion. Mallows (1980) provides a formal development of the theory underlying nonlinear smoothing.

Figures 7 and 8 present the smoothed inflation rates for the four countries which underwent a "constitutional change" in their central bank during the sample period (see Table 1): these are the U.K., Germany, Canada and New Zealand. These confirm the previous results relating to the move to a dependant central bank in U.K., Canada and New Zealand: apart from the World War I years, inflation rates have tended to be higher after the move than before it. For Germany, which moved from a dependent to an independent central bank in 1945, inflation behaviour seems to have been rather similar in both regimes, if the period of the early 1920s is ignored, this again being consistent with our previous results.

5.   CONCLUSIONS

The results set out in this paper are certainly consistent with the belief that independent central banks will deliver lower inflation than will dependent banks. This appears both from the contrasting performance of dependent and independent banks in different countries, and from the change in behaviour when the status of a central bank was altered.

Figure 7
Smoothed Inflation: U.K. and Germany

U.K.

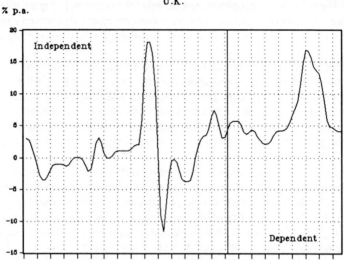

GERMANY

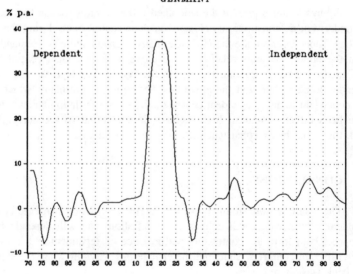

Figure 8
Smoothed Inflation: Canada and New Zealand

CANADA

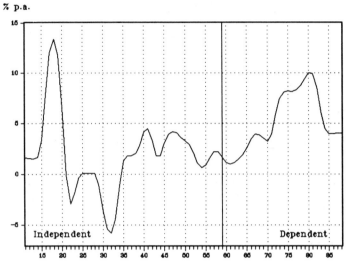

NEW ZEALAND

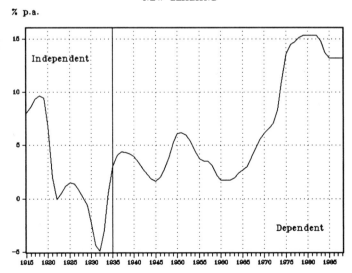

Nevertheless, these results do not in our view lead directly to the conclusion that granting central banks independence will lower inflation rates.

First, because there is clear evidence that while independence may be sufficient for low inflation, it is certainly not necessary - note in evidence of this Sweden and Germany. The former dependent bank performs almost as well as the independents, and (excluding the hyperinflation of the 1920s), Germany was a low inflation country regardless of the status of the central bank. Second, of the central banks which appear to have similar ambiguous status for similar reasons, Belgium and Italy, one produced relatively low inflation, the other high. These points suggest that something other than independence, for which independence is a good but not perfect proxy, may be important.

It should also be observed that when a central bank's status was changed, this was not, except in the case of Germany after 1945, exogenous to the previous economic history of the country. That history may therefore lie behind the change in performance, or at least contribute to it. And finally, it must be emphasised that while there is a rigorous analytical model which can explain why dependent central banks inflate, the explanation of why independent ones do not is not so satisfactory. Independence solves the time consistency problem provided central banks want low inflation. But why do they? To conclude, then, our present results do suggest that central bank independence may be important in reducing and containing inflation; but they demonstrate clearly only that the hypothesis is worth taking seriously and exploring further. What this paper has shown is that the hypothesis stands up outside of the data set which originally suggested it.

REFERENCES

Alesina, A. (1988), "Macroeconomics and Politics", *NBER Macroeconomic Annual 1988*, Cambridge, Mass.: MIT Press.

Alesina, A. (1989), "Politics and Business Cycles in Industrial Democracies", *Economic Policy*, April, 55-98.

Alesina, A. and Summers, L.H. (1991), "Central Bank Independence and Macroeconomic Performance: Some Comparative Evidence", Harvard Institute of Economic Research, Discussion Paper 1496.

Auburn, H.W. (1966), *Comparative Banking*, Waterlow & Sons.

Bade, R. and Parkin, M. (1987), "Central Bank Laws and Monetary Policy", University of Western Ontario, Department of Economics Discussion Paper.

Barro, R.J. and Gordon, D.B. (1983a), "A Positive Theory of Monetary Policy in a Natural Rate Model", *Journal of Political Economy*, 91, 589-610.

Barro, R.J. and Gordon, D.B. (1983b), "Rules, Discretion and Reputation in a Model of Monetary Policy", *Journal of Monetary Economics*, 12, 101-122.

Bernholz, P. (1986), "The Implementation and Maintainence of a Monetary Constitution", *Cato Journal*, 6, 477-511.

Capie, F.H. (1986), "Conditions in Which Hyperinflation has Occurred", Carnegie-Rochester Conference Series on Public Policy.

Capie, F.H. and Wood, G.E. (1991), "Central Banks and Inflation: An Historical Perspective", *Central Banking*, 2, Nos. 2 and 3.

Conant, C.A. (1927, reprint 1969), A History of Modern Banks of Issue, Augustus M. Kelly.

Creighton, J.H. (1933), *Central Banking in Canada*, Clarke & Stuart.

Cukierman, A. (1992), Central Bank Strategy, Credibility and Independence: Theory and Evidence, Boston: MIT Press.

Friedman, M. (1962), "Should There be an Independent Monetary Authority", in L.B. Yeager (editor), In Search of a Monetary Constitution, Boston: Harvard University Press.

Gebski, V. and McNeil, D. (1984), "A Refined Method of Robust Smoothing", *Journal of the American Statistical Association*, 79, 616-623.

Goodhart, C.A.E. (1985), The Evolution of Central Banking: a Natural Development, London School of Economics and Political Science.

Grossman, H.E. (1991), "Monetary Economics: A Review Essay", *Journal of Monetary Economics*, 28, 323-346.

Jarque, C.M. and Bera, A.K. (1980), "Efficient Tests for Normality, Homoskedasticity and Serial Independence in Regression Residuals", Economics Letters, 6, 255-259.

Kisch, C.A. and Elkin, W.A. (1932), Central Banks, London: Macmillan.

Kydland, F.E. and Prescott, E.C. (1977), "Rules Rather Than Discretion: the Inconsistency of Optimal Plans", *Journal of Political Economy*, 85, 473-491.

Lees, F.A., Botts, J.M. and Csyne, R.P. (1990), Banking and Financial Deepening in Brazil, London: Macmillan.

Mallows, C.L. (1989), "Some Theory of Nonlinear Smoothers", *Annals of Statistics*, 8, 695-715.

Masciandaro, D. and Tabellini, G. (1988), "Monetary Regimes and Fiscal Deficits: a Comparative Analysis", in Cheng (editor), *Monetary Policy in the Pacific Basin Countries*, Kluwer Academic.

McGill, R., Tukey, J.W. and Larsen, W.A. (1978), "Variations of Box Plots", *American Statistician*, 32, 12-16.

Mills, T.C. (1990), Time Series Techniques for Economists, Cambridge: Cambridge University Press.

Mitchell, B.R. (1981), European Historical Statistics 1750-1975, London: Macmillan.

Mitchell, B.R. (1982), International Historical Statistics: Africa and Asia, London: Macmillan.

Mitchell, B.R. (1983), International Historical Statistics: The Americas and Australasia, London: Macmillan.

Neufeld, E.P. (1955), Bank of Canada Operations 1935-1954, Toronto: University of Toronto Press.

Plumptre, A.F.W. (1940), Central Banking in the British Dominions, Toronto: University of Toronto Press.

Pressnall, L.S. (1974), Money and Banking in Japan, London: Macmillan.

Quintero Ramos, A.M. (1965), A History of Money and Banking in Argentina, University of Puerto Rico Press.

Sayers, R.S. (1952), Banking in the British Commonwealth, Oxford: Clarendon Press.

Sayers, R.S. (1962), Banking in Western Europe, Oxford: Clarendon Press.

Smith, V. (reprint 1990), The Rationale of Central Banking, Liberty Press.

Stokes, M.L. (1939), Central Banking in Canada, Hunter Rose & Co.

Tukey, J.W. (1977), Exploratory Data Analysis, Reading, Mass: Addison-Wesley.

Velleman, P.F. (1980), "Definition and Comparison of Robust Nonlinear Data Smoothing Algorithms", *Journal of the American Statistical Association*, 75, 609-615.

Velleman, P.F. and Hoaglin, D.C. (1981), Applications, Basics, and Computing of Exploratory Data Analysis, Boston, Mass: Duxbury.

Weston, R. (1980), Domestic and Multinational Banking, Croom Helm.

Williamson, J.H. and Wood, G.E. (1976), "The British Inflation - Indigenous or Imported?", *American Economic Review*, 76, 520-531.

Appendix

Central Bank Classifications

Argentina

Banco Central de la Republica Argentina

Est. 1935

Summary: One of the main reasons for setting up the bank was to "minimize the ups and downs which so frequently affected the Argentine economy". In order to set up an institution to deal with this problem, the government in 1933, asked the Bank of England for help. Under the leadership of Sir Otto Niemeyer, a director of the Bank of England at the time, a report was published and soon the bank was established.

		1935	1946	1988
1	Ownership	J	G	G
2	Management	J	G	G
3	Money Issue	J	S	S
4	Monetary Policy	I	D	D

Notes:

(1)   When the bank was established in 1935 the government subscribed to half the capital, of m$n 30 million, while private shareholders to the rest. The private shareholders consisted of 49 banks, including 12 foreign banks and no bank was allowed to own more than 10% of the capital. However the ownership structure was changed in March 1946 when the newly elected socialist government nationalized the bank. All shareholders prior to nationalization were expropriated through a 2.5% Treasury bond.

(2)   Prior to 1946 the President and Vice-President were appointed on the advice of the senate for a period of seven years. The senate obtained three nominations from each member bank. The rest of the twelve directors were selected for a period of three years by member banks, including two directors by foreign banks.

        Since 1946 the President and Vice President have been selected as before. The ordinary directors, which now consist of thirteen members, are all selected by the President of the country for three years. The directors can be reappointed without limitation. As from 1946 all directors have to be Argentinean by birth.

(3)   Initially the bank issued notes and coins above m$n5 only, while the government issues notes and coins below this sum. However, the government could not issue above m$n20 per inhabitant. After nationalization the bank became the sole issuer of all notes and coins.

(4)   Between 1935 and 1946 the bank acted as an agent for the government. After 1946 the bank acted solely as a department of the government.

Source: Qunitera Ramos A.M. (1965).

Austria (Austria-Hungary)

Chartered Austrian National Bank (till 1878)
Austria Hungarian Bank (till 1922)
Austrian National Bank

Est. 1816 (refers to Chartered Austrian National Bank)

Summary: The bank was formed primarily to regulate the circulation of notes and coins. The bank has always been privately owned; however it has gone through a number of changes. The main change occurred at the time of the union with Hungary, which resulted in the bank having to merge with the Austro-Hungarian Bank. When the union between the two countries was dissolved, after the first world war, the bank returned to being a purely Austrian Central Bank.

		1816	1878	1922	1988
1	Ownership	P	P	P	P
2	Management	J	G	J	J
3	Money Issue	S	S	S	S
4	Monetary Policy	D	D	D	D

Notes:

(1)   The bank is wholly owned by private shareholders.

(2)   Until 1878 the Governor and his deputy were selected by the government and the rest of the directors by the shareholders. After 1878, the Governor was appointed on the advice of both the Minister of Finance from Austria and Hungary. The ministers also appointed a deputy each, although Goodhart (1986) notes that Austria had the majority on the council.

        In 1922 a new charter was passed creating the Austrian National Bank. The bank continued to be a private concern with the Chairman appointed by the President of the country for five years. The Vice-Chairmen (of which there were two), were selected by the board on the approval of the Government. Ordinary directors were selected at general meetings by shareholders. However, there existed guidelines which made sure that certain sectors in the economy were represented. The charter allowed for foreigners to be directors but limited their number to four.

(3)   The Bank was set up as a sole issuer of notes and coins and this was its primary function. After the union with Hungary in 1867 Austrian notes and coins were legal tender in Hungary. This formed part of the agreement with Hungary as did the bank opening of branches in Hungary.

(4)   Although being a privately owned bank it has never been away from the influence of the government. By 1841 the Bank behaved more like a department of the government than an independent organization. In 1899 the government was given greater power in the management of the bank. Goodhart (1986) claims that during the period 1890 to 1910 it was the bank, "most under the thumb of the government".

Source: Conant, C.A. (1929), Goodhart C.A.E. (1986), Kirsch C.H. and Elkin W.A. (1932).

Belgium

National Bank of Belgium

Est. 1850

Summary: The historic relationship between the bank and the government is not well documented. However, the government is part shareholder in the bank with half of the representation on the council.

		1850	1945	1988
1	Ownership	J	J	J
2	Management	J	J	J
3	Money Issue	J	S	S
4	Monetary Policy	U	U	U

Notes:

(1)   The Bank is partly owned by the State (via the government) and private shareholders.

(2)   The Governor is nominated by and can be dismissed or suspended by the government. The appointment is for a fixed period but can be renewed. The rest of the board of directors appointed by the government represent various economic groups. There is also a permanent government representative who has the power to veto any decision. All members of the board of directors have to be Belgian.

(3)   The Bank is a sole issues of notes and coins.

(4)   Conant (1929) claims, "the history of banking in Belgium is a history of greater freedom from State interference and entanglement with the finances of the government than that of most other European countries". However, the government does have the right to oppose any measures which it considers contrary to the laws, statutes or the interests of the State; and therefore it is difficult to classify the bank.

Source: Conant, C.A. (1929), Goodhart C.A.E. (1986), Kirsch C.H. and Elkin W.A. (1932), Weston R. (1980).

Brazil

Central Bank of Brazil

Est. 1965

Summary: Prior to the central bank, monetary regulation was under the responsibility of the Superitendencia da Moeda e do Credito (SUMOC). The currency was issued by the Federal Treasury.

		1965+	1988
1	Ownership	G	G
2	Management	G	G
3	Money Issue	S	S
4	Monetary Policy	D	D

Notes:

(1)   Since the establishment of the bank it has been wholly owned by the government.

(2)   All the directors of the Bank are appointed by the President of the country. They are not appointed for fixed time periods but instead can be dismissed at any time.

(3)   Lees et al. note that, "the executive branch of the government retained most of its former authority [i.e. before the establishment of the central bank] in matters relating to money and credit creation. The printing of money remained under the control of the Minister of Finance".

(4)   The government has a strong influence in the central bank and also makes most of the important monetary and foreign exchange decisions. Important matters relating to monetary and foreign exchange have since 1965 been made by the 'National Monetary Council'.

Source: Lees F.A., Botts J.M. and Cysne R.O. (1990).

Canada

Bank of Canada

Est. 1935

Summary: The bank was one of the first central banks in America. The prime objective for setting up the bank was to regulate the credit and currency in the best interests of the state. The bank initially had private shareholders but then in 1938 it was nationalized after a number of capital injections by the newly elected Liberal government.

		1935	1936/7	1938	1967	1988
1	Ownership	P	J	G	G	G
2	Management	J	J	G	G	G
3	Money Issue	S	S	S	S	S
4	Monetary Policy	I	I	D	D	D

Notes:

(1)   Although initially a private bank it soon received a number of capital injections, from the government. By 1937 the government owned a substantial part of the Bank. The process was completed in 1938 when it was nationalized and all private shareholders forced to sell.

(2)   The Bank of Canada Act 1934, (i.e. the Act which led to the establishment of the Bank), states that after the first Governor and his deputy all future Governors and deputies should be selected by the directors with the approval of the Governor-in-Council. The term of office of the Governor and his deputy was supposed to be seven years with eligibility for reappointment. Between 1936 and 1938 (i.e. during the periods of capital injections) the Government had an average of ten voting rights while private shareholders had seven. The Governor had a veto.

(3)   The Bank is the sole issuer of notes and coins.

(4)   Before 1938 the Bank was largely independent from the government. From 1938 onwards, this had changed and the Bank became more government department rather than a separate organization. This relationship between the Bank and government was formalized by the Bank of Canada Act 1967. Under this Act the Bank had to consult the Minister of Finance and set out a formal procedure, and if there occurred a disagreement the government could after further consultation issue a directive.

Source: Creighton J.H. (1933), Neufeld E.P. (1955), Stokes M.L. (1939), Weston R. (1980).

United Kingdom

Bank of England

Est. 1694

Summary: The bank was originally a private institution which acted as an agent for the government. Although being quite independent from the government, it nevertheless fell victim to government pressure in return for certain favours and privileges. The newly elected Labour government of 1945 nationalized the Bank.

		1694	1844	1946	1988
1	Ownership	P	P	G	G
2	Management	P	P	G	G
3	Money Issue	M	S	S	S
4	Monetary Policy	I	I	D	D

Notes:

(1)   The Bank was a private concern until 1946 when it was nationalized by the recently elected Labour government of 1945.

(2)   The directors of the Bank consisted of 13 ordinary directors, a Governor and his deputy. The directors were selected by shareholders owning the value of £500 or more. All directors had to be natural born or naturalized British subjects. After nationalization directors were appointed by the government.

(3)   When the Bank was established there existed a number of banks which issued notes and coins. However the Bank of England Act of 1844 gave a monopoly of note issue to the Bank. Banks which had previously issued notes were allowed to continue at a fixed rate of their average level prior to 1844. This privilege to the banks would terminate at either their will, a merger or a takeover. However, this did not extend to Scottish banks who will issue their own notes.

(4)   Prior to nationalization the Bank was largely independent from the government. However, at times it obeyed the government in return for certain favours and privileges. After nationalization it was largely a dependent central bank.

Source: Goodhart C.A.E. (1986), Kirsch C.H. and Elkin W.A. (1932), Smith V. (reprint 1990).

France

Banque de France

Est. 1800

Summary: The original idea for the bank came from the Le Couteulx de Canteleu et Perregaux and it was immediately welcomed by Napoleon. Prior to the bank the Paris bankers used the Caisse des Comptes Courants, which provided some of the central bank facilities.

		1800	1801	1806	1848	1945	1988
1	Ownership	J	P	P	P	G	G
2	Management	J	J	G	G	G	G
3	Money Issue	M	M	M	S	S	S
4	Monetary Policy	D	D	D	D	D	D

Notes:

(1)   Napoleon persuaded the shareholders of Caisse des Comptes Courants to dissolve the company and merge it with the Banque de France. This provided for some of the initial capital of 36FF million while the rest was obtained from the government and private shareholders. In 1801 Napoleon sold the government holding in the bank. Later in 1945 the Bank was nationalized by the newly elected socialist government.

(2)   Prior to 1806 the directors of the Bank were selected largely by the shareholders. Due to Napoleon's dislike and distrust of the bankers and also because he assumed they were furthering their own interest; he felt that the government should elect the directors. Even after Napoleon, the government continued to select the directors of the Bank.

(3)   The Bank achieved complete note issuing monopoly in 1848 although the process had started in 1802. This monopoly was challenged for a very brief period in the 1860s by the Bank of Savoy.

(4)   The Bank has always been dependent on the government.

Source: Goodhart C.A.E. (1986), Kirsch C.H. and Elkin W.A. (1932), Smith V. (reprint 1990).

Germany (West Germany after WWII)

Reichsbank (until 1945)
Bundesbank (from 1945)

Est. 1875 (Reichsbank)

Summary: The bank was set up in order to unify and organize the note issue. The post second world war bank has been modelled on that of the USA.

		1875	1891	1945	1988
1	Ownership	P	P	G	G
2	Management	J	J	G	G
3	Money Issue	M	E	S	S
4	Monetary Policy	D	D	I	I

Notes:

(1)   The Bank was originally a private concern but was nationalized in 1945.

(2)   Prior to 1945 the directors consisted both of private shareholder appointees and governmental appointees. After 1945 the Governor and the directors of the Bank, of which there are no more than ten, have been appointed by the President. They are appointed for a fixed period of eight years, on the advice of the Council of the Bank. The Council consists of eleven presidents of the 'Land' Central Banks nominated by the parliament, the Governor and the directors of the Bank.

(3)   The main purpose of the Bank was to unify and organize the note issue. This was somewhat of a difficult task considering there were many note issuers at the time. In view of the large number of local banks issuing notes, the Federal Council decided to review the situation every ten years starting from 1891. The banks who did not agree to this law found that their notes would not be accepted outside their state. As recent as 1922 there existed more than one issuer of notes and coins. In fact the Bank Law of 1924 gave the Bank exclusive rights to issue notes in addition to giving rights to four other banks. Also notes of a value less than RM10 could be issued with the consent of the government.

Source: Conant C.A. (1929, Goodhart C.A.E. (1986), Kirsch C.H. and Elkin W.A. (1932), Smith V. (reprint 1990).

India

Reserve Bank of India

Est. 1935

Summary: The Bank was established while India was under the rule of the British and therefore it is not surprising to notice a similarity between the structure of the two banks. With decolonization and separation in 1948, India decided under Nehru to follow the Socialist path. One result of this was an end to a private Central Bank in which the shareholders elected half the board of directors. Instead came government ownership, government appointed directors and government direction.

		1935	1948	1988
1	Ownership	P	G	G
2	Management	J	G	G
3	Money Issue	S	S	S
4	Monetary Policy	D	D	D

Notes:

(1)   The Bank was established as a private bank with a capital of Rs5 million, of which Rs220,000 was reserved for the government (of India). The government holding was held by directors nominated by it. The 1948 Reserve Bank Act nationalized the Bank, and all shareholders were paid Rs118.10 per share in the form of a government promissory note bearing 3% interest per annum.

(2)   Prior to 1948 the government selected the Governor, two deputies and four directors. The government also appointed an official who was present at all board meetings. The remaining eight directors were selected by the shareholders. After nationalization all directors were appointed by the government.

(3)   The Bank took over the sole control of the note issue from the government. The new socialist government continued to keep note issue under the sale control of the Bank.

(4)   In the early years the government was the only major customer of the Bank and one with a large representation on the board. The result of this was the monetary policy was largely dependent on the government. Nationalization formalized this relationship between the Bank and government, where the former was subservient to the latter. The 1948 Act allowed the central government to give directors to the Bank which it considered to be in the interest of the public.

Source: Sayers R.S. (1952).

Italy

Banca D'Italia

Est. 1893

Summary: The Bank is a private concern which was formed as a result of a merger between the four of the six banks of issue at the time. It gained the sole right to issue notes in 1926. Any monetary policy measures by the Bank have to be approved by the 'Inter ministerial Committee for Credit and Savings'.

		1893	1926	1988
1	Ownership	P	P	P
2	Management	P	P	P
3	Money Issue	M	S	S
4	Monetary Policy	U	U	U

Notes:

(1)   The Bank was a result of a merger between four banks of issue and all previous shareholders continued to own shares in the new Bank. The Banking Law of 1936 limited ownership of the Bank to public law banks, savings banks, banks of national interest, social security institutions and insurance companies.

(2)   The Governor of the Bank is appointed for an indefinite period by the board, on the approval of the President. The remaining thirteen directors of the bank are elected by the shareholders for a three-year period with reappointment allowed.

(3)   The Bank gained the sole right to issue notes and coins in 1926, prior to which there existed many issuing banks.

(4)   The Bank has to seek approval from the Inter ministerial Committee for Credit and Savings for any monetary policy measure.

Source: Sayers R.S. (1952).

Japan

Bank of Japan

Est. 1882

Summary: After the Meiji restoration, the Japanese looked to the west for a central bank model to implement. In the National Bank of Belgium they found one. However, in practice the bank is greatly different from its model.

		1882	1885	1942	1988
1	Ownership	J	J	J	J
2	Management	G	G	G	G
3	Money Issue	X	S	S	S
4	Monetary Policy	D	D	D	D

Notes:

(1)   The government is a partner but is allowed to own only half the capital.

(2)   Prior to the second world war the Governor and his deputy were selected by the Crown on the advise of the Government. The period of governorship was fixed at five years with reappointment allowed. The government also appointed two-thirds of the ordinary directors, while the shareholders selected the remaining third. Ordinary directors were selected for a fixed period of four years. After the war the Governor and his deputy were appointed by the cabinet. The ordinary directors are selected by the Minister of Finance from recommendations of the Governor. All positions are for a fixed period with four years for the Governor and his deputy and three for the ordinary directors.

(3)   Monopoly authority to issue notes and coins was given to the Bank in May 1884, although these did not reach circulation till 1885. Prior to 1884/85 the Bank did not issue any notes or coins.

(4)   The Bank of Japan Act 1884 states that, "The Government shall control all the operations of the bank of Japan, and shall prevent not only any operation which is contrary to the Act or By-Laws, but also any measure that the Government may deem disadvantageous for the state". This tight grip on the Bank continued after the war whereby the Bank was subject to extensive supervision. Pressnell (1974) notes, "The Minister of Finance is empowered to issue general directives and may give supervisory orders to the Bank. The Minister also appoints the Comptroller of the Bank of Japan, who superintends its business. The Minister can also dismiss the officers of the Bank. In addition to this general supervision, the government has the power to permit, approve and decide various individual matters of the Bank's business, so that almost all aspects of its activities including policies, organization, note-issue and accounting, are under the government's control."

Source: Conant C.A. (1929, Goodhart C.A.E. (1986), Kirsch C.H. and Elkin W.A. (1932), Pressnell, L.S. (1974).

New Zealand

Reserve Bank of New Zealand

Est. 1933

Summary: The Bank was initially jointly owned between private shareholders and the government. However, the Labour government of 1936 nationalized the Bank and formalized the relationship between the two.

		1933	1936	1988
1	Ownership	J	G	G
2	Management	J	G	G
3	Money Issue	S	S	S
4	Monetary Policy	D	D	D

Notes:

(1)   The Bank began life as jointly owned between the government and private shareholders. Private shareholders were allowed to invest in one third of the Bank's capital of £NZ 1.5 million and the government to the remainder. No single shareholder was permitted to own more than £NZ 2500 of the Bank's capital. However the newly elected Labour government of 1936 nationalized the Bank.

(2)   Prior to 1936 the directors were selected on the basis of three by the state and four by the shareholders. After 1936 all directors are selected by the government. The changes in 1936 gave the Secretary of the Treasury voting rights which were previously denied to him.

(3)   The Bank gained is the sole issuer of notes and coins.

(4)   Before nationalization the Bank had some degree of independence from the government. In 1936 this independence was lost and the bank behaved more as a department of the government rather than a separate institution.

Source: Plumptre A.F.W. (1940)

Spain

Bank of San Fernando (until 1856)
Bank of Spain (from 1856)

Est. 1829 (Bank of San Fernando)

Summary: The bank's privileges and activities were initially restricted to Madrid and to places where it had branches. The Act of 1856 extended the bank's privileges to all parts of Spain.

		1829	1874	1931	1988
1	Ownership	J	J	J	J
2	Management	J	J	J	J
3	Money Issue	M	S	S	S
4	Monetary Policy	D	D	D	D

Notes:

(1)   The Bank Law of 1921 increased the capital of the Bank to P177 million with a facility to increase it on the approval of the shareholders and government. Shareholders receive a guaranteed 10% pa from net profits and any excess is shared with the government.

(2)   The Governor is appointed by the government and the two assistant governors by the council of the Bank. The council of the Bank consists of twenty one members of which fifteen are elected by shareholders. Of the remainder three are selected by various official organizations and three by the state. Apart from the three state appointed directors all directors have to deposit a given number of shares as guarantee. Only Spanish citizens are eligible to be directors.

(3)   The Bank law of 1874 gave the Bank the exclusive privilege to issue notes and coins. The existing banks were forced to liquidate their circulation and transfer it to the Bank of Spain.

(4)   The Bank is forced to seek the approval of the Minister of Finance on matters of monetary policy.

Source: Conant C.A. (1929), Kirsch C.H. and Elkin W.A. (1932)

Sweden

State Bank of Sweden

Est. 1656

Summary: This is the world's first central bank. The interesting aspect of this bank was that from its establishment to the 1830s it was the only bank in the country.

		1656	1668	1809	1988
1	Ownership	P	G	G	G
2	Management	P	G	G	G
3	Money Issue	M	M	S	S
4	Monetary Policy	D	D	D	D

Notes:

(1)   The bank was originally established as a private concern which later became a state institution in 1668.

(2)   The Constitution of 1809 stated that the President of the bank and his deputy should be selected by the Crown. It also stated that five ordinary directors be appointed for three years by the Riksdag (i.e. the Parliament). All directors including the president and his deputy are answerable to the Riksdag. Only Swedish citizens not directors of other banks can be directors of the Bank.

(3)   Article 72 of the 1809 constitution gave the Bank the sole right to issue notes. However, this did not become fully effective until 1904.

(4)   The 1809 constitution put the bank under the guarantee of the Riksdag. It also increased the political pressures placed on the directors. Also all matters regarding monetary policy have to be approved by the Minister of Budget and Economics.

Source: Conant C.A. (1929), Goodhart C.A.E. (1986), Kirsch C.H. and Elkin W.A. (1932)

U.S.A.

Federal Reserve System

Est. 1913

Summary: Before the Fed was established, one of the most extensive of studies regarding central banks was carried out. The study began in 1908 and ended in 1912. Soon after the study the Federal System of Banks was established. The purpose of this institution was to, "furnish an elastic currency, to afford means of redistributing commercial paper, to establish a more effective supervision of banking".

		1913	1988
1	Ownership	MB	MB
2	Management	J	J
3	Money Issue	S	S
4	Monetary Policy	I	I

Notes:

(1)   The Bank is owned by all the member banks of the Federal System.

(2)   The seven members of the Federal Reserve Board are selected by the President of the country, on the approval of the Senate for a fixed period of fourteen years. Two members from the board are selected to be the Chairman and Vice Chairman, by the President of the country, for a four year period with reappointment allowed.

(3)   Article 16 of the 1913 constitution gives the Bank the sole right to issue notes and coins.

(4)   Decisions relating to matters of monetary policy are made by the 'Open Market Committee'. This committee consists of the members of the Federal Reserve Board, the President of the Federal Reserve Bank of New York, and four presidents from the Federal Reserve Banks. The four Presidents from the Federal Reserve Banks are selected for a fixed one year period on a rotating basis. Decisions made by the committee are reached by a simple majority.

Source: Conant C.A. (1929), Goodhart C.A.E. (1986), Kirsch C.H. and Elkin W.A. (1932), Smith V. (reprint 1990)

CHAPTER 6

POLITICAL EFFECTS ON CENTRAL BANK BEHAVIOUR: SOME
INTERNATIONAL EVIDENCE[1]

David R. Johnson
Pierre L. Siklos

1.   INTRODUCTION

It has once again become fashionable in the economics literature to argue that politicians successfully manipulate the instruments of macroeconomic policy to satisfy a political objective, either the prospect of reelection or the opportunity to implement a particular economic ideology. Alesina (1988) surveys part of the literature. Other contributions include Alesina (1989), Alesina and Roubini (1990), Alesina, Cohen and Roubini (1991), Nordhaus (1989), Haynes and Stone (1990), as well as the collection of papers edited by Mayer (1990) and Willett (1988). While details about how political business cycles are generated, in particular the exact electoral shape of the cycle (Beck 1991b),[2] are somewhat unclear the literature has

[1] The second author thanks Wilfrid Laurier for financial assistance in the form of a book preparation grant, a Course Remission Grant, and a grant from the Academic Development Fund. Both are grateful to Freure Homes for a Student Assistantship and to the Social Sciences and Humanities Research Council of Canada under grant 410-93-1409. Research assistance was provided by Philip King and Ildiko Tiszvoszky. Comments by King Banaian, Neal Beck, John Boschen, Richard Burdekin, Rick Hafer, Tom Willett, Mark Wohar, and participants at Brock University, and the workshop on the Political Economy of Global Monetary Stabilization in Claremont, CA., were greatly appreciated. A version of this paper which includes an extensive appendix with information about the dating of electoral, partisan and exchange rate events, as well as additional results not presented here is available as a Wilfrid Laurier working paper.

[2] Haynes and Stone (1989, 1990) find that the electoral cycle, in the US at least, is regular and periodic with a period of four years. Beck's (1991a) empirical findings stand in contrast to those of Haynes and Stone since he finds that electoral effects take place early in the US Presidential electoral cycle.

generally argued that political influences originate from two sources: electoral and partisan effects. In the electoral scenario politicians attempt to influence economic activity in pre-election times to increase the likelihood of reelection. In the case of partisan effects only certain economic aggregates are the focus of politicians' attention before elections, depending upon their ideology.[3] Thus, for example, left-wing politicians are relatively more concerned about reducing unemployment than inflation.

Until recently, however, what stands out in this literature is that research on political business cycles has been interested in overall policy outcomes while explicitly abstracting from the behaviour of the central bank (see, however, Banaian, Laney and Willett (1983), and Alesina and Sachs (1988)). To be sure, there exists an old and sizeable literature on reaction functions of the monetary authorities. However, the bridge between central bank behaviour and the attempts by the political authorities to interfere in monetary policy actions has not usually been explored in much detail, other than perhaps for the U.S. The aim of this paper is to contribute both to the literature on political business cycles and central bank independence in a number of novel ways. First, by generating a quantitative assessment of central bank behaviour and independence for several countries using high frequency data. Second, by estimating the importance of political influence on central bank behaviour and, indirectly, on economic outcomes. Third, by expanding the set of variables through which political effects on central bank behaviour can be measured. Thus, our specification permits central banks to react to a wider array of variables in its information set than is commonly assumed in the existing literature. In small open economies the external position, as measured by the trade balance, should be incorporated into a reaction function along with inflation and unemployment. Fourth, we are mindful of the fact that central banks base their decisions on the available data. By contrast, existing studies which examine relationships over some sample implicitly provide policy makers with more information than they could possibly have had when implementing policy. We avoid this problem by estimating relevant relationships recursively. Fifth, we also recognize the endogeneity of the variables in question. To account for this possibility, we estimate vector autoregressions to derive central bank reaction functions.[4] Finally, we allow inflation performance, and thus central bank behaviour, to be influenced by the exchange rate regime.

---

[3]   A more sophisticated view of the political business cycle relaxes the assumptions that elections or partisan influences aim to maximize some objective. Instead, as in Frey and Schneider (1978a, 1978b, 1983), politicians have a satisficing objective which predicts, for example, that politicians will not care about unemployment except when it is "too high" to begin with. See Davidson, Fratianni, von Hagen (1992) for U.S. evidence since 1914.

[4]   Johnson and Siklos (1992) also use this technique, as do Bernanke and Blinder (1992) in a study we became aware of after writing this paper.

2.   POLITICAL BUSINESS CYCLES AND CENTRAL BANK
      INDEPENDENCE

Crucial to the arguments about politicians' attempts at increasing their chances for reelection is the role of voters' expectations about the variables being manipulated. Original expositions of electoral and partisan influences (Nordhaus 1975, MacRae 1977, Hibbs 1977) assumed that economic agents form their expectations adaptively. However, the principle of rational expectations, under which agents effectively evaluate a mathematical expectation of a variable conditional on some information set, has replaced adaptive expectations in models of opportunistic political behaviour. The result is that pre-electoral effects on economic activity can arise due to information asymmetry. For example, voters have difficulty distinguishing between temporary and permanent effects of government spending on debt. Cukierman and Meltzer (1986), and Rogoff (1987), are notable contributions to this literature. Under rational expectations partisan influences are possible because of the uncertainty about election outcomes. Hence, while the average voter knows what left and right-wing politicians would like to do there is uncertainty about which party will get the chance to implement its preferred policies. Much recent research has attempted, with mixed results, to corroborate the partisan view of political business cycles. See, for example, Alesina (1988), Alesina and Sachs (1988), and Havrilesky (1987). Almost all the research has been done on post-World War II samples, and usually with US data. Alesina, Londregan and Rosenthal (1991), Davidson, Fratianni and von Hagen (1992) and Siklos (1992) search for political influences on US macroeconomic data for almost a century of data.

The resurgence of interest in central bank behaviour and its connection with the political authorities is explained, first, by the largely descriptive and qualitative evidence, beginning with the seminal contribution by Parkin and Bade (1985),[5] which finds that central banks which are statutorily independent deliver relatively lower inflation rates, at least in the post World War II era. Banaian, Laney, and Willett (1983), Alesina (1988), Alesina and Summers (1992), Burdekin and Willett (1991), Cukierman, Webb and Neyapti (1992), Burdekin, Wihlborg, and Willett (1992), represent some of the many papers in this literature which has mushroomed in recent years.[6] Capie, Mills, and Wood (1992), consider over a century of data for several countries and consider the statistical relationship between central bank statutes and

---

[5] We omit an earlier literature which analyzes central bank performance in the context of theories of bureaucratic behaviour (Acheson and Chant 1973).

[6] Other studies in this area include Epstein and Schor (1986), Grilli, Masciandro and Tabellini (1991), Masciandro and Tabellini (1988), Parkin (1986), and Hochreiter (1990). Johnson and Siklos (1992) discuss the problems with the existing qualitative rankings and provide a more comprehensive survey of the literature.

inflation. Generally, this literature concludes that statutory independence is associated with lower inflation rates.

A second influence on the research on central bank behaviour comes from recent developments in Europe. Proposals include, for example, the creation of a European Central Bank[7], as well as changes in central bank acts to ensure their formal independence from governmental interference. In New Zealand, reforms have been implemented which clarify the role of that country's central bank and its relationship and duties relative to the political authorities.[8]

The literature on central bank independence either implicitly or explicitly assumes that a significant portion of the burden of economic performance with respect to inflation and unemployment is placed on the central bank. Yet, central banks control only monetary policy instruments while politicians have direct responsibility over fiscal policy.[9]

The definition of central bank independence in this study is specific as it is defined as the extent to which a central bank acts independently in monetary policy decisions. Specifically, we are interested in measuring whether central banks act independently within government. Clearly, no central bank can be entirely independent of any government because, in most countries, governments are ultimately responsible for monetary policy (Fair 1979, Swinburne and Castello-Branco 1991).

The motivation for our study stems from problems arising with studies which focus too narrowly on the legislative structure of central banks instead of central bank behaviour. This is a criticism which has been raised by Cargill (1989), and Mayer (1976). However, we should not unduly minimize the role of institutional reforms in legislation governing central bank behaviour which is an important question as

---

[7] As outlined in the Maastricht Treaty agreed to in December 1991.

[8] Where formal inflation targets have been established for the Reserve Bank to meet and independence from direct government interference has been guaranteed. See Archer (1992).

[9] This is somewhat of an exaggeration since qualitative indexes recognize somehow the interrelationship between fiscal and monetary policies but it is not entirely clear what role these effects play. There exists a literature which analyzes the separate influence of fiscal policy on macroeconomic aggregates and the interaction between fiscal and monetary policies. A partial list of contributions in this area includes Fair (1978), Hamburger and Zwick (1981), Parkin (1986), Havirilesky (1988), Burdekin and Wohar (1990), Alesina, Cohen and Roubini (1991), Grilli, Masciandaro and Tabellini (1988), and Burdekin and Langdana (1992).

Alesina and Grilli (1991), and Goodman (1989), have stressed. Instead, we believe these qualitative aspects of the relationship between a central bank and the political authorities should be supplemented with a more quantitative assessment of central bank independence. Case studies such as Toniolo (1988), and Bernanke and Mishkin (1992), as well as casual observation, suggests several instances where statutorily independent central banks behave as dependent entities while statutorily dependent central banks seem to act independently within government.

The rest of the paper is organized as follows. The econometrics of reaction functions is discussed in section 3 while our specifications are outlined in section 4. Empirical results are summarized in section 5. The paper concludes in section 6 with a summary and suggestions for future work.

3.   REACTION FUNCTIONS AND POLITICS

The standard methodology in quantitative assessments of central bank and opportunistic political behaviour has been the estimation of reaction functions.[10] A representative reaction function for policy makers, here assumed to be the central bank, specifies how an instrument of monetary policy (I) reacts to a vector which captures the relevant information set of the central bank (Z) as well as political variables (P). Because of delays in obtaining and processing data the information used by the central bank is available with a one period lag. This yields the specification

$$I_t = B(L)Z_{t-1} + C(L)P_t \qquad (1)$$

where $B(L)$ and $C(L)$ are distributed lags.[11] There are, in essence, three problems with estimation and inference of equations such as (1). One is the temporal instability of coefficients in $B(L)$ and $C(L)$. This problem has been known since Christian (1965) and Havrilesky (1967). Second, $B(L)$ and $C(L)$ confound the relationship between Z and I, the weights on achieving different objectives, as well as the value of these objectives. The identification problem makes is difficult to interpret reaction functions and not only because (1) is a reduced form specification (Khoury 1990 and Beck 1990). A final difficulty arises with the specification of the political variable P. This is a dummy variable active before elections when monetary policy is looser (Nordhaus 1975) or is defined according to the partisan preferences of the party in power as in Hibbs (1977). The existing literature is overwhelmingly concentrated on

---

[10] The literature in this area is long and varied. It begins with Reuber (1964). Alt and Chrystal (1983, ch. 6) survey the literature.

[11] Equation (1) can be formally derived from an optimal control problem where the policy maker has quadratic preferences over the outcomes and a linear model of the economy as in Friedlander (1973) and Goldfeld and Blinder (1972).

US evidence. Indeed, estimation of reaction functions for data sets of other countries is sparse (Frey and Schneider 1981, Cowart 1978, Hodgman and Ressek 1983, Woolley 1983, and Hibbs 1987, are exceptions).

Also, existing research does not generally attempt to quantify the degree of central bank independence, conditional on political influences, nor do existing studies satisfactorily address some of the econometric problems facing the reaction function approach. Moreover, there is the tendency, noted previously, for existing studies to rely heavily on classifications of the relevant legislation regarding central bank behaviour thereby occasionally leading to peculiar results.[12] The presumption is that there is a one-to-one relationship between what central banks are legislated to do and their actual performance.

4.   ECONOMETRIC SPECIFICATION

4.1   The Choice of Variables and the Econometric Model

Our central bank reaction functions are predicated upon the assumption that central banks are responsible for the conduct of monetary policy. Generally, the literature in this area has chosen a monetary aggregate of some kind as representative of a central bank's instrument (Abrams, Froyen, and Waud (1980), Bernanke and Blinder (1992), are exceptions). In contrast, the present study uses a market determined interest rate to capture the stance of monetary policy for several reasons. First, money supply and reserve data are influenced by a host of factors such as fluctuations in interbank clearings, bank crises, seasonality, changes in reserve requirements, which cannot easily be controlled for in a comparative study of the kind attempted here. Moreover, money supply changes can mask the actual stance of monetary policy which is the variable of interest. Second, interest rate developments are more likely to be the object of political scrutiny or interference than some indicator of money supply growth. Third, central banks can influence the direction of change in interest rates.[13]

---

[12] For example, Austria ranks as a relatively dependent central bank in Grilli, Masciandro and Tabellini (1990), even though the legislation governing the Austrian National Bank makes it one of the most independent central bank (Hochreiter 1990). Cukierman and Webb and Neyapti (1992) and Burdekin and Willett (1991) rank Austria much higher in terms of independence. The subtlety of the notion of independence is also evident in Lohmann's (1993) discussion of the structure and behaviour of the Bundesbank.

[13] It is true that in some countries, for example, the U.S. and Canada, the central bank has more short-term influence over its discount rate. However, changes in discount rates, at least for a significant portion of the sample considered, appear to

Central banks are assumed to respond to inflation, the unemployment rate, the balance of trade, with the latter variable defined as exports less imports, and interest rate developments in the rest of the world. Our proxy for the world interest rate is the average of the selected US, German, and Japanese interest rates. Other definitions for the world interest rate were also considered since the importance of Japanese interest rates may only be a recent phenomenon,[14] German interest rates are central in the European Monetary System (EMS), while US interest rates dominate Canadian interest rate movements (Burdekin and Burkett (1992)).

Moreover, we recognize the endogeneity of all the variables, except the world interest rate variable. Consequently, our formal econometric model postulates that a vector autoregression (VAR), written as follows, characterizes the economy:

$$Z_t = A(L) Z_{t-1} + \epsilon_t \qquad\qquad (2)$$

where $Z_t = [R_t, \pi_t, U_t, \Delta TB_t]'$. R_t is a nominal interest rate, our proxy for the instrument of monetary policy, π_t is the inflation rate, U_t is the unemployment rate, ΔTB_t is the change in the balance of trade. All the other terms in (2) have been defined previously. The variables in the vector Z are all lagged one period because the required data are usually available to policy makers with a lag.

To the extent that changes in fiscal policy influence lagged interest rates, unemployment and inflation rates, and the change in the trade balance (other than its contemporaneous effects), fiscal policy effects are indirectly incorporated into the study.[15] Expression (2) also assumes that all central banks respond only to economic events captured in Z_{t-1}. Under this restriction the timing of elections or partisan

---

to be uninformative about the stance of monetary policy because they change relatively infrequently. Moreover, it would be surprising if central banks did not care about the general level of short-term interest rates.

[14] Interest rates, of course, can proxy real or monetary factors. Sims (1980), Litterman and Weiss (1985) argue for the former view, while Bernanke and Blinder (1992) and McCallum (1983) suggest the latter is the preferred interpretation of the transmission mechanism. To the extent that interest rate behaviour incorporates the influence of monetary aggregates this eliminates the need to include a proxy in the reaction function. Nevertheless, were we to add a monetary aggregate to our specification we would, in addition to the considerations outlined already, face the problem of choosing proxies which would permit the kind of cross-country comparison we are aiming for.

[15] More direct fiscal policy proxies, comparable across countries, such as government spending or a deficit measure, were not available for most of the countries in our sample or at the monthly frequency.

influences do not matter so our specification can be estimated for even those countries where election timing is endogenous. An important innovation in our study is that the coefficients in (2) are allowed to vary over time. We accomplish this by estimating (2) over every possible sub-sample. Thus, the innovations ε are based only on information known to the monetary authority at the time the policy is carried out and can be thought of as forecast errors.[16] Finally, we recognize the fact that inflation performance will be affected by the exchange rate regime. With few exceptions, this aspect relevant to the evaluation of central bank performance has been neglected.[17]

4.2   Reaction Functions

Once a central bank has reacted to past values of the variables contained in the information set, interest rates will only be changed in the current period according to unexpected events, including political interference. This implies a reaction function of the form:

$$\Delta R_t = \alpha(L)(\varepsilon_t^{\pi}) + \beta(L)(\varepsilon_t^{U}) + \gamma(L)(\varepsilon_t^{\Delta TB}) + \delta(L)P_t + \theta(L)\Delta R_t^{w} \qquad (3a)$$

$$\alpha(L){>}0, \ \beta(L){<}0, \ \gamma(L){>}0, \ \theta(L){>}0$$

ΔR_t is the first difference in the interest rate in period t (i.e., $R_t - R_{t-1}$). This is the instrument of monetary policy. ε_t^{π}, ε_t^{U}, $\varepsilon_t^{\Delta TB}$, are the innovations in inflation, unemployment rates, and changes in the trade balance, respectively. If political interference influences central bank behaviour then $\delta(L){\neq}0$, while changes in the world interest rate (ΔR_t^{w}) may also force the central bank to adjust domestic interest rates by $\theta(L)$.

Under the assumption that the central bank achieves its desired interest rate during the period, changes in interest rates are interpreted as the policy choices made by the central bank. Thus, if $\Delta R_t > 0$, the central bank raises interest rates by more than the market expects, given Z_{t-1}. This might arise because inflation has risen unexpectedly. For an unexpected increase in unemployment, the central bank might wish to lower the nominal interest rate for a given inflation rate. A worsening trade

---

[16]   Lombra and Karamouzis (1990) use the funds rate as an instrument of the Fed's policy, and a Kalman filter approach to estimate the time varying effect of deviations of actual money growth from its target on the Federal Funds rate. However, their relationship is not a reaction function in the conventional sense. Woolley's (1988) is another attempt which goes part way in recognizing the potential importance of changing coefficients over time.

[17]   Bordo (1992) is a recent survey of international economic performance under different exchange rate regimes.

balance might be corrected by reducing interest rates which would, in concert with a depreciation of the home currency, help improve the future balance of trade. This specification also enables us to analyze differences in central bank behaviour according to whether monetary policy makers place greater weight on some economic variables more than others.[18] For example, it is conceivable that some central banks might only react to innovations in inflation. Finally, one would expect domestic interest rates to react to the world interest rate in a world with a high degree of capital mobility. This is certainly true of countries in our sample which operate under the quasi-fixed exchange rate system of the EMS, while the scope for independent nominal interest rate behaviour would be relatively greater in countries where the exchange rate is floating. The anticipated sign for each variable is shown below equation (3a), except for $\delta(L)$ which is discussed in the following section. Whether P_t, also influences interest rate is the issue of central interest in this paper, along with the nature of central bank reactions to Z_{t-1}.

Other specifications are, of course, possible. For example, the existing literature typically estimates reaction functions where the innovations in π, U, and ΔTB, are proxied by the first difference of the relevant series.[19] This results in reaction function (3b) below.

$$\Delta R_t = \alpha'(L)\ \Delta \pi_t + \beta'(L)\ \Delta U_t + \gamma'(L)\Delta^2 TB_t + \delta'(L)P_t + \theta'(L)\Delta R_t^W \quad (3b)$$

where all the terms and variables have been previously defined and Δ^2 is the second difference operator.

Finally, we consider a third reaction function equation (3c) below:

$$\epsilon_t^R = \alpha^*(L)(\epsilon_t^\tau) + \beta^*(L)(\epsilon_t^u) + \gamma^*(L)(\epsilon_t^{TB}) + \delta^*(L)P_t + \theta^*(L)\Delta R_T^W \quad (3c)$$

where ϵ_t^R replaces ΔR_t as the dependent variable. In this version, unexpected changes increases in interest rates are explained by unexpected changes in the variables in its information set. A possible difficulty with this specification is that, strictly speaking, unexpected events at the same point in time cannot be correlated.

---

[18] Subject again to the usual caveat that the weights in (3) mix central bank preferences with those of the government.

[19] Most studies use a monetary aggregate instead of R to proxy I and, while π and U are usually part of Z_{t-1}, the trade balance is not and they do not rely on the VAR specification. Also, $\theta(L)$ is typically set to zero.

4.3   Political Variables

By adding political variables to (3) we are asking whether political or electoral variables help explain central banks' behaviour beyond their reaction to lagged forecast errors in inflation and unemployment. If so, there is some evidence that the monetary authorities in that country are influenced by political forces.

As in all this literature the variable P_t, is proxied by dummy variables. Following Nordhaus (1975, 1989), a dependent central bank would reduce the nominal interest rate, all else equal, in the months preceding an election. Thus, a dummy variable is active in the pre-election period and $\delta(L)$ would be expected to be negative. Second, it may be that a politically motivated central bank defers a necessary increase in interest rates until after the election. Therefore, the relevant dummy variable is active before an election, where it takes a value of +1 and becomes -1 in the months following an election. The sign of $\delta(L)$ is, however, still expected to be negative if the central bank is dependent. If $\delta(L)$ is positive or zero for either electoral dummy this is a sign that a central bank is independent.

A second type of political variable distinguishes between the political preferences of the party in power. Parties are classified as being left-wing or right-wing following the classification of Alesina and Roubini (1990). In their scenario a switch from right to left following an election signals a looser monetary policy. This would mean an expected increase in future inflation. An independent central bank would react by raising the interest rate while a politically motivated central bank would not and possibly even reduce interest rates. Since the partisan dummy is set to +1 for a right-wing government and -1 for a left-wing government the reaction function of a dependent central bank would result in $\delta(L)$ being positive.[20]

In addition to the standard political dummy variables we also considered for inclusion in (3) several other indicators of political influence for a subset of countries. They were considered in order to explicitly capture the richness and diversity of existing political structures, particularly in parliamentary democracies. Strom (1990) lists for several countries, the tenure of each government, measured in consecutive months, the type of government as well as the length of time, again measured in consecutive months, a party is in power.[21] In addition, we also considered the date at which a government must table its annual budget.

---

[20] In the empirical section we report only the case where the partisan dummy is assumed to be only temporarily active.

[21] A party would be in power longer than a government when the leader or the prime minister changes but the same party continues to govern.

A criticism of existing partisan dummy specifications is that the right wing-left wing distinction does not adequately describe parliamentary democracies in several European countries, most notably Germany, as well as Canada and Australia. Strom (1990) classifies governments according to whether they are non-partisan, as well as whether by type of minority government. Thus, a minority coalition (MC) would consist of a cabinet where representatives are from several parties. By contrast, a substantive minority (SM) government is one in which opposition parties are not represented in cabinet but the government enjoys sufficient support to govern. In formal minority (FM) governments a single party governs but lacks sufficient support to govern as if it were a majority government. Strom (1990) finds that the FM governments are least successful (and least frequent) in office while SM governments leave under relatively more favourable conditions than MC governments. Finally, Strom found that MC governments were at least as effective in passing legislation and in governing as MP governments and typically enter election campaigns under relatively more favourable conditions. Since minority governments tend to be relatively moderate it may be assumed that they are less likely to interfere in central bank policies. The central bank is thus permitted to respond to economic fundamentals rather than to purely election or partisan considerations.[22] Since the FM type of government requires the most outside support to survive it may be expected to interfere in central bank actions relatively more often to satisfy its external supporters. Substantive minorities have more independence in a parliamentary setting and so may feel less pressure to satisfy conflicting political objectives. Majority parties operate like the two-party system implicit in existing partisan dummy specifications. Finally, majority coalitions are least likely to interfere in central bank decisions by virtue of their desire to maintain cross-party consensus to govern. Clearly, other interpretations are possible but the cases examined by Strom would appear to justify the construction of the government type dummy in the manner just described. As before, a negative value for $\delta(L)$, other things being equal, would be consistent with the behaviour of a dependent central bank.

The tenure and party variables recognize that, in a parliamentary democracy, a government or a party in power can overlap or exceed the term of a central bank governor or president.[23] These variables capture the possibility that pressure or interference in central bank actions grows the longer a government or a party is in

---

[22] Strom (1990) does not discuss the different governments' relationship with their central banks. However, because it appears that minority governments or coalitions appear less likely to pursue votes, or a particular type of policy, it seems reasonable to assume that interference in central bank actions will also be moderated under these forms of government.

[23] Cukierman, Webb and Neyapti (1992) find that the turnover rate of central bank governors is an important qualitative characteristic in explaining central bank independence.

power. Under these conditions a dependent central bank will tend to reduce interest rates, conditional on the other variables in (3), the longer the tenure of a government or a party in government and δ(L) would be negative in either case. Both definitions allows us to determine whether there are differences, if any, across governments of the same party (e.g., Reagan vs. Bush in the U.S.) as they impact on central bank behaviour.

While election timing in some countries is endogenous (e.g., Britain and Canada) the date at which a budget is tabled is not. Since a budget is occasionally interpreted as a signal of an upcoming election an independent central bank might react favourably to the fiscal policy implications of a budget. Thus, if the budget is viewed as being inflationary an independent central bank would raise interest rates in the face of this singular annual event. In the empirical section, we follow the usual aproach of, first, estimating reaction functions (3) with, alternatively, the electoral or partisan dummies. We next add the remaining political variables to examine whether additional political influences on central bank behaviour can be detected.

A final comment is in order about the role of fiscal policy in interpreting the empirical results to follow. If, in the current month, there is a pre-election fiscal expansion not captured by lagged unemployment, inflation, interest rates, or trade balance terms in the VAR, the central bank must decide whether to accommodate. If dependent, interest rates would not be allowed to rise. A positive pre-election effect could be additional evidence of independence. A zero or negative effect is evidence of dependence of the monetary authority if there is an unobserved (in our model) current fiscal expansion.

In the case of partisan changes, if a new left-wing government expanded fiscal policy, and the central bank accommodated so that interest rates did not rise a zero coefficient is evidence of dependence. A negative coefficient could, in principle, reflect a fiscal contraction of a newly elected right-wing government. This issue may not be of much practical importance, since it is difficult to imagine changes in fiscal policy enacted within a month of a new government.

4.4   The Data

Monthly data for a sample of 16 OECD countries were used. The sample usually begins in 1960.01 and ends with 1990.12. For certain countries data at the monthly frequency are sometimes unavailable until the early 1970s. The interest rate variable is usually the yield on a three month financial instrument such as a Treasury bill. Inflation is calculated on an annual basis (e.g., 100 times log (CPI_t/CPI_{t-12}), where CPI is the consumer price index. For Australia, as there was insufficient unemployment rate data the annual rate of change in the monthly industrial production index series served as a proxy, the assumption being that a rise in industrial production is generally negatively correlated with a fall in the unemployment rate. Similarly, for Italy, the number of days lost due to labour disputes is the proxy for the unemployment rate.[24]

The unemployment series poses a particular problem because in its seasonally adjusted form the data might be influenced by the choice of seasonal filters which differ across countries. Therefore, we use the raw data and seasonally adjust the data via deterministic seasonal dummies.[25] Table 1 introduces the sample of countries and provides some summary statistics for the Bretton Woods (B)/Post-Bretton Woods (P) periods. A noticeable feature in the data is that interest rates and inflation rates are almost always higher in the P period than in the B period, with the exception of Austria and Japan. Differences in inflation rates between the two samples are small for Switzerland, Germany, and the Netherlands. Finally, unemployment rates are always higher in the P portion of the sample.[26] Clearly, central bank performance differs across exchange rate regimes. Below, we explore econometrically other differences between the P and B periods in more detail.

5.   EMPIRICAL RESULTS

5.1   Bretton Woods versus Post-Bretton Woods Samples

While detailed estimates of the VAR specification (equation (2)) are not discussed, Table 2 provides some evidence that, generally, B and P periods produce different coefficient estimates for the model of the economy. The second column in the Table gives the date at which the regime shift occurred, while the remaining columns provide the likelihood ratio statistic (p-values are in parenthesis) for the test of the equality of coefficients between B and P exchange rate periods for those countries (12 of the 16 countries in our sample) where such a test was feasible given the availability of data. Overall, interest rate, inflation, unemployment, and trade balance change equations show instability although the coefficients in the inflation

---

[24] Switzerland's unemployment rate poses a special problem because of the large number of guest workers. In Johnson and Siklos (1992), a proxy for labour market conditions was considered, namely an employment index, but it had no effect on the conclusions. Hence, we used the unemployment rate.

[25] Although this approach is adequate it does ignore the possibility of unit roots at the seasonal frequency. Based on other empirical evidence (e.g., see Ghysels, Lee and Siklos 1992) this may not be too much of a problem for the unemployment rate but it is a source of possible misspecification.

[26] For Australia, the growth rate in industrial production was smaller in the post-Bretton Woods sample. However, in Italy the average number of days lost due to strikes fell marginally during the P period.

equation are unstable for considerably more countries than equations for the other variables in the VAR. Although the coefficient stability test was performed for a fixed point in time the test was repeated for several months before and after the dates shown in Table 2 to ascertain the sensitivity of test results. The results were found to be robust to changes in the dating of the break-point. Of course, the exchange rate regime is only one of several possible reasons for the coefficients in the VAR to change over time. There exist other obvious candidates such as the two oil price shocks[27] or the deflation of the second half of the 1980s. While the results in Table 2 are illustrative, clearly one does not know a priori whether there are other candidates or events which could produce model instability throughout the sample considered. It is precisely for this reason that we rely on recursive estimation of the economic model summarized in equation (2).[28]

---

[27] A closer look at the dating of the regime shift in Table 2 reveals that, in some instances at least, the first-oil price shock and the change in exchange rate regimes occurred more or less at the same time.

[28] Johnson and Siklos (1992) also report that estimating VARs for complete samples provides a central bank with more economic information than it could have had, as measured by mean squared forecast errors.

Table 1

Mean and Standard Deviation of Series[1]

Country	Bretton Woods				Post-Bretton Woods			
	Interest Rate	Inflation	Unemployment Rate[2]	Change in the Trade Balance	Interest Rate	Inflation	Unemployment Rate	Change in the Trade Balance
Canada	4.50 (1.46)	2.68 (1.34)	4.79 (1.52)	.11 (5.57)	9.34 (3.52)	6.61 (2.82)	8.05 (2.02)	.27 (42.52)
U.S.	4.20 (1.40)	2.86 (1.67)	4.88 (1.18)	*	7.87 (2.60)	6.18 (3.08)	6.83 (1.48)	*[a]
U.K.	5.15 (1.32)	4.60 (2.11)	2.17 (.52)	.04 (7.22)	10.40 (2.89)	9.70 (5.23)	6.77 (3.19)	-.36 (65.94)
Germany	4.37 (1.99)	3.08 (1.31)	.79 (.38)	.75 (56.43)	6.31 (2.74)	3.48 (2.05)	5.50 (2.21)	.48 (184.27)
France	5.55 (2.10)	4.52 (1.74)	1.00 (.49)	-1.75 (51.10)	10.22 (2.71)	7.91 (2.76)	7.69 (2.76)	-3.27 (348.67)
Denmark	INS[3]	INS	INS	INS	11.85 (3.88)	7.90 (5.36)	7.56 (2.66)	.53 (119.53)
Japan	7.50 (1.46)	5.43 (1.56)	1.26 (.26)	37.68 (3490)	6.75 (2.56)	5.29 (5.20)	2.23 (.47)	38.59 (3365)
Sweden[4]	5.65 (1.57)	4.63 (2.00)	0.70 (.35)	.49 (24.75)	9.84 (3.32)	7.94 (2.59)	3.38 (.47)	.14 (169.28)
Switzerland	2.45 (1.22)	3.35 (1.12)	.01 (.02)	-.47 (10.16)	3.16 (2.38)	4.07 (2.60)	.43 (.30)	.08 (29.07)
Belgium[5]	4.84 (1.43)	3.32 (1.43)	2.00 (.48)	.07 (423.00)	9.65 (2.93)	5.85 (3.28)	8.29 (2.98)	-6.49 (2024)
Netherlands	3.37 (1.87)	4.11 (1.88)	.88 (.45)	-.22 (16.38)	6.48 (3.03)	4.71 (3.14)	7.32 (4.06)	.75 (72.53)
Australia[6]	6.19 (1.35)	5.78 (9.66)	.45 (1.29)	.12 (4.20)	12.99 (3.20)	7.54 (11.19)	.09 (2.59)	.08 (33.30)
Norway[7]	4.87 (1.48)	6.43 (1.58)	.92 (.30)	-1.60 (46.55)	10.97 (2.90)	7.83 (2.55)	1.89 (1.12)	3.59 (146.96)
Ireland	INS	INS	INS	INS	12.34 (4.05)	8.37 (7.11)	13.23 (4.43)	.15 (9.68)
Italy	6.79 (1.04)	4.07 (1.88)	9624 (9611)	-12.55 (493)	13.32 (3.42)	11.74 (4.91)	7875 (8029)	102.42 (12008)
Austria[8]	5.07 (.77)	5.12 (1.04)	1.65 (.60)	-6.52 (74.52)	6.82 (2.09)	4.71 (2.31)	2.93 (1.61)	-2.14 (225.92)

Notes:

1. See Appendix for interest rate definition for each country. Sample usually begins in 1960.01, unless otherwise noted and ends in 1990.12. For all the series means and standard deviations of the levels are given except for the trade balance which is measured as 100* (log_t - log_{t-1}). For the dating of B and P samples, see Table 2. The P sample includes the month of the exchange rate regime change.

2. For Australia industrial production proxies the unemployment rate series; for Italy number of days lost due to strikes proxies the unemployment rate series.

3. INS means insufficient observations were available, * series was not used for the US.

4. Sample begins 1963.01.

5. Sample begins 1961.01.

6. Sample begins 1968.01.

7. Sample begins 1971.08.

Table 2

Test for Stability Between Bretton Woods and Post-Bretton Woods Periods

Country	Date of Regime Change	Interest Rate		Inflation		Unemployment Rate		Trade Balance
Canada	1970.03	23.62	(.60)	27.26	(.40)	32.40	(.18)	11.42 (.99)
U.S.	1972.04	27.48	(.09)+	28.36	(.08)+	16.42	(.63)	n.a.
U.K.	1972.05	12.06	(.99)	41.34	(.02)*	49.34	(.00)*	4.03 (1.00)
Germany	1973.02	60.26	(.00)*	45.01	(.01)*	24.91	(.52)	32.46 (.18)
France	1974.02	51.39	(.00)*	70.24	(.00)*	44.23	(.01)*	16.85 (.01)
Denmark	1973.02	CT		CT		CT		CT
Japan	1973.01	77.64	(.00)*	52.69	(.00)*	77.40	(.00)*	46.14 (.01)*
Sweden	1973.02	34.21	(.13)	35.19	(.11)	116.68	(.00)*	0.00 (.00)*
Switzerland	1971.03	35.51	(.00)+	16.38	(.93)	44.32	(.01)	13.24 (.98)
Belgium	1973.02	30.56	(.25)	47.27	(.01)*	22.30	(.67)	22.16 (.68)
Netherlands	1971.03	25.34	(.50)	90.46	(.00)*	14.37	(.97)	(1.00) 10.23
Australia	1974.02	CT		CT		CT		CT
Norway	1973.02	CT		CT		CT		CT
Ireland	1974.11	CT		CT		CT		CT
Italy	1973.01	31.41	(.21)	47.04	(.01)*	56.53	(.00)*	8.24 (.19)
Austria	1973.01	37.84	(.06)+	28.06	(.36)	35.41	(.10)+	5.95 (1.00)

Notes: Test statistic is the likelihood ratio. p-value in parenthesis. * rejection of the null of constancy in parameters at the 5% (+; 10%) level. CT = cannot test because of insufficient data.

5.2   Recursive VAR Estimates

Table 3 provides the means and standard deviations of the innovations from the recursive VAR estimates of (3c) for the complete sample. The estimates were generated by beginning with as small an initial sample as possible (the exact dates are shown at the bottom of the Table) and then increasing the sample by one observation at a time. Each time a new observation is added the VAR is reestimated. Each VAR was estimated with 6 lags, which is equivalent to two quarters. Some experimentation with shorter as well as longer lags did little to alter the conclusions. Generally, the forecast errors are small with the exception of the trade balance innovations. Comparison with the mean forecast errors of model (3b) (not shown) reveals that the VAR outforecasts a model in first differences (equation (3b)), especially for inflation and unemployment equations. There is also evidence throughout of positive serial correlation in the forecast errors although these are not large in magnitude. The results are mixed for the interest rate and trade balance series.

Tables 4 and 5 provide estimates of central bank reaction functions which omit the political variables for the B and P samples separately. Table 4 provides estimates for the Bretton Woods period relying on reaction function (3b), that is, the model in first differences of the variables. Given that relatively few observations are available for this sample there was little advantage in attempting to use the recursive approach here. Table 5, by contrast, estimates reaction function (3a) and maximizes the number of recursions by estimating the initial VAR for a sample which precedes the Post-Bretton Woods period. While this means that estimates are somewhat influenced by data from a different population, as the results in Table 2 suggest, it is nevertheless the case that central banks must have faced the same problem in conducting monetary policy shortly after the end of Bretton Woods. However, the estimates for the P segment of the sample are based only on data available to the central bank at the time of the forecast.

Results in Table 4 reveal that the world interest rate has a statistically significant impact on domestic interest rate changes for almost all the countries in our sample except Austria and Japan. In these countries, capital and other strict financial controls could explain this result although Sweden and the U.K., among other countries considered here, also had similar restrictions on the flow of capital. A one percent rise in the world rate produced a far less than one percent change in the domestic interest rate in most countries which also reflects restrictions on capital flows during the Bretton Woods period. The one exception is Germany whose interest rate overshoots a one percent change in the world interest rate. One cannot reject the hypothesis of a one percent increase in the Canadian interest rate when U.S. interest rates also rise by one percent. As far as the other variables in the reaction function it would appear that changes in the trade balance have almost no impact during the Bretton Woods period. The same holds for the unemployment rate when the sum of lagged coefficients is examined with two notable exceptions.[29] The Fed significantly reduced interest rates in response to higher unemployment as did the Bank of Japan. Both central banks responded to higher unemployment by reducing domestic interest rates. Turning to inflation, the U.S., Germany, the Netherlands, and Austria behave like independent central banks by raising interest rates in the face of higher expected inflation. Japan and the U.K. respond as dependent central banks while the coefficients are statistically insignificant for the other countries. In the Post-Bretton Woods sample changes in the world interest rate have a statistically significant impact on all domestic interest rates. However, the coefficients tend to be smaller for those countries which nominally have flexible exchange rates such as the U.S., the U.K., Japan, Sweden, Switzerland, and Norway. The view that Canada and Australia have an independent interest rate policy is clearly a fiction according to the estimates in Table 5. As in the B sample, changes in the trade balance are statistically insignificant. Interest rates in Canada and the U.S. respond negatively to higher unemployment rates. The general statistical irrelevance of domestic unemployment rates relative to the Bretton Woods era may be a reflection of the increased weight placed by central banks since the mid-1970s on domestic inflation. Indeed, reaction functions for half the countries in our sample respond to inflation innovations with statistical significance. As a result, France, the Netherlands, and Denmark respond like independent central banks while Canada, Germany, Japan, Switzerland, and Ireland respond like dependent central banks. Taken in isolation these results are considerably at variance with evidence based on central bank independence indexes which typically place Germany, Switzerland, and Japan, at the top of lists of independent central banks.

Overall, the results so far indicate some disagreement with qualitative evidence of central bank behaviour. More importantly, however, is the fact that central banks, even if they are independent domestically, do not appear to be independent from U.S. or German central banks, especially during the Bretton Woods period. Finally, there are considerable differences in the reaction functions as between the Bretton Woods and Post-Bretton Woods periods which lends further support to the earlier conclusions reached in Table 2.

---

[29] Two lags for the innovations was found to be sufficient for all the variables in the reaction functions. F-tests of the joint significance of the lags do not contradict the conclusions in Tables 4 and 5.

Table 3

Mean and Standard Deviation of Forecast Errors for Recursive VARs

Country	Interest Rate (ϵ^R)		Inflation (ϵ^Π)		Unemployment Rate (ϵ^U)		Trade Balance (ϵ^{TB})	
Canada	.01	(.55)	-.04	(.39)	.02	(.32)	-.54	(31.74)
U.S.	-.01	(.60)	-.08	(.36)	.03	(.23)	NA	
U.K.	-.05	(1.35)	-.07	(.65)	.01	(.08)	2.41	(48.24)
Germany	-.07	(.74)	-.05	(.28)	-.02	(.18)	-17.69	(137.64)
France	.03	(.59)	-.04	(.29)	-.002	(.12)	-15.89	(257.89)
Denmark	-.33	(2.26)	-.23	(1.02)	-.03	(.84)	1.01	(82.30)
Japan	.03	(.36)	.02	(.79)	.02	(.12)	12.42	(229.66)
Sweden	.12	(.97)	-.11	(.76)	-.03	(.66)	-1.83	(119.79)
Switzerland	.16	(6.24)	.04	(.51)	-.002	(.03)	-.27	(23.78)
Belgium	-.05	(.70)	-.04	(.39)	-.001	(.15)	-93.06	(1314.4)
Netherlands	-.31	(1.45)	.06	(.31)	.01	(.37)	5.75	(59.10)
Australia	.11	(1.20)	-.02	(3.09)	-.01	(2.09)	.27	(25.40)
Norway	-.02	(1.46)	.12	(.96)	.03	(.15)	7.13	(126.76)
Ireland	-.12	(2.50)	-.04	(.88)	-.01	(.24)	.36	(6.83)
Italy	.02	(.31)	-.08	(.56)	-1.47	(.44)	256.90	(9923)
Austria	.05	(.61)	.05	(.41)	.02	(.15)	6.71	(264.84)

Notes: The vector autoregressive model is estimated with six lags. A constant and a trend were also included. Sample start dates: Canada 1966.09, US 1971.11, UK 1971.12, Germany 1972.09, France 1973.09, Denmark 1972.09, Japan 1972.08, Sweden 1972.09, Switzerland 1970.10, Belgium 1972.09, Netherlands 1970.10, Australia 1973.09, Norway 1972.09, Ireland 1974.06, Italy 1972.08, Austria 1972.08.

5.3   Political Variables

Tables 6 and 7 present estimates of the reaction function (3a) and (3b) augmented with electoral or partisan variables for the Bretton Woods and Post-Bretton Woods periods, respectively. The variables in the first two columns of the Table summarize the naive and rational expectations versions of the electoral hypothesis cycle, while the third column summarizes the rational partisan view of political business cycles. The final four columns show the impact of augmenting reaction functions with additional sources of political influence. Coefficient estimates for these variables were generated by including either an electoral or a partisan dummy depending on their relative statistical significance. In most cases the choice was straightforward. In the few instances where one or more electoral or partisan dummies were found to be statistically significiant tests which allow a choice between non-nested models were applied (Greene 1993, pp. 222-25).

For the B sample (Table 6), six of the countries exhibit pre-electoral effects and, based on non-nested tests, these tend to be more important statistically than electoral effects delayed until after the election. Only 3 countries exhibit partisan effects. Of those central bank reaction functions which are statistically influenced by electoral factors, the U.K., Japan, and the Netherlands, (with Belgium in the case of post-electoral interest rate effects) can be classified as dependent central banks since pre-electoral periods are associated with a fall in the interest rate. Canada, France, and Sweden, display interest rate reactions consistent with independent central banks. In the case of partisan effects, the U.K. and Germany's central banks reduce interest rates when a "right-wing" government comes to power while Belgium's monetary authorities raise interest rates when there is a change from left to right. When a variable which recognizes different types of government is added only Canada and Italy respond to these considerations, and only for the latter country is the sign as expected. The length of time a particular government or party is in power has a negative impact on interest rates in Canada, Belgium, Sweden, the Netherlands, and Australia, but the effect is quantitatively small. For Austria, the effect from the same variable is positive, which is consistent with the independence of that country's central bank. The timing of the fiscal year, however, has no statistical effect whatsoever on domestic interest rates in any of the countries considered.

The Post-Bretton Woods case considered in Table 7 is perhaps more interesting because the results are entirely based on the recursive estimation approach outlined earlier. The first thing to notice is that, compared with the Bretton Woods sample, post-electoral and partisan influences occur more frequently than either pre-electoral effects and in many more countries than in the earlier sample. The exchange rate regime itself is one explanation of these results since floating rates permit government to pursue an independent monetary policy. As far as electoral effects are concerned, Sweden, Australia, Norway, Italy, and Austria come out as dependent central banks. Canada, Germany, Japan, the Netherlands, and Belgium appear to act as independent central banks. When partisan features are considered, Canada, the U.S., Denmark, and Belgium raise interest rates as expected when a right-wing government is in power. France, the Netherlands, and Austria reduce interest rates when right-wing governments are elected. These results may, however, be a feature of the partisan classifications, which may be inappropriate in the European context, rather than a contradiction of the meaning of right-wing/left-wing distinctions. This is especially true of Austria which, based on reaction functions which omit political variables, acts like an independent central bank. The government type variable is significantly positive for Canada, Belgium, the Netherlands, and Italy. This suggests

Table 4
Central Bank Reaction Function Omitting Political Effects
Bretton Woods Period*

Country	Sample	$\Delta\pi_{t-1}$	$\Delta\pi_{t-2}$	ΔU_{t-1}	ΔU_{t-2}	$\Delta^2 TB_{t-1}$	$\Delta^2 TB_{t-2}$	ΔR^W_t	R^2
Canada	63.01-70.02	.41 (.36)	.28 (.36)	.54 (.55)	-.03 (.55)	.04 (.03)	.04 (.03)	.80 (.28)*	.31
U.S.	62.03-72.03	.55 (.16)*	-.16 (.15)	-.61 (.21)*	-.05 (.22)	--	--	.15 (.03)*	.70
U.K.	62.03-72.04	.11 (.13)	-.23 (.13)+	-1.23 (.97)	-.41 (1.03)	-.001 (.01)	.01 (.01)	.03 (.07)	.31
Germany	62.03-73.01	.18 (.08)*	.11 (.08)	2.34 (.49)*	-1.81 (.50)*	-.001 (.001)	-.001 (.001)	1.50 (.05)*	.92
France	62.03-74.01	.29 (.18)	.08 (.18)	-9.16 (1.78)*	6.79 (1.84)*	.002 (.002)	.001 (.002)	.39 (.05)*	.56
Denmark				insufficient	data to	estimate			
Japan	62.03-72.12	-.06 (.09)	-.21 (.09)*	-2.84 (.91)*	-3.57 (.90)*	.001 (.006)	.001 (.001)	.12 (.09)	.40
Sweden	64.03-73.01	.07 (.09)	-.02 (.09)	-.15 (.11)*	-.25 (.10)	-.004 (.01)	-.001 (.01)	.40 (.08)+	.56
Switzerland	62.03-71.02	-.29 (.19)	.17 (.19)	-7.01 (7.36)	-3.39 (7.10)	-.005 (.01)	.01 (.01)	.18 (.05)*	.16
Belgium	62.03-73.01	.11 (.14)	-.09 (.14)	-4.85 (1.46)*	4.35 (1.41)*	-.0002 (.0004)	-.0001 (.0004)	.43 (.06)*	.46
Netherlands	62.06-71.02	-.03 (.06)	.16 (.05)*	2.04 (1.02)*	-2.60 (1.10)*	-.001 (.006)	.002 (.006)	.12 (.06)*	.34
Australia	70.09-74.01	.12 (.05)*	.06 (.05)	.69 (.08)*	.01 (.08)	-.03 (.04)	-.04 (.04)	.16 (.09)+	.86
Norway				insufficient	data to	estimate			
Ireland				insufficient	data to	estimate			
Italy	62.03-72.12	-.01 (.09)	.14 (.09)+	-.00001 (.00001)	.000002 (.00001)+	.0002 (.0001)+	.0002 (.0001)	.18 (.03)*	.32
Austria	71.03-72.12	.50 (.27)+	.65 (.30)+	-.27 (1.26)	.52 (1.29)	-.004 (.002)	-.005 (.003)+	.14 (.14)	.81

* For Canada and Australia, the US interest rate proxies R^W; for France, Denmark, Switzerland, Belgium, the Netherlands, Ireland, Italy, and Austria, Germany's interest rate proxies R^W; otherwise R^W is as described in the text. For Italy, unemployment is proxied by days lost in labour disputes; for Australia, industrial production proxies the unemployment rate.

Table 5*

Central Bank Reaction Function Omitting Political Effects
Dependent Variable: Change in Interest Rate
Post-Bretton Woods Period

Country	Sample	Inflation		Unemployment Rate	
		ε^{Π}_{t-1}	ε^{Π}_{t-2}	ε^{U}_{t-1}	ε^{U}_{t-2}
Canada	70.03-90.12	-1.65 (.45)*	-1.50 (.45)*	-1.20 (.55)*	-1.20 (.55)*
U.S.	72.04-90.12	.42 (.41)	-.26 (.41)	-.99 (-.60)+	-1.53 (.59)*
U.K.	72.05-90.12	.10 (.34)	-.03 (.34)	-2.44 (2.97)	-.76 (3.15)
Germany	73.02-90.12	-.90 (.29)*	-.40 (.29)	.50 (.44)	.32 (.44)
France	74.02-90.12	.68 (.47)	.82 (.48)+	-.27 (1.14)	-.13 (1.12)
Denmark	73.02-90.12	.09 (.35)	.74 (.35)*	.27 (.97)	.31 (.97)
Japan	73.01-90.12	-.75 (.22)*	-.64 (.21)*	-.01 (1.33)	1.20 (1.37)
Sweden	73.02-90.12	.01 (.30)	-.03 (.30)	-.03 (.35)	-.31 (.35)
Switzerland	71.03-90.12	-.17 (.33)	-.88 (.33)*	-2.77 (5.68)	-7.72 (5.77)
Belgium	73.02-90.12	-.07 (.42)	-.21 (.42)	-.51 (1.06)	-.14 (1.08)
Netherlands	71.03-90.12	.77 (.75)	1.24 (.75)+	-.36 (.65)	-.83 (.65)
Australia	74.02-90.12	-.02 (.04)	.03 (.04)	.04 (.05)	.04 (.05)
Norway	73.02-90.12	.02 (.22)	.09 (.22)	-.41 (1.44)	-1.78 (1.43)
Ireland	77.02-90.12	-1.24 (.41)*	-.94 (.41)*	-.13 (1.58)	-1.47 (1.56)
Italy	73.01-90.10	-.09 (.30)	.04 (.30)	-.000003 (.00003)	-.000004 (.00003)
Austria	73.01-90.12	.20 (.31)	.27 (.31)	1.31 (.87)	.72 (.87)

* See note to Table 4.

Table 5*

Central Bank Reaction Function Omitting Political Effects
Dependent Variable: Change in Interest Rate
Post-Bretton Woods Period

Country	Sample	Inflation		Unemployment Rate	
		ϵ^{Π}_{t-1}	ϵ^{Π}_{t-2}	ϵ^{U}_{t-1}	ϵ^{U}_{t-2}
Canada	70.03-90.12	-1.65 (.45)*	-1.50 (.45)*	-1.20 (.55)*	-1.20 (.55)*
U.S.	72.04-90.12	.42 (.41)	-.26 (.41)	-.99 (-.60)+	-1.53 (.59)*
U.K.	72.05-90.12	.10 (.34)	-.03 (.34)	-2.44 (2.97)	-.76 (3.15)
Germany	73.02-90.12	-.90 (.29)*	-.40 (.29)	.50 (.44)	.32 (.44)
France	74.02-90.12	.68 (.47)	.82 (.48)+	-.27 (1.14)	-.13 (1.12)
Denmark	73.02-90.12	.09 (.35)	.74 (.35)*	.27 (.97)	.31 (.97)
Japan	73.01-90.12	-.75 (.22)*	-.64 (.21)*	-.01 (1.33)	1.20 (1.37)
Sweden	73.02-90.12	.01 (.30)	-.03 (.30)	-.03 (.35)	-.31 (.35)
Switzerland	71.03-90.12	-.17 (.33)	-.88 (.33)*	-2.77 (5.68)	-7.72 (5.77)
Belgium	73.02-90.12	-.07 (.42)	-.21 (.42)	-.51 (1.06)	-.14 (1.08)
Netherlands	71.03-90.12	.77 (.75)	1.24 (.75)+	-.36 (.65)	-.83 (.65)
Australia	74.02-90.12	-.02 (.04)	.03 (.04)	.04 (.05)	.04 (.05)
Norway	73.02-90.12	.02 (.22)	.09 (.22)	-.41 (1.44)	-1.78 (1.43)
Ireland	77.02-90.12	-1.24 (.41)*	-.94 (.41)*	-.13 (1.58)	-1.47 (1.56)
Italy	73.01-90.10	-.09 (.30)	.04 (.30)	-.000003 (.00003)	-.000004 (.00003)
Austria	73.01-90.12	.20 (.31)	.27 (.31)	1.31 (.87)	.72 (.87)

Table 6

**The Impact of Political Variables on Central Bank Behaviour
Bretton Woods Period**

Equation (3b)

Country	Pre-Election	Delayed Change	Partisan	Government Type	Tenure	Budget Date	Party
Canada	1.23 (.44)*	.78 (.25)	3.32 (.50)	-.54 (.14)*	-.02 (.01)*	-.09 (.44)	-.03 (.02)
U.S.	.18 (.18)	.03 (.12)	.05 (.26)	ND[1]	ND	.07 (.21)	.002 (.002)
U.K.	-.90 (.31)*	-.34 (.18)+	-1.40 (.31)*	ND	ND	.19 (.32)	ND
Germany	.13 (.16)	.10 (.11)	-.30 (.18)+	ND	ND	-.07 (.20)	ND
France	.84 (.32)*	-.19 (.22)	ND	ND	ND	.32 (.40)	.002 (.003)
Denmark	insufficient data to estimate[2]						
Japan	-.72 (.33)*	-.48 (.23)*	NA	ND	ND	-.12 (.47)	ND
Sweden	.59 (.31)+	.15 (.21)	NA	-.021 (.12)	ND	-.11 (.43)	-.02 (.004)*
Switzerland	-.31 (.38)	.33 (.24)	NA	ND	ND	.24 (.41)	ND
Belgium	-.36 (.31)	-.38 (.21)+	1.05 (.48)*	NA[3]	-.01 (.002)*	.08 (.38)	.001 (.002)
Netherlands	-.66 (.25)*	-.34 (.19)+	.17 (.30)	-.10 (.15)	ND	-.12 (.35)	-.02 (.01)*
Australia	.54 (.34)	.04 (.26)	.39 (.42)	ND	ND	-.21 (.35)	-.02 (.01)*
Norway	insufficient data to estimate						
Ireland	insufficient data to estimate						
Italy	-.15 (.19)	.12 (.13)	.08 (.34)	.10 (.05)*	-.003 (.01)	-.02 (.24)	-.0005 (.002)*
Austria	-.67 (.45)	-.27 (.23)	NA	ND	ND	-.49 (.80)	.14 (.05)*

Notes: 1.   ND means no data were available.
         2.   Means the available sample was too small.
         3.   NA means not applicable because there were no partisan changes during the period in question.

Table 7

The Impact of Political Variables Effects on Central Bank Behaviour
Post-Bretton Woods Period[1]

Equation (3a)

Country	Pre-Election	Delayed Change	Partisan	Government Type	Tenure	Budget Date	Party
Canada	1.18 (.49)*	1.04 (.32)*	1.30 (.62)*	.71 (.19)*	-.002 (.005)	-.30 (.61)	.006 (.003)+
U.S.	-.22 (.41)	-.10 (.28)	1.36 (.54)*	ND	ND	.05 (.48)	-.008 (.004)+
U.K.	1.04 (.67)	.30 (.44)	.71 (.88)	ND	ND	-.09 (.83)	ND
Germany	.64 (.22)*	.32 (.15)*	-.43 (.45)	ND	ND	-.09 (.28)	ND
France	-.52 (.38)	-.33 (.26)	-2.50 (.36)*	ND	ND	.19 (.46)	-.003 (.001)*
Denmark	1.25 (.79)	.56 (.52)	4.40 (.135)*	-.03 (.57)	-.01 (.01)	.44 (.129)	-.01 (.02)
Japan	.60 (.42)	.56 (.52)	NA	ND	ND	.12 (.59)	ND
Sweden	.009 (.59)	-.79 (.39)*	.46 (.90)	.05 (.17)	ND	.15 (.91)	-.005 (.005)
Switzerland	-.32 (.51)	.03 (.35)	NA	ND	ND	.25 (.65)	ND
Belgium	.50 (.42)	.53 (.28)+	2.11 (.47)*	.75 (.31)*	-.009 (.003)*	.31 (.55)	.01 (.01)
Netherlands	-.64 (.63)	.74 (.40)+	-1.36 (.72)*	.61 (.35)+	ND	-.02 (.85)	-.02 (.009)*
Australia	-.63 (.27)*	-.53 (.17)	.11 (.49)	ND	ND	.07 (.40)	-.009 (.005)*
Norway	-.50 (.60)	-.68 (.40)+	-.12 (.77)	-.15 (.16)	.009 (.006)	-.29 (.78)	-.01 (.01)
Ireland	.43 (.85)	-.91 (.60)	.68 (.94)	-.28 (.20)	-.07 (.03)*	.13 (1.27)	-.01 (.02)
Italy	-.78 (.50)+	-.57 (.31)+	.04 (.67)	.88 (.22)*	.08 (.02)*	.28 (.55)	-.09 (.02)*
Austria	-1.50 (.36)*	-.03 (.24)	-1.13 (.48)*	ND	ND	.34 (.45)	-.007 (.003)*

Note: 1.   See notes to Table 6.

that the election of more politically secure governments permit central banks to act more independently than weak governments, as expected. Both the length of time a government or a party is in power tends to have a quantitatively small but statistically significant impact in most of the countries for which data were available. For Belgium, Ireland, the U.S., the Netherlands, Australia, Italy, and Austria, it was in the direction of central bank dependence. For Canada, it was in the direction of more central bank independence. Finally, as in the B sample, the timing of the government's fiscal year has no statistical effect on interest rate changes.

6.   CONCLUSIONS

The evidence of his paper points to three conclusions. First, central banks considered to be statutorily independent in qualitative studies of central bank independence appear less so in relative terms on the basis of the reaction function approach. In particular, interest rate changes in Germany, Switzerland, the U.S., and the Netherlands are consistently influenced by political and economic factors in such a way as to make those countries' central banks appear dependent. By contrast, the central banks of Canada and France, for example, appear to act more independently than would be judged by the metric of legal independence. Also, the Bank of Japan appears to be less independent than existing qualitative indexes would lead us to believe. The Japanese case has proved to be troublesome for advocates of statutory independence measures as predictors of central bank performance. Second, central bank behaviour is significantly different in the post-Bretton Woods period relative to the Bretton Woods era. Thus, existing indexes of central bank independence mask subtle changes in central bank behaviour over time. Third, there is little evidence that central banks consistently react to domestic inflation or unemployment rate considerations. Instead, interest rate developments elsewhere in the world, or in a relatively large neighbouring country, are statistically the most important determinant of domestic interest rate policy. Overall, then, the actual performance of central banks does not appear to be highly correlated with what they are legislated to do if only because the choice of exchange rate regimes and foreign monetary policies, both of which are politically influenced, appear to be important determinants. That is not to say that legal independence is not an important feature in the design of a central bank. Rather the conclusion is that the institutional features of central banks cannot be viewed in isolation of other considerations which are not typically associated with the legislation governing central bank behaviour.

REFERENCES

Abrams, R.K., R. Froyen, and R. Wand (1980), "Monetary Policy Reaction Functions, Consistent Expectations, and the Burns Era", *Journal of Money, Credit and Banking*, 12 (February): 30-42.

Acheson, K. and J.F. Chant (1973), "Bureaucratic Theory and the Choice of Central Bank Goals," *Journal of Money, Credit and Banking* 5 (May): 637-55.

Alesina, Alberto (1989), "Macroeconomics and Politics" in S. Fischer (ed.) *NBER Macroeconomics Annual* (Cambridge, Massachusetts: MIT Press).

Alesina, Alberto (1989), "Politics and business cycles in industrial democracies," *Economic Policy* 8: 57-98.

Alesina, Alberto and Jeffrey Sachs (1988), "Political Parties and the Business Cycle in the United States, 1948-1984," *Journal of Money, Credit and Banking* 20: 63-82.

Alesina, Alberto and Nouriel Roubini (1990), "Political Cycles: Evidence from OECD Economies," National Bureau of Economic Research Working Paper No. 3478.

Alesina, Alberto, G.D. Cohen, and N. Roubini (1991), "Macroeconomic Policy and Elections in OECD Democracies", National Bureau of Economic Research Working Paper No. 3830.

Alesina, Alberto, and Vittorio Grilli (1991), "Establishing a Central Bank", paper presented at the European Central Bank: Reshaping Monetary Politics in Europe Conference, Georgetown University, May.

Alesina, Alberto, and J. Londegran, and H. Rosenthal (1991), "A Model of the Political Economy of the United States", NBER Working Paper 3611.

Alesina, Alberto, and L.H. Summers (1992), "Central Bank Independence and Macroeconomic Performance: Some Comparative Evidence", *Journal of Money, Credit and Banking* (forthcoming).

Alt, James E. and K. Alex Chrystal (1983), *Political Economics* (Berkeley, Calif.: University of California Press).

Archer, D.J. (1992), "Organizing a Central Bank to Control Inflation: The Case of New Zealand", mimeo, Reserve Bank of New Zealand.

Banaian, King, Leroy Laney and Thomas D. Willett (1983), "Central Bank Independence: An International Comparison," *Federal Reserve Bank of Dallas Economic Review*, 1-13.

Beck, Nathaniel (1990), "Political Monetary Cycles", in Thomas Mayer (Ed.), *The Political Economy of American Monetary Policy* (Cambridge: Cambridge University Press, 1990), pp. 115-30.

Beck, Nathaniel (1991a), "The Fed and the Political Business Cycle", *Contemporary Policy Issues* 2: 25-38.

Beck, N. (1991b), "What is the Shape of the Electoral Cycle?", mimeo, University of California San Diego.

Bernanke, B.S. and A.S. Blinder (1992), "The Federal Funds Rate and the Channels of Monetary Transmissions", *American Economic Review*, 82 (September): 901-21.

Bernanke, Ben and Frederic Mishkin (1992), "Central Bank Behaviour and the Strategy of Monetary Policy: Observations from Six Industrialized Countries," NBER working paper no. 4082 (May).

Bordo, M.D. (1992), "The Gold Standard, Bretton Woods and Other Monetary Regimes: An Historical Appraisal", mimeo, Rutgers University.

Burdekin, R.C.K., and P. Burkett (1992), "The Impact of US Economic Variables on Bank of Canada Policy: Direct and Indirect Response", *Journal of International Money and Finance*, 11: 162-87.

Burdekin, R.C.K., and Mark E. Wohar (1990), "Monetary Institutions, Budget Deficits and Inflation", *European Journal of Political Economy*, 6, 531-551.

Burdekin, R.C.K., and Thomas D. Willett (1991), "Central Bank Reform: The Federal Reserve in International Perspective," *Public Budgeting and Financial Management* (forthcoming).

Burdekin, R.C.K., Clas Wihlborg, and Thomas D. Willett (1992), "A Monetary Constitution Case for an Independent European Central Bank," *The World Economy*, 15 (March 1992), 231-49.

Burdekin, R.C.K., and F.K. Langdana (1992), *Budget Deficits and Economic Performance*, (London: Routledge).

Capie, F., T.C. Mills and G.E. Wood (1992), "Central Bank Dependence and Inflation Performance: An Exploratory Analysis", in this volume.

Cargill, Thomas F. (1989), "Central Bank Independence and Regulatory Responsibilities: The Bank of Japan and the Federal Reserve", Solomon Brothers Center for the Study of Financial Institutions, Monograph Series in Finance and Economics, monograph 1989-2.

Christian, James W. (1965), "A Further Analysis of the Objectives of American Monetary Policy," *Journal of Finance* 23: 465-477.

Cowart, Andrew T. (1978), "The Economic Policies of European Governments, Part I: Monetary Policy," *British Journal of Political Science* 8: 285-311.

Cukierman, A. (1992), *Central Bank Strategy, Credibility and Independence: Theory and Evidence*, (Cambridge: The MIT Press).

Cukierman, A. and A.H. Meltzer (1986), "A Theory of Ambiguity, Credibility and Inflation Under Discretion and Asymmetric Information", *Econometrica* 53 (September): 1099-1128.

Cukierman, A., S.B. Webb, and B. Neyapti (1992), "The Measurement of Central Bank Independence and Its Effect on Policy Outcomes", *World Bank Economic Review*, 6(3): 353-98.

Davidson, L.S., M. Fratianni, and J. von Hagen (1992), "Testing the Satisficing Version of the Political Business Cycle 1905-84", *Public Choice* 73: 21-35.

Epstein, Gerald A. and Juliet B. Schor (1986), "The Political Economy of Central Banking," Harvard Institute of Economic Research Discussion Paper No. 1281.

Fair, D. (1979), "The Independence of Central Banks", *The Banker* (October).

Fair, D.E. (1980), "Relations between government and central bank: a survey of twenty countries" in *Appendices, Committee to Review the Functioning of Financial Institutions*, London: Her Majesty's Stationery Office.

Fair, R.C. (1978), "The Sensitivity of Fiscal Policy Effects to Assumptions about the Behaviour of the Federal Reserve," *Econometrica* 46: 1165-1179.

Frey, B. and F. Schneider (1978a), "A Politico-Economic Model of the United Kingdom", *Economic Journal*, 88: 243-53.

Frey, B. and F. Schneider (1978b), "An Empirical Study of Politico-Economic Interaction in the United States", *Review of Economics and Statistics*, 60 (May): 174-83.

Frey, B. and F. Schneider (1983), "An Empirical Study of Politico-Economic International in the United States: A Reply", *Review of Economics and Statistics*, 65: 178-82.

Frey, B. and F. Schneider (1981), "Central Bank Behaviour: A Positive Empirical Analysis," *Journal of Monetary Economics* 7: 291-315.

Friedlander, Ann F. (1973), "Macro Policy Goals in the Postwar Period: A Study in Revealed Preference," *Quarterly Journal of Economics* 87: 25-43.

Ghysels, E., H.S. Lee, and P.L. Siklos (1992), "On the (Mis)specification of Seasonality and Its Consequences: An Empirical Investigation with US Data", *Empirical Economics* (forthcoming).

Goldfeld, Stephen M. and Alan S. Blinder (1972), "Some Implications of Endogenous Stabilization Policy," *Brookings Papers on Economic Activity* 3: 585-640.

Goodman, John B. (1989), "Monetary Politics in France, Italy and Germany: 1973-85", in P. Guerriegi and P.C. Padsan (eds.), *The Political Economy of European Integration*, States, Markets and Institutions (New York: Harvester Wheatsheaf): pp. 171-201.

Gorvin, I. (Ed.) (1989), *Elections Since 1945: A Worldwide Reference Compendium* (Chicago and London: St. James Press, 1989).

Greene, W.H. (1993), *Econometric Analysis* (New York: MacMillan).

Grilli, Vittorio, Doanato Masciandaro and Guido Tabellini (1991), "Political and monetary institutions and public financial policies in the industrial countries,: *Economic Policy* 13: 342-392.

Hamburger, Michael J. and Burton Zwick (1981), "Deficits, Money and Inflation," *Journal of Monetary Economics* 7: 141-150.

Havrilesky, Thomas (1988), "Monetary Policy Signalling from the Administration to the Federal Reserve," *Journal of Money, Credit and Banking* 20: 83-101.

Havrilesky, Thomas (1987), "A Partisanship Theory of Fiscal and Monetary Regimes," *Journal of Money, Credit and Banking* 19: 308-325.

Havrilesky, Thomas (1967), "A Test of Monetary Policy Action," *Journal of Political Economy* 75: 299-304.

Haynes, Stephen E. and Joe A. Stone (1990), "Political Models of the Business Cycle Should be Revived," *Economic Inquiry* 28: 442-465.

Hetzel, Robert L. (1990), "Central Bank Independence in Historical Perspective", *Journal of Monetary Economics*, 25: 165-176.

Hibbs, Douglas A. Jr. (1977), "Political Parties and Macroeconomic Policy," *American Political Science Review* 71: 1464-1487.

Hibbs, D.A. Jr. (1987), *The Political Economy of Industrial Democracies*,

Hochreiter, Edouard (1990), "The Austrian National Bank Act: What Does it Say About Monetary Policy?", *Konjunkturpolitik*, 36 (4): 245-56.

Hodgman, Donald R. and Robert W. Resek (1983), "Determinants of Monetary Policy in France, The Federal Republic of Germany, Italy and the United Kingdom: A Comparative Analysis" in D.R. Hodgman (ed.) *The Political Economy of Monetary Policy*, Boston: Federal Reserve Bank of Boston.

International Financial Statistics, various issues, (Washington: International Monetary Fund).

Inter-Parliamentary Union (1986), *Parliaments of the World*, Vol II, Second Edition, (New York: Facts on File).

Johnson, D.R. and P.L. Siklos (1992), "Empirical Evidence on the Independence of Central Banks", mimeo, Wilfrid Laurier University.

Khoury, Salwa S. (1990), "The Federal Reserve Reaction Functions: A Specification Search", in Thomas Mayer (Ed.), *The Political Economy of American Monetary Policy* (Cambridge: Cambridge University Press), pp. 27-50.

Laney, L., and T.D. Willett (1983), "Presidential Politics, Budget Deficits, and Monetary Policy in the United States", *Public Choice*, 40: 53-70.

Litterman, R.B. and L. Weiss (1985), "Money, Real Interest Rates, and Output: A Reinterpretation of Postwar U.S. Data", *Econometrica* (January): 129-56.

Lombra, R.E. and N. Karamouzis (1990), "A Positive Analysis of the Policy-Making Process at the Federal Reserve", in T. Mayer (Ed.), *The Political Economy of American Monetary Policy* (Cambridge: Cambridge University Press), pp. 181-96.

Lohmann, S. (1992), "Designing a Central Bank in a Federal System", unpublished, Stanford University.

Mackie, T.T., and R. Rose (1991), *The International Almanach of Electoral History* (London: MacMillan, 1974, 1991).

Masciandaro, Donato and Guido Tabellini (1988), "Monetary Regimes and Fiscal Deficits: A Comparative Analysis" in Hang-Sheng Chong (ed.) *Monetary Policy in Pacific Basin Countries*, Boston: Kluwer Academic Publishers.

MacRae, C. Duncan (1979), "A Political Model of the Business Cycle", *Journal of Political Economy*, 85: 293-363.

Mayer, Thomas (1976), "Structure and Operations of the Federal Reserve System", in *Compendium of Papers Prepared for the Financial Institutions and the Nation's Economy Study*, Committee on Banking, Currency and Housing, 94th Congress, Second Session (Washington, D.C.: GPO).

Mayer, Thomas (Ed.) (1990), *The Political Economy of American Monetary Policy* (Cambridge: Cambridge University Press).

McCallum, B.T. (1983), "A Reconsideration of Sims' Evidence Concerning Monetarism", *Economics*, 13 (2-3): 167-71.

Nordhaus, W. (1975), "The Political Business Cycle," *Review of Economic Studies* 42: 169-190.

Nordhaus, W. (1989), "Alternative Approaches to the Political Business Cycle", *Brookings Papers on Economic Activity*, 2:1-68.

Parkin, Michael (1986), "Domestic Monetary Institutions and Deficits" in James M. Buchanan, Charles K. Rowley and Robert D. Tollison (eds.) *Deficits*, London: Basil Blackwell.

Parkin, Michael and Robin Bade (1985), "Central bank laws and monetary policy: a preliminary investigation" in Michael G. Porter (ed.) *The Australian Monetary System in the 1970*'s, Clayton, Australia: Manosh University.

Political Handbook of the World (1980), (New York: McGraw-Hill).

Reuber, Grant L. (1964), "The Objectives of Canadian Monetary Policy 1949-61: Empirical Trade-Offs and the Reaction Functions of the Authorities," *Journal of Political Economy* 72: 109-132.

Rogoff, K. (1987), "Reputational Constraints on Monetary Policy", in K. Brunner and A.H. Meltzer (Eds.), *Carnegie-Rochester Conference Series on Public Policy*, 24 (Amsterdam: North Holland).

Siklos, P.L. (1992), "Politics and U.S. Business Cycles: A Century of Evidence", mimeo, Wilfrid Laurier University.

Sims, C.A. (1980), "Comparison of Interwar and Postwar Business Cycles: Monetarian Reconsidered", *American Economic Review*, 70 (May): 250-57.

Strom, K. (1990), *Minority Government and Majority Rule*, (Cambridge: Cambridge University Press).

Swinburne, M. and M. Castello-Branco (1991), "Central Bank Independence: Issues and Experience", International Monetary fund working paper 91/58 (June).

Toniolo, G. (Ed.) (1988), *Central Banks' Independence in Historical Perspective* (Berlin: Walter de Gruyter).

Willett, T.D. (Ed.) (1988), *Political Business Cycles*, Durham and London: Duke University Press).

Woolley, John T. (1988), "Partisan Manipulation of the Economy: Another Look at Monetary Policy with Moving Regression," *Journal of Politics* 50: 335-360.

Woolley, John T.(1983), "Political factors in monetary policy," in D.R. Hodgman (ed.) *The Political Economy of Monetary Policy*, Boston: Federal Reserve Bank of Boston.

CHAPTER 7

REPUTATION, CENTRAL BANK INDEPENDENCE AND THE ECB[1]

Michele Fratianni
Haizhou Huang

1.   INTRODUCTION

An important message of the literature on time inconsistency is that a central bank (CB henceforth) has a strong incentive to ignore whatever commitment to price stability she makes because this commitment is bound to conflict with her desire to reduce the unemployment rate at some future date. Such a proposition was originally identified by Kydland and Prescott (1977) and Calvo (1978), using a game theoretic model where the players make only one move (one-shot game). The problem of time inconsistency may not disappear even if the game allows the players to make a finite number of repeated moves (Benoit and Krishna, 1985; Rogoff, 1987)[2].

There are at least two solutions to this problem. The first is to let the CB build reputation (Barro and Gordon, 1983). This solution works if the private sector and the CB have access to the same information. If instead one posits that the CB knows more than the private sector, there is no assurance that reputation will actually work. This is the basic insight gained from the works by Porter (1983) and Green and Porter (1984) who find that collusion based on a trigger strategy need not be sustainable if information is imperfect.[3]

When the private sector and the CB have different sets of information, three possible outcomes can arise: moral hazard because of hidden information (e.g., the CB has private information in forecasting the demand for money), moral hazard

---

[1]   We thank Jürgen von Hagen, Pierre Siklos and seminar participants at the University of Mannheim, the University of Aarhus, and the Federal Reserve Bank of Cleveland for useful suggestions and criticism.

[2]   This is true so long as there is a unique one-shot game equilibrium.

[3]   Asymmetric information implies imperfect information, but the reverse need not be true.

because of hidden action (e.g., the CB may desire to misrepresent her information), and adverse selection because the CB may want to misrepresent herself. The asymmetric information literature of game theory suggests that moral hazard can be overcome if the CB can be suitably restructured. Hence, the second solution to the problem of time inconsistency requires a change in the CB's preferences and incentives, changes that can be brought about either through the appointment of a more conservative central banker (Rogoff, 1985) or through legislative means.

Our paper makes five points. First, a monetary game with asymmetric information generates two possible equilibrium outcomes. The first is that a trigger strategy is sustainable as an equilibrium strategy if both the CB and the private sector play the monetary game for an infinite period and certain other conditions are satisfied. In a trigger strategy the private sector punishes the CB if the inflation rate goes above a certain level. The punishment takes place in the form higher wages.[4] The second equilibrium outcome is that, under specified conditions, the monetary game with asymmetric information has only a noncooperative equilibrium --i.e., the CB and the private sector play the noncooperative equilibrium strategy of a one-shot game in each period.

Second, we prove that the noncooperative equilibrium is absolutely robust, whereas there is no assurance that a trigger strategy equilibrium is robust.

Third, we obtain a specific solution for the value of the trigger level under the assumption that the CB's forecast error of the demand for money follows a normal distribution.

Fourth, since one cannot rely on reputation alone to solve the problem of time inconsistency the solution to the latter requires altering the CB's preferences and incentives either through the appointment of a more conservative central banker (i.e., an independent central bank with an appropriate but not overwhelming emphasis on the price stability objective) or through legislative means. We argue that the first option is preferable to the second for a variety of reasons.

Fifth, central bank independence and the sole objective of price stability cannot be jointly set. According to the Maastricht Treaty -- which is yet to be ratified -- the future European Central Bank (ECB) will be constituted to be both independent of government and to pursue exclusively price stability. We argue, instead, that an

---

[4]   According to the literature, a noncooperative game has a cooperative equilibrium when a trigger strategy applies. Throughout our paper we will use interchangeably cooperative strategy and trigger strategy. A cooperative equilibrium is the outcome of a trigger strategy in our model. This equilibrium, however, does not preclude periodic inflationary episodes, even if the CB were always running the ideal monetary policy.

excessive weight on price stability by the ECB can be counterproductive to the Community's goal of actually achieving price stability.

The paper is organized as follows. We review Canzoneri's (1985) version of the Barro-Gordon monetary game model under symmetric and asymmetric information in Section II. There we take up the issue of whether the CB could credibly precommit to a low-inflation target, leaving to Section III the development of the solution under asymmetric information. Our formal answer lays out two fundamental propositions. We also offer a specific example, based on a normal distribution of the CB's forecast error of the demand for money, of why reputation may not work, as well as provide a closed-form solution of the trigger level. In Section IV we broaden the discussion concerning the limitation of reputational effects in solving the time inconsistency problem; there we submit that an independent central bank, with an appropriate but not overwhelming weight on the price stability goal, is preferable to a legislative approach. In Section V, we discuss the policy implication of central bank independence to the ECB. Conclusions are presented in Section VI.

2.   THE BARRO-GORDON-CANZONERI MODEL

We let the private sector and the CB play a monetary game repeatedly using two alternative information regimes: the symmetric (as in Barro and Gordon) and the asymmetric (as in Canzoneri).

2.1   The Model with Symmetric Information

This model is summarized in Table 1, where equation (1) is an output supply function, equation (2) determines the wage rate in terms of the price level expected when labor contracts are negotiated, and equation (3) is the simple money market that closes the model. The utility functions of the wage setters and the CB are given by (4) and (5), respectively. The CB deems the output rate generated by the private sector, $\bar{y}$, to be too small (because of distortions such as tax rates and unemployment compensation schemes) and aims at a higher output goal, $k\bar{y}$, $k > 1$. Given the incentive of the CB to deviate from the equilibrium rate of output, $\bar{y}$, there is a conflict between (4) and (5) concerning the optimal levels of real wages, employment, and output. As a result, the problem of time inconsistency emerges.

The second term on the right-hand side of (5) can be justified by the fact that inflation redistributes income among different groups, distorts incentives, and extracts a seigniorage. In addition, when inflation deviates from the socially optimal value, π^*, the CB faces pressure from the private sector to return to it.

The monetary game assumes that the wage setters move first. The Nash equilibrium strategy for a one-shot game can be solved by the following procedure.

Since there is no uncertainty in this model, the first difference of (3) becomes $g_t - \pi_t = 0$; using this condition in the output function, we obtain $y_t = \bar{y} + \theta(p_t - p_t^e) = \bar{y} + \theta(\pi_t - \pi_t^e)$. As a result, the public's utility function becomes $UP_t = -(p_t - w_t)^2 = -(y_t - \bar{y})^2/\theta^2 = -(\pi_t - \pi_t^e)^2$ and the CB's $UF_t = -\theta^2(g_t - \pi_t^e - y^*)^2 - s(g_t - \pi^*)^2$. Then maximizing UF_t, taking π_t^e as given, we find that the CB's decision rule is $g_t = (\theta^2\pi_t^e + s\pi^* + \theta^2 y^*)/(\theta^2 + s)$, which is

Table 1

The Canzoneri Version of the Barro-Gordon Model

$$y_t = \bar{y} + \theta(p_t - w_t), \tag{1}$$

$$w_t = p_t^e, \tag{2}$$

$$m_t - p_t = \bar{y}, \tag{3}$$

$$UP_t = -(p_t - w_t)^2, \tag{4}$$

$$UF_t = -(y_t - k\bar{y})^2 - s(\pi_t - \pi^*)^2. \tag{5}$$

The Nash solution of the model is:

$$g_t = \pi^* + y^*/f, \tag{6a}$$

$$y_t = \bar{y}, \tag{6b}$$

$$\pi_t = \pi^* + y^*/f, \tag{6c}$$

$$EUF_t^{nc} = -(1+\frac{\theta^2}{s})\theta^2 y^{*2}, \tag{6d}$$

$$EUP_t^{nc} = 0. \tag{6e}$$

Legend

y_t, p_t, m_t and w_t are the natural logarithms of output, the price level, the money supply and the contract wage respectively; θ and s are positive constants and $\bar{y}$ is the equilibrium rate of output corresponding to the natural rate of employment; $k > 1$; the superscript e denotes expectation conditional on information available at the beginning of the contract period; $\pi_t = p_t - p_{t-1}$ is the rate of inflation and π^* is its socially optimal value; $y^* = (k-1)\bar{y}/\theta$ and $f = s/\theta^2$ for short notations.

a function of the wage setters' actions. In turn, taking the CB's decision rule as given, the wage setters obtain their utility maximizing rule $\pi_t^e = g_t^e = \pi^* + y^*/f$. The Nash equilibrium solution is shown in Table 1. In a one-shot game the CB's precommitment is not credible. For example, the CB could precommit to the optimal inflation rate, π^*. If the wage setters believed in this announcement, then the CB would find it in her interest to set the money supply at $yg_t = \pi^* + \theta^2 y^*/(\theta^2+s)$. As a result, the actual inflation rate would be $\pi_t = g_t = \pi^* + \theta^2 y^*/(\theta^2+s) > \pi^*$, with the CB's utility increasing from $-\theta^2(\theta^2+s)y^{*2}/s$ to $-\theta^2 s y^{*2}/(\theta^2+s)$ because $(\theta^2+s)/s > 1 > s/(\theta^2+s)$; on the other hand, the wage setters' utility would decrease from 0 to $-\theta^4 y^{*2}/(\theta^2+s)^2$. This problem was first identified by Kydland and Prescott and Calvo. It is easy to show that there is only one unique equilibrium for the one-shot game. As a result, the problem of time inconsistency exists even if the game is played for a finite period.[5]

However, if the game is played infinitely, then, a cooperative strategy can be sustained as an equilibrium based on the Folk theorem (Barro and Gordon).

2.2   The Model with Asymmetric Information

In the real world a monetary game is more likely to be characterized by asymmetric than symmetric information. Following Canzoneri, we add a stochastic disturbance to the money market:

$$g_t - \pi_t = \delta_t, \tag{7}$$

where δ_t is white noise.

As in Canzoneri, $\delta_t = e_t + \varepsilon_t$, where e_t is the CB's forecast of the demand for money shock.[6] The noncooperative Bayesian equilibrium in a one-shot game can be solved as follows. Taking g_t^e as given, the CB maximizes her expected utility. Through the first-order condition, the CB derives her decision rule or optimal strategy as a function of g_t^e. Then, wage setters maximize their utility by taking the CB's decision rule as given. The solution is summarized in Table 2.

---

[5] If there is more than one equilibrium in a one-shot game, then a cooperative strategy may be sustained as the subgame perfect equilibrium strategy for a finite period game. See Benoit and Krishna (1985) and Rogoff (1987) for more details.

[6]   Actually, three situations can arise based on three different information structures: one in which the CB knows δ_t while the wage setters do not; a second in which the CB knows some of δ_t, e_t, because of inside information or superior forecasting but wage setters do not; and finally the case where δ_t is known to neither the CB nor the wage setters. Canzoneri focuses on the second case because it is the most realistic.

Note that the Bayesian equilibrium has an inflation bias equal to y*/f. As Canzoneri points out, there is an ideal solution -- the cooperative and efficient solution -- which would eliminate the inflation bias without changing the rate of output (see Table 2). In this instance the wage setters' equilibrium utility level is the same as in the noncooperative case, but the CB's utility is instead higher. Therefore, the cooperative solution is Pareto dominant and, hence, efficient.

But this cooperative equilibrium is not sustainable if the game is played for only one period because the CB has an incentive to cheat. Indeed, if wage earners set $g_t^e = \pi^*$, the optimal solution is given by (9a) to (9f) in Table 2. Clearly, the CB gains over the cooperative solution and, consequently, the problem of time inconsistency arises.

2.3   Could the CB Credibly Precommit?

The main contribution of Barro and Gordon is to have offered a solution to the time inconsistency problem under symmetric information. If the monetary game can be played infinitely, the trigger strategy is sustainable because the CB can make a credible precommitment or build a reputation. The latter is the key to the solution of the problem of time inconsistency.

With asymmetric information, Canzoneri claimed that the CB can still credibly precommit and solve the problem of time inconsistency through reputation. There is a difference in the equilibrium outcome between the symmetric and asymmetric information cases.

Under asymmetric information the CB, even though she chooses her precommitted strategy before being punished by the private sector, knows that punishment will occur in later periods. Again, punishment takes the form of wage setters renegotiating higher wage rates in the next period, the so-called reversionary period. That is, a commitment to an ideal policy does not preclude bouts of higher inflation rates.

Canzoneri's argument goes as follows. Since the private sector can observe the money demand disturbance δ_t at the end of each period but cannot decompose it into the CB's forecast, e_t, and the residual, ε_t, it cannot revert to inflationary wage setting when g_t is greater than $g_t^{eF,c} = \pi^* + e_t$. However, the private sector can construct a trigger strategy such that if g_t is greater than $\pi^* + \delta_t + \bar{\varepsilon} = g_t^{eF,c} + \varepsilon_t + \bar{\varepsilon}$, where $\bar{\varepsilon}$ is a target value chosen by the private sector.

Table 2

Noncooperative, Cooperative and Cheating Solutions

NONCOOPERATION

$$g_t^{eF,nc} = \pi^* + e_t + y^*/f, \tag{7a}$$

$$g_t^{e,nc} = \pi^* + y^*/f, \tag{7b}$$

$$y_t = \bar{y} - \theta\varepsilon_t, \tag{7c}$$

$$\pi_t = \pi^* + y^*/f - \varepsilon_t, \tag{7d}$$

$$EUF_t^{nc} = -(s+\theta^2)\sigma_\varepsilon^2 - (1+\frac{\theta^2}{s})\theta^2 y^{*2}, \tag{7e}$$

$$EUP_t^{nc} = -\sigma_\varepsilon^2. \tag{7f}$$

COOPERATION

$$g_t^{eF,c} = \pi^* + e_t, \tag{8a}$$

$$g_t^{e,c} = \pi^*, \tag{8b}$$

$$y_t = \bar{y} - \theta\varepsilon_t, \tag{8c}$$

$$\pi_t = \pi^* - \varepsilon_t, \tag{8d}$$

$$EUF_t^c = -(s+\theta^2)\sigma_\varepsilon^2 - \theta^2 y^{*2} > EUF_t^{nc}, \tag{8e}$$

$$EUP_t^c = -\sigma_\varepsilon^2 = EUP_t^{nc}. \tag{8f}$$

CHEATING

$$g_t^{eF,ch} = \pi^* + e_t + y^*/(1+f), \tag{9a}$$

$$g_t^{e,ch} = \pi^*, \tag{9b}$$

$$y_t^{ch} = \bar{y} + \theta y^*/(1+f) - \theta\varepsilon_t, \tag{9c}$$

$$\pi_t^{ch} = \pi^* + y^*/(1+f) - \varepsilon_t, \tag{9d}$$

$$EUF_t^{ch} = EUF_t^c + y^{*2}/(1+f), \tag{9e}$$

$$EUP_t^{ch} = EUP_t^c - y^{*2}/(1+f). \tag{9f}$$

Legend

The superscript eF denotes the CB's expectation while e denotes the wage setters' expectation conditional on information available at the beginning of the contract period; the superscripts nc, c and ch stand for noncooperative, cooperative and cheating solutions, respectively. The rest of the notation is the same as in Table 1.

As a result, the probability of a reversion in period t+1 is[7]

$$P(g_t - g_t^{eF,c} - \bar{\varepsilon}) = Pr(\varepsilon_t < g_t - g_t^{eF,c} - \bar{\varepsilon}), \qquad (10)$$

where $P(\cdot)$ is the cumulative distribution function of the CB's forecast error ε_t and $Pr(\cdot)$ denotes probability. Canzoneri argued that the wage setter can find an $\bar{\varepsilon}$ such that if the CB considers raising g_t marginally above $g_t^{eF,c}$, then the expected gain in period t for the CB will be offset by the expected loss in period t+1. By looking at the CB's expected utility over the next two periods starting from a current non-reversionary period,

$$U(g_t, \bar{\varepsilon}) = EUF_t^c + PEUF_{t+1}^{nc} + (1-P)EUF_{t+1}^c, \qquad (11)$$

Canzoneri found that it would be incentive compatible for the CB not to renege if $p(-\bar{\varepsilon}) \geq 2/(y^*/f)$. If y^*/f is greater than 2, then an optimal $\bar{\varepsilon}$ can be chosen such that the CB has no incentive to renege. In other words, reputation yields a credible precommitment, even though in equilibrium there may be some periodic inflationary episodes.

Our position is that the reputation effect is not sufficiently robust; that is, the CB cannot credibly precommit to policy under a broad range of circumstances. In the next section we prove our point.

3.   REPUTATION MAY NOT WORK

3.1   Changes in the Model

Our basic point of departure is that the CB, by playing a game for an infinite period, should consider her expected present discounted utility. The structure of the game goes as follows. The central bank starts with a non-reversionary period (period t) and faces the same trigger strategy as in Canzoneri (see equation (10) above). If $g_t < \pi_t^* + \delta_t + \bar{\varepsilon}$, the CB's expected utility will increase by the discount factor, β, times $(1-P)$ times the value of the utility, and the game is repeated. If, instead, $g_t > \pi_t^* + \delta_t + \bar{\varepsilon}$ a reversionary period will take place, the CB's utility will increase by P times β times EUF_{t+1}^{nc}. Since a reversion is assumed to last only one period, both players will choose a cooperative strategy in the next period and the expected utility will increase by P times β^2 times the value of the utility. The structure of the game is summarized in Figure 1 (see Porter (p. 317) for a similar formulation applied to cartel behavior). In sum, we have

---

[7]   See equation (22) in Canzoneri.

$$V(g_t, \bar{\varepsilon}) = EUF_t^c + (1 - P)\beta V(g_t, \bar{\varepsilon}) + P[\beta EUF_{t+1}^{nc} + \beta^2 V(g_t, \bar{\varepsilon})]$$

$$= \frac{EUF_{t+1}^{nc}}{1 - \beta} + \frac{EUF_t^c - EUF_{t+1}^{nc}}{1 - \beta + P\beta(1 - \beta)}, \tag{12}$$

where $V(g_t, \bar{\varepsilon})$ is the CB's expected present discounted utility. We assume that the CB at time t commits not to change money growth rates in the future. The crucial difference with respect to Canzoneri's formulation is that in our case the CB does discount her future utility, with $0 < \beta < 1$. For $\beta = 1$ expression (12) is not defined; the economic reason is that today's CB actions are taken by either a selfless governor who cares about the future or by a governor who cares about being reappointed tomorrow (Fratianni, von Hagen and Waller, 1992a).

The optimal trigger money supply, g_t, will maximize the CB's expected present discounted utility $V(\cdot)$, given by equation (12), and subject to the incentive constraint that neither the CB nor the wage setters gain by deviating during cooperative periods. Given that wage setters cannot control g_t and have an incentive to cooperate with the CB so long as $g_{t-1} \leq \pi^* + \delta_{t-1} + \bar{\varepsilon}$, the CB can choose the optimal trigger money supply to maximize her $V(\cdot)$, subject to the incentive constraint that the CB cannot gain by deviating in cooperative periods.

3.2   Main Findings

Using the first and second-order conditions of the above-mentioned maximization problem -- see Appendix -- we derive two fundamental propositions. The first is that the equilibrium strategy in a one-shot game, $g_t^{eF,nc} = \pi^* + e_t + y^*/f$ and $g_t^{e,nc} = \pi^* + y^*/f$, is an equilibrium strategy in cooperative periods for any values of the trigger level and of the model's parameters. In contrast (and this is the second proposition), the ideal policy, $g_t^{eF,c} = \pi^* + e_t$ and $g_t^{e,c} = \pi^*$, has a limited range of applications, since there are values of the model's parameters for which it cannot hold. The proof of these two propositions is relegated to the Appendix; here we emphasize less technical or more intuitive aspects of these propositions.

The degree of CB conservativeness in the ideal policy is given by

$$s = \beta\theta^2 y^* p(-\bar{\varepsilon})/2[1 + P(-\bar{\varepsilon})\beta]. \tag{13}$$

which has an upper bound because β, θ and y* have upper bounds. Furthermore, the path of s cannot violate the second-order constraint

$$(\theta^2 + s)p(-\bar{\varepsilon}) - \theta^2 y^* \cdot \frac{\partial^2 P(-\bar{\varepsilon})}{\partial g_t^2} > 0. \tag{14}$$

This constraint can be made more precise by assuming that the CB's forecast error of the demand for money follows a random distribution. Under these conditions (14) becomes:

$$\theta^2 + s - \theta^2 y \cdot \frac{\bar{\varepsilon}}{\sigma_\varepsilon^2} > 0. \tag{15}$$

Equation (15) states that a trigger strategy is more likely to occur the higher s, the more uncertain is the forecast error of the demand for money σ_ε^2, the smaller $\bar{\varepsilon}$ and the smaller y*. No precise statement can be made about the relationship between the trigger strategy and the coefficient of the inflation surprise, θ, without additional restrictions. Furthermore, the discount rate β is irrelevant to the second-order condition (15), given the normal distribution, but not to the first-order condition (13). These conditions have very intuitive economic meaning.

Figure 1
The Infinite Period Game Tree

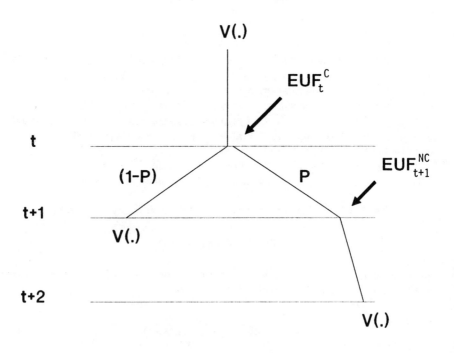

A higher value of s means that the CB cares more about the inflation and that her preference is getting closer to that of the wage setters. Intuitively, this translates to a weaker conflict between the CB and the private sector, making the cooperative strategy (i.e., the ideal policy) more sustainable in the noncooperative game. The upper bound of s works like the conservative CB in Rogoff (1985) and Fratianni, von Hagen and Waller (1992b). However, there are differences between these formulations. In ours output stabilization does not enter the private sector's utility function; this in turn sets an upper bound to the degree of CB's conservativeness. The discount factor in our paper substitutes for output stabilization in the private sector's utility. A lower β can be interpreted as the CB caring less about the future and more about current events, including current output stabilization; a lower β implies a less conservative CB. Hence, our results are consistent with those of Fratianni, von Hagen and Waller (1992b). A larger variance of the CB's forecast error of the demand for money implies that the CB has less inside information about money demand. The result is that the CB has less of an incentive to cheat and, consequently, a cooperative strategy is more sustainable in the noncooperative game.

A lower value of $\bar{\varepsilon}$ implies a lower trigger level of g_t, which in turn implies an increase in the probability of an inflation reversion in period t+1. Consequently, the CB has a smaller incentive to increase the money supply and the ideal policy is more sustainable as a noncooperative equilibrium strategy.

A lower value of y* means that the CB's output target becomes closer to the equilibrium output $\bar{y}$. Again, there is less conflict between the goals of the CB and those of the private sector, leading to a cooperative strategy being more sustainable in the noncooperative equilibrium.

So far we have treated the trigger level as given. We can endogenize $\bar{\varepsilon}$, on the assumption that it is normally distributed. Using (13) and the normality assumption yields that

$$\bar{\varepsilon} = -\frac{2s\sigma_\varepsilon^2}{\theta^2 y^*}. \tag{16}$$

Substituting (16) in (15), the second-order condition simplifies

$$\theta^2 + 3s > 0. \tag{17}$$

Not only this condition is always satisfied, but now we can state unequivocally that the trigger strategy is more likely to be sustained the higher the value of the inflation surprise coefficient. In turn, since θ is positively related to the frequency with which the CB has used money surprises in the past (Lucas, 1973; Fratianni and Huang, 1992), the minimum degree of conservativeness is higher for a CB that has "abused" money surprises than a CB which has not.

In sum, when the error of the CB's forecast of the demand for money is normally distributed, the ideal policy, $g_t^{eF,c} = \pi^* + e_t$ and $g_t^{e,c} = \pi^*$, is less likely to be an equilibrium strategy in cooperative periods if s and σ_ε^2 decrease, and if $\bar{\varepsilon}$, y* and θ increase.

The above result states that a cooperative strategy, the ideal policy, may not be sustainable as a noncooperative equilibrium strategy in cooperative periods. Even if it initially were sustainable, changes in the values of s, σ_ε^2, θ and y* can render it unsustainable. It is also quite possible that condition (13) and (14) can never be satisfied for some probability distribution function $P(\cdot)$.

In addition, our model assumes that the probability distribution function $P(\cdot)$ is common knowledge to both the CB and the private sector. Should this assumption not hold, the ideal policy will also not hold. For example, if the private sector did not know the distribution function of the CB's forecast errors of the demand for money, it would have strong reasons to doubt that conditions (13) and (14) were satisfied. As a result, it would want to choose a noncooperative strategy because of its dominance (i.e., it holds for all kinds of probability distribution functions of the CB's forecast errors and for all value of $\bar{\varepsilon}$). A similar argument holds if s, θ, β, k or $\bar{y}$ are not common knowledge.

4.   REPUTATION VS INDEPENDENCE

We have just demonstrated that, in the presence of asymmetric information, a noncooperative strategy is sustainable as an equilibrium strategy for all kinds of distribution functions of the CB's forecast errors, all values of the trigger and all values of parameters s, θ, β, k and $\bar{y}$ within their defined ranges. In contrast, under the same circumstances, a cooperative strategy, which is the ideal policy, may not be sustainable as an equilibrium strategy. This implies that the problem of time inconsistency may not be easily resolved with reputation, as it is true in a world of symmetric information (Barro and Gordon). Canzoneri's solution turns out to be an incomplete answer to the problem: his trigger strategy may or may not work, depending on the distribution functions of the CB's forecast errors, the trigger level and values of other parameters.

Our results can also be interpreted in terms of the robustness of the equilibrium outcomes. In our model, there are two equilibria: the noncooperative equilibrium, if both parties play the noncooperative equilibrium strategy of a one-shot game, and the ideal equilibrium, if the CB plays her ideal policy and the public plays a trigger strategy which is designed to make the ideal policy incentive compatible. The first equilibrium exists, regardless of the distribution functions of the CB's forecast errors, the trigger level and the values of the other parameters. Therefore, the first equilibrium is absolutely robust. The second equilibrium, on the other hand, may or may not exist, depending on the distribution functions of the CB's forecast errors, the trigger level and the values of the other parameters. It follows that there is no guarantee that the second equilibrium is robust. The robustness of one equilibrium, coupled with the non-assurance of the robustness of the second equilibrium, means that one cannot exclude that both players, even though they start playing the game cooperatively, will switch to a noncooperative equilibrium strategy, due to some disturbance in the model.

The fact that the time inconsistency problem cannot be solved by applying a trigger strategy in an environment of asymmetric information does not mean that the problem cannot be solved. The inflation bias and the time inconsistency problem exist because policymakers and institutions cannot credibly and effectively precommit to an inflation target; in other words, the ultimate cause is an institutional deficiency. There are two possible solutions to the problem. The first is to create, through a constitutional amendment, an independent CB having the same status as the other three branches of government (legislative, executive and judiciary). In our paper independence means that the CB can autonomously set the relative weight on the price stability objective, s. The second entails for Congress or Parliament to legislate incentive-compatible rules. These rules, would not only change the incentives of the private sector and of the CB, but would also constrain the players' strategies. As an example, the legislative branch could prescribe that the CB adhere to a Friedman's k-percent rule (Canzoneri, p. 1066).

There are several reasons for preferring the independent CB to the legislative approach. To begin with, in an environment of asymmetric information, the Congress is bound to be less informed than the CB and, as a consequence, to have less reputation than the CB. Second, a legislative approach implies that the Congress would have to formulate an explicit policy objective for the CB to carry out. In other words, it would have to precommit indirectly to a low-inflation strategy. But there is an inevitable contrast between the interests of elected politicians and those of the CB and this conflict gives rise to the inflation bias. Politicians are primarily concerned with using monetary policy to ensure that output and employment levels are favorable for their reelection (i.e., political business cycle considerations), while the CB is more concerned with price stability (Fratianni and von Hagen 1992). The more subservient is the CB to either the legislative or the executive branches of government, the less credible is her commitment to price stability and, consequently, the higher is her inflation bias. Furthermore, in representative democracies elected officials shun precision, because that means accountability and running the risk of being blamed by the public (Cukierman and Meltzer, 1986).[8] Finally, the legislative approach, in contrast with an independent CB, implies high monitoring costs. In sum, an

---

[8] Cukierman and Meltzer study reputational effects under imperfect information, but their main concern is the role played by ambiguity in the Fed's selection of an optimal policy.

independent central bank holds more promise in delivering consistently low-inflation outcomes than either reputation or legislative means.

The empirical literature in the field tends to corroborate the hypothesis that inflation performance is correlated with the independence status of the CB, especially for those CBs which are classified as the most independent. Bade and Parkin (1987), building on previous work, summarize in an index form the independence characteristics of the CBs of twelve industrial countries. Their methodology, like much of this literature, relies on a legal interpretation of CB statutes. Germany and Switzerland turn out to have the most independent CBs, while Australia the least independent. The index of CB independence is used as an input in an autoregressive model of the inflation rate to check whether inflation is country specific. The significant conclusion is that central bank laws affect inflation only in the highest range of the independence index, namely Germany and Switzerland.[9]

Alesina and Summers (1990) go beyond inflation and key on other macroeconomic variables such as output growth, the rate of unemployment and the real rate of interest and their respective variances. Their methodology is "visual" in the sense that they plot a measure of CB independence developed by Grilli, Masciandaro and Grilli (1991) against each of the variables under consideration. The authors conclude that "the monetary discipline associated with central bank independence reduces the level and variability of inflation but does not have either large benefits or costs in terms of real macroeconomic performance." (p. 6).

Burdekin and Laney (1988) estimate an interacting three-equation system to study the effect of CB independence on money growth, budget deficit and the rate of inflation. Independence is measured with a dummy variable and exists for Germany, Switzerland, the U.S. and Canada and does not exist for all other countries. The relevant empirical finding is that both the rate of inflation and the budget deficit are lower in the presence of CB autonomy.

Cukierman (1992, Ch. 19) reviews extensively the literature on the measurement of CB independence and proposes three alternatives of his own: one based on the legal criterion, a second based on the actual turnover of CB governors and a third based on the results of a questionnaire answered by specialists of monetary policy. In Chapter 20 he uses his three measures to assess the hypothesis

---

[9]   Banaian, Laney and Willett (1983), using cross-sectional data for the post-1960 period, had found evidence that also the United States, in addition to Germany and Switzerland, was enjoying the benefits of an autonomous CB in terms of a lower rate of inflation. Alesina (1989) arrives at similar conclusions by comparing a modified Bade-Parkin index of CB independence with the average inflation rate in the period 1973 to 1986.

that countries with more independent CBs have lower rates of inflation. His conclusions are that:

> "CB independence affects the rate of inflation in the expected direction, but that there are other factors as well .... discrepancies between actual and legal independence are larger in developing than in developed countries." (p.90).

The historical study by Capie and Wood (1991) is the most skeptical about the difference in inflation performance between countries with an independent CB and countries with a dependent CB. The authors conclude that Latin American countries account for a great deal of the observed positive association between CB dependency and inflation rates. When these countries are excluded -- as the authors believe they should because of the extremity of their inflation rates -- the expected association between CB independence and inflation performance is tenuous.

Table 3 and Figures 2 and 3 provide a useful summary of much of the empirical literature we have cited. In the second column of the table we have constructed an independence index based on nine different measures of CB independence: one each from Epstein and Schor (1986), Bade and Parkin (1987), Alesina (1989), Burdekin, Wihlborg and Willett (1991), and Capie and Wood (1991), and two each from Grilli, Masciandaro and Tabellini (1991) and Cukierman (1992).[10] Country coverage differs from study to study. To be included in our index a central bank had to appear in at least four of the nine measures of CB independence.[11] The German Bundesbank was the unanimous choice for the most independent CB; it became our benchmark with a value of unity. We assigned values to the other CBs by calculating the distance of each CB from the German Bundesbank, where the $distance = \sqrt{(average - 1)^2 + variance}$ and average and variance are obtained from the nine separate measures of independence.

---

[10] We selected the political and economic indicators by Grilli, Masciandaro and Tabellini (1991) and the legal and questionnaire indicators by Cukierman (1992).

[11] This is the reason why, for example, Austria and New Zealand were omitted from the list in Table 3. The Austrian National Bank represents an almost unique case of a CB whose objectives are specifically directed at maintaining price and exchange rate stability (Burdekin and Willett, 1991). Yet, its degree of independence is ranked below that of the Bundesbank by Burdekin, Wihlborg and Willett (1991), Capie and Wood (1991), and Cukierman (1992). New Zealand passed a law in 1989 according to which the Reserve Bank of New Zealand is instructed to meet the single objective of price inflation. The target inflation value is agreed by the Governor of the Bank and the Minister of Finance, and it is a matter of public record (Burdekin and Willett, 1991).

Not surprisingly, Switzerland is very close to Germany, wherea Italy and Australia are at the farthest from the Bundesbank.[12]

Table 3

CB Independence, Macroeconomic Performance
and Statutory Objectives
1960-1990

Country's CB	Independence Index	Inflation rate average	Inflation rate variance	Output growth average	Output growth variance	Statutory objectives
Germany	1.00	3.47	3.34	3.08	4.73	multiple
Switzerland	0.98	3.95	4.89	2.72	6.90	multiple
U.S.	0.62	5.13	10.33	3.10	5.11	multiple
Denmark	0.39	7.23	10.14	2.91	5.85	multiple
Ireland	0.33	8.66	34.75	3.93	4.64	multiple
Netherlands	0.19	4.73	8.05	3.26	5.22	price
U.K.	0.19	8.06	29.08	2.46	8.18	none
France	0.15	6.77	12.97	3.72	3.29	none
Canada	0.15	5.59	10.37	4.22	4.88	multiple
Sweden	0.12	7.07	9.24	2.83	3.71	none
Japan	0.11	5.68	37.00	6.28	10.96	multiple
Spain	0.06	10.15	29.44	4.65	8.82	none
Belgium	0.04	4.97	9.61	3.36	4.77	none
Italy	0.04	9.12	37.69	3.88	6.29	none
Australia	0.03	7.07	16.35	3.88	5.00	multiple

Notes and Sources

The independence index was calculated applying the distance formula to the average and the standard deviation of nine separate measures of CB independence obtained from the following studies: Epstein and Schor (1986), Bade and Parkin (1987), Alesina (1989), Grilli, Masciandaro and Tabellini (1991), Burdekin, Wihlborg and Willett (1991), Cukierman (1992), Capie and Wood (1991). Statutory objectives were assigned from a reading of central bank laws (Aufricht, 1961; Vol II, 1967). The inflation rate is the annual percentage change in the consumer price index; the output growth is the annual growth rate of either real GDP or GNP; the averages were computed at continuously compounded rates. The real GNP series of Australia and the Netherlands come from the Main Economic Indicators of the OECD; the remainder of the series from the International Financial Statistics of the IMF.

---

[12]   Country symbols are as follows: D=Germany, CH=Switzerland, U.S.=United States, DK=Denmark, IR=Ireland, NL=Netherlands, U.K.=United Kingdom, F=France, CA=Canada, SW=Sweden, J=Japan, SP=Spain, B=Belgium, I=Italy and AL=Australia.

Figure 2

CB Independence and Inflation Rate

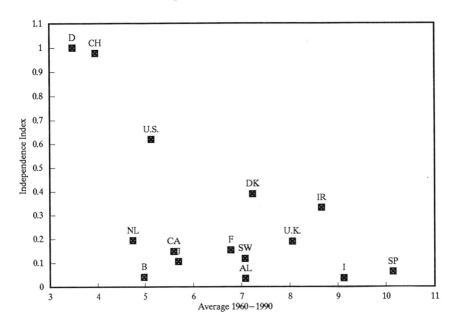

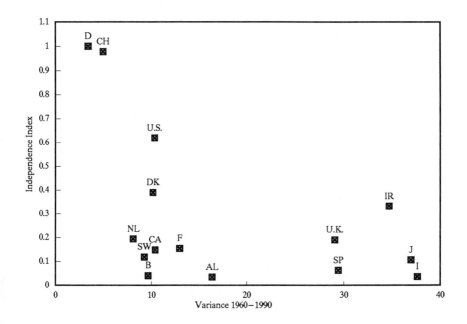

Figure 3

CB Independence and Output Growth

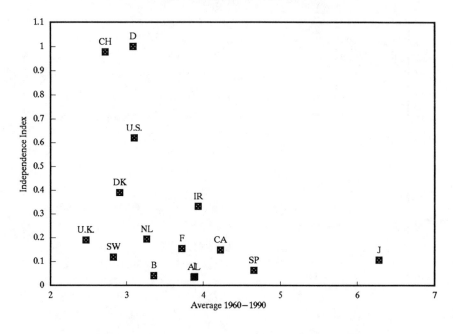

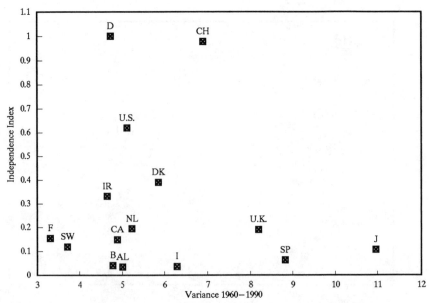

Columns three to six show the mean and the variance of inflation and of national output over the 1960-1990 period, which includes years of fixed, flexible and managed exchange rates. We made no attempt to differentiate among these regimes.[13] To facilitate the reading, each of the four series is plotted against our index of CB independence in Figures 2 and 3. CB independence and inflation, both in the mean and the variance, are negatively and significantly related; on the other hand, CB independence and output growth are not.[14]

A careful look at Figure 2A reveals that our index of CB independence "penalizes" countries like Belgium, the Netherlands, Canada and Japan in the sense that these countries' inflation performance has been much better than is implied by the index.

Such outcomes reflect the limitation of a measurement that is grounded in a legal interpretation of the CB statutes. Belgium and the Netherlands, while endowed with fairly dependent CBs, have in fact delegated monetary policy to the German Bundesbank, the most independent CB in the world, since the late 1970s through the working of the European Monetary System. The Bank of Japan is a dependent institution in the sense that the Ministry of Finance has the final say on monetary policy. Yet, the Ministry of Finance is subject to less political pressure from the rest of the government than the Fed is from the White House (Cargill, 1989).

Despite the difficulty of properly measuring CB independence and the incompleteness of the empirical results, we can state that inflation performance is related to the degree of CB independence, especially at the extreme ends of the index. There is also some evidence that CB independence exerts discipline on fiscal authorities to generate smaller budget deficits (for a review of the literature read Burdekin, Wihlborg and Willett, 1991).[15]

---

[13]   Johnson and Siklos (1992), instead, estimate central bank reaction functions for separate sub-periods of fixed and flexible exchange rates.

[14]   The t values of the regression of CB independence on a constant and one of the four series are: 2.71 for average inflation, 2.05 for the variance of inflation, 1.6 for average output growth and 0.4 for the variance of output growth.

[15] Puzzling aspects of this literature are worth noting. Fischer (1988, p. 130), in his comments to Tabellini (1988) who proposes a model of monetary dominance applied to Italy, notes that "the inflation regressions are not consistent with the implications of the model. Remarkably, deficits seem to be more inflationary in the 1980s than before." In their eight-country study, Burdekin and Wohar (1990) find that there is no deficit accommodation by the monetary authorities of Germany, Switzerland and the U.S. --which is consistent with monetary dominance-- but the very dependent Bank of Italy does not accommodate budget deficits either.

5.   IMPLICATIONS FOR THE EUROPEAN CENTRAL BANK

The European Council, at the Maastricht Summit of December 1991, agreed to revise the EC Treaty so as to incorporate in it monetary union, price stability, and sound public finance (Fratianni, von Hagen and Waller, 1992b).[16] It has also set the institutional machinery leading to monetary union in the Community. At the beginning of Stage Two (1994), the European Monetary Institute will be created to administer the EMS and prepare instruments and procedures that the ECB will use in the third and final stage. The European Monetary Institute will cease to exist as the ECB starts operations.

For the purpose of this paper, two aspects of the future ECB are particularly relevant: her degree of independence and the weight that the institution will place on price stability. Article 7 of the ECB statutes addresses the issue of independence:

> neither the ECB, nor a national central bank, nor any member of their decision-making bodies shall seek or take instructions from Community institutions or bodies, from any government of a Member State or from any other body. The Community institutions and bodies and the Governments of the Member States undertake to respect this principle and not to seek to influence the members of the decision-making bodies of the ECB and of the national central banks in the performance of their tasks.

Article 2 refers to the objectives of the ECB:

> The primary objective of the System shall be to maintain price stability. Without prejudice to the objective of price stability, the System shall support the general economic policy of the Community. The system shall act consistently with free competitive markets.

In essence, the ECB will be a very independent institution dedicated primarily, if not exclusively, to achieving price stability. In the language of our model, the ECB will operate with a mandate to place a large value on the weight of the price stability objective, that is $s - s^{high}$. We shall argue that this constraint on the weights of the CB's preferences can be counterproductive in achieving low inflation outcomes.

Our argument proceeds as follows. It is clear that the ECB needs to work cooperatively with the public if such cooperation to be sustained in the noncooperative monetary game. In a world of symmetric information, there is no

---

[16]   The fate of the Maastricht Treaty remains uncertain, since Denmark has rejected it and other member countries have yet to ratify it. We assume that the parts of the Treaty dealing with monetary union and the ECB will remain intact.

restriction on the value of s because many trigger strategy equilibria are sustainable according to the Folk theorem (see also Barro and Gordon).

Under asymmetric information, however, s must satisfy both equations (13) and (14). Consequently, the degree of conservativeness s has an upper bound $\bar{s}$ which is defined by the upper bounds of β, θ, y^*, the distribution function of the ECB's forecast error and the public's trigger level. It is clear that if the ECB's primary goal is set so that $s_{high} > \bar{s}$, the cooperative strategy collapses and the only equilibrium in the monetary game is the noncooperative strategy equilibrium. In other words, an overly restrictive weight on price stabilization can switch the monetary game from a cooperative to a noncooperative equilibrium. In particular, so long as information is asymmetrically distributed between the ECB and the private sector, perfect price stabilization is not feasible. In a cooperative equilibrium, the inflation rate π_t is defined by equation (8d), $\pi_t = \pi^* - \varepsilon_t$. While in noncooperative equilibrium, the inflation rate π_t defined by equation (7d), $\pi_t = \pi^* + y^*/f - \varepsilon_t$, is obviously higher than that in the cooperative equilibrium because of the inflation bias.

The economic intuition underlying the switch from a cooperative to a noncooperative equilibrium lies in the fact that the public at large (in contrast to the wage setters) values not only price stabilization, but also output stabilization. Too high a value of s is likely to contradict the search for an optimum tradeoff between the two objectives, a result which is consistent with those of Rogoff (1985) and Fratianni, von Hagen and Waller (1992b).

It is not surprising that virtually all CB statutes are relatively vague about the weighting scheme of the CB's objectives. Eight of the 15 CBs surveyed in Table 3 have multiple objectives, six have no stated objective and only one, the Netherlands, refers to price stability as the primary goal of monetary policy. The Federal Reserve Act of 1913, for example, charges the Fed with the task "to furnish an elastic currency"; the Reform Act of 1977 gives the Fed a multiplicity of objectives. The National Bank of Switzerland, the second most independent and second best inflation performer in the group, is supposed "...to regulate the country's monetary circulation, facilitate payments transactions, and implement a credit and monetary policy serving the general interests of the country." (Aufricht, 1967, Vol II, p. 705). Even the Bundesbank, the standard of independence and inflation performance, is not encumbered by rigid objective constraints: "...shall regulate the note and coin circulation and the supply of credit to the economy with the aim of safeguarding the currency and shall ensure appropriate payments through banks within the country as well as to and from foreign countries." (Aufricht, 1967, Vol II, p. 252). Similarly for the Reserve Bank of New Zealand, the much heralded objective of price stability is not iron clad. In fact, the inflation target can be renegotiated if the economy is subject to large changes in housing prices, interest rates, indirect taxes or terms of trade (Burdekin and Willett, 1991). These escape clauses are consistent with our argument that the optimal degree of conservativeness is not infinite.

It remains an unexplored area of research why central bank statutes appear to be much more detailed on instruments and procedures of monetary policy than on objectives. The ECB has been labelled as a carbon copy of the Bundesbank, when in fact it is not. As it is pointed in Fratianni, von Hagen and Waller (1992b, p. 41) "The BBK model is restrictive in the choice of instruments, vague in the formulation of the objective, and gives a well-defined conditionality clause. The ECB, in contrast, has a concrete objective, a vague conditionality, and an unrestricted choice of instruments." Our model suggests that the institutional design of the Bundesbank is better suited to a reputation-building mechanism than that of the ECB.

6.   CONCLUSIONS

Noncooperative equilibrium, based on both players playing their equilibrium strategies in a one-shot game, is robust under any condition. That is, the noncooperative strategy is an equilibrium strategy regardless of the distribution function of the CB's forecast error of the demand for money function, the trigger level and the values of the other parameters of the model. In contrast, the ideal policy, which is the cooperative strategy or time inconsistent policy in a one-shot game, may or may not be an equilibrium strategy, depending on the distribution function of the CB's forecast errors, the trigger level and the values of the other parameters of the model.

We have shown that, after adding asymmetric information to Barro and Gordon's model, there is no assurance that reputation may work for the CB. Therefore, the solution to the problem of time inconsistency cannot rely on letting the CB and the public play the monetary game for an infinite period of time.

Canzoneri's solution based on reputation is incomplete, because there is a wide range of circumstances for which the ideal policy is not sustainable as an equilibrium strategy.

The result of this paper indicates that there is no guarantee that the problem of time inconsistency, in a world of asymmetric information, can be solved by a highly reputable CB. We consider the alternatives of an independent CB, with an appropriate but not overwhelming emphasis on the goal of price stability, and of the legislative branch of government directly supervising monetary policy, and conclude in favor of the former.

The results of our paper bear critically on the design of the ECB. The Maastricht Treaty accords the ECB maximum independence from government and a very high weight on the price stabilization objective. This design, while well motivated, is likely to overburden the ECB in the specific sense that this institution will not be free to optimize between the weight placed on output growth stabilization and that on inflation stabilization. Consequently, the ECB will run the risk of losing reputation and induce wage setters to play the game noncooperatively in every period. It is not surprising that virtually every central bank in the industrial world, including those with the best inflation performance, have statutes that state either multiple or no objectives.

REFERENCES

Alesina, Alberto, "Politics and Business Cycles in Industrial Democracies," *Economic Policy*, 8, 1989, pp. 55-98.

Alesina, Alberto and Summers, Lawrence, "Central Bank Independence and Macroeconomics Performance: Some Comparative Evidence," mimeo, 1990.

Aufricht, Hans, *Central Bank Legislation: A Collection of Central Bank, Monetary and Banking Laws*, International Monetary Fund, Washington, D.C., 1961; Volume II, 1967.

Bade, Robin and Parkin, Michael, "Central Bank Laws and Monetary Policy," mimeo, 1987.

Banaian, King, Laney, Leroy O. and Willett, Thomas D., "Central Bank Independence: An International Comparison," *Federal Reserve Bank of Dallas Economic Review*, 1983, 1-13

Barro, Robert and Gordon, David, "Rules, Discretion and Reputation in a Model of Monetary game," *Journal of Monetary Economics*, 1983, 12, 101-122.

Benoit, Jean-P and Krishna, Kala, "Finitely Repeated Games," *Econometrica*, 1985, 53, 890-904.

Burdekin, Richard C.K. and Laney, Leroy O., "Fiscal Policymaking and the Central Bank Institutional Constraint," *Kyklos* 41, 1988: 647-662.

Burdekin, Richard C.K., Wihlborg, Clas and Willett, Thomas D., "A Monetary Constitution Case for An Independent European Central Bank," typescript, July 1991.

Burdekin, Richard C.K., and Willett, Thomas D., "Central Bank Reform: The Federal Reserve in International Perspective," *Public Budgeting and Financial Management*, 1991, forthcoming.

Burdekin, Richard C.K. and Wohar, Mark E., "Monetary Institutions, Budget Deficits and Inflation: Empirical Results for Eight Countries," *European Journal of Political Economy 6*, 1990: 531-551.

Calvo, Guillermo, "On the Time Inconsistency of Optimal Policy in a Monetary Economy," *Econometrica*, 1978, 46, 1411-1428.

Canzoneri, Matthew B., "Monetary Policy Game and the Role of Private Information," *American Economic Review*, 1985, 75, 1056-1070.

Capie, Forrest and Wood, Geoffrey E., "Central Bank Dependence and Performance: An Historical Perspective," City University London, July 1991.

Cargill, Thomas F., *Central Bank Independence and Regulatory Responsibilities: The Bank of Japan and the Federal Reserve*, Monograph 1989-2, Solomon Brothers Center for the Study of Financial Institutions, New York University, 1989.

Cukierman, Alex, *Central Bank Strategy, Credibility and Independence: Theory and Evidence*, MIT Press, Cambridge, 1992, forthcoming.

Cukierman, Alex and Meltzer, Allan, "A Theory of Ambiguity, Credibility, and Inflation under Imperfect Information," *Econometrica*, 1986, 53, 1099-1128.

Epstein, Gerald A. and Schor, Juliet B., "The Political Economy of Central Banking," Discussion Paper N. 1281, Harvard Institute of Economic Research, July 1986.

Fischer, Stanley, "Monetary and Fiscal Policy Coordination with a High Public Debt: A Comment." In Francesco Giavazzi and Luigi Spaventa (eds.), *High Public Debt: The Italian Experience*. Cambridge: Cambridge University Press, 1988.

Fratianni, Michele and Huang, Haizhou, "Central Bank Independence and Optimal Conservativeness," Indiana University, mimeo, December, 1992.

Fratianni, Michele, von Hagen, Jürgen, "European Monetary Union and Central Bank Independence," *Regional Science and Urban Economics Journal*, 1992, forthcoming.

Fratianni, M., von Hagen, Jürgen and Waller, Christopher, "Central Banking as a Political Principal-Agent Problem," Indiana University, 1992a.

Fratianni, M., von Hagen, Jürgen and Waller, Christopher, *The Maastricht Way to EMU*. Essays in International Finance N. 187, June 1992b. Princeton, N.J.: International Finance Section.

Green, Edward and Porter, Robert, "Noncooperative Collusion under Imperfect Information," *Econometrica*, 1984, 52, 87-100.

Grilli, Vittorio, Masciandaro, Donato and Tabellini, Guido, "Political and Monetary Institutions and Public Finance Policies in the Industrial Democracies," *Economic Policy*, 1991.

Johnson, David R. and Siklos, Pierre L., "Empirical Evidence on the Independence of Central Bank," mimeo, 1992

Kydland, Finn and Prescott, Edward C., "Rules rather than Discretion: the Inconsistence of Optimal Plans," *Journal of Political Economy*, 1977, 85, 473-90.

Masciandaro, Donato and Tabellini, Guido, "Monetary Regimes and Fiscal Deficits: A Comparative Analysis." In Hang-Sheng Cheng (ed.) *Monetary Policy in Pacific Basin Countries*, Kluwer Academic Publishers, Boston, 1988.

Neumann, Manfred J.M., "Precommitment by Central Bank Independence," *Open Economies Review*, 1991, 2, 95-112.

Porter, Robert, "Optimal Cartel Trigger-Price Strategies," *Journal of Economic Theory*, 1983, 29, 313-338.

Rogoff, Kenneth, "Reputational Constraints on Monetary Policy," *Carnegie-Rochester Conference Series on Public Policy*, 1987, 26, 141-181

Rogoff, Kenneth, "The Optimal Degree of Commitment to an Intermediate Monetary Target," *Quarterly Journal of Economics*, 1985, 100, 1169-1190.

Tabellini, Guido, "Monetary and Fiscal Policy Coordination with a High Public Debt." In Francesco Giavazzi and Luigi Spaventa (eds.), *High Public Debt: The Italian Experience*. Cambridge: Cambridge University Press, 1988.

Appendix

The maximization of (12) in the text yields the first-order condition:

$$\frac{[1-\beta+P\beta(1-\beta)]\dfrac{\partial EUF_t^c}{\partial g_t} - (EUF_t^c - EUF_{t+1}^{nc})(1-\beta)\beta\dfrac{\partial P}{\partial g_t}}{[1-\beta+P\beta(1-\beta)]^2} = 0, \qquad (A1)$$

and the second-order condition

$$\frac{\partial^2 V(g_t,\bar{\varepsilon})}{\partial g_t^2}\Big|_{g_t=g_t^{eF,c}} = \frac{\dfrac{\partial^2 EUF_t^c}{\partial g_t^2}\Big|_{g_t=g_t^{eF,c}}}{1-\beta+P\beta(1-\beta)} < 0. \qquad (A2)$$

The proposition that the equilibrium strategy in a one-shot game is an equilibrium strategy in cooperative periods regardless other conditions can be proved as follows. For any value of $\bar{\varepsilon}$, for any distribution function $P(g_t-g_t^{eF,c}-\bar{\varepsilon})$, and for any values of parameters s, θ, β, k and $\bar{y}$, within their defined ranges, if both wage setters and the CB are playing a noncooperative strategy in every period, then $EUF_t^c = EUF_t^{nc}$ at EUF_t^{nc}. As a result, $\partial EUF_t^c/\partial g_t = \partial EUF_t^{nc}/\partial g_t = 0$. Noting that $EUF_t^{nc} = EUF_{t+1}^{nc}$, it is straightforward that equation (A1) can always be satisfied. Furthermore, for any value of $\bar{\varepsilon}$, for any distribution function $P(g_t-g_t^c-\bar{\varepsilon})$ and for any value of s, θ, β, k and $\bar{y}$, within their defined ranges, the second-order condition, (A2), can always be satisfied because of $1-\beta+P\beta(1-\beta)>0$ for $0<\beta<1$ and $0 \leq P \leq 1$ and the strict concavity of the CB's utility function.

If a strategy is an equilibrium strategy, conditions (A1) and (A2) must be satisfied. The second proposition in the text says that, for any strict concave utility function of the CB, the ideal policy cannot be an equilibrium strategy in cooperative periods regardless other conditions. This proposition can be proved as follows. Evaluating equation (A1) at $g_t^{eF,c} = \pi^* + e_t$ and $g_t^{e,c} = \pi^*$, we obtain

$$(1+P\beta)\partial EUF_t^c/\partial g_t\big|_{g_t=g_t^{eF,c}} - [\beta(EUF_t^c-EUF_{t+1}^{nc})\partial P/\partial g_t]\big|_{g_t=g_t^{eF,c}} = 0,$$

or

$$p(-\bar{\varepsilon}) = \frac{2[1+P(-\bar{\varepsilon})\beta]s}{\beta\theta^2 y^*}, \qquad (A3)$$

where $p(-\bar{\varepsilon})$ and $P(-\bar{\varepsilon})$ are the probability density and cumulative distribution functions evaluated at $-\bar{\varepsilon}$, respectively. Furthermore, the second-order condition, (A2), evaluated at $g_t^{eF,c} = \pi^* + e_t$ and $g_t^{e,c} = \pi^*$ becomes

$$2[1+P(-\bar{\varepsilon})\beta](\theta^2+s) + \beta\frac{\theta^4}{s}y^* \cdot \frac{\partial^2 P(-\bar{\varepsilon})}{\partial g_t^2} > 0. \qquad (A4)$$

Equations (A3) and (A4) set two constraints on the value of $\bar{\varepsilon}$, the cumulative distribution function $P(g_t - g_t^{eF,c} - \bar{\varepsilon})$ and the values of parameters s, θ, β, k and $\bar{y}$. If either (A3) or (A4) cannot be satisfied, then the ideal policy cannot be sustained as an equilibrium strategy. In other words, the reputation effect cannot work.

Assuming a normal distribution function of the CB's forecast error of the demand for money

$$P(-\bar{\varepsilon}) = \int_{-\infty}^{-\bar{\varepsilon}} \frac{1}{\sqrt{2\pi}\,\sigma_\varepsilon} \exp(-\frac{\varepsilon_t^2}{2\sigma_\varepsilon^2}) d\varepsilon_t, \tag{A5}$$

(A1) becomes

$$\frac{\beta\theta^2 y^*}{s\sqrt{2\pi}\,\sigma_\varepsilon} \exp(-\frac{\bar{\varepsilon}^2}{2\sigma_\varepsilon^2}) = 2[1 + \beta \int_{-\infty}^{-\bar{\varepsilon}} \frac{1}{\sqrt{2\pi}\,\sigma_\varepsilon} \exp(-\frac{\varepsilon_t^2}{2\sigma_\varepsilon^2}) d\varepsilon_t]. \tag{A6}$$

By substituting (A5) in (A4), we obtain expression (15) in the text.

The closed-form solution of $\bar{\varepsilon}$ can be derived from (A6). Taking the derivative of the both sides of (A6) with respect to $\bar{\varepsilon}$, we obtain

$$\frac{\beta\theta^2 y^*}{s\sqrt{2\pi}\,\sigma_\varepsilon} (-\frac{\bar{\varepsilon}}{\sigma_\varepsilon^2}) \exp(-\frac{\bar{\varepsilon}^2}{2\sigma_\varepsilon^2}) = 2\beta \frac{1}{\sqrt{2\pi}\,\sigma_\varepsilon} \exp(-\frac{\bar{\varepsilon}^2}{2\sigma_\varepsilon^2}).$$

After simplification, we have

$$\bar{\varepsilon} = -\frac{2s\sigma_\varepsilon^2}{\theta^2 y^*}. \tag{A7}$$

Substituting (A7) into (15) in the text, we obtain $\theta2 + 3s > 0$.

CHAPTER 8

AN INSTITUTIONAL ANALYSIS OF THE PROPOSED EUROPEAN CENTRAL BANK WITH COMPARISONS TO THE U.S. FEDERAL RESERVE SYSTEM[1]

Nathaniel Beck

1.   INTRODUCTION

Analyzing the proposed European Monetary Union ("EMU") and the proposed European Central Bank ("ECB") is a growth industry, one (rightly) dominated by economists. Many of the issues surrounding the EMU are technical economic issues about which political science tells us nothing. Among such issues are the optimal scope of monetary union, the efficiency gains from a single European currency, and the relationship between the instruments of ECB policy-making and economic outcomes of interest. A political scientist's contribution on these issues can only be to remind his colleagues that the world is a complicated place, and modesty is called for. My discipline stresses how little we understand complex phenomena, and how hard it is to control such phenomena, even in a world where the controller is a dictator.

But political science has much more to contribute. Central banking is a political activity. When central banks make decisions to tighten monetary policy, some citizens (those who become unemployed) are clearly hurt, at least in the short run; a surprise ease in policy, conversely, helps those same workers. Low or zero inflation may be efficient, in that the gains from such a policy would allow the winners to compensate the losers. Since such compensation is typically not paid, central banks must be seen as making political decisions.[2]

---

[1] Thanks to Richard Burdekin, Suzanne Lohmann, Pierre Siklos and Thomas Willett for comments on an earlier draft.

[2] This argument is spelled out more fully in the American context in Beck (1988). Applications of that argument to the Fed are in Beck (1984; 1987; 1990b; 1990a; 1991). I only briefly set forth all the arguments of those papers here.

We can see the political nature of central banking even in the leading mathematical models. These models, derived from Rogoff's (1985) model of monetary commitment, assume that output is partially determined by surprise inflation, and that nation's have a welfare function which is a function of output and inflation. In all of these models, optimal monetary policy is affected by the parameters of that welfare function. But politics is exactly about (in stylized form!) how nations choose welfare functions. Central banking can only be apolitical if optimal policy is independent of value trade-offs.

On a less lofty plane, questions about the design of governmental institutions, such as the ECB, are clearly political. One set of questions has to do with the degree of independence of the ECB and the implications of independence for price stability.[3] There is little question that the proposed rules for the ECB make it as **formally** independent of its principal, the European Council, as any central bank is independent of its government. The design of the ECB is different from other central banks, in that a large portion of the ECB Council is made up of national Central Bank Governors, who are themselves in an agency relationship with their own governments.

Thus we need to ask whether the formal independence of the ECB will translate into behavioral independence, and whether that behavioral independence will translate itself into greater price stability. Section -- looks at some arguments for why independence should improve policy and the empirical evidence that independence leads to lower inflation. Section -- then discusses some general issues about formal vs. behavioral independence, and Section -- discusses the consequences of making monetary policy by subgovernmental agents. Much of this latter discussion draws on what we know about the United States Federal Reserve System ("Fed").

These questions lead to a much more general question: why should EC citizens accept the dictates of the ECB as authoritative? From whence comes the legitimacy of the ECB? We can examine the legitimacy of the various central banks, but we have little evidence about central banks created *de novo* in the current political-economic environment. The issue of legitimacy is key for the success of the ECB. This question is treated in Section --, which also concludes the paper.

---

[3] The Maastricht Treaty also requires that member nations joining the European System of Central Banks to meet various conditions on the independence of their own central bank, particularly with respect to minimum terms of appointment. It has been argued that this institutional change should also improve European price stability. All the arguments presented in this paper about independence are obviously also relevant to that conjecture.

2.   WHY INDEPENDENCE

The issue of central bank independence is grounded in the theory of agency. Central banks are agents with the central government being the principal.[4] The literature on agency is filled with methods of writing contracts to ensure that the agent will not "shirk", that is, to ensure that the agent will act in the principal's interest. The agency problem is an interesting one when it is costly for the principal to monitor the agent's behavior.

By the standards of agency theory, even the most dependent central banks appear quite independent. Monitoring central banks is difficult, and central banks have a tremendous information advantage over the executive. Thus, for example, even the very (legally) dependent Bank of England in the 1960's had much latitude to manoeuvre because the Bank had a monopoly on monetary information and expertise (Hall 1986). This is especially true in the short-run; central banks experience little, if any, interference with their day to day operations.

It would be possible to write contracts to make the central bank a reliable agent if we know the preferences of the principal. Thus, for example, if the principal wanted the bank to provide minimum inflation, central bank salaries could be tied to the rate of inflation. But most political economists do not want the central bank to be a reliable agent. If the central bank is a reliable agent of the central government, it will make policy to maximize the short term interests of that government at the expense of the long-run well-being of the economy.

One way to get around this problem would be to write a contract to force the agent to follow some rule which would yield the desired result. Such a rule might, as Milton Friedman long ago proposed, mandate a specified growth rate in some monetary aggregate, or might, as the bill introduced in the US Congress by Rep. Stephen Neal (HJR 409) mandating zero inflation within five years. Whatever the merits of such proposals, they do not allow the central bank the flexibility to deal with economic shocks (Burdekin et al. 1992). Hence the search for a type of contract which allows the agent (the bank) to shirk (in terms of the demands of its principal, the government), without writing a contract which leaves the agent no discretion to deal with unforeseen events. Hence the interest in rules which make the central bank independent of the central government.

Central banks are independent of their governments if they can act independently of that government. The ability to act independently is "behavioral" independence. Behavioral independence is very close to what Dahl (1961) called

---

[4] In the US, for example, it is unclear if the principal is the president or Congress, but for purposes here this is irrelevant. For simplicity I shall take the principal as the executive.

'power'; the central bank is behaviorally independent when it can do something even if the central government wants it to do the opposite. Behavioral independence is very hard to measure, because we do not know the preferences of the central government.[5] Scholars typically resort to examining "formal" (legal) independence, that is, whether the rules that govern the central bank are of the type that *should* lead to behavioral independence.[6] Among these rules are length of bank governor term, the appointment process of governors, whether the bank has a legal mandate to ensure price stability and the responsibility of the bank to finance government debt.

The issue of central bank independence is unusual in that the typical issue in agency theory is how to make the agent act in the principal's interests; the issue in central banking is how to avoid this. Why don't we want central banks to be good agents (of the executive)? The fear is that the executive has incentives to undertake policies that lead to excess inflation. Coupled with this fear is that the hope that central banks, given independence, will provide greater price stability. While there is some basis for both this fear and this hope, both need to be examined more critically. I start with the fear, then take up the hope.

2.1   Seigniorage

The oldest argument that central governments will provide excess inflation is based on seigniorage, that is the possibilities for governments to raise real revenues via inflation. The fear is that, if the executive (or the sovereign) could freely print (or coin) money, then there would be no var on what the executive could do (and particularly, no var on the power to make war). Executives who must pay for projects and adventures via taxation are limited, both by taxpayers preferences and by the need of the executive to gain legislative approval; paying for projects by running the printing presses certainly avoids the latter hurdle. In a more modern guise, the central government can pay for projects via a tax on cash balances, that is, by inflation.

---

[5] In one of the few comparative studies that tries to assess behavioral independence, Johnson and Siklos (1992) study whether central banks respond either to changes in the party controlling the executive branch or whether they ease monetary policy before elections so as to aid the incumbent's re-election chances. Their results are mixed. But, more importantly, no matter how ambitious this study, identifying the preferences of the executive with either its party or a desire for easy policy before elections hardly exhausts the possibilities for executive preferences about policy.

[6] This measurement issue causes grave problems for the Fratianni, von Hagen and Waller (1992, 31-2) suggestion that the independence condition for whether a nation is eligible for the EMU be judged by behavioral, not formal, independence. Fratianni, von Hagen and Waller do not tell the European Monetary Institute how to make such an evaluation.

Inflation also makes the central government better off by reducing the real value of its debt (which is typically not indexed). Finally, central government revenue increases with inflation, both through 'bracket creep' and because capital gains are taxed on a nominal rather than a real basis. Thus the central government gains by inflation, and hence has an incentive to provide too much inflation from the standpoint of citizen welfare. An independent central bank has no such incentive.[7]

If seigniorage revenues were important, then we might well prefer an independence central bank that does not gain from such a revenue source. But seigniorage revenues do not seem all that important. Looking at the United States, Summers (1991, 626-7) concludes that "[o]ptimal tax theory has little to do with optimal monetary policy. Tax revenues from seigniorage in the United States were just 0.2 percent of GNP in 1989 and have never exceeded 0.5 percent of GNP in peacetime... . Inflation as a Ramsey tax may be the most overstudied issue in macroeconomics."

Aiyagari (1990) takes this argument further, and argues that even if seigniorage revenue were an important component of total government revenue, seigniorage is an efficient form of taxation. This is because the principal holders of cash balances are criminals. Aigagari also argues that if inflation distorts the tax system, the problem is caused by failure to index the tax code. This problem can be alleviated by changes in the tax code, not changes in the independence of the Fed. The possibility of the government earning revenue from seigniorage thus does not seem to be a strong argument, in practice, for an independent central bank.

2.2   Political Business Cycles

A second alternative is that the incumbent executive can increase his chances of re-election via an inflationary strategy. This is the theory of the 'political business cycle' (Nordhaus 1975). Here governments exploit voter myopia and short term Phillips curve type trade-offs between unemployment and inflation to increase their chance of re-election by pursuing an early term deflationary strategy and a pre-

---

[7] If the income of the central bank is derived from seigniorage, it too might have an incentive to provide excess inflation. Toma (1982) makes this argument for the Fed. But the Fed, at least since the Accord of 1951, uses only a portion of its revenues to cover expenses, returning any excess to Treasury, this argument does not hold up. The situation may have been different in the early years of the Fed. Open market operations were actually initiated during the first decade of the Fed because Reserve Bank revenues from discounting operation were insufficient to cover expenses (Chandler 1958; Eichengreen 1991). Such a situation could lead to excess inflation. The Maastricht Treaty is a bit vague on the exact financing arrangements for the ECB, but it does appear as though Article 33 makes it unnecessary for the ECB to engage in inflationary finance to cover its expenses.

election inflationary strategy. In the long run society is made worse off by such cycles, but the incumbent does benefit. An independent central bank, not subject to election pressures, would yield superior price performance.

The political business cycle argument has fallen on hard times because its theoretical basis is inconsistent with modern macroeconomic theorizing. There have been some valiant efforts to provide for a rational expectations political business cycle, but these do not have the intuitive appeal of the Phillips curve based arguments.

Whatever its theoretical interest, empirical support for the political business cycle is weak. The cycle has been most investigated for the U.S. in the post World War II period. While there is some evidence for such cycles (Haynes and Stone 1990), the overall effects (on output), even when found, are not large, and the bulk of the studies do not find statistically significant evidence for the cycle. To cite but one recent study, Siklos (1992) found that while elections might have influenced business cycles in the pre-World War II period, they do not seem to have an effect during the post-War period; these findings are consistent with the recent findings of Alesina, Londergan and Rosenthal (1991b).[8] The findings for other countries are even weaker. In a study of OECD nations, Alesina and Roubini (1992) found evidence for a political business cycle in output in only Germany, New Zealand and possibly Japan.[9]

Turning specifically to the instruments of monetary policy, there is more evidence for the political business cycle theory. My own work on the US (Beck 1991) finds a political business cycle in M1 for the post-War US, Alesina, Cohen and Roubini (1991a) have similar evidence for the OECD countries. The magnitude of the cycles is not large (with a total impact well under 1 point in the growth of M1). Alesina, Cohen and Roubini (1991a, 27) conclude "that although these cycles are not strong in any particular country, they occur at least occasionally in many OECD democracies." Johnson and Siklos (1992) also get mixed results in a cross-national study of political business cycles in interest rates; interestingly, their country by country results do not coincide with the Alesina, Cohen and Roubini results using monetary aggregates, indicating that the cycle in monetary policy is not robust.

---

[8] The post-War period is of most importance, since there was no economic understanding of the relationship of government policy and the economy for much of the pre-War period.

[9] Japan is complicated by the problem of endogenous election timing. The evidence for Japan is that elections are called during good economic times, but there is little evidence for systematic pre-electoral manipulation of the Japanese economy (Cargill and Hutchison 1991).

A more independent central bank would, presumably be less likely to help create a political business cycle by manipulating its own policy instruments. But the cross-national evidence is hardly overwhelming in favor of this supposition. Both Alesina and Roubini and Johnson and Siklos find some evidence of political business cycles in Germany, which has a very independent central bank; my work and that of Johnson and Siklos finds evidence of a cycle in US monetary policy, again with a formally independent central bank. Both Johnson and Siklos and Alesina and Roubini also find cycles in countries with dependent central banks. But there is simply no evidence of a clear relationship between central bank (formal) dependence and political business cycles.

2.3   Partisan Cycles

A third argument for independence is that a dependent central bank will change policy with changes in partisan control of the government. Such a theory is associated with Hibbs (1987), who argued that left-wing governments provide more inflation and less unemployment than do their right-wing counterparts. Hibbs' argument is not consistent with rational expectations. Alesina and Sachs (1988) have modified the Hibbs argument so that the effect of partisan change occurs early in a term (when is it a surprise); after government policy is anticipated, it no longer has an effect ('rational partisan theory').

Presumably an independent central bank would not change policy with the coming to power of a new party. Hence independence would lead to a more stable monetary policy. Stable monetary policy has much to recommend it, but it is not obviously optimal. If there were one correct monetary policy (such as a Friedman monetary rule or zero inflation), then obviously following such a policy regardless of who controls the government would make sense. But if there were a 'correct' monetary policy, central banking would not be the political issue that I have argued it is.

If central banking involves making political choices, then changing those choices with changing voter preferences (signalled by a change in whom voters choose to run the country) is sensible. Thus the existence of a Hibbs-type partisan effect on economic policy has no implications (either positively or negatively) for the non-optimality of dependent central banks.

The situation is different if there is a rational partisan cycle. Since the output effect of such cyclic policy is short-lived, while its inflationary consequences go on forever, such a cycle can hardly lead to optimality. If there are rational partisan cycles, then we ought to prefer an independent central bank. But it should be noted that the argument for a rational partisan cycle rests heavily on the policy ineffectiveness argument; in fact, it is not the existence of partisan cycles, but the assertion that anticipated left- or right-wing monetary policy has no effect, that leads to the argument for independent central banks. Since the policy ineffectiveness argument has received (at best) mixed support, we might not wish to buttress an argument for central bank independence on this argument.

The rational partisan model has also received mixed empirical support. Looking at outcomes, Alesina and Roubini (1992, 683) conclude that the theory is "consistent with the empirical evidence[,] particularly for a subset of countries with a bi-partisan system or clearly identifiable movements from left to right and vice-versa. The theory is less applicable, and in fact tends to fail, in countries with large coalition governments with frequent government collapses. The 'partisan theory' with permanent effects on output and unemployment is generally rejected." But Johnson and Siklos (1992, 21) find few partisan effects *in the right direction* on monetary policy. In short, we have little evidence that dependent modern central banks lead to inferior monetary outcomes. Is there evidence that independent banks actually provide superior outcomes; in particular, do they provide less inflation?

2.4   Implications for the ECB

Would political business or partisan cycles be likely to present a problem for the EC and the ECB? The strongly federated status of the EC should decrease such fears. The staggered timing of European national elections, and the lack of any clearcut partisan change in control of the EC should make either political business cycles and partisan cycles unlikely occurrences, at the EC level. This should be the case, whether or not the ECB has a high level of formal independence. There are other types of arguments to support a preference for legal independence, but these arguments should not be based on fear of political cycles.

2.5   Does formal independence lead to lower inflation?

Since the pioneering study of Parkin and Bade (1978), there have been several excellent cross-national analyzes of central bank independence and its policy consequences (Banaian and Willett 1983; Burdekin et al. 1992; Cukierman et al. 1992; Grilli et al. 1991). These have focused almost entirely on formal independence.[10] These studies have invariably found a relationship between price stability and central bank independence.

Cross-national studies are not causal. As these authors are well aware, it is not possible to use their studies to infer a causal relationship between independence and low inflation rates. Nations with a preference for low inflation may also choose to have independent central banks. Since nations seldom change their central banking institutions, it is hard to design a study to infer whether the association between independence and price stability is causal.

---

[10] The Cukierman study also used expert assessments of independence where possible.

Thus, for example, has Germany had low inflation rates because the Bundesbank is independent, or has an inflation averse population supported the independence of the bank? Has the Bundesbank successfully thwarted attempts by the government to interfere in monetary policy because it is independent, or because such governmental attempts are politically costly in the German politico-economic environment. This question cannot be answered within the methodology of the various cross-national studies.

The cross-national studies are also puzzling on their own terms. Most studies compile a single index of (formal) independence, but Grilli, Masciandaro and Tabellini (1991) disaggregated independence into political and economic independence; the former has to do with appointments and bank-government relationships while the latter is largely determined by whether the central bank participates in the primary market for government debt and the nature of monetary instruments available to the bank.

The regressions reported in that paper show a clear relationship between economic independence and low inflation, but no relationship whatsoever between political independence and low inflation. This result is very puzzling, because a central bank can easily purchase government debt on the open market in almost all of the OECD nations. Why does it matter if the Fed directly finances the US deficit, or if it does so by providing reserves for private agents to buy government paper? (Burdekin et al. 1992, 238). But it appears as though it is economic independence, for whatever reason, that drives good price performance.

Studies of institutional reform are not causal. There have been a few cases where nations have changed their central banking institutions. The two well known cases of a move towards independence are the Italian 'divorce' of 1981 (Goodman 1991) and the New Zealand statutory commitment to zero inflation of 1989 (Burdekin et al. 1992; Archer 1992). Goodman does report some initial monetary tightness as a result of the divorce, but both he and Burdekin, Wihlborg and Willett are skeptical about the long term price stability consequences of the Italian divorce. Burdekin, Wihlborg and Willett and Archer report some initial success of the New Zealand experiment but the experiment is recent.

But it is very difficult to know whether even the initial success of these reforms was due to the change in institutions. Nations presumably reform their institutions when they are not working; they presumably reform their central banking institutions when inflation is excessive. Thus following the reform we can expect a decrease in inflation due to regression towards the mean; we cannot infer that any post-reform lessening of inflation is due to the institutional changes.

It is also the case that reforms reflect changes in societal preferences about price stability. In Italy, for example, Goodman (1991, 341) reports that "[a] noticeable shift had occurred in the preferences of major social actors [in the early 1980's]." The

New Zealand reform was brought about by legal changes introduced by the central government; there was no apparent conflict between the central bank and the Treasury on this issue.[11]

In short, while formal independence may lead to lower (and less variable) inflation rates, there is no way we can treat this as an appropriately verified law of political economy. Germany and Switzerland do have both the most independent central banks and low rates of inflation. But there is no way we can be sure that a newly created central bank will deliver more price stability if it is more formally independent.

3.   FORMAL VS. BEHAVIORAL INDEPENDENCE

Formal independence is not the same as behavioral independence. While we might expect formal independence to lead to behavioral independence, the relationship between the two is complicated. Formal independence is often measured by two separate components, political independence is measured by characteristics of the appointment process (term length, whether board members are appointed by the central government), the statutory relationship between the central bank and the government (whether government officials are on the central bank board, whether the bank must consult with the central government) and the constitutional status of the central bank (whether price stability is the legally mandated goal, whether the bank must follow government policy). Economic independence is measured by whether the central bank can or must participate in government debt financing. How do these factors relate to behavioral independence, the ability of the central bank to pursue its desired policies regardless of governmental demands? While this cannot be answered in general, it is instructive to look at this relationship among existing central banks. Here I look at the Fed.

The Fed is regarded by all observers as being a relatively formally independent central bank (as independent as all but the Deutsche Bundesbank and the Swiss National Bank). The behavioral independence of the Fed is less clear. Most observers find that the president eventually gets the monetary policy he desires. The

---

[11] Interestingly, the New Zealand reforms do not make the bank independent; instead they tie the hands of the bank. All sanctions in the reform are on the Bank Governor; there are no sanctions on Treasury if the inflation target is not met. A formal analysis of the New Zealand reform, which might be misleading, would lead to the conclusion that the problem in New Zealand was the Bank, not Treasury.

president doesn't always get his way, but he often does.[12] Let us look at the various components of formal independence and see how they relate to the behavioral independence of the Fed.

3.1   Actual vs. legal term length

The president can influence the Fed by appointing new Governors (Havrilesky 1992). Fed Governors have a 14 year term to limit this influence. But regardless of statutory term, recent history has seen Governors serve, on average, under four years. If we ignore the Chair,[13] there are six Fed Governors. With a 14 year term,[14] we would expect a president, to be able to fill two positions each term. But Reagan made five appointments in his second term (following two in his first term), Carter made five appointments and the Nixon/Ford administration made seven appointments (following two appointments by Nixon in his first term).

Whatever the legal length of term for Governors, the question for behavioral independence is the number of appointments available during an administration. This depends both on the legal term of appointment, but also on the attractiveness of the position and the other career possibilities available to Governors. These issues cannot be legislated.

Obviously the issue of term renewability is important. If a governor or chair wishes reappointment then he or she will have to accede to the demands of whoever is doing the reappointment. As Alt (1991) has argued, this can be critical to understanding the behavior of the Fed. The non-renewability of appointments to the ECB is therefore an important legal consideration in understanding behavioral independence.[15]

---

[12] Excellent treatments of this issue are Woolley (1984) and Havrilesky (1992).

[13] The Chair is a governor serving a 14 year term, but the chair is only appointed for four years, and no chair who has not been reappointed has continued to serve as governor.

[14] A governor appointed to fill out an unexpired term is only appointed for the unexpired time, so legally the average term is not really 14 years.

[15] Central bank governors may be re-appointed. They may also be appointed to the Executive Committee. Executive Committee members serve an eight year term, and may not be re-appointed. (Article 109a).

3.2   Informal consultation with government

It is not necessary for the central government to formally consult with bank governors for the bank to know what the government desires. As Havrilesky (1988; 1992) has shown, the central government can signal its policy preferences to the Fed, and the Fed has often, although not always, responded to those signals.

It will not even be necessary for the EC Council to signal the ECB through the media, as the White House does the Fed. The Maastricht Accord allows the President of the EC Council and one member of the EC Commission to attend ECB Council meetings (with non-voting status). The ECB Council should have no difficulty interpreting the signals of the EC Council.

Presidents can also appoint close advisors or confidants to the Fed. Is there any way to have prevented Arthur Burns from having consulted with Richard Nixon? How can this type of behavior be legislated? Even if we could somehow prevent Burns and Nixon from talking directly, is it even conceivable that Burns would not have known of Nixon's policy desires?

Article 8 of the Maastricht Protocols does not allow the ECB Council members to take any instruction from either the EC or member state governments.[16] This gives members of the ECB Council the right to ignore member state instructions, if they so wish. It cannot prevent consultation if the governors wish to consult. This depends on the behavioral relationship between Council members and their governments, not the formal statute.

3.3   Government-Bank disputes

The Fed and the president may disagree. But the president has tremendous political advantages over the Fed, and the president can, if he wishes, win any battle with the Fed. It would obviously be easier for the president to simply instruct the Fed, but the Fed must know that in any battle with the president it will likely lose.

The best example of this is Lyndon Johnson's desire to fight the Vietnam War and the War on Poverty with little or no economic pain. This meant a policy of easy money. When the Fed objected, the Johnson administration used its tremendous power (Woolley 1984). The result was a war financed by inflation.

It is unlikely that any independent central bank can stand against the central government for very long and still maintain its independence. Goodman (1991, 342)

---

[16] As Fratianni, von Hagen and Waller (1992, 39) point out, the Maastricht Accord does instruct the ECB to 'consult' with both national governments and the EC Council. Thus there is an inconsistency.

argues that after the divorce, the Italian central bank was "careful not to jeopardize its independence." Kane (1980) has made a similar argument for the Fed. The ECB Protocols may countenance ECB/European Council disagreements, but it is unclear if ECB will have the political power to actually take advantage of this right. The only saving grace for the ECB here is that we have a little idea about the political power of either the post-1999 European Council and/or Parliament.

3.4   Budgetary independence

The Fed is not subject to the annual budgetary process of the US Congress. This is because the Fed pays its expenses out of its income (primarily interest on its portfolio). It has been argued (McCubbins and Schwartz 1984) that the annual appropriations process gives Congress significant oversight power over the various administrative agencies; the subcommittee chairs on the Appropriations Committees often have more power over the various agencies than do the chairs of the substantive committees. Thus the budgetary independence of the Fed significantly increases the Fed's behavioral independence. The Fed, like the ECB, must report to its legislative masters; these legislative masters would have more power if they could signal their displeasure by cutting the central bank's budget. It appears that the Maastricht Treaty allows the ECB budgetary independence similar to that enjoyed by the Fed, but this is not fully spelled out. Such arrangements may prove very important in maintaining ECB behavioral independence.

3.5   Independence as an end

We might expect independence to enable the Fed to pursue its own monetary goals. But it appears that the Fed's goal may be to maintain its independence, and that monetary policy may be the tool to achieve that end. This argument has been made most forcefully by Kane (1980). He argues that the Fed eases monetary policy to avoid political pain to powerful political actors, so that those powerful actors will not threaten its prized independence. Given that the Fed's grant of independence is by simple act of Congress, and not a part of the Constitution, this threat to Fed independence is taken seriously by the Fed. So independent central banks, whose independence is not constitutionally mandated, may behave just like a dependent central bank, in order to maintain their independence.[17]

---

[17] It is hard to know how to apply this argument to the ECB. The independence of the ECB is enshrined in the Maastricht Treaty, but we do not know enough about how the European Council will operate to know whether it can threaten ECB independence.

3.6   Central bank incentives

Many scholars include in the definition of central bank independence a constitutional mandate for the bank to have price stability as its only, or at least its major, goal. An agency with a constitutionally imposed goal can hardly be called independent. Economists include the constitutional mandate in list of requisites for independence because they presumably believe that an independent central bank would provide for price stability, and so any constitutional mandate for price stability will give the central bank more power to do that it would prefer to do. Economists also may believe that the central government is not as interested in price stability as is the central bank, and so the legal mandate makes the bank more powerful vis-a-vis the government.

Whether central banks prefer price stability depends on the incentives of central bank governors. As many have noted, tying governors' salaries to the rate of inflation, or requiring resignation if inflation exceeds a specified level, would provide such an incentive. So far only academics seem happy with these types of incentives, and no central banks is subject to such incentives.[18] There is no such set of incentives in the ECB Statute.[19]

There are countries which mandate that the central bank have price stability as its goal. Would we expect such a mandate to have an independent effect on lowering inflation rates. Governments seem to have little difficulty in flouting constitutional rules about balanced budgets and other unpleasant matters.[20]

A mandate of price stability would be of aid to a central bank that wanted to provide price stability. But what do central banks (or bankers) want? We don't know the answer to that question. The public choice school (Chant and Acheson 1972; Toma 1982) argues that central bankers pursue their narrow (economic) self-interest, but that view seems overly narrow (Beck 1988).

---

[18] While it is often claimed that New Zealand has this arrangement, Archer (1992) reported this not to be the case. His explanation for not including this provision is the fear of governmental embarrassment if the bank governor's pay went up while the rest of New Zealand endured a monetarily induced recession designed to lower inflation.

[19] Vaubel (1990) regards this as a major flaw in the Statute.

[20] Obviously the US Congress' attempt to eliminate the deficit via the Gramm-Rudman Act comes to mind, but also witness the creative way that state legislatures avoid constitutionally mandated balanced budgets.

It surely is far from clear that price stability is the only goal of the Fed. The work of Havrilesky and his associates (summarized in Havrilesky, forthcoming) indicates that Bank Presidents on the Federal Open Market Committee ("FOMC") are more likely to be concerned about inflation than are the Governors. It also appears as though FOMC members with academic backgrounds may be more concerned about inflation than are non-academics; FOMC members with government service backgrounds appear to have been less concerned with price stability.

This is consistent with impressionistic evidence of Fed goals. Under William Martin 1951-70) the Fed was concerned with providing 'orderly' market conditions (Woolley 1984). Under Arthur Burns the concern seems to have been interest rate stability and under William Miller the concern seems to have been low rates of unemployment. The chairmanships of Paul Volcker and Alan Greenspan may have been marked more by attempts to fight inflation, but even here the Fed pursued other goals.

Thus, for example, when the stock market crashed in October, 1987, the Fed clearly provided extra liquidity to ensure no general collapse of financial markets. Concern for financial markets and institutions has long been a hallmark of Fed policy, from concern with the impact of Chrysler's default in the commercial paper market to propping up huge but weak banks (Continental Illinois) via the discount window to concern with the status of Latin American loans on the books of money center banks in September of 1982.

The systematic evidence on Fed goals based on reaction functions is less clear. However, almost all reaction functions find that the Fed was influenced by both output shortfalls and fiscal policy. Khoury (1990, 38), summarizing 42 reaction function studies, concluded that "[t]he only independent variables [showing] consistent and significant results were the federal debt and unemployment."

This is not an argument that it is wrong for the Fed to be concerned with the stability of financial markets, just an argument that price stability is not the only goal of the Fed, regardless of its independence. Would a law mandating such a goal make the Fed any less concerned with the stability of the financial markets? Would such a lack of concern make the economy better off?

This argument about the Fed appears to hold true for other leading central banks. In a study of six major central banks, Bernanke and Mishkin (1992, 5) concluded:

> "First, in their conduct of monetary policy, central bankers appear to be pursuing multiple economic objectives; they care not only about the behavior of inflation and unemployment but sometimes also, independently, about the behaviour of variables such as exchange rates and interest rates. Further, central bankers' objective

functions sometimes look to be almost lexicographic: A large part
of the monetary policy-maker's attention at any given time is
devoted to the variable that is currently 'in crisis', to the neglect
of other concerns."

Based on this evidence, it is not obvious that independence will lead to greater price
stability.

3.7   Implications for the ECB

Formal independence may have behavioral consequences. A dependent
central bank will do what its government wants (if the government can solve the
agency problem). Independent central banks may be able to act against the wishes of
the central government. This depends on the relative political power, broadly defined,
of the two actors. Several features of the Maastricht Treaty (non-renewability of
Executive Committee, mandate of price stability) give the ECB advantages over the
Fed, but at present we cannot assess the relative political strength of the ECB and EC
Council.

There are, however, several factors that might make the ECB behaviorally
more dependent than might be expected, given the formal independence set up in the
Statute. Of particular importance is the makeup of the ECB Council and the voting
rules on the Council. This issue is dealt with in the next section.

4.   VOTING ON THE ECB

The Council of the ECB has 18 voting members, with six (the Executive
Board) being appointed by the European Council and the rest being the Governors of
the member Central Banks.[21] Unlike most EC councils, which use weighted voting,
the ECB Council uses simple majority voting (with the chair having the tie-breaking
vote).

---

[21] Here I assume that all 12 member nations have met the conditions for
EMU membership. As Fratianni, von Hagen and Waller (1992) argue, this assumption
is not likely to be met by 1999, if ever. Many observers argue, however, that the
desire for all EC nations to be part of the ECB is part of a political, not an economic,
agenda, and is the opening wedge towards federating the EC nations. In such a case
we might see nations in the ECB even though they have not met all the convergence
criteria. Even now there is discussion of allowing Belgium to fail to meet the criterion
based on the ratio of national debt to GDP. See Fratianni and von Hagen (1992, ch.
2) for a discussion of the political versus economic reasoning behind the ECB
proposals.

The ECB Statute maintains that no Council member shall be instructed by either a member state of the EC central apparatus. As argued above, this does not mean that the Council members will ignore their national interests. How might they be expected to vote?

4.1   Voting behavior of Council members

Thanks primarily to the work of Thomas Havrilesky and his associates (in numerous articles summarized in Havrilesky Forthcoming) we know a fair bit about the characteristics that determine FOMC voting behavior in the US.[22] Havrilesky has studied two different issues: what background factors lead to voting for relatively contractive policies and what background factors lead to voting consistent with the preferences of the appointing president.

Voting for contractive policies. Governors are more likely to vote for easy policy than are Bank Presidents; those with government careers are more likely to vote for easy policy than are those with regional Bank careers: academics are less likely to vote for easy policy.

The structure of the ECB Council is very different from the structure of the FOMC. The Six members of the Executive Board are appointed by the EC Council with the other twelve being the member central bank governors. It seems likely that the Executive Committee will resemble Fed Governors, that is, they will be likely to favor ease over tightness.[23] If most of the Executive Committee are not professional economists, then they are also likely to be unreliable, that is they will change positions as the position of the EC Council changes.

This problem will be compounded if the Executive Committee members do not serve out their full eight year terms. Looking at the Fed, it seems likely that at least some of them will not serve out their terms, giving the EC Council even greater influence over the ECB Council.

---

[22] It would be interesting to study dissent voting on the Deutsche Bundesbank Council, which has up to 10 central government appointees and 11 Land Bank representatives. Since the Bundesbank does not publish its votes, such a study cannot be done.

[23] Obviously it is hard to make firm predictions on this issue. The argument is that the Executive Committee members will follow career paths similar to the US Governors. It may be the case that only monetary expertise will be considered in making these appointments, but one would not always expect this based on examination of the Fed appointment process. Monetary expertise is only one of many factors in the US appointment process.

What about the 12 central banks governors? Will they look like US Bank Presidents, that is, will their preferences be contractive? Fratianni, von Hagen and Waller (1992, 35) argue yes. "Realizing that the common monetary policy is unfit to meet regional output and employment targets, the [governors] will be naturally inclined to give higher priority to the low-inflation target of the common monetary policy than the Executive Board, by virtue of the fact that it represents a federal or Community institution, will define its responsibility in terms of Community aggregates. Therefore, Board members in the ECB Council will push for more active, discretionary output and employment stabilization at the federal level than the governors of the member banks."

My own guess is that the answer is no. Member nation central bank governors are more likely to look like Fed Governors than Bank Presidents in terms of previous experience. One does not get to be a central bank governor by ignoring the preferences of the central government.

But more importantly, the 12 governors will represent constituencies with fairly clear preferences about growth/inflation trade-offs. This is very different than the situation on the FOMC, where the Bank Presidents do not represent constituencies with clear preferences. No studies of the FOMC show a high growth bloc of Bank Presidents based on their geographic position.

Obviously there will be differences in preferences among the 12 central bank governors. Presumably some of these differences will be due to national preferences about the costs of inflations. The German governor will probably prefer to fight inflation at the cost of output loss, while the governors from the poorer EC nations might well have the opposite preferences.

Table 1 shows inflation rates in the EC countries from 1985 through 1990. It is easy to see that inflation rates differ dramatically across the community. Perhaps some of the high inflation countries have those rates because they have dependent central banks. But it seems more likely that many of the high inflation countries are pursuing more rapid growth strategies. If those countries join the EMU, would we expect their governors to vote for contractive policies?

If the governors would differ in their preferences,[24] as I think they would, what would the median preference be? It clearly would not be that of Germany. Seven EC members had average inflation rates of under about 4% in the last half decade; the other five experienced rates over 6%. Thus the preferences of the

[24] The claim here is not that governors are choosing a point on a Phillips curve type trade-off, but that each society has a loss function as in the Rogoff (1985) model. All that is critical here is that nations, and governors, may have different preferences about the optimal rate of monetary growth.

Executive Committee members would be critical. But if the ECB led to a single EC
rate of inflation, it would almost certainly exceed the 1-2% rate of inflation seen in
the most price stable nations.

It is possible that such a situation might not come to pass. An EC national
must meet four economic 'convergence' criteria before it can joint the EMU.
Fratianni, Von Hagen and Waller (1992, 27) argue that Greece, Italy, Portugal and
Spain are unlikely to ever meet the conditions for EMU membership, and, of course,
whether the UK wants to join the EMU is very unclear.

Table 1

Table 1: Inflation Rates of EC Nations, 1985-1990							
	1985	1986	1987	1988	1989	1990	Average
Belgium	4.9	1.3	1.6	1.2	3.1	3.5	2.6
Denmark	4.7	3.7	4.0	4.6	4.8	2.7	4.1
France	5.8	2.5	3.3	2.7	3.5	3.4	3.5
Germany	2.2	-.1	.2	1.3	2.9	2.7	1.5
Greece	19.3	23.0	16.4	13.5	13.7	20.4	20.1
Ireland	5.4	3.8	3.1	2.2	4.0	3.4	3.8
Italy	9.2	5.9	4.8	5.1	6.3	6.5	6.3
Luxembourg	4.1	.3	-.1	1.5	3.4	3.7	2.2
Netherlands	2.2	.1	-.7	.8	1.1	2.5	1.0
Portugal	19.3	11.7	9.4	9.6	12.6	13.4	13.6
Spain	8.8	8.8	5.7	4.8	6.8	6.7	6.9
United Kingdom	6.1	3.4	4.2	4.9	7.8	9.5	6.0
Source: International Financial Statistics, Variable 64X							

These five countries are exactly the five high inflation countries in Table 1. But the
other seven countries have done quite well without the EMU, and so an EMU made
up of these seven would not lead to major changes in European price stability.

4.2 The imperative of unanimity

What if one or two of the high inflation nations are allowed EMU
membership, even if they have not met the convergence criteria? (This would reflect
the political agenda discussed above). Since their votes would not change the median

preference very much, would we then not see improved price stability in the newly joined nations at little cost to price stability of the original EMU members? If the Council really operated by majority rule, the answer to this question is yes. Is there any reason for a median voter result not to apply?

Looking at the FOMC, which formally operates by majority rule, we see results which make it appear as though majority rule is not really operating. There were approximately 500 FOMC decisions in the four post-Accord decades. Of these, 60% were unanimous. Looking only at the 40% of the decisions that were split, the modal number of dissenters (by a wide margin) is one. Thus, almost all FOMC decisions were either unanimous or eleven to one.

This could simply reflect consensus on monetary policy. If monetary policy is neutral and technical, a panel of experts ought to be able to agree on the appropriate policy. If monetary policy is political, then we would expect many more divided votes.

Reading Fed memoranda of discussion, it appears as though there is often disagreement in the FOMC. However, there is often unanimous, if grudging, agreement to a directive of 'no change'. Anecdotal evidence has Arthur Burns carefully crafting his proposed directives so that they could receive a unanimous vote.

Why this imperative towards unanimity? My guess is that it is to preserve the illusion of the Fed as a neutral, technical body. A series of dividend votes would threaten the legitimacy of the Fed. If FOMC members can disagree, why should we allow the unelected Fed to administer its distasteful economic medicine?

The US Supreme Court faces a similar position. While it, unlike the Fed, enjoys constitutional status, its authority, like the Fed's, is based on its legitimacy. If five judges read the Constitution one way, while four read it the opposite way, why should political actors feel obligated to obey the Court? In major political cases, such as that ending school segregation, the Court has achieved unanimity.

The Court isn't always successful in reaching unanimity, but its leadership does appear to try hard not to decide important cases by a five to four vote. The leading scholar of judicial strategy, Walter Murphy (1964) has argued:

> "Once majority acquiescence has been obtained, the marginal value of any additional votes declines perceptibly, as would the price which an opinion writer should be willing to pay. However, the marginal value of another vote is never zero, though the asking price may exceed its real value and may have to be rejected. [Thence follows a long footnote, with the relevant portion being] ... While the price any politician would rationally pay for increments of support declines sharply after 50.1 percent, there is usually a

psychological, if not material, advantage in 'winning big'. This is especially true in a political system where power is fragmented among different institutions of government. In such a situation there is great need for an appearance of consensus. ... (p. 65)

"Where a Justice has reason to foresee a political reaction which will be dangerous to his policy or the Court if a case is decided a certain way or if the opinion announces a particular policy, he still might decide to pursue a 'damn the torpedoes' strategy and forge ahead. ... The status of the prestige and reputation of the Court would be among the most crucial factors [in making the assessment of whether to do this], as would the size of the majority on the Court. It is far more difficult to invoke the sacred mysteries of the cult of the robe for 5-4 rulings than for those which are unanimous or nearly so." (p. 172)

If the US Supreme Court faces such an imperative, the Fed must face an even stronger one. The Court has equal constitutional status to the President and Congress. The Fed was created by Congress in this century. The Fed was designed as a lender of last resort, not the principal arbiter of economic policy. Lacking legitimacy, the Fed should have an even stronger aversion to close votes than does the Court. This imperative will be especially strong when the Fed is imposing a painful anti-inflationary tight money policy. It is at such times that the legitimacy of the Fed is most likely to be challenged. (Political actors seldom complain about a regime of easy money).

4.3   Implications for the ECB

If this is correct, and if the ECB faces the same legitimacy problems, then the one or two governors with a preference for more rapid monetary growth (or less distaste for inflation vis-a-vis output growth) would have more power than the median voter model suggests. If unanimity were required, these governors would have a veto power. Dissents are clearly allowed, so this would not be the case. But these governors could force easier policy than the median model would suggest, leading to higher rates of inflation than that model would suggest.[25]

One way to limit this problem would be for the ECB to maintain a strict policy of not announcing either the vote division or the positions of the Council members. The Fed does make public (with some delay) both of these; the

---

[25] As argued above, close votes in favor of ease would involve much less of a threat to ECB legitimacy, and so the imperative to unanimity is asymmetric in the direction of higher rates of inflation.

Bundesbank, on the other hand, has been able to maintain secrecy.[26] It would also be the case that the ECB would have to maintain a strict policy against informal 'leaks' of the vote. The Fed has not been able to maintain such a policy, while the Bundesbank seems to have been more successful in this regard.

5.   CONCLUSION: THE LEGITIMACY OF THE ECB

It is hard to make predictions about central banks being created *de novo*. Studies of the Bundesbank and the Fed show that their current status is at least partially determined by historical contingencies. The Fed, for example, was created in 1913; it was assumed that the Fed would prevent banking panics through rediscounting operations. Open market operations were undertaken in the 1900's to increase the inadequate revenue of the regional Federal Reserve Banks (Chandler 1958). This was a decade before the theory of open market operations as a tool of monetary policy was formulated (Eichengreen 1991, 5) and several decades before open market operations became the dominant tool of monetary policy-making. Eichengreen (1991, 5-7) also notes that it took the Federal Reserve System over two decades to sort out the institutions responsible for carrying out open market operations, and that the institutional structure decided upon in 1935 was undreamt of in 1913. What contingencies and new theories await the ECB?

The Bundesbank was, of course, created after World War II, emerging in its current form in 1957 (Goodman 1991). As detailed by Goodman, the Bundesbank early on had to fight to maintain its independence. Fortunately, for the Bundesbank, the German populace is inflation averse, and so its struggle for legitimacy was, perhaps, not so difficult. In any event, it was very successful in restraining inflation, and this, in concert with the economic 'miracle', has given the Bundesbank great legitimacy.

Can we expect such success for the ECB? Much obviously depends on the early success of the ECB. A major mistake would have grave consequences for the new institution. Also much depends on clever political leadership of the ECB. An overly timid ECB will do little to establish its importance, but an overly aggressive ECB may endanger its status before it has established political allies. An established central bank may have much greater political leeway than does a new one.

The ECB has some advantages in obtaining legitimacy, vis-a-vis the Fed, but it also faces some disadvantages. The advantage of the ECB is the decline of Keynesianism, with a rise in the belief that inflation brings no good, but only harm. Thus inflation fighting institutions have an advantage. Offsetting inflationary fiscal policies might have been politically difficult in the 1960's, but by the late 1970's such

---

[26] The Maastricht Treaty is silent on the issue of voting secrecy.

action would have a much easier time obtaining, at least, intellectual support. Such support should translate into political support.

The disadvantage of the ECB is that it is being formed at a time when political actors pay a great deal of attention to monetary policy. The Fed has the luxury of toiling in political obscurity for decades. Legislatures and executives have only recently begun to acquire their own sources of monetary information and expertise. A central bank is most powerful when it is obscure. It may be least powerful when monetary policy is seen as the only way for governments to influence the economy. This bodes poorly for the behavioral independence of the ECB.

REFERENCES

Aiyagari, S. 1990. "Deflating the case for zero inflation." *Federal Reserve Bank of Minnesota Quarterly Review* Summer: 2-11.

Alesina, A., G. Cohen, and N. Roubini. 1991a. "Macroeconomic policy and elections in OECD democracies." Working Paper 3830 National Bureau for Economic Research.

Alesina, A., J. Londregan, and H. Rosenthal. 1991b. "A model of the political economy of the United States." Working Paper 3611 National Bureau of Economic Research.

Alesina, A., and N. Roubini. 1992. "Political cycles in OECD countries." *Review of Economic Studies* 59: 663-88.

Alesina, A., and J. Sachs. 1988. "Political parties and the business cycle in the United States, 1948-1984." *Journal of Money, Credit and Banking* 20: 63-82.

Alt, J. 1991. "Leaning into the wind or ducking out of the storm: U.S. monetary policy in the 1980's." In A. Alesina and G. Carliner (Eds.), *Politics and Economics in the Eighties* 41-77. Chicago: University of Chicago Press.

Archer, D. 1992. "Organizing a central bank to control inflation: The case of New Zealand." Paper presented at the 1992 Annual Meeting of the Western Economic Association, San Francisco, July, 1992.

Banaian, K. and Laney, L., and T. Willett. 1983. "Central bank independence: An international comparison." *Economic Review (Federal Reserve Bank of Dallas)* 1-13.

Beck, N. 1984. "Domestic political sources of American monetary policy: 1955-1982." *Journal of Politics* 46: 787-815.

Beck, N. 1987. "Elections and the Fed: Is there a political monetary cycle?" *American Journal of Political Science* 31: 194-216.

Beck, N. 1988. "Politics and monetary policy." In T. Willett (Ed.), *Political Business Cycles: The Political Economy of Money, Inflation and Unemployment.* Durham: Duke University Press.

Beck, N. 1990a. "Congress and the Fed: Why the dog doesn't bark in the night." In T. Mayer (Ed.), *The Political Economy of American Monetary Policy* 131-50. New York: Cambridge University Press.

Beck, N. 1990b. "Political monetary cycles." In T. Mayer (Ed.), *The Political Economy of American Monetary Policy* 115-30. New York: Cambridge University Press.

Beck, N. 1991. "The Fed and the political business cycle." *Contemporary Policy Issues* 9(2): 25-38.

Bernanke, B., and F. Mishkin. 1992. "Central bank behavior and the strategy of monetary policy: Observations from six industrialized countries." Working Paper 4082 National Bureau for Economic Research.

Burdekin, R., C. Wihlborg, and T. Willett. 1992. "A monetary constitution case for an independent European Central Bank." *World Economy* 15: 231-49.

Cargill, T., and M. Hutchison. 1991. "Political business cycles with endogenous election timing — evidence from Japan." *Review of Economics and Statistics* 73: 733-739.

Chandler, L. 1958. *Benjamin Strong Central Banker*. Washington, D.C.: Brookings.

Chant, J., and K. Acheson. 1972. "The choice of monetary instrument and the theory of bureaucracy." *Public Choice* 12: 13-33.

Cukierman, A., S. Webb, and B. Neyapti. 1992. "The measurement of central bank independence and its effect on policy outcomes." *World Bank Economic Review* 6:353-98.

Dahl, R. 1961. *Who Governs*. New Haven: Yale University Press.

Eichengreen, B. 1991. "Designing a central bank for Europe: A cautionary tale from the early years of the Federal Reserve System." Working Paper 3840 National Bureau of Economic Research.

Fratianni, M., and J. von Hagen. 1992. *The European Monetary System and European Monetary Union*. Boulder, Co.: Westview Press.

Fratianni, M., J. von Hagen, and C. Waller. 1992. "The Maastricht way to EMU." Technical Report 187 Essays in International Finance, Department of Economics, Princeton University.

Goodman, J. 1991. "The politics of central bank independence." *Comparative Politics* 23: 329-49.

Grilli, V., D. Masciandaro, and G. Tabellini. 1991. "Political and monetary institutions and public financial policies in the industrial countries." *Economic Policy* 13: 341-92.

Hall, P. 1986. *Governing the Economy*. New York: Oxford University Press.

Havrilesky, T. 1988. "Monetary policy signalling from the administration to the Fed." *Journal of Money, Credit and Banking* 20: 83-101.

Havrilesky, T. 1992. *The Pressures on Federal Reserve Monetary Policy*. Boston: Kluwer Academic.

Haynes, S., and J. Stone. 1990. "Political models of the business cycle should be revived." *Economic Inquiry* 28: 442-65.

Hibbs, D. 1987. *The American Political Economy: Macroeconomics and Electoral Politics in the United States*. Cambridge: Harvard University Press.

Johnson, D., and P. Siklos. 1992. "Empirical evidence on the independence of central banks." Working paper, Wilfrid Laurier University.

Kane, E. 1980. "Politics and Fed policy-making: The more things change, the more they remain the same." *Journal of Monetary Economics* 6: 199-212.

Khoury, S. 1990. "The Federal Reserve reaction function: A specification search." In T. Mayer (Ed.), *The Political Economy of American Monetary Policy* 27-50. New York: Cambridge University Press.

McCubbins, M. and T. Schwartz. 1984. "Congressional oversight overlooked: Police patrols versus fire alarms." *American Journal of Political Science* 28: 165-179.

Murphy, W. 1964. *Elements of Judicial Strategy*. Chicago: University of Chicago Press.

Nordhaus, W. 1975. "The political business cycle." *Review of Economic Studies* 42: 169-90.

Parkin, M., and R. Bade. 1978. "Central bank laws and monetary policies: A preliminary investigation." In M. Porter (Ed.), *The Australian Monetary Systems in the 1970's*. Clayton, Australia: Monash University.

Rogoff, K. 1985. "The optimal degree of commitment to an intermediate monetary target." *Quarterly Journal of Economics* 100: 1169-90.

Siklos, P. 1992. "Politics and U.S. business cycles: A century of evidence." Working paper, Wilfrid Laurier University.

Summers, L. 1991. "How should long-term monetary policy be determined." *Journal of Money, Credit and Banking* 23: 625-33.

Toma, M. 1982. "Inflationary bias of the Federal Reserve System." *Journal of Monetary Economics* 10: 163-190.

Vaubel, R. 1990. "Currency competition and European monetary integration." *Economic Journal* 100: 936-46.

Woolley, J. 1984. *The Federal Reserve and the Politics of Monetary Policy*. New York: Cambridge University Press.

CHAPTER 9

MONETARY UNION AND MONETARY POLICY: A REVIEW OF THE GERMAN MONETARY UNION

Jürgen von Hagen

1.   INTRODUCTION

On July 1, 1990, East and West Germany formed a monetary union which made the Deutsche Mark (DM) the only legal tender and the German Bundesbank the sole monetary authority in the unified currency area. While East Germany continued to exist as a political entity until October 2 of the same year, its currency, the Mark, was replaced by the DM immediately. For the socialist East German economy, monetary union meant the introduction of a modern financial and banking system, an essential step in the transition to a market economy, together with the adoption of a stable, convertible and reputable currency. For the Bundesbank, monetary union brought the challenge to conduct monetary policy in an enlarged currency area, in which the empirical qualities of a sizeable part of the aggregate demand for and supply of money were unknown.

Under the socialist regime, the only financial assets available to East Germans were cash, interest-paying savings deposits which were also usable as transactions accounts, and a basic form of life insurance, which was quantitatively negligible.[1] The ratio of cash holdings to bank deposits was smaller than in West Germany - 0.061 in May 1990 comparing to 0.51 in West Germany -, in part because East German businesses were obliged to funnel all payments through the state banking system, without using any cash at all.[2] East German banks were essentially book-keeping operations for the state bank, without any autonomous financial activity.

---

[1] As of May 1990, their total volume amounted to seven percent of the financial assets of private non-business residents.

[2] Note that the West German ratio of cash holdings to demand deposits plus savings deposits, which may be more comparable to the East German figure that the ratio of currency to demand deposits, was 0.20 in May 1990, i.e., it still exceeded the East German figure substantially.

Only bank deposits of East German residents were made eligible for conversion into Deutsche Mark on July 1, 1990, so that - apart from small coins remaining in circulation until July 1991 - the immediate cash supply could only come about by withdrawing cash from accounts converted into DM balances. To prepare this step, the Bundesbank gave East German residents the opportunity to convert Mark balances into claims on DM cash some time before July 1st; these claims were then redeemable in the first few days of the monetary union at a large number of auxiliary bank counters.

With the rapid move of West German commercial banks into East Germany - by the end of 1991 22 percent of all bank branches in East Germany were owned by West German or foreign banks - and the transfer of Western bank management know how through personnel and training, the whole array of financial assets available to West Germans became quickly available to East Germans. To adjust the hybrid, East German type of bank deposits to the West German bank law, the treaty on monetary union ruled that these deposits had to be converted into either demand deposits, which pay no or only a nominal fixed interest rate, or savings deposits, which pay higher interest but have limitations on withdrawal. Most of these conversions took place as of December 31, 1990; a smaller, final adjustment occurred as of June 30, 1991.

Monetary union confronted the Bundesbank with three main sources of uncertainty in the conduct of monetary policy. The first one can be called structural uncertainty: Little was known about the portfolio choices East Germans would make in their new financial environment, both with regard to the demand for money and with regard to the desired structure of their monetary portfolios, i.e., the desired relative amounts of currency, demand deposits, time and savings deposits. The other two sources are data uncertainty: Even if the basic relationships between the demand for money, interest rates, prices and output had been known, the actual level of the demand for money and, therefore, the appropriate money supply would have been largely unknown, because the level of real output and the price level were (and remain) measurable only with large margins of error due to the lack of a national accounting system appropriate for a market economy and the severe allocative distortions caused by the socialist regime which required large adjustments of demand patterns and relative prices.

This paper intends to review the monetary developments in Germany since monetary union. The next section provides a brief overview of the main monetary trends since 1989. Another section III characterizes the Bundesbank's monetary policy regime and provides empirical estimates of the money demand functions and the money multiplier characterizing the money supply process up to unification. Section IV analyzes the behavior of money demand and the multiplier in the following six quarters. The final section closes with an interpretation of German monetary policy since July 1990.

2.   GERMAN MONETARY TRENDS SINCE 1989

Table 1 provides an overview of the main monetary developments in Germany since 1989. The five quarters prior to monetary union can be characterized as a period of relatively strong, mildly inflationary, real growth. Real GNP grew by almost four percent in real terms throughout 1989. Prices rose by almost three percent, a return from the short period of price stability in the mid-1980s, and at an increasing rate, reflecting the increasing degree of capacity utilization.

Annual money growth rates measured in terms of M1 (currency held by non-banks and demand deposits) or M3 (M1 plus time deposits with maturities under four years and savings deposits at statutory notice) exceeded real GNP growth throughout 1989, fell to a low of 2.4 percent for M1 and 3.9 percent for M3 in the first quarter of 1990, and picked up slightly in the second quarter. The growth rate of the adjusted monetary base increased from five to above seven percent in the first three quarters of 1989, but fell through the second quarter of 1990 to an annual rate of 3.1 percent.[3] For West Germany, monetary union thus occurred in a period of strong real growth and at the turn from a relatively lax to a relatively restrictive monetary policy.

During the first three quarters of 1989, long-run interest rates hovered around seven percent, while the short-term money market rate increased by about 130 basis points. The fourth quarter of 1989 showed a first reaction to the opening of East Germany on November 9. Long-run interest rates jumped up about 60 basis points, followed by another jump of 100 basis points in the first quarter of 1990. The money-market rate increased by about 80 basis points in the last quarter of 1989. At the same time, the external value of the DM appreciated by almost six percent.

The beginning of the monetary union added immediately additional monetary balances to the DM area. This *level effect* can be approximated by an increase in M1 balances by 13.4 percent of the West German balances of June 30, an increase in M3 balances by 15.0 percent of West German balances and an increase in the monetary base by 11.6 percent of the West German base on June 30. In contrast, the monetary union added an estimated 8.8 percent real output to the currency area.

---

[3]   We define the adjusted monetary base as currency in circulation plus commercial bank deposits at the Bundesbank plus liberated reserves, with the latter adjusting the base for changes in required-reserves ratios. We measure liberated reserves by cumulating the item 'changes in the supply of central bank money due to changes in required-reserves ratios' from the Bundesbank's Monthly Reports (Table I.3).

Table 1

Monetary Developments in Germany, 1989 - 91

	M1 growth	M3 growth	adjusted base growth	money market rate	bond rate	exch. rate	GNP Defl.	real GNP
1989,I	9.1	6.8	5.0	5.59	6.8	174.7	2.6	5.0
II	4.7	5.1	7.1	6.21	7.0	173.8	2.4	3.7
III	5.1	5.1	7.4	6.86	6.9	174.6	2.7	3.5
IV	5.5	5.5	5.5	7.69	7.5	180.2	3.0	3.3
1990,I	2.4	3.9	4.1	7.69	8.5	185.0	3.1	3.5
II	3.4	4.3	3.1	7.78	8.9	185.0	3.6	4.4
III	9.1	5.1	3.1	8.03	8.9	185.0	4.1	5.6
IV	17.0	5.2	1.3	8.20	9.0	187.1	3.4	4.5
1991,I	14.7	5.6	9.8	8.66	8.7	188.1	3.4	3.7
II	12.0	4.8	7.3	8.74	8.5	180.2	5.0	2.1
III	8.8	4.5	6.9	8.94	8.9	180.9	5.1	2.0
IV	3.4	6.3	3.9	9.02	8.9	184.2	5.2	0.8

Note: All growth rates and interest rates are annual rates in percent. 'Money market rate' in the Frankfurt interbank rate on overnight money. 'Bond rate' is the average yield on government securities. 'External value' is an index of the weighted foreign currency price of the DM vis-a-vis Germany's 18 largest trading partners.

In view of this discrepancy, the Bundesbank repeatedly argued, during the following quarters, that monetary union had created an excess supply of money and, thereby, a potential for a price-level increase. Obviously, this view assumes that the velocity of money in East Germany would be similar to or even higher than pre-union velocity in West Germany.

The money and output growth rates shown in Table 1 for the third quarter of 1990 and from there on are all adjusted for the level effect of monetary union, allowing us to focus on the underlying monetary trends.[4] The table shows that the broad aggregate M3 continued to grow at rates around five percent, conforming to the Bundesbank's monetary target. In contrast, monetary base growth fell to 1.3 percent in the last quarter of 1991, rose strongly in the first three quarters of 1991 and then came down again. M1 growth was very rapid until mid-1991, and then came down very strongly.

While West German real GNP grew by a record of 5.6 percent annually, total real output growth in Germany fell in all subsequent quarters to reach a mere 0.8 percent in the final quarter of 1991. Behind this lies a strong divergence of real growth in East and West Germany: The East experienced a severe real contraction until the third quarter of 1991, while output in the West grew at falling rates. By the end of 1991, real output in West Germany fell, while East German output stabilized.

During the 18 months after monetary union, the growth rate of the (West German) GNP deflator rose to about five percent annually. Following another jump of 40 basis points in the second quarter of 1990, long-run interest rates peaked at nine percent in the fourth quarter of that year. In contrast, the money market rate kept increasing throughout the period to reach nine percent in the last quarter of 1991. While the rise in interest rates is compatible with either a rise in inflation expectations or a higher real interest rate due to the simultaneous fiscal expansion, the appreciation of the DM shown in the table suggests that the latter explanation is the dominating one. Finally, the table indicates a flat yield curve towards the end of the period under consideration.

3.   GERMAN MONETARY POLICY BEFORE MONETARY UNION

3.1   A Characterization of the Bundesbank's Policy Regime

With the breakdown of the Bretton Woods system in the early 1970s, the Bundesbank adopted a policy regime of monetary targeting.[5] Within this regime, the Bundesbank aims mainly at achieving price stability - defined as a permanent growth

---

[4]   The following adjustment was made: First, the estimated level effect of monetary union on Germany's GDP and money supply was added to the observed, West German data from the third quarter of 1989 to the second quarter of 1990. The following growth rates were then computed as logarithmic differences between the data from the third quarter of 1990 to the second quarter of 1991 and the appropriate level-adjusted data from the third quarter of 1989 to the second quarter of 1990.

[5]   For a detailed analysis see von Hagen (1989) and Neumann and von Hagen (1991).

rate of the price level of two percent.

The Bank's regime can be described on the basis of the following model.[6] It is convenient to define the basic control period as one month, since monetary stock data is available, in Germany, on a monthly basis. Let p_t be the price level, M_t the money stock, y_t real output and v_t the velocity of money, all defined in logs. Starting from the quantity equation, the monthly change in the price level is

$$\Delta p_t = \Delta M_t + \Delta v_t - \Delta y_t = \Delta M_t + \Delta x_t. \tag{1}$$

We allow for short-run price stickiness and real effects of monetary policy by assuming that the short-run elasticities of the velocity of money with respect to nominal money and real output, v_{ms} and v_{ys} are constrained by $-1 < v_{ms} < 0 < v_{ys} < 1$, while both elasticities are zero in the long run. Similarly, the short-run elasticity of real output with respect to nominal money, $y_{ms} > 0.$, while the corresponding long-run elasticity is zero. Decomposing the growth rates of output and velocity into a permanent $(\tau + X_t)$ and a transitory component (ε_{1t}),

$$\Delta x_t = \tau + X_t + \varepsilon_{1t}; \quad \Delta X_t = \varepsilon_{2t} , \tag{2}$$

where ε_{1t} and ε_{2t} are serially and mutually uncorrelated, normally distributed random shocks with expectation zero and τ is a constant parameter, we define the rate of inflation as the permanent rate of change in the price level,

$$\pi_t = \Delta M_t + \tau + X_t. \tag{3}$$

At the beginning of a year, the Bank derives a target rate for the money supply, $\Delta_{12}M^*_{t+12}$ from a projection of the trend rate of change of the velocity of money, the projected rate of growth of potential real output, and the annual target rate of inflation, π^*,

$$\Delta_{12}M^*_{t+12} = \pi^* - E\Sigma_{j=1,12}X_{t+j} = \pi^* - 12(\tau + X_t) \tag{4}$$

This annual target is publicly announced in the form of a corridor, between two and three percent wide, to give the Bank some discretionary flexibility of monetary policy throughout the year; the announcement is usually revised in the middle of the year.[7] Next, a series of monthly monetary targets is derived from (4) and allowing for reactions to recent permanent output and velocity shocks as

---

[6] See von Hagen (1988), Neumann and von Hagen (1987).

[7] Note that the starting point for a target corridor in year t is the actual money supply in year t-1. Thus, if the Bank overshoots its targets consistently over time, a base drift problem occurs.

perceived from the observation of Δx_{t-1}, $E(X_{t-1}|\Delta x_{t-1})$ and to recent monetary control errors $\varepsilon_{Mt-1} = \Delta M_{t-1} - \Delta M^*_{t-1}$,

$$\Delta M^*_{t+j} = (1/12)\Delta_{12}M^*_{t+12} - \lambda_1\varepsilon_{Mt+j-1} - \lambda_2(\Delta x_{t+j-1} - \tau - X_t), \tag{5}$$

$j = 1, ..., 12.$

This yields an actual annual inflation rate

$$\Sigma_{j=1,12}\pi_{t+j} = \pi^* + \Sigma_{j=1,12}[(1-\lambda_1)\varepsilon_{Mt+j-1} + (1-\lambda_2)(X_{t+j-1}-X_t)- \tag{6}$$

$$\lambda_2\varepsilon_{1t+j-1}] + \varepsilon_{Mt+12} + \Delta_{12}X_{t+12}.$$

Assuming that $E\varepsilon_{Mt-j}\Delta x_{t-k} > -0.5\sigma^2_m$ k, j = 0, 1, ..., where σ^2_m is the variance of the monetary control error, equation (6) implies that, to minimize the variance of the actual around the targeted rate of inflation, the Bundesbank needs a monetary control procedure with a minimal variance of the monthly error ε_{Mt} and, since Δx_t includes the forecast error about the velocity of money, a reliable, stable money demand function.[8] Furthermore, standard stochastic control theory (e.g. Muth, 1960) implies that, to minimize the variance of inflation, the Bundesbank should react less to observed output and velocity shocks in the recent past, if the contribution of transitory shocks to the total variance of Δx_t increases.

During a month, the Bank controls the growth rate of the money supply using a short-term money market rate, z_t, as an operating target, i.e., a guide for its daily policy actions. Dividing the monthly growth of the money supply into the change of the money multiplier, Δm_t, and the change in the adjusted monetary base, ΔB_t, the Bank needs a projection for the money multiplier $E(\Delta m_{t+1} | \Delta z_{t+1}, \zeta_t) = \beta\Delta z_{t+1} + g(\zeta_t)$, where the stochastic vector ζ_t stands for all relevant information used at time t, and a relationship between the monetary base and the operating target, $\Delta B_{t+1} = \alpha\Delta z_{t+1} + f(\zeta_t)$. This yields the initial target value at the beginning of a month for the money market rate,

$$\Delta z^*_{t+1} = [\Delta M^*_{t+1} - g(\zeta_t) - f(\zeta_t)]/(\alpha + \beta). \tag{7}$$

If this target was strictly implemented throughout the month, the monthly monetary control error would be the sum of the forecast errors for the monetary base, $\varepsilon_{B,t+1} = \Delta B_{t+1} - \alpha\Delta z^*_{t+1} - f(\zeta_t)$ and the forecast error for the multiplier, $\varepsilon_{m,t+1} = \Delta m_{t+1} - \beta\Delta z^*_{t+1} - g(\zeta_t)$, i.e., $\varepsilon_{Mt+1} = \varepsilon_{B,t+1} + \varepsilon_{m,t+1}$. However, since the development of the monetary base is observable for the central bank throughout the month, the operating

---

[8] The assumption $E\varepsilon_{Mt-j}\Delta x_{t-k} < -0.5\sigma^2_m$ would have the implausible implication that the Bank can reduce the variance of inflation by increasing the variance of the monetary control error.

target can be adjusted during the month and the multiplier forecast can be updated, using the daily observations of the money market rate and the monetary base. This implies that the standard deviation, σ_m, of the monthly forecast error $\epsilon_{m,t+1}$ can be regarded as an upper limit of the standard deviation of the monthly money stock control error - the achievable standard deviation must be smaller since the Bank can use more information than what is contained in $E(\Delta m_{t+1} | \Delta z_{t+1}, \zeta_t)$. We will use this implication to estimate the minimum degree of control precision achievable before and since monetary union empirically.

3.2   Estimates of Money Demand and Multiplier Models

As in the US, there has been a lively debate over the existence of a stable money demand function for West Germany since the early 1970s. Many authors claimed that the demand for money was empirically instable because they had found significant parameter variation in their estimated money demand functions.[9] Thus, they concluded that the Bundesbank's monetary strategy was not well-grounded. Neumann and von Hagen (1987) and von Hagen and Neumann (1988), in contrast, argued that this result was a statistical artefact mainly due to dynamic misspecification. Using the methodology developed by Hendry (1980) and Hendry et al. (1982, 1984), they developed empirical representations of the velocity of money over the period from 1962 through 1984 which pass a large number of tests addressing various alternative forms of instability. Furthermore, they showed that the right-hand-side variables of their regressions passed tests for strong and weak exogeneity relative to the dependent variable, which justified the interpretation of these models as empirical representations of the demand for money. Recently, Röger and Herz (1990) have shown that the dynamic specifications used in these two papers - which include error-correction terms and fairly extensive short-run dynamics - can be greatly simplified, if one recognizes a shift in the seasonal pattern of the income variable in the mid-1970s.

Here, we follow their approach and estimate the following general model for the velocity of money:

$$(1 - \gamma_3(L))\Delta v_t = \gamma_0 + \Sigma_{j=1,3}\gamma_{1,j}S_{j,t} + \Sigma_{j=1,3}\gamma_{2,j}S^*_{j,t} + \qquad (8)$$

$$\gamma_4(L)\Delta y_t + \gamma_5(L)\Delta i_t + \gamma_6(L)\Delta\Delta p_t + \gamma_7 v_{t-1} + \gamma_8 y_{t-1} + \gamma_9 i_{t-1} + u_t,$$

---

[9] In contrast, Langfeldt and Lehment (1980) define stability as irrelevance of 'special factors' such as changes in the ratio of currency to demand deposits in the money demand function. They find that their money demand function is empirically unstable. Buscher (1984) allows for stochastic parameter variation and defines stability as stationarity of the parameter process. He finds that stationarity cannot be rejected empirically.

where the regression error u_t is defined as a serially uncorrelated, normally distributed random variable with expectation zero and stochastically independent of the other arguments. The terms $\gamma_j(L)$ are polynomials in the lag operator, L. $S_{j,t}$ and $S^*_{j,t}$ are seasonal dummy variables; the variables S^* are zero up to the first quarter of 1973, they capture the change in the seasonal pattern reported by Röger and Herz.

Our empirical work uses quarterly data. Money, either M1 or M3, is measured as averages over three end-of-month balances; the interest rate variable is the quarterly average yield of government bonds. In the German financial system, where private non-banks have no access to interbank money markets and a short-term T-bill market does not exist, the yield on government bonds can be regarded as the appropriate opportunity cost variable in the demand for money. While M1 balances do not include interest-bearing deposits in Germany, it would be desirable to net out the interest paid on savings deposits and time deposits from the opportunity cost in the demand for M3. Data limitations do not, however, allow us to do that. The fact that interest rates on savings deposit have almost no variance during the sample period means that for this part of M3 the use of the bond yield does not create a serious measurement problem. Output is defined as GNP, measured at annualized rates. Although, in a study of money demand, national income may be regarded as a more satisfactory transactions variable, we use GNP since national income data does not yet exist for East Germany. Inflation is defined in terms of the rate of change of the consumer price level.[10]

The last line of equation (8) contains the error-correction term, which represents the long-run relationship between money, prices, and output. This relationship can be expressed by solving the error-correction term for the long-run equilibrium price level,

$$p^* = m - (1/\gamma_7)[(\gamma_7 + \gamma_8)y + \gamma_9 i]. \tag{9}$$

Note that, in a recent study of the long-run relationship between money, output and prices in Germany, the Bundesbank has argued that the typical lag between an increase in p^* and an increase in the actual price level is ten quarters (Monatsbericht, January 1992).

To investigate the impact of German monetary union, we first estimate velocity models of this type using data from 1965 through the second quarter of 1990. Table 2 summarizes our estimates. We begin with broad specifications allowing for up to five lags in each of the lag polynomials γ_3 to γ_6. The table indicates that these

---

[10] The price index used is the index of cost of living of average households of employed persons; it includes seasonal items such as food and energy.

specifications pass tests for serial correlation of and normality of the residuals.[11] Next, we reduce these specifications. The stepwise elimination of regressors is guided by the triple condition that each reduction must not lead to violations of the serial non-correlation and the normality characteristics of the residuals, nor worsen the information content of the empirical model as measured by Aikaike's AIC criterion. The resulting, preferred specifications are highly significant, with R^2s of 0.94 for the M1 velocity and of 0.77 for the M3 velocity.

Next, we subject these specifications to a number of specification and stability tests. The ARCH statistics report tests for fourth-order ARCH effects, they indicate no such effects in both cases. H_{73} and H_{79} report the result of White's (1980) test for heteroskedasticity of the residuals before and after 1973, the breakdown of the Bretton Woods system, and 1979, the start of the EMS. For the M1 velocity, we found a significant increase in the standard error by 41 percent after 1973. The estimates and statistics shown in table 2 for the preferred specification of this velocity all refer to GLS estimates adjusting for the change in variance.

The M3 velocity does not exhibit heteroskedasticity. The S_{73} and S_{79} statistics show no evidence of structural breaks in 1973, nor in 1979. The NLin test looks at the significance of the squared regressors in the velocity equations to check for possible non-linearities. Trend and AR are the statistics of tests for time-trending parameters and stochastic parameter variation with a first-order autoregressive parameter structure; no evidence for a violation of the constant-parameter assumption is found.[12]

Finally, the statistics FOR(8) are out-of-sample prediction tests for structural stability.[13] The test statistics indicate no parameter variation.

---

[11] Neumann and von Hagen (1987, 1988) and von Hagen (1986) report test statistics showing that velocity and multiplier have unit roots, so that differencing the data is appropriate to achieve stationarity. Here, we do not reproduce those tests. Note, however, that the absence of serial correlation of the residuals of the model in first differences is consistent with the stationarity assumption.

[12] Note that the latter three tests include all parameters except the intercept and seasonal dummy.

[13] For these tests, we estimate the models using data only up to the last quarter of 1987. The parameter estimates thus obtained are taken to compute out-of-sample prediction errors for the eight quarters up to the last quarter of 1989.

Table 2

Estimates of Velocity Functions, 1965 - 89
M1 velocity

$(1 - .05L^1 - .07L^4)\Delta VM1_t = -.012 + .069S_1 + .013S_3 + .015S_1^* + .021S_2^* + .021S_3^*$
   (1.9) (2.3)   (2.4) (12.9) (2.9) (2.0)   (3.5)   (4.1)

$+ .45(1 + .29L^2 + .46L^3 - .31L^3S^*)\Delta Y_t + .0036\Delta i_t$
(9.4) (2.9)   (3.1)   (1.6)   (4.1)

$- .017(VM1_{t-1} - .125i_{t-1})$
(5.8)   (4.7)

Broad specification: AIC = -413; S.E. = 0.010; $Q_{12}[\chi^2(7)] = 7.9$; $P_{normal} > .15$

Selected specification: AIC = -439   S.E. = 0.097

$R^2 = 0.94$	$F_{86,10} = 89.6$	$P_{normal} > 0.15$
$ARCH[\chi^2(4)] = 7.0$	$Q_{12}[\chi^2(10] = 15.0$	$S_{73}[\chi^2(8)] = 10.5$
$S_{79}[\chi^2(7)] = 9.6$	$NLin[\chi^2(8)] = 9.9$	$Trend[\chi^2(8)] = 7.7$
$AR[\chi^2(8)] = 4.7$	$H_{73}[\chi^2(1)] = 0.0$	$H_{79}[\chi^2(1)] = 1.1$
$FOR(8)[\chi^2(8)] = 10.1$		

M3 velocity

$(1 - .15L^3 - .20L^4)\Delta VM3_t = .12 + .021S_1 + .015S_2 + .018S_3 + .01S_2^* + .006S_3^*$
   (2.2) (3.0)   (1.2) (6.7) (3.5)   (4.3)   (2.2)   (1.4)

$+ .89(1 - .13L^2)\Delta y_t + .005\Delta i_t$
(8.6) (1.5)   (2.9)

$-.06(VM3_{t-1} + .32y_{t-1} - .041i_{t-1})$
(2.3)   (1.4)   (3.2)

Broad specification: AIC = -448; S.E. = 0.0088; $Q_{12}[\chi^2(7)] = 10.6$; $P_{normal} > .15$

Selected specification: AIC = -465   S.E. = 0.0085

$R^2 = 0.77$;	$F_{81,13} = 21.9$;	$P_{normal} > .15$
$ARCH[\chi^2(4)] = 2.8$; $Q_{12}[\chi^2(10)] = 8.0$;		$S_{73}[\chi^2(8)] = 6.7$
$S_{79}[\chi^2(8)] = 6.3$:	$NLin[\chi^2(8)] = 7.2$	$Trend[\chi^2(8)] = 12.3$
$AR[\chi^2(8)] = 7.9$	$H_{73}[\chi^2(1)] = 0.0$	$H_{79}[\chi^2(1)] = 0.7$
$F\ OR(8)[\chi^2(8)] = 3.4$		

Table 2 (cont'd)

Notes: Absolute t-ratios in parenthesis. F is the F-test on model significance, P_{normal} the marginal probability of a test on normality of the residuals, ARCH the test statistic for 4th order ARCH, Q_{12} the Box-Ljung statistic for 12th order resiudal autocorrelation, S_{73} and S_{79} the tests for structural breaks in 1973 and 1979, NLin the statistic for model-nonlinearity, Trend the statistic for time-trending parameters, AR the statistic for first-order autoregressive, stochastic parameter variation, H_{73} and H_{79} White's statistics for heteroskedasticity before and after 1973 and 1979, respectively, FOR(8) the eight-quarter out-of-sample prediction test. $[\chi^2(k)]$ indicates that a statistic has a χ^2 distribution with k degrees of freedom under the Null. The dummy variable S^* on Δy_{t-3} in the VM1 equation is zero before 1979 and one thereafter.

Note that the seasonal dummies take significantly different values after 1973. Furthermore, the parameter on real GNP lagged by three quarters in the M1 equation changes values after 1979. Both findings can be attributed to the changes in the seasonality pattern of real GNP in the mid-1970s pointed out by Röger and Herz.

In sum, we corroborate earlier results of a stable, constant-parameter empirical representation of German demand for money in the form of a velocity equation. Table 2 shows that the parameter estimates have the expected signs. The short-run income elasticity of money demand is found significantly below one, as indicated by the significant coefficients on current and lagged real income, a result that is in line with earlier findings. The error-correction term in the model for M1 indicates, however, that the long-run elasticity of the demand for money is one with respect to both the price level and output, it is 0.125 with respect to the government bond yield. The long-run elasticity of the demand for M3 is less interest-elastic, while its long-run elasticity with respect real output is below one, but not significantly so; finally, the long-run elasticity with respect to the price level is, again, one.

Next, we turn to the development of money multiplier forecast models, using time-series techniques. Table 3 summarizes the results. Both multipliers were differenced to remove trend and seasonality. The transfer function input Z_t is the money market rate on overnight money, the Bundesbank's operating target, differenced in the same way as the multipliers. The table reports the results of some basic specification tests. Residuals pass tests for serial correlation, normality and ARCH effects measured up to six lags. The table indicates standard deviations of the multiplier forecast errors of 2.3 percent for M1 and 2.4 percent for M3. This confirms previous results for the early 1980s (von Hagen, 1986). Since the monetary target is expressed in quarterly terms, it is worth noting that these estimates imply a standard control error of 1.3 percent for M1 and 1.4 percent for M3.

4.   UNIFICATION EFFECTS

In a completely integrated national economy, the concept of a regional demand for and supply of money is empirically not well-defined, since residents in one part of the country can hold and make use of deposits at commercial banks in other parts of the country and banks with branches across the country can use central bank deposits as reserves against deposits irrespective of where the depositor resides or his deposits was made. With the inception of the monetary union in Germany, therefore, money demand and supply would only be relevant concepts for East and West Germany together.

Table 3
Multiplier and Components Forecast Models

Var.	Model	Q_{12}	P_n	STD	ARCH$_6$
$\Delta\Delta_{12}m$ 1	$x_t = (1-.72L)(1+.18L^6)(1-.76L_{12})\varepsilon_t - .0059Z_t$ (11.2) (2.0) (12.5) (2.2)	5.9	>.15	.023	4.8
$\Delta\Delta_{12}m$ 3	$x_t=(1-.73L)(1-.79L_{12})\varepsilon_t - .012(1.0 + 1.0L)Z_t$ (11.0) (12.0) (2.6) (2.9)	10.7	>.15	.024	2.8
$\Delta\Delta_{12}k$	$(1+.90L)(1+.60L^2)x_t = .005Z_t + (1 - .69L)\varepsilon_t$ (12.8) (8.6) (2.4) (10.5)	14.7	>.15	.020	3.1
Δr	$(1+.15L^4)x_t = 0.047(1+.69L)^{-1}Z_t + (1-.54L)\varepsilon_t$ (1.7) (4.7) (6.5) (7.1)	14.3	>.15	.051	10.4
$\Delta\Delta_{12}t$	$(1+.18L)x_t = (1-.25L^4)(1-.43L^{12})\varepsilon_t + .029Z_{t-1}$ (2.0) (2.7) (4.9) (5.6)	9.2	>.15	.032	7.1
$\Delta\Delta_{12}s$	$x_t = (1-.58L)(1+.43L^3)(1-.42L^{12})\varepsilon_t +.0039Z_{t-1}$ (7.6) (5.0) (4.3) (1.8)	9.0	>.15	.016	12.3

Note: Q_{12} is the Box-Ljung portemanteau statistic for serial correlation with 12 lags, it is $\chi^2(12)$ under the Null of no correlation. P_n is the marginal probability level of a test for normality of the residuals. STD is the standards deviation of the monthly forecast error. ARCH$_6$ is the ARCH test statistic with six lags, it is $\chi^2(6)$ under the Null.

Note that this error is biased upwards by the use of end-of-months data for the money supply and the monetary base; Neumann and von Hagen (1987) show that the standard forecast errors are about half that if the base is measured in terms of monthly averages of daily data. The same table also reports time-series forecast models for the components of the multipliers, the ratio of currency held by non-banks to demand deposits, k, the ratio of time deposits to demand deposits, t, the ratio of savings deposits at statutory notice to demand deposits, s, and ratio of bank reserves to demand deposits, r. This allows us to identify the main sources of uncertainty in the multiplier forecasts. The table shows that the savings deposit ratio and the currency ratio are better predictable than the other two, the reserves ratio yielding the largest forecast error.

The particularities of the German monetary union, however, allow us to consider the two regions separately at least for a while: With the lack of modern tele-communications in East Germany, the need to build up a modern banking industry, including a payments system, largely from scratch and integrate it into the West German one, and the fact that only bank accounts of East German residents were converted into DM, it is plausible to assume that, at least for some time after monetary union, bank deposits at East German banks are held by East German residents, and that East Germans do not hold large deposits at banks in West Germany. With this in mind, we can look at deposits at East German banks in 1990 and 1991 to infer the behavior of the regional demand and supply of money. Such data is provided by the Bundesbank through December 1991.[14] Cash holdings of East German non-bank residents are, of course, not directly observable. Therefore, to estimate an East German and a West German M1, we assume that the currency ratio is the same in both parts of the country.

To express the demand for money in terms of velocity, an appropriate transactions variable must be found. Since the relevant consideration is the use of money as a medium of exchange in purchases of goods and services, the transactions variable should reflect the volume of the domestic transactions made by domestic residents. In a closed economy, nominal GNP can be used as a proxy, since GNP is the same as domestic absorption. Normally, GNP remains a good proxy in an open economy, since the difference between absorption and GNP (exports less imports or capital inflows) is relatively small. This is not true, however, for East Germany in 1990 and 1991: For example, in 1991, domestic aggregate demand exceeded GNP by about 100 percent, reflecting the inflow of capital though private markets and, most of all, the fiscal system. One may, therefore, argue that domestic absorption is the better transactions variable in East Germany. Subsequently, we will calculate velocity on the basis of absorption in East Germany.[15]

---

[14] Since January 1992, East German banks are no longer required to report their regional deposits on a monthly basis. Quarterly figures will still be published for some time.

[15] For this purpose, we need quarterly estimates of aggregate demand and nominal GNP. Quarterly estimates of East German GDP at prices of the second half of 1990 are available from DIW (1992a). Estimates of semi-annual nominal GNP and aggregate demand are published in DIW (1992b) for 1991 and in Statistisches Bundesamt (1992) for the second half of 1992. Our estimates of quarterly GNP and aggregate demand use these figures and assume that the quarterly pattern of the nominal aggregates is the same as that of real GNP. Our estimates of quarterly real aggregate demand used subsequently assume that the relevant price deflator is the West German GDP deflator. Note that the velocity for West Germany continues to be computed on the basis of GNP.

Figure 1 shows the M1 velocity from 1988 through 1991. Apart from the more pronounced seasonal drop in the last quarter of 1991, the behavior of the East German velocity parallels the West German one in a striking way. Figure 2 shows the corresponding picture for the velocity of broad money, M3. East German M3 velocity followed the seasonal drop in late 1990, but then rose by about fifty percent in the following two quarters, stabilizing only towards the end of 1991. Comparing the two figures suggests that the demand for broad money has been more strongly affected by adjustment processes since currency unification than the more transactions-oriented demand for narrow money, M1. At the same time, the figures show that the velocity of money for the entire currency area was less volatile and less subject to lasting level adjustments than the velocity measured separately for either part of the currency area. This suggests that the financial integration of the two parts proceeded quite rapidly and implies that an attempt to target 'West German M3' as the Bundesbank undertook it in 1990 in spite of the currency union, may lead to more interest rate and price level instability than targeting the money supply for the entire area right after currency unification.

Figure 1
M1 Velocity 1988-91

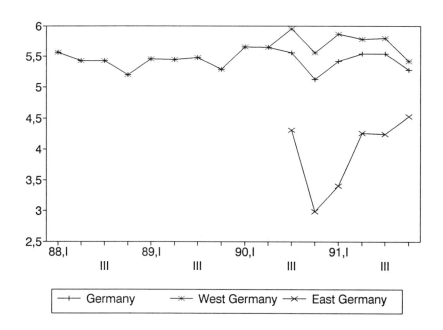

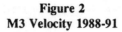

Figure 2
M3 Velocity 1988-91

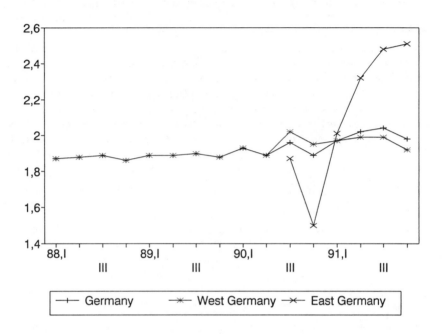

To see how unification affects the performance of our velocity equations, we compute the six-quarter out-of-sample prediction errors using our preferred specifications from table 2.

Figure 3 plots these errors and compares them with the (in-sample) errors from 1988 through 1990, II. The largest prediction errors occurred for the M1 velocity immediately after unification. The errors for the M3 velocity are smaller in late 1990 but larger in early 1991. Table 4 summarizes the statistical characteristics of these residuals. Clearly, unification has added monetary policy uncertainty in the sense that the standard error of quarterly velocity estimates has increased. Note, however, that the relative increase in uncertainty is larger for the M3 velocity, with standard errors a rising by 263 percent, than for the M1 velocity, whose standard error rises by 118 percent. In contrast, the absolute increase in uncertainty is quite similar for both velocities, namely 1.11 percentage points for M1 and 0.92 for M3. This suggests that targeting the narrow, more transactions-oriented aggregate would have been preferable to targeting M3 from the point of view of minimizing the additional monetary policy uncertainty after currency unification.

Figure 3
Residuals from Velocity Equation 1988-91

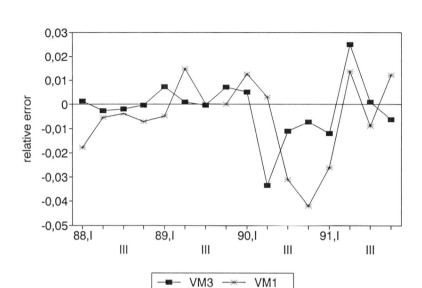

Table 4 also indicates that our estimated velocity equations continue to track the velocities on average, i.e., the mean prediction error does not turn statistically different from zero after unification. However, the stability tests FOR(6) indicate that the hypothesis of parameter stability must be rejected for the M3 velocity. In contrast, it can be statistically accepted for the velocity of narrow money. This indicates that the more transactions-oriented demand for money underwent an increase in volatility with unification, but no significant structural break in the sense of a change in the income or interest elasticities. To pursue this argument further, we estimate our velocity functions over the enlarged sample period including 1991, IV, and add two dummy variables to the model, one, K1, which is one after 1990,II, and one, K2, which is one in 1990,III, minus 1 in 1990,IV and zero thereafter.

These dummies are significant in the M1 velocity equations: The parameter estimates (t-ratios) are -0.037 (4.49) and 0.022 (1.94). Next, we take the squared residuals from this estimation and regress them on the dummy K1. The $\chi^2(1)$ statistic for heteroskedasticity obtained from this regression is 5.9, which is significant at the one-percent level. Finally, we divide the 1991 out-of-sample errors by the appropriate adjustment factors to remove the heteroskedasticity and recalculate the out-of-sample prediction test statistics for parameter stability based on these residuals.

The resulting number is 3.12 and is not statistically significant. This corroborates the conclusion that the demand function for M1 is stable up to an increase in stochastic variation. Regressing the M3 velocity on the same dummies results in no significant parameters. Hence, we have to reject stability of the velocity equation. Thus, our earlier hypothesis, that the demand for M3 was more strongly affected by adjustment processes than the demand for M1 is supported by the statistical evidence.

Table 4

Residuals from Out-of-Sample Velocity Estimation

	1988,I - 1990,I		1990, III - 1991, IV		
	mean (percent)	STD (percent)	mean (percent)	STD (percent)	FOR(6) [$\chi^2(6)$]
VM1	-0.1	0.94	-1.1	2.05	9.0
VM3	0.2	0.35	-0.2	1.27	14.4

Note: FOR(6) is the six-quarter out-of-sample predicition test for structural stability of the velocity equation. Errors have been computed adjusting for the shift in the level of real GNP in 1990:III. STD is the standard deviation.

This is consistent with the view that 'learning' processes with regard to the new portfolio choices in a modern financial environment affect the more speculative-oriented part of the demand for money (savings and time deposits) more than the transactions-oriented part. It is plausible if one assumes that the former are closer substitutes for non-monetary assets - which were unavailable before monetary union - than transactions balances.[16]

Figure 4 provides a picture of the money multipliers shortly before and after unification. Note that the M1 multiplier started to rise immediately after unification. Altogether, its increase contributed about 20 percent to the rise in M1 in the last two quarters of 1990. At the beginning of 1991, the M1 multiplier fell sharply. From then on, it seems to move around an average of about 1.93, compared to about 1.83 prior to unification, but with much more pronounced seasonal spikes in the mid-year and at the end of the year. Thus, unification seems to have had two basic effects on the multiplier: an upwards shift of around five percent, and a stronger seasonal element. The effect on the M3 multiplier was similar. Here, we see again a lasting shift in the

---

[16]   Insofar as it suggests the existence of a well-behaved household demand function for narrow money in East Germany before monetary union, this result is also consistent with Lane's (1992) results for pre-reform Poland.

mean, although of a smaller size and occurring earlier than the shift in the M1 multiplier. Again, an increase in the volatility of the multiplier is recognizable and the post-unification seasonal spikes may be more pronounced.

Figure 4
Money Multipliers, Germany, 1988-92

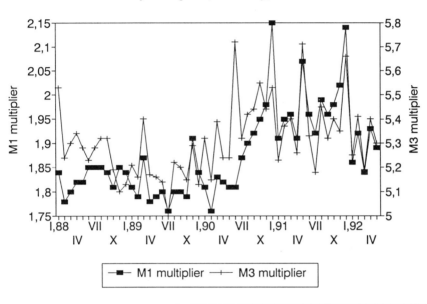

To see how unification affected the central bank's ability to target the nominal money supply, we take our multiplier forecast models from table 3 and run an ex-ante forecasting experiment starting in January of 1989. For each month, the models are estimated using data available up to the forecast period.[17] Thus, the experiment mimics the Bundesbank's task of predicting the multiplier. Following unification, we allow for level adjustments of the multiplier by introducing dummy variables. The variable F1 is zero up to July 1990 and one from then on, the variable F2 is one in July 1990 and zero elsewhere. Both are introduced for the multiplier forecasts after July 1990, after unification occurred. That is, we overestimate the true forecast error in July 1990 by assuming that the multiplier effect of currency unification was completely unexpected. A similar pair of dummies is introduced in the same way after January 1991, to account for the effect of the conversion of former East German savings deposits.

---

[17] This assumes that the central bank's operating target, Z_t, is held equal to its desired value throughout the month.

Figure 5 plots the ex-ante prediction errors. It is obvious that the unification and the conversion effect at the end of 1990 lead to large spikes. Since the multiplier models are mainly of a moving-average type, these large errors would carry through the predictions in subsequent months. To remove this carry-over effect, we adjust the models by replacing the large errors in July and December 1990 and January 1991 in the later predictions by an assumed error of one standard deviation in the same direction. Since the relevant prediction occurs at least one month after observing the errors estimated originally, this procedure is admissible, as the central bank would have had the information necessary to do the same, and would likely have done so to smooth subsequent forecasts. The figure indicates that, apart from the spikes at unification and at the turn of the years, there is some increase in the forecasting

Figure 5
Multiplier Forecast Errors 1989-91

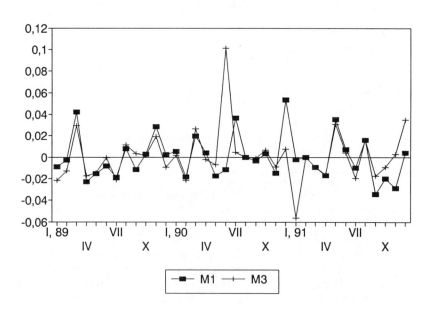

uncertainty. This is confirmed in table 5, which shows that the standard M1-multiplier forecast error increases by about 27 percent from 1.74 percent in the first 18 months of the experiment to 2.22 percent in the post-unification period, while the standard M3-multiplier forecast error rises by about 24 percent, from 1.58 percent to 1.96 percent. Both post-unification standard errors do not exceed the sample averages shown in table 3. Thus, apart from the level adjustments of the multipliers around the two critical dates, our models continue to capture the development of both multipliers with reasonable precision. This implies that the control uncertainty with respect to the money supply has not increased significantly with monetary union.

5.   MONETARY POLICY WITH UNIFICATION

The main results of the previous section can be summarized in the following three propositions: (1), Monetary union increased the volatility of velocity shocks in the following quarters; (2), the stability of the money demand function must be rejected for the broad monetary aggregate M3 but can be accepted for M1 conditional on the appropriate choice of the transactions variable; (3), following a level adjustment in the portfolio coefficients and, hence, the money multipliers, post-union monetary control uncertainty does not exceed pre-union levels significantly.

These propositions imply that the central bank's operating regime for targeting the money supply remained viable after monetary union and that monetary targeting remained an appropriate monetary strategy to reach price stability. However, the greater stability of the M1 velocity after monetary union means that a narrow monetary target would have been preferable. Furthermore, the increase in the variance of transitory shocks to the change in velocity suggests that the Bundesbank should have lessened its response to recently observed changes to avoid unwarranted reactions to monetary fluctuations.

Actual monetary policy continued to target West German M3 in the two quarters following monetary union. In fact, in its December 1990 report, the Bank argued that the enlargement of the currency area had proceeded rather smoothly and that the monetary developments in East Germany had not posed any serious problems. In view of this, the Bank felt that it could continue its policy without major adjustments. Yet, in the discussion of the considerations leading to its monetary target for 1991, the Bank admitted an increase in monetary uncertainty from the money-demand side. However, it argued that the signalling effect of a monetary target was all the more important to assure the public of the continuity of the Bank's price stability-oriented policy and to avoid a rise in inflation expectations (Report, December 1990).

Table 5

Ex Ante Multiplier Forecast Errors

	January 1989 - June 1990		July 1990 - December 1991	
	mean (percent)	STD (percent)	mean (percent)	STD (percent)
m1	-0.1	1.74	0.09	2.22
m3	-0.2	1.58	-0.2	1.96

Note: STD is the standard deviation.

For 1991, the Bundesbank announced a target M3 growth rate of four to six percent for Germany as a whole, based on a target inflation rate of two percent (Annual Report, 1990). This target was revised downwards by 100 basis points in July. The Bank argued that this was consistent with a target rate of increase in the price level of two percent for 1991 (Monthly Report, July 1991) and would not harm real output performance in West Germany (Monthly Report, September 1991).

Yet, a restrictive effect is indeed very likely, if the targeted money growth rate of four percent is held against the real output growth rates of early 1991.

To assess the performance of monetary policy since monetary union, we use our velocity models and solve the long-run parts for the equilibrium price level, see equ. (11). Figure 6 shows the equilibrium price levels computed from the velocity models. The graph based on M1 shows an acceleration in the equilibrium price level already as a result of the monetary expansion in late 1989. This and the monetary union caused a shift in the equilibrium price level until the third quarter of 1990. Assuming a lag of about six quarters between changes in the growth of the equilibrium and the actual price level, which is consistent with the Bundesbank's estimate, table 1 indicates that this acceleration occurs in the actual price level in early 1991. Following this level adjustment, the equilibrium price level fell in early 1991 to remain flat for the rest of the period. Thus, judging from the equilibrium indicated by our empirical model, monetary policy was, indeed, overly restrictive in 1991 and likely contributed to the downturn in economic growth. The graph based on M3 leaves a similar impression.

Figure 6, then, poses the question, why did the Bundesbank conduct an overly restrictive policy in a period where real growth was badly needed to over-come the problems of German unification? The explanation we propose rests on

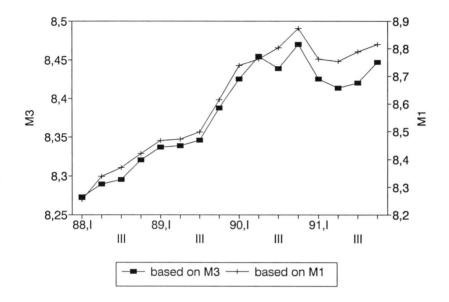

Figure 6
Equilibrium Price Level 1988-91

institutional grounds. The months following monetary union confronted the Bundesbank with a strategic dilemma. As indicated in Table 1, the gap between the overall increase in the money stock due to monetary union and the increase in total output created a potential for price level adjustment. It is clear that, in contrast to the Bank's repeated suggestions (e.g. Annual Report 1990, Monthly Report July 1991), this potential remained even if the East German money stock M3 declined soon after July 1990, since on a macro level this decline only reflects a redistribution of the total monetary balances in Germany. In fact, the West German money stock increased faster than the average rates indicated in the table. This monetary pressure for a price level adjustment was further augmented by a rise in excise taxes in mid-1991, which, according to the Bundesbank, contributed an estimated effect of 50 basis points (Monthly Report, July 1991), and the need for a real exchange rate appreciation in the presence of fixed nominal rates with Germany's most important trading partners to accommodate the fall in the current account balance.

Theoretically, the Bundesbank's response could have been to accept this need for a level adjustment, since a one-time shift in the price level does not affect its policy target, the underlying rate of inflation.[18] Thus, there was no need for a restrictive monetary policy in 1991. But this simple conclusion presupposes that the private sector looks at the situation in the same way and does not change its inflation expectations although the observed rate of change in the price level accelerates. That is, the private sector can distinguish level changes from the underlying trend and the credibility of the Bundesbank's monetary policy remains unaffected by monetary union. Even if the former is assumed, however, the Bundesbank may have feared that monetary union did weaken its credibility and, hence, caused an increase in inflation expectations. Apart from the increase in monetary uncertainty, two policy factors contributed to this perceived credibility loss: The public conflict with the Federal Government over the appropriate terms of monetary union, which left the impression that the Bank was overruled by the government, and, from the Fall of 1990 on, the Bank's repeated public statements that German fiscal policy posed an immediate threat to monetary stability, which created the impression of a lasting conflict between the Bank and the government with an uncertain outcome. The public impression of a conflict between the Bank and the Federal Government was strengthened by the fact that the President of the Bundesbank, Mr. Pöhl, left the Bank quite unexpectedly in the Summer of 1991, being replaced in the Bundesbank Council by Mr. Tietmeyer, a former Finance Ministry official designated to become Bundesbank president after a brief *interregnum* of Mr. Schlesinger, and by the fact that the Bank repeatedly overestimated the public sector deficit in 1990/91 by margins of 20 to 30 percent of the deficit in its attacks on the stance of public finances. In addition, the Bank began to argue publicly against wage policies in Germany which it considered to be an important cause of the acceleration in the price level since early 1991. In this situation, tightening monetary policy in response to the acceleration in the price level gave the Bank an opportunity to reassure the public of its firm position on low inflation and to reassert publicly its political independence. Thus, the dilemma was a choice between a neutral monetary policy, accepting the price level increase and sticking to a rate of monetary expansion consistent with the target inflation rate and strong economic growth, and a restrictive monetary policy to restore the perceived credibility damages from monetary union at the risk of losing real output growth. The developments of 1991 suggest that the Bundesbank decided to give greater weight to its institutional interest in credibility.

---

[18] Sargent and Velde (1990) argued in this way to point out that the much-debated conversion rate of Marks into DM was irrelevant from the point of view of inflation.

6.   CONCLUSIONS

This paper has presented an empirical analysis of Germany's experience with monetary union. Judging from the empirical results, monetary union has increased monetary uncertainty in the sense of greater volatility of velocity shocks and money multiplier forecast errors. The portfolio adjustment processes have affected the demand for broad money more strongly than the demand for narrow money. Overall, however, the Bundesbank's monetary strategy of targeting a monetary aggregate was not invalidated. However, a re-orientation of the strategy towards the use of a narrow target aggregate and less reaction to short-term price, output and velocity fluctuations would have been desirable. For the conduct of monetary policy in other socialist economies in transition, our results suggest that targeting a transactions-oriented monetary aggregate is a viable monetary strategy to achieve monetary stability. For a future European monetary union, which would make additional choices for speculative monetary assets available to the private sector, a similar suggestion holds, namely that targeting a European transactions-oriented money stock would be preferable to targeting a broad aggregate.

At the same time, reviewing the conduct of monetary policy after German monetary union reveals a basic institutional problem: How to prevent an independent central bank, which is now generally viewed as desirable to achieve longrun monetary stability, from making policy choices which serve its institutional interest in preserving its credibility more than contributing to macro-economic stability. Obviously, this problem does not arise if the central bank enjoys complete credibility. Short of a good suggestion of how this can be achieved, we conclude that the German experience indicates that there is a real cost of imperfectly credible central bank independence.

REFERENCES

Buscher, Herbert (1984), 'The Stability of West German Demand for Money', *Weltwirtschaftliches Archiv* 120, 256-78.

Deutsche Bundesbank, *Monthly Reports*, various issues.

Deutsche Bundesbank (1991), *Geschäftsbericht für 1990*, Frankfurt.

Deutsche Bundesbank (1992), *Geschäftsbericht für 1991*, Frankfurt.

Deutsches Institut für Wirtschaftsforschung (DIW) (1992a), 'Gesamtwirtschaftliche und unternehmerische Anpassungsprozesse in Ostdeutschland'. *Wochenbericht* 59, No. 12/13

Deutsches Institut für Wirtschaftsforschung (DIW) (1992b), 'Die Lage der Weltwirtschaft und der deutschen Wirtschaft im Frühjahr 1992'. *Wochenbericht* 59, No. 16/17.

Hendry, David F. (1980), 'Predictive Failure and Econometric Modelling in Macroeconomics: The Transactions Demand for Money' in: Paul Ormerod (ed.), *Modelling the Economy* London.

Hendry, David F., Adrian R. Pagan and J. D. Sargan (1983), 'Dynamic Specification'. in: Zvi Grilliches and Michael D. Intrilligator (eds.) *Handbook of Econometrics* Amsterdam: North Holland.

Hendry, David F., and Jean F. Richard (1982), 'On the Formulation of Empirical Models in Dynamic Econometrics' *Journal of Econometrics* 20, 3-34.

Lane, Timothy D. (1992), 'Household Demand for Money in Poland: Theory and Evidence'. Working Paper WP/92/6, International Monetary Fund

Langfeldt, E. and Harmen Lehment (1980), 'Welche Bedeutung haben Sonder faktoren für die Erklärung der Geldnachfrage der BRD?' *Weltwirtschaftliches Archiv* 116, 669-84.

Neumann, Manfred J. M. and Jürgen von Hagen (1987), 'Theoretische und empirische Grundlagen von Geldmengenzielen' in: A. Gutowski (ed.) *Geldpolitische Regelbindung: theoretische Entwicklungen und empirische Befunde.* Berlin: Duncker & Humblodt.

Neumann, Manfred J. M. and Jürgen von Hagen (1991), 'Monetary Policy in Germany' in: Dominick Salvatore and Michele Fratianni (eds.), *Handbook of Monetary Policy*, London: Greenwood Press.

Röger, Werner, and Bernhard Herz (1990), 'Evaluating Conflicting Stability Results in German Money Demand Regressions', *Weltwirtschaftliches Archiv* 126, 691-708.

Sargent, Thomas J. and Velde, F. R. (1990), 'The Analytics of German Monetary Unification'. Federal Reserve Bank of San Francisco *Economic Review.*

Statistisches Bundesamt (1992), *Statistisches Jahrbuch für das vereinte Deutschland.* Wiesbaden.

von Hagen, Jürgen (1986), *Strategien kurzfristiger Geldmengensteuerung* Hamburg: Weltarchiv.

von Hagen, Jürgen (1988), 'Alternative Operating Regimes for Money Stock Control in West Germany: An Empirical Evaluation'. *Weltwirtschaftliches Archiv* 124, 89-109.

von Hagen, Jürgen (1989), 'Monetary Targeting Under Exchange Rate Constraints: The Bundesbank in the 1980s'. Federal Reserve Bank of St. Louis *Review* 71 No. 5, 53-69.

von Hagen, Jürgen and Manfred J. M. Neumann (1988), 'Instability vs. Dynamics: A Study in West German Demand For Money'. *Journal of Macroeconomics* 10, 327-49.

CHAPTER 10

DESIGNING A CENTRAL BANK IN A FEDERAL SYSTEM: THE DEUTSCHE BUNDESBANK, 1957 - 1992

Susanne Lohmann

1.   INTRODUCTION

Deutsche Mark und Deutsche Bundesbank -- mit einem dunklen Rätsel nähern sich beide ihrem Ende.[1] In November 1990, the presidents of the central banks of the member states of the European Community (EC) published a proposal for the statute of a European central bank (ECB). According to this proposal, the primary objective of the bank will be to maintain price stability. The bank will be required to support the economic policy of the Community, but without prejudice to the objective of price stability. The ECB and its national member banks will be granted independence from political interference. The bank's directorate will be composed of a president, a vice-president and four other members, all of which will be appointed by the European Council for eight years without the possibility of renewal. These appointees will form the bank's council together with the twelve presidents of the national central banks. Decisions will be made by simple majority rule. Generally one member will have one vote, the president a tie-breaking vote; but for some issues weighted voting will apply.[2]

This proposal is not primarily based on theoretical considerations. Instead the design for the ECB mimics, by and large, the design of the Deutsche Bundesbank and is motivated by the celebrated monetary policy performance of its German counterpart. The implicit argument is that Germany's low-inflation monetary policy

---

[1]   Balkhausen 1992, p. 18. ("Shrouded in dark mystery, both the Deutsche Mark and the Deutsche Bundesbank are nearing their end.") German expressions are translated by the author unless otherwise indicated.

[2] See Ausschuß der Präsidenten der Zentralbanken der Mitgliedstaaten der Europäischen Wirtschaftsgemeinschaft (1990) and Fratianni, von Hagen and Waller (1992, pp. 31/32).

is due to the Bundesbank's independence; that the source of the Bundesbank's independence lies in the institutional arrangements underlying German monetary policy; and that these institutional arrangements can be replicated at a European level, resulting in a low-inflation European monetary policy.

There are, however, a number of problems with this line of argument. First, there is some dispute whether institutions or preferences are the driving factor for Germany's low-inflation monetary policy. According to Goodman (1992), the crucial institution is given by the independent Bundesbank that is required by law to pursue the goal of price stability. Other scholars point to Germany's historical experience with hyperinflation. The German public's aversion to inflation and its suspicion of politicians and political parties are invoked as an explanation of why the Bundesbank's independence is a taboo subject in German political discourse (Caesar 1981, pp. 199/200 and 202/203). While the Bundesbank law can in principle be replicated at the European level, the same does not obviously hold for the preferences or attitudes of the German public.

Second, the legal autonomy of the Bundesbank is in fact quite limited.[3] Article 12 of the Bundesbank law stipulates that the Bundesbank is independent of instructions from the federal government, but it also requires the Bundesbank to support the general economic policy of the federal government. This article does not formally specify how a potential conflict between the mandated goal of price stability and competing policy objectives of the government should be resolved. Moreover, the formulation of the price stability goal is ambiguous. Article 3 requires the Bundesbank to "safeguard the currency." This objective could be interpreted as standing for the external stability of the currency (that is, fixed or stable exchange rates) or for its internal stability (that is, a low average inflation rate or a low variability of the price level). Furthermore, the federal government has retained the authority to determine exchange rate arrangements and parities. This division of power has constrained the Bundesbank's discretionary powers, given that Germany was part of the Bretton Woods system and is now a member of the European Monetary System (EMS).[4] Finally, until recently the Bundesbank's independence was not constitutionally guaranteed.[5] The Bundesbank itself can be dissolved at any time by a simple federal law, as stipulated by Article 44 of the Bundesbank law.

---

[3] Indeed, several other central banks have a similar or higher degree of de jure independence (Caesar 1981, p. 167).

[4] The EMS was originally constructed as a system involving symmetric intervention reponsibilities, but de facto the Deutsche Mark has become the anchor currency of the EMS. This development has loosened the constraints on the Bundesbank's discretionary powers.

[5] The revision of the German constitution necessitated by the 1992 Maastricht Treaty will stipulate that the Bundesbank can be replaced only by an independent central bank.

This chapter examines whether Germany's low-inflation monetary policy is due to preferences or institutions. I argue that the public plays the role of an umpire in cases of conflict between the federal government and the Bundesbank. However, the institutional arrangements underlying German monetary policy also matter. The central hypothesis of this chapter is that the federal components of the Bundesbank institution -- in particular, the presence of Land (regional state) appointees on the Bundesbank's council -- are an important source of its autonomy.

In the next section, I review some of the theoretical underpinnings of central bank independence. I then analyze the 1957 replacement of the Bank deutscher Länder by the Deutsche Bundesbank and the 1992 changes to the Bundesbank law necessitated by German unification. Based on the evidence assembled in these two case studies, I assess the empirical contribution of the theories reviewed earlier. Finally, I examine the proposed design for the ECB in the light of the Bundesbank experience.

2.   THEORETICAL   FOUNDATIONS   OF   CENTRAL   BANK AUTONOMY

The Bundesbank is granted some degree of political independence by law; and this chapter will argue that the institutional arrangements underlying German central banking contribute to its independence. Both the Bundesbank law and the Bundesbank institution were devised by German politicians. At first blush, it is surprising that the political principals of the Bundesbank would deliberately design the law and the institution to ensure that the Bundesbank is (at least partially) independent. After all, monetary policy has huge efficiency and distributional effects on the wealth and well-being of political constituencies. Two motivations for such an abdication of political power to a central bank have been identified in the literature: the time-consistency problem and political business cycles in monetary policy.

2.1   The Time-Consistency Problem

The classic time-consistency problem in monetary policy arises from a policymaker's futile attempt to stimulate output above the natural level, resulting in an inflationary bias to discretionary monetary policy (Kydland and Prescott 1977; Barro and Gordon 1983). As a consequence, the policymaker faces a time-consistency problem when she sets monetary policy at her discretion. Wagesetters know that the policymaker has an incentive to stimulate employment and output above the natural level by inflating. They write an inflationary markup into their nominal wage contracts that is sufficiently high to give the inflation-averse policymaker disincentives to stimulate employment and output. As a result, the natural levels of employment and output are achieved on average, while the inflation rate exhibits an inflationary bias.

It is often argued that an appropriately designed central banking institution can mitigate this credibility problem (Taylor 1983, Tabellini 1987).[6] Most prominently, Friedman (1945) proposes that the discretionary powers of the monetary authority should be constrained by the imposition of a simple monetary growth rule.

Friedman's simple rule solves the time-consistency problem in monetary policy but at the price of precluding a flexible response to shocks and unforeseen contingencies. His proposal thus fails to allow for a stabilization role for monetary policy. An appropriately designed central banking institution would retain some flexibility to employ monetary instruments to stabilize employment and output and deal with unforeseen contingencies. A number of institutional arrangements have been proposed that are associated with different tradeoffs between credibility and flexibility considerations (Lohmann 1992).

Flood and Isard (1990) modify Friedman's simple rule, suggesting that the policymaker should follow the simple zero-inflation rule in normal times and deviate from the rule when extreme shocks are realized.[7] If the distribution of shocks is unbounded, such an escape-clause is implemented if the policymaker can ex post renege on the rule at a strictly positive but finite cost. This arrangement mitigates the deadweight loss arising from simple rule's insensitivity to shocks; but the average time-consistent inflation rate is strictly positive.

Rogoff (1985) instead proposes a modification of the discretionary regime. He argues that the inflation bias could be mitigated if the policymaker delegated power to a conservative central banker who places a higher weight on inflation stabilization than does the policymaker. When setting monetary policy at his discretion, the central banker implements a lower average time-consistent inflation rate. However, he does not offset shocks as much as would his political principal.
According to this approach, the degree of central bank conservativism (as reflected in the central banker's relative weight on the output versus inflation objective) is a political choice variable. To ensure that the central bank is controlled by conservatives, the central bank's political principal could make use of the heterogeneity in the society. If the members of the society are heterogeneous and differ in their monetary policy preferences, the policymaker could select a conservative "type" to head the central bank. For example, individuals with professional backgrounds as economists or bankers might be appointed. Another possibility is that a "nonclassical" sector characterized by nominal wage contracts places a higher weight on the stabilization objective than does a "classical" sector

---

[6] Bendor and Lohmann (1993) examine the validity of the assumption implicitly underlying such institutional "solutions" to the time-consistency problem, namely that a policymaker can credibly commit to a central banking institution even though she does not have the ability to make credible monetary policy commitments.

[7] See, however, Lohmann's (1990) critique of Flood and Isard's model.

characterized by competitive labor markets. In this situation, the policymaker could appoint a representative of the classical sector (Waller 1992b). Alternatively, the policymaker could encourage the central bank to be "captured" by interest groups that favor a low-inflation monetary policy. For example, the policymaker could design the central banking institution to ensure that central bankers' career paths are controlled by external interest groups with conservative preferences (Maxfield 1992). Finally, central bankers' preferences could be formed by a strong corporate culture that emphasizes the importance of price stability.

Lohmann (1992) modifies Rogoff's proposal, suggesting that a conservative central banker should be granted only partial independence. The deadweight loss induced by the central banker's distortionary response is larger for extreme shocks. If the policymaker retains the option to override the central banker's decisions at some strictly positive but finite cost, she would induce the central banker to implement a nonlinear policy rule. In normal times, the central banker would set the inflation rate independently at his discretion. In extreme situations, he would implement a flexible escape-clause: the more extreme are the shocks, the more the central banker will be forced to accommodate the policymaker's ex post demands in order to avoid being overridden.

Moreover, Lohmann shows that the discretionary regime, the regimes of full or partial commitment to a simple rule and the regime of a fully independent conservative central banker can be formalized as special cases of her model; these other arrangements are dominated by the regime of a partially independent conservative central banker.

Lohmann's approach is based on the assumption that the degree of central bank independence (corresponding to the political cost of overriding the central banker's decisions) is a political choice variable. To grant some independence to the central bank, the policymaker could make use of legislative transaction costs. If central bank independence were legislated, changes to the legislation would be costly, but not prohibitively so in extreme situations. Moreover, policymakers with different constituencies may have heterogeneous preferences over monetary policy outcomes and consequently over central banking institutions. Legislative transaction costs are arguably higher, the more policymakers with heterogeneous preferences are involved in passing legislation. Even in the absence of a law, if multiple heterogeneous policymakers have a stake in the institution, some of them may have incentives to resist political attempts to override the central bank's decisions. Finally, the policymaker could ensure that future disagreements with the central bank are carried out in public. As a consequence, the policymaker may lose political capital when she publicly attempts to force the central bank to comply with her wishes.

A different line of argument suggests that the desired monetary policy rule could be implemented via an appropriately designed incentive contract for central bankers (Walsh 1992). Such a contract would link the budget of the central bank or the income of central bankers to observable monetary policy outcomes. In practice, however, the contract that optimally trades off credibility and flexibility considerations would be extremely complicated. Moreover, it is not obvious what a contractually specified response to unforeseen contingencies would look like. Thus, due to transaction costs or bounded rationality, it may be impossible for the policymaker to negotiate, legislate and enforce such a contract.

In this situation, Kreps (1990) proposes that the corporate culture of an organization can provide guidelines for the actions to be taken when specific and possibly unforeseen contingencies are realized. Applied to central banking, such a culture would motivate central bankers to follow a low-inflation monetary policy that is nevertheless responsive to real shocks and other contingencies.

2.2   Political Business Cycles

An alternative motivation for central bank independence is based on the notion that   policymakers have incentives to use monetary instruments for opportunistic or partisan political goals. The resulting variability in monetary policy can be reduced or eliminated if central bankers are isolated from electoral or partisan pressures.

Nordhaus (1975) develops the opportunistic hypothesis according to which an incumbent policymaker has incentives to follow an expansionary monetary policy prior to an election to stimulate employment and output and thereby increase her chances of reelection.[8]

This hypothesis motivates an institutional design that isolates central bankers from pressures to manipulate the economy prior to elections. This end could be achieved in two ways. First, central bankers' terms of appointment could be delinked from the terms of appointment of their political principals. Central bankers could be appointed for life or given a nonrenewable contract. If central bankers' terms were renewable, they may have incentives to generate electoral cycles in order to increase the likelihood that their contracts will be renewed. Of course, both life-time and nonrenewable contracts are associated with down-side risks. In the presence of incomplete information about preferences, a central banker who is appointed for life cannot be replaced if it turns out that he has the "wrong" preferences. Moreover, central bankers who cannot make a career in central banking because of nonrenewable contracts may have incentives to make monetary policy decisions that favor external groups who control their future careers.

---

[8] The Nordhaus model is based on the assumptions of adaptive inflation expectations and naive retrospective voting. Recent variants of the opportunistic hypothesis rely on the assumptions of rational inflation expectations and rational retrospective voting (see Cukierman and Meltzer 1986, Rogoff and Sibert 1988, Persson and Tabellini 1990).

Alternatively, in a federal system with staggered elections, policymakers could delegate monetary policy to a committee that makes its decisions by simple majority rule (Lohmann 1993a). The members of this committee could be appointed by federal and regional state policymakers whose electoral incentives do not coincide. If the federal appointees form a minority on the committee, then at any given time only a minority of the political principals of the members of the central bank council would be up for reelection so that a majority of the council would vote against any opportunistic attempts to manipulate the money supply for electoral gain.

The alternative hypothesis of a partisan business cycle is developed by Hibbs (1977) and Alesina (1987).[9] Two parties with different policy objectives succeed each other in power, thereby creating a partisan business cycle in inflation, employment and output.

The partisan hypothesis implies that non-partisan central bankers should be appointed or that central bankers should be isolated from the pressures of partisan political principals and their constituencies. One institutional solution is provided by Waller (1992a), who argues that monetary policy outcomes are moderated when partisan appointments are staggered. Alternatively, output uncertainty could be mitigated by longer terms of appointment for partisan central bankers (Waller 1989).[10]

In implementing these proposals, partisan policymakers could again make use of the presence of staggered elections in a federal system (Lohmann 1993a). They could delegate monetary policy to a committee that makes its decisions by simple majority rule and is composed of a minority of federal appointees and a majority of regional state appointees. Changes in the partisan identity of the median voter on the central bank committee over time would then be determined by the electoral fortunes of the political parties in federal and regional state elections.

3.   TWO CASE STUDIES OF INSTITUTIONAL CHANGE

3.1   The German Political System

Perhaps the central political feature of the Federal Republic of Germany is given by its federal organization (Bulmer 1989). Until 1990, the republic consisted

---

[9] Alesina (1987) reformulates the Hibbs model in a rational expectations framework.

[10] Waller's 1989 and 1992 proposals are based on competing hypotheses about the decision making process in a central bank council. The 1989 proposal is based on a median voter model, the 1992 proposal on a bargaining model.

of eleven states; five additional states joined the system after German unification.[11] The states are heterogeneous in population, political preferences and economic conditions. For example, Baden-Württemberg, the rising star among the states, has a population of over nine million. Its government has been dominated by the Christian Democrats. In contrast, Bremen is a city state in economic decline controlled by the Social Democrats, with a population of under 700,000. The system of government is parliamentary. There are two houses of parliament, the Bundestag and the Bundesrat (see Figure 1). The members of the Bundestag are elected by the people according to a mixed system of proportional representation. The Bundestag elects the chancellor by simple majority rule, and the chancellor then forms the cabinet. The delegates to the Bundesrat are nominated by the state governments and subject to their principals' instructions. The large states have a higher number of delegates than do the small states, but full proportionality is not achieved. For example, Baden-Württemberg has five seats in the Bundesrat, while Bremen has three seats.[12]   State elections are staggered between national elections. A multi-party system that allows for occasional entry of new parties has emerged. Parties typically form coalition governments, both at the national and state levels. The dominant right-of-center parties are the Christian Democratic Union (CDU), organized in all states except for Bavaria, and the Christian Social Union (CSU), organized only in Bavaria. These two parties form a permanent coalition at the national level, the Christian Union Parties (CDU/CSU). The largest left-of-center party is the Social Democratic Party (SPD). Of the smaller parties, the most important one is the moderate, free market oriented Free Democratic Party (FDP). At the national level, the CDU/CSU or SPD typically form a coalition with the FDP.

Party discipline is strong, since political careers depend on the support of the party leadership. Voting in the Bundestag generally follows party lines. At the state level, politicians are attentive to constituency interests, but many of them have national ambitions and thus have incentives to pay attention to the wishes of the party leadership.

The constitution of the Federal Republic of Germany assigns extensive rights and responsibilities to the states, not the least of which allow for the participation of the states in the forming of national legislation via the Bundesrat. The federal structure was deliberately imposed by the drafters of the constitution in a successful attempt to avoid the excessive concentration of power that characterized the Third Reich (Bulmer 1989).

---

[11] Prior to German unification, the city state of West Berlin was associated with the Federal Republic of Germany but did not have all the rights and responsibilities of the other states.

[12] Prior to German unification, the representatives of West Berlin were appointed to the Bundestag and the Bundesrat and had very limited voting rights.

Figure 1
The German Federal System

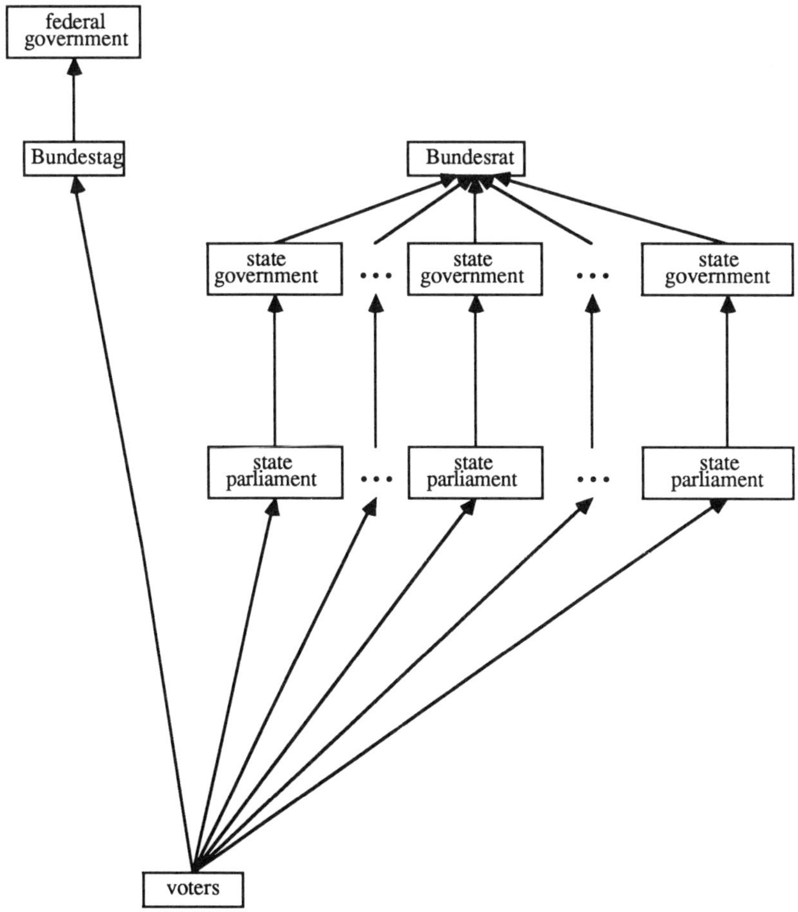

Each level of government is endowed with independent responsibilities for some policy areas, whilst other responsibilities are shared. Moreover, the Bundesrat has extensive veto powers -- both suspensive and absolute -- regarding legislation made by the Bundestag. Constitutional amendments require a two-thirds majority of the Bundesrat. The Bundesrat has an absolute veto regarding legislation that affects the states.

If a simple majority of the Bundesrat vetoes legislation passed by the Bundestag, a conciliation committee may be called upon to make a compromise proposal. If this proposal is rejected by a simple majority of the Bundesrat and the underlying issue does not affect the vital interests of the states, then the Bundesrat veto can be overturned by a simple majority of the Bundestag. In this case, the effect of the Bundesrat's veto and the associated conciliation procedure is to delay legislation. Note that this delay per se has the potential to prevent legislation that is motivated by very short-run political interests. If a qualified majority of the Bundesrat vetoes a law, such a veto can only be overturned by a corresponding two-thirds majority of the Bundestag. With the exception of the government supported by the grand coalition of CDU/CSU and SPD in 1967-69, no federal government has been supported by a qualified majority of the Bundestag. Thus, a Bundesrat veto passed by two-thirds of the Bundesrat has the potential to prevent legislation from being passed.

Moreover, for legislation that affects the vital interests of the states -- so-called *zustimmungsbedürftige Gesetze* (laws requiring consent) -- a Bundesrat veto can only be overturned by a qualified majority in the Bundestag, even if the veto was supported by a simple majority of the Bundesrat only. Whether a law is to be classified as *zustimmungsbedürftig* (requiring consent) can be a matter of dispute and would ultimately be decided by the constitutional court. The court would be more likely to find that a law affects the vital interests of the states if the law affects the appointment powers or other rights and responsibilities of the state governments.

It follows that if the national opposition parties succeed in winning a sufficient number of state elections, they can effectively influence national legislation via the Bundesrat. One stylized fact about German elections is that the dominant national opposition party regularly gains votes in state elections (Brady, Lohmann and Rivers 1992). As a consequence, the federal government often faces an opposition at the state level and in the Bundesrat. A few states have been dominated by one party over time, but none of the two large parties has had a lock on the federal government or on a majority of the state governments over the post-war period.

3.2   The 1957 Bundesbank Law

After the collapse of the Third Reich, the U.S., British and French military governments set up Land Central Banks (regional central banks) in the western occupied zones of Germany. The Bank deutscher Länder, a joint subsidiary of the regional central banks, was created by the U.S. and British occupation forces in March 1948. The Land Central Banks in the French zone joined the system later on.

The new central banking system had a two-tier, decentralized organizational structure. The two-tier organization form meant that the Land Central Banks were de jure autonomous entities coordinated by the Bank deutscher Länder in Frankfurt. The organizational structure was decentralized in the sense that the supreme decision making body of the system was dominated by the presidents of the Land Central Banks: they formed the central bank council together with two further members of their choice, the president of the central bank council and the president of the directorate. The Bank deutscher Länder was formally independent of the federal government and gained its independence from the Allied Bank Commission in August 1951.

Article 88 of the German constitution of 1949 gave the federal government a mandate to replace military law with German law and establish a central bank. The public discussion about the institutional design of the central banking system began soon thereafter and continued through two legislative periods, only to be resolved with the passing of the Bundesbank law in 1957.

The main players in this discussion were the finance and economics ministries, the cabinet, the leaderships of the political parties, the state governments and their delegates in the Bundesrat, the directorate of the Bank deutscher Länder and the presidents of the Land Central Banks. The debate was dominated by one issue: the degree of centralization of the central banking system -- that is, one-tier centralized or two-tier decentralized. In a one-tier system, the Land Central Banks would lose the formal independence from their central headquarters they enjoyed under the two-tier Bank deutscher Länder system. In a centralized system all (or a majority of) the members of the central bank council would be appointed by the federal government, while in a decentralized system comparable to the Bank deutscher Länder all (or a majority) would be appointed by the state governments.

Between 1949 and 1957, the federal government was supported by a coalition of CDU/CSU and FDP, and the CDU and CSU controlled a majority of the state governments, some of them in grand coalition with the SPD.[13]

In March 1950, the finance ministry developed a proposal for a decentralized design of a future central bank. The economics ministry was internally split, with the department for basic questions of economic policy favoring a decentralized organization form, while the department for money and credit preferred a centralized design. Since Minister Ludwig Erhard was a proponent of centralization, the economics ministry came out with a centralized proposal. The cabinet, however, voted in favor of the finance ministry's decentralized proposal, and this proposal was passed on to the Bundestag. The CDU/CSU and FDP coalition supporting the government was also internally split. The FDP fraction in the Bundestag introduced a competing bill that was based on the centralized proposal made by the economics ministry.

---

[13] In the legislative period 1949-53, the FDP formed a coalition with the Deutsche Partei (DP) at the national level, in 1953-57 with the DP and the Block der Heimatvertriebenen und Entrechteten (BHE). Both the DP and the BHE were minor parties that eventually dropped out of the Bundestag.

Meanwhile, the Bundesrat voted in favor of the decentralized design, after making a few changes in the direction of more decentralization. The FDP then petitioned the constitutional court in 1953 for a finding that a vote of the Bundesrat was not necessary to pass the central bank legislation; its petition was rejected.

Dr. Otto Pfleiderer, the president of the Land Central Bank of Württemberg-Baden proposed a two-tier decentralized central banking system that would correspond to the Bank deutscher Länder.[14] While his proposal was supported by the other Land Central Bank presidents, the directorate of the Bank deutscher Länder favored a one-tier centralized design.

In the Bundestag, the competing proposals were referred to the committee for money and credit, chaired by CDU parliamentarian Hugo Scharnberg, in consultation with the economic policy committee. The legislation languished in the committee until the next legislative period.

In the meantime, the Bank deutscher Länder followed a very restrictive monetary policy from the Summer of 1955 to the Spring of 1956. The resulting conflicts between the federal government and its central bank shaped the tendency towards more centralization that is apparent in the Bundesbank law of 1957 (Könneker 1957, p. 796). Chancellor Konrad Adenauer had become unhappy with the perceived failure of the Bank deutscher Länder to support economic reconstruction. In a well-publicized speech in May 1956, he criticized the Bank deutscher Länder on the grounds that high interest rates were hurting small business, farmers and blue collar workers. More ominously, Adenauer questioned the legitimacy of the bank's independence (Deutsche Bundesbank 1988, p. 116/118).

Against this background, the economics ministry once again made a centralized proposal in September 1955, and this time its proposal was accepted by the cabinet. The Bundesrat rejected this proposal and made a decentralized counterproposal. The federal government in turn rejected the Bundesrat's proposal, and its centralized proposal found a majority in the Bundestag. In November 1956, the legislation was again referred to the committee for money and credit.

Meanwhile, due to the upcoming national election in 1957, the federal government was under considerable pressure to pass a central bank law. Adenauer wanted to exploit the prestige associated with the future central bank for electoral

---

[14] The Land Central Bank that Pfleiderer presided over was named "Land Central Bank of Baden-Württemberg" from 1952 to 1957 and "Land Central Bank in Baden-Württemberg" after 1957. In 1952, the states Württemberg-Baden, Württemberg-Hohenzollern and Baden were consolidated to form the state Baden-Württemberg. In the two-tier Bank deutscher Länder system, the Land Central Banks were referred to as "Land Central Bank of Berlin," "Land Central Bank of Bremen" and so on, while in the one-tier Bundesbank system, they were renamed "Land Central Bank in Berlin," "Land Central Bank in Bremen" and so on.

purposes and appoint its president before the election in case his party lost. Thus, the Scharnberg committee moved fast and suggested a compromise: a one-tier, partially decentralized central bank. This compromise, the *Gesetz über die Deutsche Bundesbank* (Bundesbank law), was passed by the Bundestag on July 4, 1957, and by the Bundesrat on July 19, 1957.[15] The Bundestag vote was unanimous. In the Bundesrat, only two states, Bavaria and the Rhineland-Palatinate, voted against the law. There is no obvious partisan pattern in the vote.[16] Up to the end, there was considerable disagreement regarding the question of whether the law was *zustimmungspflichtig*. This question remained unanswered when the law was passed by a qualified majority in the Bundesrat.

The Bundesbank law of 1957 stipulates that the Land Central Banks are purely administrative main offices of the Bundesbank. The supreme decision making body is the central bank council. The members of the council give instructions to the directorate, in cases of internal conflict by simple majority rule. Until the Bundesbank law was modified in 1992, the council consisted of a president, a vice-president and up to eight further members of the directorate, all nominated by the federal government, and eleven Land Central Bank presidents, chosen by their respective state governments (see Figure 2).[17]

The case study evidence assembled so far can be used to assess the empirical contribution of the theories reviewed earlier. Incentive contracts for central bankers played no role in the discussion. Moreover, the idea of legislatively constraining the Bundesbank to follow a monetary targeting rule was explicitly rejected on the grounds that the commitment to such a rule would prevent a flexible response to shocks that cannot be clearly defined or are not fully understood.[18] There was a consensus among the members of the academic advisory council to the federal

---

[15] The law is documented in Deutsche Bundesbank 1989.

[16] At the time, Bavaria was governed by a coalition of SPD, FDP and some smaller parties, the Rhineland-Palatinate by a coalition of CDU and FDP. Some of the states that voted in favor of the Bundesbank law in the Bundesrat were dominated by the SPD, others by the CDU.

[17] Formally, the president of the Federal Republic appoints all members of the central bank council. The members of the directorate are nominated by the federal government; the Land Central Bank presidents are formally nominated by the Bundesrat but de facto proposed by the state governments.

[18] Since December 1974, the Bundesbank has publicly announced monetary targets. These targets were not legislated. Moreover, the Bundesbank frequently failed to achieve its targets, suggesting a lack of full commitment to its targets.

Figure 2
The Composition of the Council of the Deutsche Bundesbank

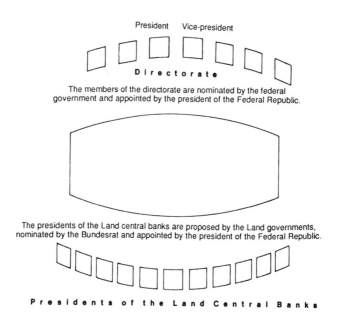

President   Vice-president

D i r e c t o r a t e

The members of the directorate are nominated by the federal
government and appointed by the president of the Federal Republic.

The presidents of the Land central banks are proposed by the Land governments,
nominated by the Bundesrat and appointed by the president of the Federal Republic.

P r e s i d e n t s   o f   t h e   L a n d   C e n t r a l   B a n k s

Source: Adapted from Deutsche Bundesbank (1988, p. 7).

government that monetary policy is too complex to be summarized by a rule. Indeed, the members of the council found that even the tasks of a central bank could not be legislated in detail (Becker 1982, p. 56/57). The imposition of a legislative limit to the money supply was also rejected after being attacked as "irrelevant" and "ridiculous" (Deutsche Bundesbank 1988, p. 208). Overall, the participants in the discussion about the Bundesbank law were sceptical about the effectiveness of legislative "solutions" to the possibility of incompetent or irresponsible behavior on the part of future members of the central bank council. Several institutional features were discussed that might affect the central bankers' monetary policy preferences in the sense of Rogoff (1985). The possibility of forming an advisory council staffed with representatives of the private sector was considered and rejected. Dr. Wilhelm Vocke, a member of the directorate of the Bank deutscher Länder, argued that a central bank should be independent from the pressures of external interest groups (Deutsche Bundesbank 1988, p. 132). Instead, advisory councils were formed at the state level and staffed with representatives of regional banks, industry and labor. These councils play an important role in providing information about the state of the regional economies. While these councils can potentially exert pressures on their respective Land Central Bank presidents, the possibility for strong, centrally organized interest group pressure is muted. The banking and exporting industries later became important constituencies of the Bundesbank and exerted considerable -- and occasionally counterproductive -- influence on German monetary policy (Becker 1988, p. 14). Overall, however, the issue of private sector influence on monetary policy played a secondary role in the public discussion of the Bundesbank law. Instead, the legislative design of the relationship between the central government and its central bank was at the center of the debate. The appointees to the directorate are required to have a professional background that makes them "suitable" for appointment. In fact, the members of the directorate have typically been lawyers, economists or bankers, and many of them have been promoted from within the Bundesbank organization (Lohmann 1993c). Moreover, the federal government is required to consult with the central bank council when nominating candidates. One might conjecture that such a consultation requirement would create a potential for the central bank council to replicate itself over time. However, the central bank council has repeatedly spoken out against "party political" candidates selected by state governments on the grounds that they lacked the necessary professional background; but in each case the candidates were appointed in spite of the council's objections.

Economists are generally disdainful of "cultural" explanations (and often rightfully so), but the evidence suggests that the corporate culture of the Bundesbank is an important factor shaping German monetary policy, even if it is not easily accessible to economic analysis. The corporate culture of the Bundesbank biases its decisions towards price stability and serves to mute partisan political pressures. The Bundesbank is the ultimate example of a "well-trained bureacracy of good standing and tradition, endowed with a strong sense of duty and a no less strong esprit de corps" (Schumpeter 1976 [1943], p. 293). This proud culture, however, also has a downside. It provides a rationale for the Bundesbank to immunize itself against public criticism: the silencing of critical journalists, academics and members of the banking sector has been justified on the grounds that their criticism undermines the Bundesbank's reputation and independence.

The factors underlying the creation or emergence of the Bundesbank's corporate culture are not well understood. One institutional feature that appears to contribute towards this culture is the renewability of the central bankers' eight-year contracts. Renewal is in many cases routine so that almost all members of the central bank council stay with the Bundesbank for the full duration of their careers. Similarly, other employees of the Bundesbank system typically make a career out of being a "Bundesbanker." Both job and monetary security ensure that the members of the Bundesbank organization are not personally dependent on outside groups who might otherwise control their future career paths.

Partisan political appointments have been made, especially at the state level, but the Bundesbank is generally thought of as remarkably free of party politics. There is a consensus among Bundesbank watchers that even appointees who are strongly identified with a political party are ultimately influenced by the "force of assimilation" in the central bank council (Könneker 1957, p. 798).

The Bundesbank law grants the Bundesbank formal independence from the federal government. The formulators of the law were aware of the tradeoff between achieving price stability by granting independence to the Bundesbank, on the one hand, and the dangers of creating an unaccountable but powerful institution that could undermine the economic policy of the federal government, on the other hand. With few exceptions, the German political and economic establishment supported the idea of central bank independence, although it was also clear that "in critical times the independence of the central bank must always end" (Deutsche Bundesbank 1988, p. 131). In the end, the legislators chose to grant the Bundesbank independence and at the same time require that it support the general economic policy of the federal government.

The formulators of the Bundesbank law deliberately chose not to specify how a conflict between the government and its central bank should be resolved. In their view, a public "dramatization" of the conflict was desirable, with the public (represented by the media) serving as an umpire (Becker 1982, p. 69). The outcome of such a conflict would then depend on the public's relative trust in its elected political representatives and in the appointed defenders of the currency.

In fact, in the next few decades both the federal government and the Bundesbank would enter into a public conflict only when the stakes were high, given the considerable political costs associated with such a conflict. The federal government is aware that a public conflict can threaten its stability: in three cases, the Bundesbank directly or indirectly contributed to the resignation of a chancellor or the collapse of a coalition government (Marsh 1992, p. 225).[19] On the other hand, the Bundesbank knows that it can endanger the legitimacy of its independent status if it publicly quarrels with elected officials.

The following two cases illustrate that the relative popularity of the chancellor's and the Bundesbank's policies are an important determinant of the outcome of a public conflict. In the first case, the governing coalition was relatively unpopular, and the conflict between the chancellor and the Bundesbank contributed to the collapse of the government. In the second case, the chancellor followed a very popular policy, and the conflict between the chancellor and the Bundesbank ended with the resignation of the president of the Bundesbank.

---

[19] The three cases are given by Ludwig Erhard 1966, Kurt Georg Kiesinger 1969 and Helmut Schmidt 1982.

In 1980/81 the Bundesbank followed an extremely restrictive monetary policy that was associated with an unprecedented level of firm bankruptcies and unemployment.[20] The SPD/FDP coalition government, the trade unions and all five national economic research institutes argued that the Bundesbank's policy was excessively restrictive. Nevertheless, the Bundesbank was able to withstand the pressures of the German political and economic establishment. Its restrictive monetary policies are thought to have contributed to the collapse of the ailing and unpopular government coalition in 1982.[21]

In February 1990 Kohl took the Bundesbank by surprise by publicly announcing his plans for a German monetary union without prior consultation with the Bundesbank. The idea of a monetary union was extremely popular with the East German public, but the Bundesbank feared its inflationary effects. Kohl's announcement embarrassed the president of the Bundesbank, Karl Otto Pöhl, who on the previous evening had publicly declared German monetary union to be a fantasy that would not solve a single economic problem of East Germany. Kohl's action also violated the consultation requirements laid out in the Bundesbank law. The Bundesbank subsequently complied with the chancellor's wishes in implementing the monetary union. Dr. Wilhelm Nölling, the president of the Land Central Bank in Hamburg, publicly criticized the federal government for giving the impression that the autonomy of the Bundesbank had ceased to be in force for the duration of unification (Marsh 1992, p. 288). Only in March 1991 did Pöhl himself publicly criticize the union as an economic disaster, and he was then severely chastised by Kohl. Pöhl unexpectedly resigned in May 1991 (Marsh 1992, Chapter 8; Balkhausen 1992, p. 173/174).

This incident suggests that the Bundesbank law per se does not guarantee the Bundesbank's independence. This law does not exist in a political vacuum: political factors affect the Bundesbank's behavioral independence over time (Lohmann 1993a).

It is apparent that the central issue in the public debate was the organization form of the Bundesbank. According to Goodman (1991, p. 337)

"no one directly called the independence of the future central bank into question ... At issue, instead, was the degree of centralization in the new

---

[20] One motivation for the Bundebank's tight monetary policy was that the West German current account was negative for the first time in decades; the establishment of external balance is one of the official goals of German economic policy.

[21] In fact, Chancellor Helmut Schmidt suspected that the anti-inflationary policy of the Bundesbank was due to the fact that a majority of the state appointees on the Bundesbank council had been appointed by Christian Democratic governments (Balkhausen 1992, p. 140).

banking system ... the vehemence of the debate throughout West German
political and social life indicated that significant interests were ... at stake."

In fact, the legitimacy of central bank independence was questioned by some
participants in the debate, most prominently by Chancellor Konrad Adenauer. More
importantly, however, the evidence suggests that central bank independence is
intricately linked to the degree of centralization of the central banking system.

Dr. Otto Pfleiderer, the president of the Land Central Bank of Baden-
Württemberg, celebrated the decentralized structure of the central bank as "an
institutional guarantee of its independence" (Deutsche Bundesbank 1988, p. 171). In
his view, the "pluralism" of the appointing bodies, the participation of the states in
the appointment process and the principle of collegiality among the members of the
central bank council contribute to the central bank's autonomy (Deutsche Bundesbank
1988, p. 171). His sentiments were echoed by his colleague Pankraz Geiselhart, the
president of the Land Central Bank of Northrhine-Westphalia. Geiselhart proposed
that central bankers who are not subject to a "unified political will" are more
independent (Deutsche Bundesbank 1988, p. 169). Similarly, Alfred Hartmann,
secretary of state in the finance ministry, argued that the independence of the central
bank is strengthened if the states carried some responsibility for monetary policy via
their appointment powers (Deutsche Bundesbank 1988, p. 172).[22] These arguments
are typical of the sentiments expressed by the proponents of a decentralized central
banking system.

The principle of central bank independence vis-à-vis the government and
economic interest groups was deemed crucial for the safeguarding of the currency
(Wagenhöfer 1957, p. 26). In Wagenhöfer's view, this principle should be legislated,
but it should also be institutionally guaranteed by the federal elements in the central
bank's internal organization structure. The federal components would create legislative
hurdles that would make future amendments to the Bundesbank law difficult and
time-consuming. This argument was empirically supported by the fact that the
Bundesbank law of 1957 was characterized by the "stamp of compromise" due to the
"retarding influence of the states" (Könneker 1957, p. 796).

Moreover, in the course of the debate the value of the principle "one Land,
one Land Central Bank" became apparent. A strong link between the federal structure
of states and the structure of the Bundesbank was associated with a higher likelihood
that the states would resist any attempts of the federal government to change the
Bundesbank law or force the Bundesbank to do its bidding.

The degree of centralization -- as reflected in the dispersion of appointment
powers -- played a greater role in the debate than did the issue of a one- versus two-
tier organization of the central bank. Von Spindler (1957, p. 168/169) noted that the

---

[22] This quote is dated February 1953, at which time the federal government supported a
decentralized organization form for the central bank.

dispersion of appointing powers and the two-tier construction of the central bank were separate issues, although both would tend to strengthen the bank's independence. It was primarily the presidents of the Land Central Banks who argued that the formal independence of the Land Central Banks from their central headquarters was important for the independence of the system vis-à-vis the government (Deutsche Bundesbank 1988, p. 154).

Given the link between central bank independence and the degree of centralization, it is not surprising that the federal government pushed in favor of a more centralized central banking system when it felt that its economic policy had not been sufficiently supported by the Bank deutscher Länder. However, the proponents of centralization did not publicly admit that their goal was to reduce the independence of the central bank. Instead, they argued that a modern economy required a unified monetary policy and thus a centralized central bank. Efficiency and cost effectiveness arguments were also invoked.

To isolate the Bundesbank from party political pressures, the members of its council were granted eight year appointments. The requirement that only a portion of the seats can be filled in any one legislative period ensured that the appointments would be staggered.

Moreover, Könneker (1957, p. 798) argued that the extent to which monetary policy is politicized depends on the degree of centralization. Könneker predicted that the Bundesbank would be more susceptible to party political pressures than was the Bank deutscher Länder, because there would be more federal government appointees on the Bundesbank council. In his view, the Land Central Bank presidents would also be political appointments, but their competing partisan interests would keep each other in check.

Interestingly, this hypothesis contrasts with the conventional wisdom held by Bundesbank watchers (see, for example, Sturm 1989). It is commonly claimed that the appointment process for Land Central Bank presidents has become more politicized over time, as measured by the number of party members on the Bundesbank's council. These developments are often said to threaten the Bundesbank's impartial pursuit of the price stability goal and its independence, although there exists little if any systematic evidence to support this claim. The directorate is said to have been more successful in isolating itself from party politics (Sturm 1989, p. 4).

In assessing the validity of these arguments, it is important to distinguish between factors that affect the monetary policy preferences of central bankers in the sense of Rogoff (1985) and factors that affect the degree of central bank independence in the sense of Lohmann (1992). A politicization of the appointment process at the state level may increase the number of members of the central bank council who place a relative higher weight on employment and output objectives than on the inflation objective. But it may also increase the political weight of the states in Bundesbank decision making, as a consequence of which the Bundesbank may become more independent. The net effect on the average time-consistent inflation rate is ambiguous.

The public debate on the Bundesbank law emphasized the importance of isolating the central bank from partisan pressures. In contrast, the concern that monetary policy could be used for electoral gain did not play a prominent role. The mixed composition of the central bank council and the staggeredness of the regional state elections has the potential to isolate the Bundesbank from electoral pressures. This effect is, however, undermined by strong party discipline: state representatives care about the electoral performance of their party at the national level. Empirically, there is some evidence for the existence of a Nordhaus cycle in German monetary policy (Lohmann 1993a).

Finally, one of the central assumptions underlying the economic analysis of institutions is inconsistent with the evidence. According to this approach, institutions affect political outcomes, and policymakers' preferences over central banking institutions are derived from their preferences over monetary policy outcomes. In fact, it is empirically more descriptive to think of the players in the Bundesbank debate as maximizing their power or protecting their turf.

The presidents of the Land Central Banks who stood to lose power under a more centralized design favored a decentralized design along the lines of the Bank deutscher Länder. Moreover, they were the main proponents of a two-tier design that would retain their formal autonomy from their central headquarters. The directorate of the Bank deutscher Länder could expect to gain under a more centralized design, and it did in fact support centralization.

Similarly, the FDP is politically more powerful at the national level, and it preferred a more centralized design. The SPD held power in a number of states, and it supported a more decentralized solution. The CSU was relatively strong at the state level (in Bavaria), and some CSU parliamentarians favored a decentralized design. The same holds for some members of the CDU, although the party leadership of CDU favored a centralized design, at least after the federal government experienced some conflict with its central bank.[23]

Moreover, the power motive appears to have dominated ideological motives. It is ironic that Ludwig Erhard -- the father of the social market philosophy and ideologically a strong proponent of decentralized economic decision making -- favored a centralized central bank. On the other side, the SPD was a proponent of central planning for some sectors of industry, and yet it favored a decentralized

---

[23] See also Goodman (1991, p. 337).

central bank.

It is also interesting to note that in the early fifties the finance ministry came down on the side of a more decentralized central banking system, while the economics ministry favored a more centralized design. Compared to other ministries, the finance ministry is less susceptible to interest group pressures. As the guardian of the budget, its task is to impose fiscal discipline on the "spending" ministries (von Hagen 1992). A more decentralized and thus more independent central banking system enhances fiscal discipline. Thus, the finance ministry appears to be the only player whose institutional preferences can be derived from its preferences over policy outcomes.

3.3   The 1992 Modification of the Bundesbank Law

On October 3, 1990, the five East German states officially joined the Federal Republic of Germany. The unification treaty of August 1990 required the Bundesbank law to be modified by October 3, 1991, with the objective of integrating the new states into the Bundesbank system. However, due to the fierce public dispute between the federal government and the states about the organization form of the new central banking system, the deadline failed to be met. The changes to the Bundesbank law were passed in July 1992 to become effective on November 1, 1992.

At this time the federal government was supported by a CDU/CSU and FDP coalition in the Bundestag, while the SPD controlled a simple majority of the Bundesrat. As before, the central issue was the degree of centralization of the central banking system, and this issue was discussed by the same cast of players.

In response to the stipulations of the unification agreement, Karl Otto Pöhl, the president of the Bundesbank, developed two solutions. The first solution specified that the system would have seven Land Central Banks and seven members of the directorate. The president of the Bundesbank would gain power, for he or she would be able to cast a tie-breaking vote. To implement this solution, the Land Central Banks of all except the largest three states would be consolidated. This solution was immediately rejected as too centralistic. By giving a majority to the federal government appointees, it would destroy the "parallelogram of forces" between the directorate and the Land Central Bank presidents (Dickertmann 1991, p. 21).

Pöhl then modified his proposal to allow for eight Land Central Banks, with no change to the size of the directorate. At the time the directorate only had seven members and would thus form a minority on the central bank council if the proposal were implemented. However, the 1957 Bundesbank law allowed the federal government to appoint up to ten members to the directorate so that the federal government appointees could form a majority in the future.

This second proposal found a majority in the central bank council. The individual votes on the council are not publicly known, but it became apparent that the directorate must have formed a coalition with a minority of the Land Central Bank presidents. A majority of seven Land Central Bank presidents strongly opposed the Pöhl proposal. Under the leadership of Reimut Jochimsen, the president of the Land Central Bank in Northrhine-Westphalia, they publicized a letter of protest to Chancellor Helmut Kohl (see Jochimsen et al. 1991). Such a public display of dissent within the central bank council was unprecedented.

It is interesting to note that five of the seven Land Central Bank presidents who spoke out against the proposal represented SPD-controlled states. The remaining two represented a CDU state (Norbert Kloten of Baden-Württemberg) and a CSU State (Lothar Müller of Bavaria), and both were known as strong and independent-minded Land Central Bank presidents. Without exception all four Land Central Bank presidents who supported the Pöhl proposal expected to gain power: the proposal specified that their Land Central Banks would service the states that would lose their Land Central Banks.[24]

In June 1991, the finance ministry modified the Pöhl proposal, raising the number of Land Central Banks to nine and reducing the maximum possible size of the directorate to eight, thus ensuring that the directorate could never outvote the Land Central Bank presidents. Moreover, for political reasons the finance ministry's proposal did not specify which states would in fact lose their Land Central Bank.

Meanwhile, a two-thirds majority of the Bundesrat rejected the proposal of the federal government and instead supported a proposal embodying the principle "one Land, one Land Central Bank." According to this proposal, each of the new states would get its own Land Central Bank, and each of the new Land Central Bank presidents would be given a seat on the Bundesbank council. Since the maximum size of the directorate was to remain fixed, this proposal amounted to a strengthening of the state component in the central bank council.

In March 1992 the Bundestag passed the finance ministry's proposal by simple majority, largely along party lines. The members of the CDU/CSU and the FDP in the Bundestag supported the proposal of their government, while the opposition parties voted against it; a handful of legislators abstained. In April 1992 a large majority of the Bundesrat rejected that proposal and initiated the conciliation

---

[24] Dr. Wilhelm Nölling, the president of Land Central Bank in Hamburg, was known as an outspoken member of the informal SPD opposition on the central bank council and thus might have been expected to join the opposition against the Pöhl plan. In fact, Hamburg's Land Central Bank publicly defended the proposal to centralize the Bundesbank, invoking rationalization, cost and efficiency arguments (Dickertmann 1991, p. 10). After all, it stood to gain responsibility for Schleswig-Holstein and Mecklenburg-Vorpommern. In the course of the political bargaining over the Bundesrat votes, however, Hamburg lost its Land Central Bank and Nölling lost his job.

procedure. At this point, there was considerable uncertainty whether a compromise proposal of the conciliation committee would be rejected by a two-thirds majority in the Bundesrat. The Social Democrats controlled a simple majority of the Bundesrat, but not a two-thirds majority. Some representatives of CDU-dominated state governments were torn between following the party line and supporting the proposal of the federal government, on the one hand, and representing the interests of their state, on the other. For example, Christine Lieberknecht, a representative of Thuringia in the Bundesrat, expressed support for the general thrust of the federal government's proposal, but criticized some of the details (Bundesrat 1992, pp. 147/148). In particular, she argued that Thuringia (an East German state) would be at a disadvantage if it were consolidated with Hesse (a West German state) in terms of forming a joint Land Central Bank instead of with Saxony (another East German state). Although Thuringia and Saxony were both controlled by the CDU, their representatives in the Bundesrat called on the conciliation committee to become active and modify the legislation to the advantage of their states.

On June 5, 1992, a simple majority of the Bundesrat rejected the proposal of the conciliation committee and declared the law to be *zustimmungspflichtig*. The vote followed party lines, with the representatives of SPD-dominated states voting against the federal government's proposal. The initially close to united front of states had broken up: some of the state representatives in the Bundesrat who had initially voted in favor of the Bundesrat's decentralized proposal had switched their support to the federal government's proposal. To undermine the opposition in the Bundesrat, the federal government had modified its proposal to "pay off" some states and get their vote in the Bundesrat (Dickermann 1991, p. 30). For example, the representatives of Thuringia and Saxony ended up voting in favor of the federal government's proposal after the proposal was modified to have Thuringia and Saxony form a joint Land Central Bank. It was probably not a coincidence that three SPD-governed states and only one CDU-governed state had to give up their Land Central Banks (Frankfurter Rundschau 1992; Bundesrat 1992, p. 147). The federal government only had to marginally modify its proposal to convince CDU-controlled states to support its bill. It would have been more expensive to "pay off" SPD representatives to vote against their party line. Overall, it is clear that the consolidation and specific location of the Land Central Banks was determined by political and not technocratic considerations (Dickertmann 1991).

If a two-thirds majority of the Bundesrat had voted against the proposal of the conciliation committee or if the law had been classified as *zustimmungspflichtig*, then the Bundestag would have had to counter with a qualified majority, and the federal government did not have such a majority in the Bundestag. Based on the presumption that the law was not *zustimmungspflichtig*, a simple majority of the Bundestag then proceeded to pass the *Viertes Gesetz zur Änderung des Gesetzes über die Deutsche Bundesbank* (fourth law modifying the Bundesbank law) on June 17,

1992.[25]

The SPD-controlled state government of the Rhineland-Palatinate then threatened to call on the constitutional court to establish that changes to the Bundesbank law are *zustimmungspflichtig*. In 1962 the constitutional court had declared changes to the Bundesbank law to not be *zustimmungspflichtig*. Nevertheless, there was some uncertainty about how the court would decide if called on in 1992. According to a standard commentary to the Bundesbank law, any centralization attempts to the Bundesbank organization would be confounded by the Land Central Bank construction. In the end, the state government of the Rhineland-Palatinate backed off, perhaps because it had also been "paid off": the Land Central Bank in the Rhineland-Palatinate gained responsibility for the Saarland (Frankfurter Rundschau 1992).

The modified Bundesbank law specified up to eight members of the directorate and nine Land Central Banks. The states Baden-Württemberg, Bavaria, Hesse and Northrhine-Westphalia are each represented by their own Land Central Bank, while the states Berlin and Brandenburg, the Rhineland-Palatinate and the Saarland, Saxony and Thuringia each share a Land Central Bank. The states Bremen, Lower-Saxony and Saxony-Anhalt are represented by one Land Central Bank; the same holds for Hamburg, Mecklenburg-West Pomerania and Schleswig-Holstein.

Many of the arguments expressed decades ago were now presented once again. As before, the forces in favor of the "one Land, one Land Central Bank" principle argued that this principle is an important institutional guarantee of the Bundesbank's autonomy (Jochimsen et al. 1991).

The supporters of centralization viewed the 1957 compromise as having two main weaknesses: inhomogeneous central bank districts and a too large and unwieldy central bank council. The 1992 modification of the Bundesbank law was taken as an opportunity to create a more centralized central bank system that would be more efficient and cost effective. Indeed, and with some justification, they criticized the state-level opposition to the new law as being based narrow self-interest, as expressed by the sentiment "Protect our nice jobs with the Land Central Bank" (Reuter 1992). The proponents of a more centralized system rejected the argument that the independence of the Bundesbank had to be institutionally guaranteed through an appropriately designed organization structure. In their view, it was sufficient for the independence of the Bundesbank to be guaranteed by law (Grünewald 1992). In a speech to the Bundesrat in April 1992, the secretary of state in the finance ministry, Dr. Joachim Grünewald, argued that the influence of the states via the appointment process undermined the independence of the Bundesbank (Bundesrat 1992, pp. 149-150). In his view, the Bank deutscher Länder, the predecessor organization of the

---

[25] The law is documented in Deutscher Bundestag 1992.

Bundesbank, had been controlled by the states for historical reasons only, and there was no technocratic justification for state involvement in monetary policy. According to Grünewald, the regional components of the administrative organization of the Bundesbank (that is, the existence of regional administrative offices) were justifiable, while the federalist components (that is, the political link to the state system via the appointment powers of the state governments) were not.

As in the fifties, neither side was moved by the arguments of the other side. Their preferences over institutional arrangements appear to have been fixed in advance, determined by power and turf considerations (Einecke 1992).

One new aspect played a role in the 1991/92 debate. Both sides invoked Germany's gradual integration into the EC and the possible creation of the ECB in the future as an argument in favor of their side. The Bundesrat proposal was criticized on the grounds that it would be wasteful to create five new Land Central Banks when European integration would require a reorganization of the German states (Bundesrat 1992, p. 149). The opponents of the modified Bundesbank law suggested that it would be wasteful to implement major organizational changes to the Bundesbank system that would become obsolete within a few years (Bundesrat 1992, p. 146).

Kaltenthaler (1993) argues that the ruling Christian Democrat-Free Democrat government coalition and members of the Bundesbank directorate used the demands of European (monetary) integration as a strategic rationalization to hone the Bundesbank into a more centralized and less federal structure. Under the pretext of developing a more efficient Bundesbank decision making structure, they could thus reduce the power of the Land Central Bank presidents who in the past opposed monetary policies that would accommodate the economic policies of the federal government.

In any case, in the long run the political importance of the German states and their Land Central Banks will fade, as the Federal Republic of Germany becomes one state in the European system, and the president of the Bundesbank becomes one of many regional central bank presidents in a European central banking system.

4.   IMPLICATIONS FOR THE DESIGN OF A EUROPEAN CENTRAL BANK

Given the large body of empirical research on the Federal Reserve, it is not surprising that the U.S. experience is typically invoked in discussions of the proposals for a ECB. For example, Beck (in this volume) argues that the central bank presidents of the European member states who would be appointed to the council of the ECB will tend to favor a more expansionary policy because they are political appointees. On the other hand, Fratianni, von Hagen and Waller (1992) propose that these appointees will tend to vote in favor of a more restrictive monetary policy because they realize that a common monetary policy is unfit to meet regional output and employment targets. Although these scholars come to opposite conclusions, both claims are consistent with the U.S. evidence that regional district bank presidents (who are not political appointees) tend to favor a more restrictive policy than do presidential (political) appointees. A dispute of this kind can only be resolved empirically -- with reference to the German system that is more similar to the proposed ECB. I now use the case study evidence assembled in this chapter to assess the potential of the proposed ECB to replicate the monetary policy of the Bundesbank.

Incentive contracts for central bankers and monetary targeting rules are rejected. Instead, the crucial factors shaping German monetary policy appear to be given by the central bank law, the political institutions the central banking system is embedded in, the internal corporate culture of central bank and the attitudes of the general public.

The proposed ECB would have a stronger legislative mandate to follow the price stability goal independently of political interference than does the Bundesbank. The formulation of the price stability goal in the Bundesbank law is ambiguous, and this law does not explicitly prioritize the two goals of safeguarding the currency and supporting the general economic policy of the federal government. In the statute for the ECB, the price stability goal is formulated quite unambiguously, as is the priority of the price stability objective over other objectives. Similarly, the Bundesbank is granted some independence from the federal government, while the ECB, its member banks, and the members of its decisionmaking bodies will be legally independent from the political pressures of EC institutions, the governments of EC member countries and any other political body.

Moreover, the German experience suggests that the credibility of a law is (at least in part) due to legislative transaction costs that make it difficult and time-consuming to change the law. Thus, the legal independence of the ECB would be strengthened if changes to the statute of the ECB are made subject to complicated and lengthy procedures with a variety of built-in veto points.

The low-inflation preferences of the members of the Bundesbank council appear to be associated with its corporate culture (Lohmann 1993c). I conjecture that this culture is created by the fact that the career paths of the members of the Bundesbank council by and large lie in central banking, due to their long terms of appointment and the norm of reappointment. In contrast, the statute for the ECB specifies that the central bankers' terms will be nonrenewable, and this feature will affect the career paths of the members of the ECB council. Nonrenewability implies that the members of the central bank council will not have incentives to do the bidding of their political principals in order to increase their chances of renewal. However, they may be susceptible to the pressures of outside groups who control their future careers. If they are "captured" by groups with low-inflation preferences, a low-inflation monetary policy would result. It appears more likely, however, that the members of the ECB council will be part of a European elite of politicians and technocrats whose career path lies in the institutions of the EC. In this case, the central bank would be highly vulnerable to political pressures.

The designers of the ECB appear to have found a new way of implementing Rogoff's (1985) conservative central banker. According to the 1992 Maastricht Treaty, a country that wishes to become a member of the future European Monetary Union is required to fulfill specific entry requirements.[26] For example, the average CPI inflation rate must be no more than 1.5 percentage points above the inflation rate of the three countries with the lowest inflation rates. Similarly, the general government deficit to GDP ratio must not exceed three percent, and the gross debt to GDP ratio must lie below 60 percent. It is often claimed that the purpose of these rules is to prevent the European Monetary Union from being destabilized when the economic fundamentals in one of its member countries are not compatible with the stringent constraints implied by a fixed exchange rate regime (Bean 1992). However, economic fundamentals also affect the monetary policy preferences of policymakers. A policymaker whose country satisfies the Maastricht conditions might be more conservative (in the sense of Rogoff) than is a policymaker whose country does not. As a consequence, the voting behavior of their appointees to the council of the ECB might be more conservative.[27]

The evidence compiled in this chapter suggests that the ECB will also enjoy a high degree of independence by virtue of the political institutions it will be embedded in. The principle of federalism is valued in the EC, and the member countries of the EC are fiercely protective of their national entitlements and rights vis-à-vis the center. The proposed design for the ECB follows the successful "one Land, one Land Central Bank" principle that has only recently been rejected for the Bundesbank. Rather than form homogeneous central bank districts that would be delinked from the federal structure of the member countries of the EC, the statute for the ECB specifies weighted majority voting on critical issues. As suggested in this chapter, the political link between the central bank and the member states of the EC

---

[26] The treaty is documented in Council of the European Communities and Commission of the European Communities 1992.

[27] At this point, it is not clear to which extent the entry requirements specified by the Maastricht Treaty constrain potential future candidates to the European Monetary Union. By the end of 1996, a qualified majority of the European Council must decide on the basis of reports by the European Monetary Institute and the European Commission and the opinion of the European parliament whether a majority of the member states fulfills the necessary conditions for the adoption of a single currency and whether to proceed on the path to monetary union. There is presumably a discretionary element in such a decision, and it is possible that the decision will be made on political rather than technocratic grounds.

via the appointment powers of the member state governments has the potential to strengthen the independence of the ECB. Depending on the number of member states joining the monetary union, the presidents of the central banks of the EC member countries may form a larger majority on the ECB council than do their German counterparts on the Bundesbank council. In conclusion, the ECB may be more independent than is the Bundesbank, especially given the recent changes to the Bundesbank law in the direction of more centralization.

Moreover, the EC will also be characterized by staggered European and regional elections. Thus, the system has the potential to prevent opportunistic and partisan political business cycles from emerging. In Germany, Nordhaus cycles have nevertheless emerged, probably due to strong party discipline (Lohmann 1993a). Party discipline is likely to be weaker in the EC, since the political parties have different ideologies, traditions and experiences. In the past, the Socialist and Social Democratic parties have cooperated with each other to a greater extent than have Conservative parties, suggesting that the system might be biased in favor of left-of-center parties. To the extent that these parties have more inflationary preferences, the resulting European monetary policy will tend to be more inflationary. However, Lohmann (1993a) finds no evidence for such partisan effects on German monetary policy, suggesting that the competing partisan interests of state representatives may keep each other in check.

Finally, the public support of the Bundesbank's independence has clearly played an important role in Germany, especially in situations of conflict between the Bundesbank and the federal government. The European public may be less uncritically supportive of its central bank. It is not obvious that the attitudes of the German public can be exported. For this reason, it is all the more important that the institutional features of the Bundesbank that have contributed to its independence are replicated at a European level.

REFERENCES

Alesina, Alberto, 1987, "Macroeconomic Policy in a Two Party System as a Repeated Game," Quarterly Journal of Economics 102: 651-678.

Ausschuß der Präsidenten der Zentralbanken der Mitgliedstaaten der Europäischen Wirtschaftsgemeinschaft, 1990, "Entwurf des Statuts des Europäischen Systems der Zentralbanken und der Europäischen Zentralbank," Mimeograph, November 27.

Balkhausen, Dieter, 1992, *Gutes Geld und Schlechte Politik: Der Report über die Bundesbank*, Düsseldorf: ECONVerlag.

Barro, Robert, and David B. Gordon, 1983, "Rules, Discretion and Reputation in a Model of Monetary Policy," *Journal of Monetary Economics* 12: 101-121.

Bean, Charles R., 1992, "Economic and Monetary Union in Europe," *Journal of Economic Perspectives* 6: 31-52.

Beck, Nathaniel, in this volume, "An Institutional Analysis of the Proposed European Central Bank: A Political Scientist's Perspective."

Becker, Wolf-Dieter, 1982, "Diskussion über ein Bundesbankgesetz im Wissenschaftlichen Beirat beim Bundeswirtschaftsministerium," *Beihefte zu Kredit und Kapital* 7: 61-77.

Becker, Wolf-Dieter, 1988, "Vierzig Jahre Geldpolitik: Erinnerungen, Tendenzen und Probleme," Mimeograph, Technical University of Aachen.

Bendor, Jonathan, and Susanne Lohmann, 1993, "Institutions and Credible Commitment," Mimeograph, Stanford University, February.

Brady, David, Susanne Lohmann and Douglas Rivers, 1992, "Party Identification, Retrospective Voting, and Moderating Elections in a Federal System: West Germany 1961-1989," Graduate School of Business Research Paper No. 1231, Stanford University, December.

Bulmer, Simon, 1989, "Territorial Government," in: *Developments in West German Politics*, eds. Gordon Smith, William E. Paterson, Peter H. Merkl, Durham: Duke University Press: 40-59.

Bundesrat, 1992, "Sitzungsbericht: 641. Sitzung - 3. April 1992," Mimeograph, Bonn.

Caesar, Rolf, 1981, *Der Handlungsspielraum von Notenbanken*, Baden-Baden: Nomos Verlagsgesellschaft.

Council of the European Communities and Commission of the European Communities, 1992, *Treaty on European Union*, Luxembourg: Office for Official Publications of the European Communities.

Cukierman, Alex, and Allan Meltzer, 1986, "A Positive Theory of Discretionary Policy, the Cost of Democratic Government, and the Benefits of a Constitution," *Economic Inquiry* 24: 367-388.

Deutsche Bundesbank, 1989, "Die Deutsche Bundesbank: Geldpolitische Aufgaben und Instrumente," Sonderdrucke der Bundesbank Nr. 7, 5th edition, Frankfurt am Main, February

Deutsche Bundesbank, 1988, "Dreißig Jahre Deutsche Bundesbank: Die Entstehung des Bundesbankgesetzes vom 26. Juli 1957," Frankfurt am Main.

Deutscher Bundestag, 1992, "Viertes Gesetzes zur Änderung des Gesetzes über die Deutsche Bundesbank (4. BBankGÄndG)", Mimeograph, Bonn, July 15.

Dickertmann, Dietrich, 1991, "Deutsche Bundesbank: Landeszentralbanken vor einer Strukturreform?" Universität Trier, FB IV: Schwerpunkt Finanzwissenschaft/ Betriebliche Steuerlehre Arbeitspapier Nr. 24, October.

Einecke, Helga, 1992, "Bundesbank wird erheblich schlanker," *Süddeutsche Zeitung*, August 21.

Flood, Robert, and Peter Isard, 1990, "Monetary Policy Strategies," *International Monetary Fund Staff Papers* 36: 612-632.

Frankfurter Rundschau, 1992, "Leere Worte," August 5.

Friedman, Milton, 1945, "A Monetary and Fiscal Framework for Economic Stability", *American Economic Review* 38: 245-264.

Fratianni, Michele, Jürgen von Hagen, and Christopher Waller, 1992, "The Maastricht Way to EMU," Essays in International Finance No. 187, Princeton University, June.

Goodman, John, 1991, "The Politics of Central Bank Independence," *Comparative Politics* 23: 329-349.

Goodman, John, 1992, *Monetary Sovereignty*, Ithaca: Cornell University Press.

Grünewald, Joachim, 1992, "Die Neue Bundesbankorganisation," *Börsen-Zeitung*, June 19.

Hibbs, Douglas, 1977, "Political Parties and Macroeconomic Policy," *American Political Science Review* 7: 1467-1487.

Jochimsen, Reimut, et al., 1991, "Zur Anpassung des Bundesbankgesetzes gemäß Einigungs vertrag," *Wirtschaftsdienst* XI: 554-559.

Kaltenthaler, Karl Christian, 1993, "The Bundesbank and German Federalism: The Politics of Institutional Change," Mimeograph, Washington University in St. Louis.

Könneker, Wilhelm, 1957, "Vom Zentralbanksystem zur Deutschen Bundesbank," *Zeitschrift für das gesamte Kreditwesen* 20: 796-798.

Kreps, David M., 1990, "Corporate Culture and Economic Theory," in: *Perspectives on Political Economy*, eds. James E. Alt and Kenneth A. Shepsle, Cambridge: Cambridge University Press.

Kydland, Finn E., and Prescott, Edward C., 1977, "Rules Rather than Discretion: The Inconsistency of Optimal Plans", *Journal of Political Economy* 85: 473-491.

Lohmann, Susanne, 1990, "Monetary Policy Strategies - A Correction: Comment on Flood and Isard," *International Monetary Fund Staff Papers* 37: 440-445.

Lohmann, Susanne, 1992, "Optimal Commitment in Monetary Policy: Credibility versus Flexibility," *American Economic Review* 82, March 1992.

Lohmann, Susanne, 1993a, "Federalism and Central Bank Autonomy: Political Business Cycles in West Germany, 1960-1989," Mimeograph, UCLA, October.

Lohmann, Susanne, 1993b, "Institutional Sources of Central Bank Autonomy: The Politics of German Monetary Policy, 1960-1989," Mimeograph, UCLA, October.

Lohmann, Susanne, 1993c, "Testing the Conservative Central Banker Hypothesis: The Deutsche Bundesbank, 1960-1989," Mimeograph, UCLA, October.

Marsh, David, 1992, *Die Bundesbank: Geschäfte mit der Macht*, Munich: C. Bertelsmann.

Maxfield, Sylvia, 1992, "Private Constituencies and the Power of the State: Monetary Authorities in Newly Industrializing Countries," Mimeograph, Yale University, January.

Persson, Torsten, and Guido Tabellini, 1990, *Macroeconomic Policy, Credibility, and Politics*, Chur: Harwood Academic Publishers.

Reuter, 1992, *Reuter Monitor*, Mimeograph, June 17.

Rogoff, Kenneth, 1985, "The Optimal Degree of Commitment to an Intermediate Monetary Target," *Quarterly Journal of Economics*: 1169-1189.

Rogoff, Kenneth and Anne Sibert, 1988, "Elections and Macroeconomic Policy Cycles," *Review of Economic Studies* 55: 1-16.

Schumpeter, Joseph A., 1976 [1943], *Capitalism, Socialism and Democracy*, London: George Allen & Unwin.

Sturm, Roland, 1989, "The Role of the Bundesbank in German Politics," *West European Politics* 12: 1-11.

Tabellini, Guido, 1987, "Reputational Constraints on Monetary Policy: A Comment," *Carnegie-Rochester Conference Series on Public Policy* 26: 183-190.

Taylor, John B., 1983, "Comments on 'Rules, Discretion and Reputation in a Model of Monetary Policy'," *Journal of Monetary Economics* 12: 123-125.

Vaubel, Roland, 1993, "Eine Public-Choice-Analyse der Deutschen Bundesbank und ihre Implikationen für die Europäische Währungsunion," in: *Europa vor dem Eintritt in die Wirtschafts- und Währungsunion*, eds. Dieter Duwendag and Jürgen Siebke, Berlin: Duncker and Humblot.

von Hagen, Jürgen, 1992, "Budgeting Procedures and Fiscal Performance in the European Communities," Mimeograph, University of Mannheim, May.

von Spindler, Joachim, 1957, "Der Kampf um die Bundesnotenbank," *Zeitschrift für das gesamte Kreditwesen* 5: 167-169.

Wagenhöfer, Carl, 1957, "Der Föderalismus und die Notenbankverfassung," in: *Festschrift zum 70. Geburtstag von Dr. Hans Ehard*, München: Richard Plaum Verlag.

Waller, Christopher J., 1989, "Monetary Policy Games and Central Bank Politics," *Journal of Money, Credit and Banking* 21: 422-431.

Waller, Christopher J., 1992a, "A Bargaining Model of Partisan Appointments to the Central Bank," *Journal of Monetary Economics* 29: 411-428.

Waller, Christopher J., 1992b, "The Choice of a Central Banker in a Multisector Economy," *American Economic Review* 82: 1006-1012.

Walsh, Carl, 1992, "Optimal Contracts for Central Bankers," Mimeograph, University of California at Santa Cruz, July.

CHAPTER 11

RULES, DISCRETION, AND CENTRAL BANK INDEPENDENCE: THE GERMAN EXPERIENCE, 1880-1989

Bernhard Eschweiler
Michael D. Bordo

1.   INTRODUCTION

Theories of rules and discretion have become a corner stone in the formulation of macroeconomic policy. They suggest that monetary policy rules are first best in terms of social welfare. However, if commitment is not feasible, delegating monetary policy to an independent and conservative central bank can be second best. Monetary policy in Germany during the past one hundred years provides an excellent case to assess the empirical evidence on the use of rules and central bank independence in monetary policy making. Since the creation of a central monetary authority in 1876, Germany has participated in four monetary regimes: the pre-war gold standard, the inter-war gold standard, the Bretton Woods system, and the floating exchange rate regime. With the exception of the two world war periods German monetary policy was geared primarily towards maintaining price stability and characterized by a high degree of formal and practical central bank independence.[1]

The period under investigation begins with the first German unification (1871) and ends just before the second German unification (1989). This time period can be divided into three parts: The pre-war period from 1871 to 1913 which coincides with the Classical Gold Standard; the inter-war period between 1924 and 1933, which is also the period of the second gold standard; and the post-war period from 1949 to 1989, which can be divided into two subperiods, the Bretton Woods period (1949 to 1973) and the floating exchange rate period (1974 to 1989).

Policy rules are only feasible when a commitment environment exists. Bordo and Kydland (1992) argued that the Classical Gold Standard established such a commitment environment, and the regression results in section 2 confirm that the Reichsbank, Germany's central bank at the time, adhered to the gold standard rule, although it violated the so-called 'rules of the game'. The Reichsbank's commitment

---

[1] See Holtfrerich 1988a.

to the gold standard reduced the risk of public debt repudiation through inflation to a minimum and allowed the government to borrow funds in the private capital market. This, according to Bordo and Kydland, was the main motivation for the gold standard rule.

The departure from the gold standard during World War I and hyperinflation after the war diminished the government's credibility. The Reichsbank was made independent to limit the government's access to central bank credit. Germany joined the reestablished gold standard and the Reichsbank, as the regression results in section 3 show, was fully committed to the new monetary policy rule. Nevertheless, the government faced severe problems in raising funds in the capital markets despite the Reichsbank's new independence and commitment to the gold standard. The simple monetary policy rule was no longer sufficient to appease the public's suspicion that the government could default on its debt again. The government's failure to restore its credibility following hyperinflation deprived it of an important funding resource at a time when fiscal flexibility was needed the most.

Following World War II the monetary authority in West Germany, first the Bank Deutscher Länder and later the Deutsche Bundesbank, was made independent once again. In addition, the Allies forced the new government to balance its budget. West Germany joined the Bretton Woods system which perhaps may be viewed as a new commitment regime. However, over time the Bundesbank was not willing to accommodate the inflationary bias of the Bretton Woods system. The regression results in section 4 show that the Bundesbank shifted its emphasis from pegging the dollar to domestic price stability, and thus contributed to the collapse of Bretton Woods.

Bretton Woods was the last commitment regime in Germany if it was one at all. After its collapse the policy environment was pure discretion. At this point the long tradition of central bank independence became most important. The second part of section 4 examines whether the Bundesbank actually behaved as an independent and conservative central bank. The regression results, which are used to compare the reaction function of the Bundesbank with the reaction function of the government, suggest that the Bundesbank was independent and conservative in the sense of Rogoff's 1985 model.

The bottom line of our analysis is that monetary policy in Germany was always geared towards maintaining price stability with the exception of the two world war periods. Germany relied both on rules and discretion with central bank independence to achieve the goal of price stability. Which regime was more efficient remains unclear. Theory predicts that rules should deliver a better outcome. A comparison of the Classical Gold Standard regime with the floating exchange rate regime in section 5 suggests that society under the floating exchange rate regime with central bank independence was better off. However, this comparison ignores the historical difference in output shocks and the possibility that society became more inflation averse over time. Adjusting for such differences could mean that rules are first best after all.

In the remainder of this section the theoretical framework of monetary policy rules and central bank independence is explained. Section 2 assesses Reichsbank policy under the Classical Gold Standard. Section 3 analyses the Reichsbank's commitment to the inter-war gold standard and the government's credibility problems following hyperinflation. Section 4 considers the Bundesbank's declining commitment to the Bretton Woods system and investigates whether the Bundesbank was actually independent and conservative. The conclusion in section 6 provides a tentative comparison of the efficiency of the different policy regimes.

1.1 Monetary Policy Rules, Central Bank Independence, and the Phillips Curve

In principle, every equilibrium policy in a model in which the private sector must form expectations about policy decisions must satisfy two requirements. It must be optimal for the policymaker and credible to the public. The latter is called the credibility constraint. Whether credibility constraints are binding for the policymaker depends on the policy environment. Two policy environments are considered, one where credibility constraints are not binding and one where they are.

In the first policy environment credibility constraints are not binding because of a commitment technology that effectively ties the policymaker's hands. Policy is chosen once-and-for-all before the public makes its decisions. Once a policy plan is chosen it becomes too costly to reverse it for economic, political, or other reasons. According to the literature, the policy is chosen under commitment. Monetary systems such as the gold standard contain a commitment technology since it is very costly for the participants to renege.

In the second policy environment, the costs of deviating from a policy plan are very low and not sufficient to offset the incentives to surprise the private sector. The policymaker can change the policy plan after the public has made its decision. In other words, the policy is chosen under discretion. Yet, since the policymaker's hands cannot be tied, the policy plan must be credible because the private sector does not expect any policy plan to be carried out which leaves an incentive for the policymaker to surprise later on. This means furthermore that policy results under discretion cannot be better than those under commitment since the policymaker faces an additional constraint.

In a simple Phillips curve framework where the government tries to stabilize inflation and output[2]

(1.1) $y = (\pi - \pi^e) - \varepsilon$

both policy regimes produce the same degree of output stability (variance of output),

(1.2) $L = E[\pi^2 + \mu(y - k)^2]$

(1.3) $y = -\dfrac{1}{1 + \mu}\varepsilon$

but discretion results in a higher rate of inflation (equation 1.4 is the rate of inflation under commitment and equation 1.5 shows the inflation rate under discretion).

(1.4) $\pi(\varepsilon) = \dfrac{\mu}{1 + \mu}\varepsilon$

(1.5) $\pi(\varepsilon) = \mu k + \dfrac{\mu}{1 + \mu}\varepsilon$

The two equilibrium inflation rates differ by the constant μk, which is called the inflation bias under discretion. However, the policy outcome under discretion is identical to the outcome with commitment if k=0. In other words, being able to make a commitment means that the policy maker can commit to an output target not different from the natural level of output. This allows us to estimate the policymaker's reaction function in its discretionary form and then test the null hypothesis whether commitments are feasible (H0: k=0).

In reality, policymakers often cannot enter into binding commitments. Thus, the relevant policy regime is more likely to be discretionary. However, it is possible that simple institutional changes improve the discretionary equilibrium. One such institutional change is the appointment of a conservative independent central banker, first proposed by Rogoff (1985).

---

[2] Equation 1 represents a standard Lucas supply function. The private sector forms inflation expectations not knowing the output shock ε. The government, on the other hand , minimizes equation 2 after observing ε and using actual inflation as its policy instrument. (Also: μ is the relative weight assigned to output stabilization and k denotes the target level of output which exceeds the natural level of output.)

According to equation 1.5, the inflation bias under discretion increases in proportion to the weight parameter μ. Yet, a higher μ also reduces the variance of output. Rogoff (1985) showed that the government could exploit this trade-off by appointing a central banker who puts a smaller but non-zero weight on output stabilization[3] Compared to pure discretion, where inflation is too high, it is optimal to accept some additional output variation in exchange for a lower inflation rate. Nonetheless, the equilibrium under the independent conservative central banker is still second best to the commitment regime since the credibility constraint remains binding leaving the outcome under discretion with central bank independence inferior to the one with commitment where the credibility constraint is not binding. Moreover, if commitments are feasible (k=0), appointing an independent conservative central banker is not optimal since the inflation bias is zero anyway but a lower μ reduces output stability.

2.   THE REICHSBANK AND THE CLASSICAL GOLD STANDARD

This section analyzes the policy of the Reichsbank during the 'Classical Gold Standard' (1880-1913). The gold standard is seen as a contingent monetary policy rule and the question is raised whether the Reichsbank adhered to this rule or departed from it by following other domestic policy targets. It is shown that the Reichsbank never suspended or endangered convertibility although it violated the so-called 'rules of the game'.

2.1   The Gold Standard As A Contingent Rule

Bordo and Kydland (1992)[4] argue that the gold standard besides functioning as an international exchange rate arrangement and providing macro stability worked as a contingent rule to constrain government policy action. In their model the government uses debt to smooth distortionary taxes over time. In addition to choosing

---

[3] It should be noted that this regime is not purely discretionary although it is still characterized by the Nash equilibrium conditions and the credibility constraint. In this regime it is assumed that the government can effectively commit to an independent central banker implying that the cost of reneging must be infinite. This suggests two possibilities. First, central bank independence requires an economic policy environment in which the costs of breaking the commitment to the independence of the central bank are infinite. Such costs could be that the independence of the central bank is guaranteed in the constitution, is commonly accepted by society, and has enjoyed a long tradition. Second, switching from pure discretion to central bank independence is not feasible unless the previous requirements have been met before.

[4] See also Giovannini (1993) and De Kock and Grilli (1989).

optimal taxes the government can also choose an optimal default rate on its outstanding debt (here the inflation tax). In a commitment regime the government can force itself to honor its outstanding debt and not default via inflation or suspension of payments. If the government cannot engage into a binding commitment - in other words, if it follows a discretionary regime - rational bond holders expect the government to have an incentive to completely default on its outstanding debt. Hence, in a discretionary equilibrium bond holders will not buy any government debt.

Bordo and Kydland argue that the gold standard functioned exactly as such a commitment mechanism. Once a country went on the gold standard it became extremely costly to leave it because of economic and political pressures from both within the country and abroad. Bordo and Kydland also maintain that the gold standard was not a fixed but a contingent rule. The cost of adhering to a fixed rule in the face of large shocks (wars, natural catastrophes, financial crises, or other contingencies) is not optimal. Under a contingent gold standard rule the government maintains the gold standard under all circumstances except when a contingency appears. The gold standard (convertibility) is suspended or relaxed for the duration of the contingency plus an adjustment period (specified in advance) and afterwards resumed under the old conditions.

The success of the gold standard as a contingent rule depends on the reputation of the government or monetary authority's ability to stick to its commitment. Several types of policy action can be seen as a violation of the commitment[5]: repeated devaluation of the currency in terms of gold; outright suspension of convertibility; and delayed resumption or devaluation after a contingency.

Furthermore, certain operating procedures can be considered inappropriate under the gold standard. For example, not playing by the so-called 'rules of the game' is viewed as inconsistent with adhering to the gold standard rule. The 'rules of the game', first used by Keynes, define monetary policy operating procedures for the participants of the gold standard. Unfortunately, there is no unique definition of the 'rules of the game'. Henceforth, it should not be surprising that findings of violations of the 'rules of the game' vary with the definition used.[6] Nevertheless, adherence to the 'rules of the game' can be assumed if monetary policy accelerates the adjustment of the balance of payments or stabilizes the exchange rate around parity to avoid a violation of the gold export points.

---

[5] Bordo and Kydland (1992) call these actions 'discretion under the gold standard'.

[6] See Nurkse (1944), Bloomfield (1959), McGouldrick (1984), Giovannini (1986) and McKinnon (1993).

Besides violating the 'rules of the game', keeping insufficient reserves and maintaining a small liquidity ratio (ratio between reserves at the central bank and notes issued) was considered inappropriate. Devaluation, suspension, and delayed resumption were not a problem in Germany during the period of the 'Classical Gold Standard'. However, many scholars claim that the Reichsbank violated the 'rules of the game' and did not maintain a stable liquidity ratio.[7]

2.2   The Reichsbank's Discount Rate Policy, Convertibility, and the 'Rules of the Game'

Although the Reichsbank used various other policy instruments, the discount rate was by far its most important policy tool.[8] The Reichsbank, like many other central banks at the time, followed the so-called 'real bills doctrine' and considered it to be its duty to discount all bills of exchange as long as they met the legal requirements.[9] Since the Reichsbank tried under all circumstances to avoid rationing of central bank credit, the discount rate was the most effective tool to regulate the demand for Reichsbank credit.[10]

Besides regulating domestic money demand, the discount rate was also used to influence the flow of capital and gold between home and abroad. A temporary or permanent increase of the discount rate relative to the discount rates in other countries caused an inflow of short-term and long-term capital respectively. The Reichsbank also used devices to promote gold imports, but with limited success.[11] With the

---

[7] See Bloomfield (1959), Bopp (1954), McGouldrick (1984), Mosbacher (1974), Plenge (1913), Seeger (1968), and Sommariva and Tullio (1987).

[8] 'The adjustment of the 'discount rate' is the only effective means for regulating the domestic demand for money. For influencing cash movements between home and abroad,'the discount rate', it is true, is not the only means, but, the most important and effective.' See 'The Reichsbank, 1876-1900' p.205.

[9] Max Schinkel testifying before the 'German Banking Inquiry of 1908' said: 'if the quality of the bill satisfies the Reichsbank, it takes any amount that is sent to it, at the official rate'; See 'German Banking Inquiry of 1908' vol.I, pp.377/8.

[10] 'As the Bank cannot, without great severity, arbitrarily refuse applications for credit, provided they meet the requirements of the Bank Act, it has no other alternative but to regulate calls for credit indirectly by adjusting the interest rate at which it is ready to grant credit.' See 'The Reichsbank, 1876-1900' pp.204/5.

[11] See 'The Reichsbank, 1876-1900' p.205 and Bopp (1954) pp.186/7. The Reichsbank could only hinder gold exports by refusing to redeem its notes at branch offices, however, it was required at all times to redeem its notes at the headquarters in Berlin.

discount rate the most important instrument of the Reichsbank, the question naturally arises whether the Reichsbank's discount rate policy was consistent with its commitment to the gold standard.

According to the traditional story, a central bank adhered to the 'rules of the game' if it used monetary policy to maintain external balance. Two objectives were important to maintain external balance. First, to stabilize the exchange rate around parity. Second, to speed up the adjustment process of the balance of payments. Maintaining exchange rate stability indirectly serves the objective of reducing gold flows since it prevents the exchange rate from depreciating below the gold-export point or appreciating above the gold-import point. This implies that a central bank playing by the 'rules of the game' was supposed to increase its discount rate when faced with a depreciating currency or a balance of payments deficit. Rising interest rates would lower the price level and thus decrease the trade deficit - cause the price specie flow mechanism to operate - and attract capital from abroad. A central bank was supposed to decrease the discount rate when experiencing a balance of payments surplus and appreciating exchange rates. Furthermore, a central bank's credit policy geared primarily to movements in central bank's reserves was supposed ... to have the effect of increasing central bank holdings of income earning assets when holdings of external reserves rose, and of reducing domestic assets when reserves fell'.[12]

Bloomfield (1959) analyzed these relations for Germany and ten other countries during the 'Classical Gold Standard' period. He found that while the discount rate rose when the liquidity ratio fell, the Reichsbank's holdings of earning assets in more cases moved in the opposite than in the same direction to reserves. Bloomfield concluded that the Reichsbank tried to stabilize the liquidity ratio but at the same time violated the 'rules of the game'.[13]

The short-coming of the traditional 'rules of the game' approach is that it focuses only on the outcome of monetary policy relative to some ad-hoc criteria but does not investigate whether a central bank's monetary policy was consistent with convertibility. In particular, analyzing the correlation of target variables like gold reserves or exchange rates with policy instruments like central bank credit or interest rates, relative to some ad-hoc benchmark, cannot determine whether a central bank's objectives are inconsistent with maintaining convertibility. To test a central bank's commitment to the gold standard it seems important to analyze its reaction function. The reaction function in turn should be derived from an explicit optimization problem that contains a trade-off between maintaining convertibility and some other target.

---

[12] See Bloomfield (1959) p.47.

[13] See Bloomfield p. 30 and p. 49.

For this purpose, a simple model of exchange rate determination must be found. The simplest exchange rate model is probably based on the uncovered interest parity assumption. According to uncovered interest parity, the expected change of the exchange rate is identical to the interest rate differential.

$$(2.1) \quad e_t - e_{t+1}{}^E = -(d_t - d_t^{UK})$$

Equation 2.1 is the uncovered interest parity identity,[14] e_t is the log of the current period's exchange rate (M/£), $\bar{e}_{t+1}{}^E$ is the log of next period's expected exchange rate, d_t is the domestic discount rate, and d_t^{UK} is the foreign (British) discount rate. Under the commitment regime, it can be assumed that the expected exchange rate and the parity exchange rate are identical ($e_{t+1}{}^E = \bar{e}$). If the Reichsbank was committed to maintain convertibility it would have stabilized the exchange rate around parity. A prolonged deviation of the exchange rate from parity would have implied a regime shift from commitment to discretion. Thus, the Reichsbank's objective function can be formulated as a quadratic loss function.[15]

$$(2.2) \quad \min \quad (d_t - \bar{d}_t)^2 + \mu(e_t - \bar{e})^2$$

Equation 2.2 specifies the Reichsbank's objective function with a trade-off between stabilizing the exchange rate around parity and smoothing the discount rate around some target $\bar{d}_t$. The parameter μ measures the weight of the exchange rate target in the objective function. A zero weight would indicate that the Reichsbank did not stabilize the exchange rate and therefore violated its commitment to convertibility.

Choosing discount rate smoothing as an alternative objective of the Reichsbank is not arbitrary. The heads of the Reichsbank and leading German monetary economists at the time thought that it was the main responsibility of the Reichsbank to accommodate the demand for central bank credit in order to stabilize

---

[14] For a derivation of equation 1 see Rivera-Batiz and Rivera-Batiz (1985) pp. 70/1.

[15] The quadratic loss function is commonly used as a utility or objective function in micro and macroeconomic applications. Most appealing is its simplicity and certainty equivalence property. However, the use of quadratic loss functions for regression purposes can cause an estimation bias if asymmetries exist.

the money market.[16]

The Reichsbank adapted its money supply to the fluctuations of money demand by keeping its discount rate as low and stable as possible.[17] The Reichsbank's discount rate reaction function is found by solving its minimization problem subject to equation 2.1.

$$(2.3) \quad d_t = \frac{1}{1+\mu}(\overline{d}_t + \mu d_t^{UK})$$

Equation 2.3 has been estimated using a non-linear least squares method. The regression is based on a monthly sample from 1880 to 1913. The discount rate target $(\overline{d}_t)$ is specified as a 12 month moving average of the discount rate. Table 1 contains the regression results of equation 2.3.[18]

Table 1

Reichsbank Reaction Function (equation 2.3), 1881:1 - 1913:12, Seas. Adj.

μ	R^2	Q(19)[a]
0.144*	91	15.5
0.021		

Standard deviations are in the second row ,below the parameter estimates
[a] Ljung Box Q-statistic for autocorrelation
* significant at the 1% level

---

[16] Helfferich (1899) p.315: 'The adaption of the quantity of money in circulation to the fluctuations of the demand for means of payments is, as is generally recognized, the most important task of central banks.' Von Lumm in 'Die Stellung der Notenbanken in der Volkswirtschaft' said: '... in times of money scarcity, surprisingly large quantities of commercial paper have been thrown into the portfolio of the Reichsbank which the latter could not prevent it.' Cited in Flink (1929) p. 26.

[17] Von Lumm (1912) p.135: 'In the general interest of stimulating national economic activity, the central bank must constantly take into consideration maintenance of as low and stable a discount rate as conditions permit.' Von Lumm's statement must be taken with a bit of caution. By 'stimulating national economic activity' he did not mean that the central bank should pursue an activist monetary policy in the modern sense but merely accommodate credit demand.

[18] The data sources are discussed in the appendix. All the variables used are stationary and seasonally adjusted.

The weight parameter for the exchange rate target in table 1 is significantly different from zero. On average, to justify a deviation of the discount rate from target by 1 percentage point the expected depreciation of the exchange rate from parity must be at least 2.6%. This basically means that the Reichsbank did not use the discount rate to correct temporary violations of the gold points and, thus, did not play by the 'rules of the game'.[19] The fact that the M/£ exchange rate violated the gold points only on a few occasions[20] must be attributed to factors other than the Reichsbank's direct efforts to stabilize the exchange rate. Most stabilizing were probably exchange rate expectations by market participants who were convinced that the government was committed to maintaining convertibility. Indeed, temporary violations of the gold points are not inconsistent with convertibility as long as the average exchange rate does not deviate from parity over time. The fact, that the Reichsbank was willing to increase its discount rate permanently by two percentage points to avoid a 5% depreciation suggests that it was committed to keeping the exchange rate close to parity. This result becomes even more evident when using annual rather than monthly data. Table 2 presents the estimation results of equation 2.3 using annual instead of monthly data.

Table 2

Reichsbank Reaction Function (equation 2.3, annual data), 1983 - 1913

μ	R^2	Q(6)
0.41*	47	7.67
0.22		

* significant at the 5 % level

According to table 2, maintaining convertibility at parity has a positive and significant weight. To justify an increase in the discount rate by a full percentage point over the year, the Reichsbank had to expect the exchange rate to deviate by 1.5% from parity. In other words, the Reichsbank would increase the discount rate by 3.3% to avoid a permanent devaluation of the Mark by 5%, which means effectively doubling the average level of the discount rate. This indicates clearly that

---

[19] Gold export points were usually 0.5 % above parity, see Giovannini (1993) figure 4. In other words, the Reichsbank would increase the discount rate by only 0.19 percent points in response to a violation of the gold export point.

[20] See Giovannini (1993) pp.31/2. During the period from 1880 to 1913 the M/£ exchange rate was on average 0.006 M/£ below parity (20.43 M/£), the variance of the deviation from parity was just 0.002.

the Reichsbank's discount rate policy was consistent with maintaining gold convertibility and the gold standard rule.

Summarizing, these findings give rise to the following conclusion. Judged by its discount rate policy, the Reichsbank did not really play by the 'rules of the game' since it did not pay much attention to temporary violations of the gold points. However, violating the 'rules of the game' does not necessarily mean that the Reichsbank was not committed to the gold standard rule. The 'rules of the game' are merely an operating procedure and are not a necessary precondition for the gold standard rule. By temporarily departing from the 'rules of the game' flexibility can be obtained to accommodate fluctuations in the credit market. As long as this practice does not threaten convertibility, it is not inconsistent with the gold standard rule. The regression results, on the other hand have clearly demonstrated that the Reichsbank was fully committed to convertibility.

3.   THE REICHSBANK IN THE INTER-WAR PERIOD

The Reichsbank's involvement in economic policy making changed after 1923 compared to the period before currency stabilization and even the pre-war period. The Reichsbank was made completely independent from the government and became actively involved in economic policy. Under the leadership of its president, Schacht, the influence and power of the Reichsbank increased to such an extent that it has been labeled the 'Extra Government'.[21] During the inter-war gold standard the Reichsbank became the symbol for currency stability in Germany. Despite increasing internal and external pressures the Reichsbank defended its commitment to the gold standard successfully. However, critics of the Reichsbank point out that the price for this uncompromising policy was too high, namely depression and the loss of democracy in Germany.

The Reichsbank's commitment to currency and price stability, can be tested using the macroeconomic model described in section 1.

$$(3.1) \quad y_t = z_t + \alpha(p_t - w_t) + u_t$$

$$(3.2) \quad m_t - p_t = y_t + v_t$$

Equation 3.1 is the aggregate supply function which incorporates a trend term (z_t, which captures technical progress and other supply conditions), a real wage term (p_t-w_t), and a random shock term (u_t). Equation 3.2 is the aggregate demand function

---

[21] See Müller (1973) pp. 38/43.

which is based on the quantity theory of money.[22] Wage setters are supposed to stabilize the expected real wage around some target (ω_t). Thus, each period they set the nominal wage equal to the expected price level (p_t^e) plus their real wage target.

(3.3) $w_t = p_t^e + \omega_t$

Inserting equation 3.3 into equation 3.1 yields a standard Lucas supply function.

(3.4) $y_t = z_t + \alpha(p_t - p_t^e) - \alpha\omega_t + u_t$

In equilibrium output and prices are determined as follows:

(3.5) $y_t = z_t + \dfrac{\alpha}{1+\alpha}(m_t - m_t^e) - \alpha\omega_t + \dfrac{1}{1+\alpha}u_t$

(3.6) $p_t = -z_t - v_t + \alpha\omega_t + \dfrac{1}{1+\alpha}(m_t + \alpha m_t^e - u_t)$

Supposing the monetary authority can actually observe the output shocks (u_t) after wages have been set implies that it can stabilize output. Whether the monetary authority would do so depends on its preferences between, say, price stability and output stability.

(3.7) $\min (p_t - p_{t-1})^2 + \mu(y_t - g_t)^2$

(3.8) $g_t = y_{nt} + \beta = z_t - \alpha\omega_t + \beta$

Equation 3.7 specifies the monetary authorities objective function. The output target (g_t) is defined as the natural rate of output (y_{nt}), derived by taking the mathematical expectation of equation 3.5, plus some scale factor (β). The solution to the optimization problem in equation 3.7 depends on the policy environment. As demonstrated in section 1, if the output target is identical with the natural output the outcome under discretion is identical to the outcome with commitment. Thus, assuming that setting the output target equal to natural output is only feasible under commitment provides a powerful test method for distinguishing the commitment policy environment from the discretionary policy environment. In other words, by first

---

[22] v_t is the reciprocal of the log of money velocity. To simplify the model, v_t is assumed to be non-stochastic.

deriving the reaction function under the assumption that the policy environment is discretionary and then testing whether β is zero, it is possible to determine the policy environment. Equation 3.9 is the monetary authority's reaction function that minimizes the quadratic loss function under discretion and subject to equations 3.5 and 3.6 using money supply (m_t).[23]

$$(3.9) \quad m_t = p_{t-1} + v_t + z_t - \alpha\omega_t + \alpha\mu\beta + \frac{1-\alpha\mu}{1+\alpha^2\mu}u_t$$

Equation 3.9 has been estimated in a two step procedure. In the first step, equation 3.1 has been estimated to obtain estimates for z_t, α, and u_t.[24] In addition, the real wage target (ω_t) has been approximated by a lag function of the actual real wage plus a constant and a trend. In other words, ω_t is equal to the real wage minus the regression residual of the following regression:

$$(3.9a) \quad w_t - p_t = \rho_o + \rho_1 t + \sum_{i=1}^{4} \sigma_i(w_{t-i} - p_{t-i}) + \varepsilon_t$$

Table 3

Aggregate Supply Function (equation 3.1), 1926:1 - 1932:4

constant	trend	y_{t-1}	y_{t-2}	y_{t-3}	y_{t-4}	α	R^2	LM[a]	$Q(5)$[b]
0.161****	0.0095***	0.94*	-0.33	0.09	0.13	1.05**	84	2.07	3.46
1.04	0.0052	0.19	0.28	0.28	0.22	0.46			

[a] Breusch - Godfrey LM first order autocorrelation statistic;
[b] Box - Pierce Q - statistic for serial autocorrelation
*, **, ***, **** significant at the 1, 2.5, 5, 10 % level

[23] The Reichsbank controlled its money supply primarily using the discount rate and credit restrictions. See Northrop (1938) pp. 265-9.

[24] z_t in equation 1 has been approximated by a constant, trend, and four quarterly lags of y_t. Further lags of y_t were not included since the inclusion did not improve the regression results but limited the sample size unnecessarily.

Table 4
Real Wage Target (equation 3.9a), 1926:1 - 1932:4

ρ_0	ρ_1	σ_1	σ_2	σ_3	σ_4	R^2	LM
-0.013	0.0067*	0.47*	-0.20	0.14	0.01	95	2.32
0.018	0.0031	0.20	0.21	0.21	0.20		

* significant at the 5 % level

According to table 3, the real wage elasticity of supply (α) is close to minus one. The trend of the aggregate supply function is positive, consistent with the fact that productivity actually increased throughout the period. The results in table 4 suggest that labor unions set the growth rate of the real wage target equal to one half the growth rate of the real wage in the previous period plus 0.7 percentage points.

In the second step the results of tables 3 and 4 have been used to estimate equation 3.9. Given the estimates for z_t, α, u_t, and ω_t, the only parameters to be estimated are β and μ.[25] Table 5 contains the regression results of equation 3.9.

Table 5
Reichsbank Reaction Function (equation 3.9), 1926:1 - 1932:4

β	μ	R^2	DW
-0.6	0.08	70	1.27
0.11	0.09		

Both parameters are not statistically different from zero. Commitment was feasible and the Reichsbank adhered to the gold standard ($\beta=0$). However, if this was the case the Reichsbank should not have put a zero weight on its output stabilization objective ($\mu=0$). In section 1 it had been shown that under commitment an independent central bank should be as inflation averse as the public and not more. An independent and conservative central bank under commitment is inefficient. In other words, if monetary policy bears any responsibility for the economic instability in the inter-war period the main reason seems to be that the Reichsbank was overly concerned about price stability and failed to concentrate appropriately on output stabilization.

The fact that the Reichsbank overemphasized its commitment to price stability and the gold standard likely reflects a lack of commitment on the part of the government. In contrast to the Reichsbank, the government did not seem much concerned with reestablishing its credibility and demonstrating its commitment to

---

[25] v_t has been computed using the equation of exchange.

price stability. Such a lack of commitment implies that the government should have had difficulty in borrowing funds. In fact, the inter-war government had tremendous difficulties in raising funds from the capital market.

Borchardt (1978) challenged the traditional view that Brüning, chancellor from 1930 to 1932, was primarily responsible for the collapse of the Weimar Republic because of his deflationary budget policy. Borchardt claims that Brüning's manoeuvrability was too restricted to adopt a Keynesian policy solution.[26] Holtfrerich (1982) criticized Borchardt's thesis, claiming that Brüning had a policy option but deliberately chose the route of fiscal deflation.[27]

Our purpose is not to participate in this discussion in any detail but to link the events in Germany during the depression with the predictions of economic theories that emphasize the role of rules in economic policy-making. In section 2 it had been shown that fiscal policy faces a credibility constraint unless the government possesses a commitment technology that prevents it from defaulting on its outstanding debt. The German government broke its gold standard commitment when it decided to continue its inflationary policy after the war. As a result, the government lost its credit rating. A successful return to the capital market was only possible if the government restored its credibility. Redemption of the old debt and commitment to a new and credible rule seem necessary conditions for a successful comeback.

---

[26] Borchardt argued that Brüning had no alternatives to his policy of fiscal deflation because the government was forced to balance the budget since it could not get any credit from either the capital market or the Reichsbank. Domestic and foreign creditors, according to Borchardt, stopped lending to the government because the latter made itself uncreditworthy through excessive borrowing during the boom of 1927; See Borchardt (1990) pp. 112/7. Secondly, financial support through the Reichsbank was not feasible, according to Borchardt, because the autonomous Reichsbank was committed to currency stability and changing the Bank Act was not at Germany's discretion since the Bank Act was part of a system of international treaties; See Borchardt (1979) pp. 168/74.

[27] According to Holtfrerich, Brüning could have pursued an alternative policy. Holtfrerich bases his hypothesis on three arguments. First, he argues that Borchardt's 'inevitability' hypothesis is bound to overlook the 'factor of freedom of action in history - that is the possibility to do otherwise than was done.' Second, he points out that alternative policy plans were discussed among cabinet members and could not have been unknown to Brüning. Third, he maintains that Brüning choose his policy of fiscal deflation deliberately since he wanted to discipline wage demands, lower social expenditures, and force the Allies to drop their reparation demands. See Holtfrerich (1982) pp. 613/31.

a)   **Redemption of Old Government Debt:**

The redemption of old government debt following hyperinflation was regulated under the Loan Redemption Act of 1925. At that time, the total government debt was approximately 82 billion RM.[28] Existing loans were converted into new loans at a rate of 40:1. With the exception of 'old holders' (those who bought bonds before July 1, 1920 and held them continuously since then), annuities were not prescribed and interest payments were postponed until the extinction of the reparations liability. 'Old holders' (about 60% of the total debt) participated in a lottery each year. The lottery each year selected the holders of 3.5% of the debt held by 'old holders'. Selected holders were paid five times the value of the revalued debt (i.e. 12.5% of the original debt) plus 4.5% annual interest on the revalued debt.[29]

b)   **New Commitment Technology:**

Germany under the pressure of the Allies joined the new internationalgold standard. To enforce the gold standard commitment and protect the central bank from the credit demands of the government, the Reichsbank was made independent from the Reich but remained subject to foreign control. In addition, credit to the government was limited to a small amount. Compared with the pre-war gold standard, this new commitment technology seemed much stronger in the sense that it limited the government's access to central bank credit. Moreover, the regression results demonstrate clearly that the Reichsbank was fully committed.

Nevertheless, despite partial redemption and a new monetary policy rule the government had severe problems in raising funds in the domestic capital market. The budget surpluses of the stabilization years (1924-1925) began to erode as early as 1926. In fiscal year 1926-1927 the public sector deficit amounted to 1.7 billion RM (2.3% of GNP). The surge of the public deficit was largely the result of increased spending by local and regional authorities which were given more fiscal autonomy by the fiscal law of February 1924. Foreign capital played an important role in the funding of the rising public deficit.[30] However, when the Reich floated a loan of 500 million RM at 5% interest in 1927 the market value of the new bonds fell from

---

[28] See Wunderlich (1929) p. 32.

[29] See Holtfrerich (1986) pp. 327/30.

[30] Capital inflows from abroad were basically triggered by the large interest rate differential between Germany and the United States, as well as by regained international confidence in the RM following the stabilization years. The Reichsbank welcomed the use of foreign funds to rebuild Germany's industrial base but was very critical of the use of foreign funds by public authorities.

92.0RM to 86.9RM within five months and the loan had to be converted to 6% interest to maintain the price.[31] Yet, the government's low credit rating did not become fully visible until 1929 when the supply of foreign funds began to dry up.

Table 6

Increase in German Government Debt, million RM

Fiscal year*	1926/7	1927/8	1928/9	1929/30	1930/1	1931/2	1932/3
Increase in public debt	1742	1075	3561	3159	2704	155	170
as % of GNP	2.3	1.3	4.0	3.6	3.4	0.2	0.3

Source: James (1986) p.52
* April 1 to March 31

Against warnings by the Reichsbank, the Reich floated a 500 million RM loan in 1929 (the so-called Hilferding Loan) of which only 177 million RM could be placed despite huge tax incentives (no wealth, inheritance, and income tax on the loan).[32] The Hilferding Loan was the last loan the Reich attempted to float domestically and after the Young Loan in 1930 the Reich issued no further bonds abroad. The strength of Borchardt's hypothesis that the government was forced to balance its budget is its consistency with the theoretical prediction. The experience of hyperinflation had taught the German public that exploding public deficits increase the temptation for the government to monetize the debt. The Reichsbank's independence and Commitment to the gold standard reduced the risk that the government could use monetary policy to finance its expenditures. Nonetheless, the Reichsbank's commitment to the gold standard did not guarantee that the government would exercise fiscal discipline. The public probably remained suspicious that rising deficits could eventually cause the government to break the Reichsbank's independence and use monetary policy to finance its government's credit rating. In fact, one could argue that 'through the light-minded borrowing during the boom

---

[31] German bond prices began to slip abroad at the same time. During the fiscal year of 1927/8 German first class bond prices began to fall in New York while Moody's AAA U.S. bond prices rose; See Balderston (1983) p. 407. Part of the decline of German bond prices in New York was the result of Parker Gilbert's (the Agent General for Reparations) public criticism in October 1927 of the conduct of German public finances.

[32] See James (1985) p. 53.

Germany has made itself uncreditworthy during the recession'.[33] A fiscal policy rule that would have ensured that deficits remained limited would probably have improved the government's credit rating, which would also have increased the Reichsbank room to target output and inflation. Furthermore, the partial redemption of old debt was probably insufficient to restore the government's credibility.

In summary, the pre-war government was able to borrow funds without difficulties by simply committing itself to the gold standard. The same, so it seems, was not true for the inter-war government. Although the Reichsbank was made independent and was clearly committed to the gold standard, the government had severe problems in raising funds in the capital market. This suggests that by breaking the gold standard commitment through hyperinflation the government lost all its credibility. It could not be restored through the Reichsbank's independence and commitment to the gold standard. This aggravated the problems of the inter-war period. The Reichsbank saw itself isolated in its attempt to secure currency and price stability. As a result, it ignored output stabilization completely. The government, on the other hand, deprived itself of an important resource of funding, constraining its flexibility at a time when fiscal spending was needed the most.

4.   THE DEUTSCHE BUNDESBANK DURING THE POST-WAR PERIOD

After more than thirty years of political and economic instability post-war Germany enjoyed high and stable growth and one of the lowest inflation rates world wide. These developments have inpart been attributed to the stability of Bundesbank policy. This section shows that the Bundesbank was primarily focused on controlling inflation. The first part assess the growing conflict between the Bundesbank's inflation objective and the Bretton Woods system. The main conclusion is that the Bundesbank by adhering to its inflation target probably contributed to the collapse of the Bretton Woods system. The second part tests the properties of central bank independence in the case of the Bundesbank. The results suggest that the Bundesbank is independent in the sense that it is more inflation averse than the government and has not been influenced by electoral or partisan politics.

4.1   The Deutsche Bundesbank and the Bretton Woods System

Germany's experience with the Bretton Woods system was marked by a persistent balance of payments surplus, constant fear of imported inflation, and the struggle over revaluation. During the Bretton Woods period, inflation in Germany was lower and productivity growth and real interest rates were higher than in most

---

[33] Letter from Prof. M.J. Bonn to State Secretary Schäffer, September 10, 1931; cited in Borchardt (1990) p. 116.

industrialized countries.[34] As a result, Germany's balance of payments tended to be in surplus most of the time. The balance of payments surplus, in turn, had an expansionary impact on Germany's money supply, threatening price stability.

The Bundesbank attempted to solve this dilemma by sterilizing foreign reserve inflows and isolating the capital account from the effects of higher real interest rates. The latter was accomplished through capital controls, especially high reserve requirements on foreign deposits. This strategy was quite successful until the return to convertibility in 1958.[35] Convertibility and increasing capital mobility made it more difficult to sterilize foreign reserve inflows. In response, Germany resorted to tighter capital controls.[36] However, by the late 1960s and early 1970s it became nearly impossible to prevent large inflows of speculative capital attracted by high real interest rates and expectations of currency revaluation.[37] As a result, the Bundesbank was left with two alternatives: either to support the Bretton Woods system and to adjust its money supply to the balance of payments disequilibrium or follow a purely domestic policy and risk the break-up of the exchange rate system.

The hypothesis that the Bundesbank was not willing to adjust its monetary policy to external disequilibria can be tested using a simple reaction function model. In a fixed exchange rate regime, external disequilibria occur whenever the fixed value of the currency and its fundamental value depart (here assumed to be determined by purchasing power parity). Thus maintaining an external equilibrium without adjusting the parities requires adjusting the fundamental value of the currency to its fixed value. Using the purchasing power parity concept, the fundamental value of the currency is simply the difference between the domestic and the foreign price level. If the Bundesbank was primarily interested in maintaining an external equilibrium then stabilizing the exchange rate at parity should have been of much higher priority than, say, controlling inflation. Thus, the Bundesbank's optimization problem could be characterized as follows.

---

[34] See Bordo (1993) Table 1 and Obstfeld (1993) Table 1.

[35] See Obstfeld (1993).

[36] The controls included measures such as prohibiting interest payments to foreigners, higher reserve requirements on foreign deposits, restrictions on borrowing abroad, and restrictions on the purchase of domestic bonds by non-residents. See Marston (1993).

[37] See Obstfeld (1993) and Kindelberger (1976) pp. 142/6.

(4.1) $\min \pi_t^2 + \mu(e_t - \bar{e}_t)^2$

(4.2) $e_t = p_t - p_t^*$

(4.3) $m_t - p_t = \gamma + \phi y_t - \lambda i_t$

Equations 4.1 to 4.3 specify the Bundesbank's optimization problem.[38] The Bundesbank minimizes a quadratic loss function by controlling the money supply (m_t) subject to the purchasing power parity condition and the money demand function.[39] The resulting reaction function is given in equation 4.4.

(4.4) $m_t = \gamma + \phi y_t - \lambda i_t + \dfrac{p_{t-1} + \mu(p_t^* + \bar{e}_t)}{1 + \mu}$

Any estimation of equation 4.4 requires the assumption that the Bundesbank in fact used money supply as its control variable. In practice, however, the Bundesbank did not use any monetary aggregate as control or intermediate target variable before 1975. Instead, it targeted banks' liquidity positions.[40] Nonetheless, the use of central bank money[41] as the Bundesbank's control variable can be justified for two reasons. First, although the Bundesbank did not officially target central bank money before 1975 it controlled it indirectly to determine the supply of money. Second, compared to other monetary aggregates central bank money had a stable relation with the price level, output, and interest rates making it an ideal control variable.[42]

---

[38] $\pi_t = p_t - p_{t-1}$ (quarterly inflation rate).

[39] All variables are in logs except for the interest rate (i_t). The exchange rate (e_t) is the DM/\$ rate and the foreign price level (p_t^*) is the U.S. price level.

[40] See Schlesinger and Bocklemann (1973) pp. 171/81.

[41] Currency plus minimum reserves which commercial banks must hold at the central bank. This is identical to a weighted average of the components of M3 with weights 1 for currency, 0.166 for demand deposits, 0.124 for savings deposits, and 0.081 for time deposits.

[42] See Deutsche Bundesbank (1989) and Trehan (1988).

Unit root tests of all variables in equation 4.4 indicate that they are non-stationary but integrated of first order.[43] Engle and Granger (1987) have shown that variables which are non-stationary might have a linear combination which is stationary. Engle and Granger call variables with this property co-integrated and develop several test methods to test for co-integration. Interpreting the relation of co-integrated variables as a long-run equilibrium implies that deviations from equilibrium are stationary. Engle and Granger also show that if a number of variables are co-integrated there exists a specific error correction model that describes the short-run behavior of these variables.

The application in this case is as follows. Although all variables in equation 4.4 are non-stationary there could be a linear combination which is stationary. This relationship would describe the Bundesbank's long-run behavior. The question is whether the inflation target, the exchange rate target, or both targets are included in this long-run relationship. This can be tested by imposing certain restrictions on the co-integration vector.

$$(4.4a) \quad m_t = \gamma + \phi y_t - \lambda i_t + \alpha p_{t-1} + (1-\alpha)(p_t^* + \bar{e}_t) \; ; \quad \alpha = \frac{1}{1+\mu}$$

Equation 4.4a is the linearized form of equation 4.4. Three different combinations can be tested for co-integration: first, no restriction on α; second $\alpha=1$; third $\alpha=0$. According to Engle and Granger co-integration can be detected in a two step procedure. In the first step the co-integrating vector is estimated using standard OLS or NLS. In the second step the regression residuals are tested for stationarity using the Dickey-Fuller regression. Table 7 contains the estimation and test results for the three versions of equation 4.4a which have been estimated using quarterly data for the time period from 1962:1 to 1971:1.[44]

---

[43] Unit root hypotheses were not rejected at the 10% level for all variables using the standard Dickey-Fuller unit root test. However, after taking first differences the unit root hypotheses were rejected at the 1% level for all variables.

[44] The test statistics for the Dickey-Fuller regressions for co-integration are from Engle and Yoo (1987).

Table 7
Long-Run Reaction Functions of the Bundesbank (equation 4.4a),
1962:1-1971:1

α	γ	ϕ	λ	R^2	DW	DF[a]
0.84	-9.05	1.21	0.002	99	1.70	-5.27**
0.21	0.58	0.05	0.003			
1.00	-9.15	1.21	0.003	99	1.75	-5.21*
	0.56	0.04	0.003			
0.00	-8.53	1.17	-0.004	98	1.01	-3.55
	0.67	0.05	0.003			

[a] Dickey-Fuller test statistic for no co-integration
* significant at the 1% level, ** significant at the 5% level

Table 7 suggests that focusing exclusively on the exchange rate target ($\alpha=0$) was not a long-run equilibrium for the Bundesbank. Instead, the long-run behavior with the highest probability is the one where the Bundesbank focuses entirely on the inflation target ($\alpha=1$). Yet, the test results show also that the Bundesbank, though with a smaller probability, possibly focused on both targets but assigning a relatively larger weight to the inflation target ($\alpha=0.84$). All in all, the Bundesbank seemed not willing to adjust its monetary policy to stabilize the Bretton Woods system, which comes as no surprise since the Bundesbank continuously complained that the Bretton Woods system suffered from an inflationary bias.[45]

However, the question still remains how to square these findings with the Bundesbank's complaints that it had to react on many occasions to external pressures.[46] Most likely the Bundesbank adjusted its money supply only partly to changes in the desired money supply and otherwise reacted to short-term shocks. This can be assessed using the error correction representation of the Bundesbank's money supply function.

---

[45] 'It may, from all the experiences in the post-war period, be safely said that our present international system has a clear inflationary bias and a clear bias to the disadvantage of surplus countries.' See Emminger (1967) p. 518.

[46] See Emminger (1976) pp.514/17 and Schlesinger and Bockelmann (1973) pp. 181/202.

$$(4.5) \quad \Delta m_t = a + \sum_{i=0}^{n} (b_i \Delta y_{t-i} + c_i \Delta i_{t-i} + d_i \Delta p_{t-1-i} + f_i \Delta p_{t-i}^* + g_i \Delta \bar{e}_{t-i} + h_i \Delta m_{t-1-i}) - k \, EC_{t-1}$$

Equation 4.5 is the error correction form of the Bundesbank's money supply function based on the co-integration model. All terms but the last in equation 5 capture the Bundesbank's short-run reaction to internal and external shocks. The last term (error correction term) captures the adjustment from the deviation from the long-run money supply in the previous period.[47]

Table 8

**Error Correction Representation of the Bundesbank's
Money Supply Function
(equation 4.5), 1962:4 - 1971:1**

k	a	c_7	d_3	f_6	h_5	R^2	LM[a]
0.22*	0.029*	-0.004**	-0.33**	0.43***	-0.54*	62	0.13
0.05	0.003	0.002	0.15	0.21	0.15		
k	a	c_7	d_6		h_5	R^2	LM
0.14*	0.029	-0.006*	-0.22		-0.42*	53	0.38
0.05	0.003	0.002	0.14		0.16		

[a] Breusch-Godfrey first order autocorrelation statistic
*, **, *** significant at the 1, 5, and 10% levels

Table 8 contains the regression results for two error correction models. The first corresponds to the co-integration relation where the Bundesbank focuses on inflation and the exchange rate ($\alpha=0.84$). The second corresponds to the co-integration relation where the Bundesbank focuses only on inflation ($\alpha=1$). In both cases equation 4.5 was first estimated with eight lags for all first differences. Lags that were insignificant were then eliminated, taking care that this did not induce residual autocorrelation.

In the first case the coefficient on the error correction term (k) reveals that 22% of the previous quarter's discrepancy between the actual and the desired money supply was corrected each quarter. In other words, the Bundesbank reacted to other factors in the short-run and adjusted only a portion of its money supply towards the desired level. The reaction to interest rate changes is consistent with the prediction of the money demand function although the lag seems very long. The Bundesbank apparently did not react to output shocks, indicating that it did not attempt to fine-tune the economy. The negative reaction to domestic price changes three quarters

---

[47] The error correction term (EC_{t-1}) is the difference between the actual money supply and the desired money supply (equation 4.4a) in the last period.

earlier as well as the positive reaction to foreign price changes six quarters earlier are consistent with the predictions of the long-run model. The Bundesbank also reacted quite significantly to money supply shocks five quarters lagged. These money supply shocks could possibly have been caused by external factors such as balance of payments disequilibria.

In the second case most reactions are similar to the first case. The adjustment to errors in the previous period is somewhat smaller. Moreover, the reaction to changes in the domestic price level, though consistent, is not very significant and much more delayed. All in all, the results in both configurations seems to be consistent with the Bundesbank's complaints that it had on occasion to adjust to external disequilibria.

4.2 Monetary Policy and Central Bank Independence in the Post Bretton Woods Period

During the Bretton Woods period, the Bundesbank already possessed statutory independence,[48] after the breakdown of the Bretton Woods system the Bundesbank became completely independent. The first formal argument that central bank independence can actually improve economic policy making was given by Rogoff (1985). Based on the articles by Kydland and Prescott (1979) and Barro and Gordon (1983a,b), he showed that appointing an independent conservative central banker is actually in the interest of both the public and the government.[49]

The concept of central bank independence contains several testable implications. The argument made by Rogoff would predict that compared to fiscal policy, monetary policy would react more strongly to inflationary pressures and less to output shocks. Furthermore, average inflation should be lower in countries with

---

[48] Here, statutory independence is defined as formal independence from the executive branch of the government. A central bank is independent from the government if the latter cannot (1) determine the formation and execution of monetary policy, (2) elect and recall officials of the central bank at will, and (3) require the central bank to finance the budget deficit or exercise financial control over the central bank in any other way. Along these criteria, the Bundesbank has been ranked the most independent central bank besides the Swiss central bank by all studies in this area; See Bade & Parkin (1985), Alesina (1988), Grilli, Masciandaro, & Tabellini (1991), Cukierman, Webb, & Neyapti (1991).

[49] See section 1.

independent central banks.[50] In addition, an independent central bank should be less inclined to accommodate fiscal deficits and its policy should not be correlated with the electoral cycle or partisan changes in government.

Demopoulos et.al. (1987) and Burdekin and Laney (1988) analyzed the relation between fiscal deficits and monetary constitutions in a cross-country comparison. Both studies concluded that only the independent central banks did not accommodate government budget deficits.[51] Alesina et.al. (1991) and Johnson and Siklos (1992) studied the effects of electoral and partisan variables on monetary policy in OECD countries. All find relatively little evidence for electoral or partisan influence on monetary policy for independent as well as dependent central banks. Nevertheless, they detect that monetary policy in Germany eased before elections in the post Bretton Woods period.

The relation between average inflation and central bank constitutions has been studied by several authors.[52] All find that lower average inflation is associated with higher central bank independence. They also find that the Bundesbank, which is usually ranked as the most independent central bank, does best on this score. Finally, many monetary reaction functions have been estimated to study whether different monetary constitutions have an effect on how central banks react to inflation, unemployment, or fiscal deficits.[53] The results confirmed that the more independent

---

[50] Simple cross-country comparisons of inflation and output growth performances can be misleading if one cannot distinguish differences in inflation and output growth that were caused by different policies from those caused by different economic conditions. In the Rogoff framework, only the mean of inflation is a function of policy variables alone. The variance of inflation as well as of output growth are functions of policy as well as country specific structural variables while the mean of output growth is only a function of country specific structural variables (natural rate). For example, the variance of output growth can be smaller in the country with the more independent central bank because the variance of its output shocks is smaller.

[51] Demopoulos et.al. (1987) actually show that the Bundesbank did accommodate the seasonal increases in the budget deficit. However, using seasonally adjusted data they find that the Bundesbank did not accommodate the budget deficit.

[52] See for example Banaian, Laney, & Willet (1986), Bade & Parkin (1985), and Alesina & Summers (1991).

[53] These studies all differ in their choice of dependent and independent variables. However, most of them use either money growth or the interest rate as the dependent variable and a combination of inflation, real growth, unemployment, and fiscal deficit as the independent variables. A summary of most estimation results is given in Bade and Parkin (1985). A more recent attempt to estimate cross country monetary reaction functions has been made by Johnson and Siklos (1992).

central banks reacted more strongly to inflationary pressures, however, they also tended to ease money supply whenever unemployment rose and accommodated fiscal deficits to some degree. This pattern was particularly strong in the case of Germany.[54]

These findings raise the question whether the so-called independent central banks are actually so independent. Simple cross-country comparisons might be misleading since they only reveal how central banks of varying degrees of statutory independence behave. Yet, their behavior could be a pure reflection of structural differences between countries. Following Rogoff, the degree of independence can best be tested by comparing the reaction of the monetary authority to inflation and unemployment with that of the government in each country separately. The testable implication would be that an independent central bank should react more strongly than the government to inflationary pressures but more weakly to rising unemployment.[55]

Fiscal policy in the form of the budget deficit is certainly a good representative of the government's economic policy. Then, assuming that fiscal and monetary policy both have inflation and output control as policy targets, monetary policy is independent and conservative if it has a higher preference for inflation control. The model for deriving the reaction functions for the Bundesbank (BB) and the fiscal authority (FA) is given by:[56]

---

[54] See Bade and Parkin (1985) p. 27.

[55] To be sure, the idea is not that fiscal policy could actually have a long-run impact on inflation, output, or employment independent from monetary policy. Instead, the purpose of this test is to test whether the government has a different attitude towards inflation and unemployment.

[56] This model is a modification of the model used by Bradley and Potter (1986) who analyzed the reaction functions of the Federal Reserve Bank and the U.S. Treasury. The structure of the theoretical framework is the same for both authorities, however, preferences and views on the economy may differ. Thus, those parameters that may be different are indexed (i=BB,FA).

The constraints (equations 4.7, 4.8, and 4.9) represent only each's authorities view on the economy and not necessarily the true structure of the economy. Furthermore, the model implies that fiscal policy makers think that they could have a permanent effect on inflation and output independent from monetary policy. This certainly neglects the budget constraint of fiscal policy. In reality, this would only be possible if the budget deficit was monetized by the central bank.

(4.6) $\min L_i = (\Delta p_t - \Delta \bar{p}_t)^2 + \mu_i(\Delta y_t - \Delta \bar{y}_t)^2 + \lambda_i(\Delta e_t - \Delta \bar{e}_t)^2$

(4.7) $\Delta p_t = \alpha_i \Delta m_t + \beta_i D_t + \Delta p_t^f$

(4.8) $\Delta y_t = \gamma_i \Delta m_t + \delta_i D_t + \Delta y_t^f$

(4.9) $\Delta e_t = \rho_i \Delta m_t + \sigma_i D_t + \Delta e_t^f$

When i=BB, equation 4.6 is the Bundesbank's loss function which it minimizes subject to equations 4.7, 4.8, and 4.9 using the growth rate of money supply (Δm_t). The loss function consists of three components; an inflation target (Δp_t), a growth target (Δy_t), and the DM/$ exchange rate (Δe_t).[57] The exchange rate target has been included since DM/$ exchange rate developments at times had significant impacts on the Bundesbank's monetary policy.[58] When i=FA, equation 4.6 is the fiscal authority's loss function which it minimizes subject to the same constraints using the budget deficit (D_t). Equations 4.7, 4.8, and 4.9 reflect the Bundesbank's and the fiscal authority's view of the structure of the economy. In this case, both use the same model but different parameter values; the rate of inflation, output growth, and the exchange rate changes are each determined by their forecasted values (Δp_t^f, Δy_t^f, Δe_t^f) and the two policy variables. The two reaction functions for the Bundesbank and the fiscal authority are the following:

(4.10) $\Delta m_t = g_{10} + g_{11}\Delta p_t^f + g_{12}\Delta y_t^f + g_{13}\Delta e_t^f + g_{14}D_t$

(4.11) $D_t = g_{20} + g_{21}\Delta p_t^f + g_{22}\Delta p_t^f + g_{23}\Delta e_t^f + g_{24}\Delta m_t$

---

[57] The variables in equations 4.6 to 4.9 are the following: p_t is the log of the price level, y_t is the log of real GNP, e_t is the log of the DM/$ exchange rate, Δ is the first difference operator, m_t is the log of central bank money, and D_t is the public sector deficit.

[58] See Bundesbank annual reports 1986-88.

Where: $g_{10} = M^{-1}(\alpha_{BB}\Delta\bar{p}_t + \mu_{BB}\gamma_{BB}\Delta\bar{y}_t + lamda_{BB}\rho_{BB}\Delta\bar{e}_t)$

$g_{11} = -M^{-1}\alpha_{BB}$

$g_{12} = -M^{-1}\mu_{BB}\gamma_{BB}$

$g_{13} = -M^{-1}\lambda_{BB}\rho_{BB}$

$g_{14} = -M^{-1}(\alpha_{BB}\beta_{BB}+\mu_{BB}\gamma_{BB}\delta_{BB}+\lambda_{BB}\ \rho_{BB}\sigma_{BB})$

$M = \alpha_{BB}{}^2 + \mu_{BB}\gamma_{BB}{}^2 + \lambda_{BB}\ \rho_{BB}{}^2$

$g_{20} = L^{-1}(\beta_{FA}\Delta\bar{p}_t + \mu_{FA}\delta_{FA}\Delta\bar{y}_t + \lambda_{FA}\sigma_{FA}\Delta\bar{e}_t)$

$g_{21} = -L^{-1}\beta_{FA}$

$g_{22} = -L^{-1}\mu_{FA}\delta_{FA}$

$g_{23} = -L^{-1}\lambda_{FA}\sigma_{FA}$

$g_{24} = -L^{-1}(\alpha_{FA}\beta_{FA}+\mu_{FA}\gamma_{FA}\delta_{FA}+\lambda_{FA}\rho_{FA}\sigma_{FA})$

$L = \beta_{FA}{}^2 + \mu_{FA}\delta_{FA}{}^2 + \lambda_{FA}\sigma_{FA}{}^2$

Equations 4.10 and 4.11 are actually nonlinear but are presented as simple linear functions, since each function is underdetermined. The signs of the g coefficients depend upon the signs for the parameters of the constraints. In this case, it is simply assumed that expansionary monetary policy and fiscal deficits increase inflation and output and cause a depreciation of the currency ($\alpha,\gamma,\rho>0$; $\beta,\delta,\sigma<0$), thus money supply growth should react contractionary to predicted increases in inflation, output growth, and currency depreciation ($g_{11},g_{12},g_{13}<0$), the budget deficit should react expansionary to predicted decreases in inflation, output growth, and currency depreciation ($g_{21},g_{22},g_{23}>0$).

Before the reaction functions can be estimated, values for predicted inflation, output growth, and currency depreciation must be constructed. Following Bradley and Potter (1986), forecasts are constructed using a rolling ARMA model for each variable. This is done in a two step procedure. First, an ARMA specification is identified for each variable.[59] Second, each ARMA is estimated for a certain sample and the one-period forecast is stored. Step two is repeated until each forecast series is complete moving the sample one period forward at a time.

---

[59] The inflation rate has been identified as an ARMA(1,8) with Q(8)=5.2, GNP growth as an ARMA(1,6) with Q(8)=3.5, and DM/\$ rate changes as an ARMA(1,4) with Q(8)=2.8.

Three modification of equations 4.10 and 4.11 have been made before estimation. First, the lagged fiscal deficit has been included into the Bundesbank's reaction function to control for the possibility that the Bundesbank monetizes the budget deficit.[60] This is important since fiscal policy cannot have an effect on inflation and output in the long-run without accommodation by monetary policy. Second, lagged values of the dependent variables have been included in each reaction function to allow for partial adjustment. Third, two dummy variables have been added to test the impact of elections and regime shifts on monetary and fiscal policy.[61] Given these modifications, equations 4.10 and 4.11 are rewritten as:

$$(4.12) \quad \Delta m_t = g_{10} + g_{11}\Delta p_t^f + g_{12}\Delta y_t^f + g_{13}\Delta e_t^f + g_{14}D_t + g_{15}D_{t-1} + g_{16}\Delta m_{t-1}$$
$$+ g_{1e}d_e + g_{1p}d_p$$

$$(4.13) \quad D_t = g_{20} + g_{21}\Delta p_t^f + g_{22}\Delta y_t^f + g_{23}\Delta e_t^f + g_{24}\Delta m_t + g_{25}D_{t-1} + g_{2e}d_e + g_{2p}d_p$$

Equations 4.12 and 4.13 have been estimated by two stage least squares using seasonally adjusted quarterly data for the 1975:1 - 1989:4 period.[62]

The results in table 9 show that the Bundesbank primarily focused on price stabilization. The second most important objective seems to be the DM/$ exchange rate. The sign for the output growth target is positive but not significant. These results confirm that the Bundesbank primarily tried to safeguard the value of the currency as is required by the Bundesbank Act. Yet, not consistent with this objective is the fact that the Bundesbank seems to have been accommodating the government's budget deficit (g_{14} and g_{15} are negative). The estimates also suggest that contrary to earlier findings by Alesina et.al. (1991) and Johnson and Siklos (1992) the

---

[60] The inclusion of past fiscal deficits has been limited to the one period lagged fiscal deficit since others were statistically not significant.

[61] The election dummy (d_e) takes the value one for the election quarter and the three quarters preceding the election and zero otherwise. For the 1983 election only the first quarter preceding the election takes the value one since a change in government occurred in the second quarter. The regime shift dummy (d_p) is zero for the SPD/FDP coalition government (1975:1-1982:3) and one for the CDU/FDP coalition government (1982:4-1989:4).

[62] The sample begins in 1975 for two reasons. First, the Bundesbank began to control central bank money in 1975. Second, no quarterly data for the total public sector deficit is available before 1974. The sample ends in 1989 to avoid the distortions in money supply caused by German monetary unification in 1990.

Bundesbank did not ease its money supply before elections.[63] On the other hand, the change in government in 1982 had a significant effect on monetary policy.

Table 9

Bundesbank Reaction Function with Election and Partisan Dummies (equation 4.12), 1975:1 - 1989:4

0 g_{10}	g_{11}	g_{12}	g_{13}	g_{14}	g_{15}	g_{16}	$g_{1\bullet}$	g_{1p}	R^2	LMᵃ
0.013*	-0.56*	-0.08	-0.07***	-0.10	-0.28***	0.31*	-0.0009	-0.005*	40	0.16
0.004	0.18	0.11	0.04	0.17	0.18	0.12	0.0018	0.002		

FA reaction function with election and partisan dummies (equation 4.13), 1975:1 - 1989:4

g_{20}	g_{21}	g_{22}	g_{23}	g_{24}	g_{25}	$g_{2\bullet}$	$g_{2\bullet}$	ρ^b	R^2	LMᵃ
-0.002	-0.21***	0.09	0.03	0.005	0.70*	-0.0005	-0.0005	-0.50**	29	0.005
0.003	0.14	0.09	0.03	0.095	0.13	0.0011	0.0013	0.26		

ᵃ Breusch-Godfrey test for first order autocorrelation;
ᵇ autocorrelation coefficient
*,**,*** significant at the 1, 5, 10 % levels.

The fiscal authority reacted to changes in forecasted output growth in the predicted manner, though the sign is not very significant. It is surprising that the fiscal authority increased its budget deficit when the inflation forecasts rose. The most obvious explanation seems to be that rising inflation reduces the real deficit leaving room for increases in the nominal deficit. Furthermore, the fiscal authority did not react to changes in money supply, suggesting that the fiscal authority determined its policy without direct consideration of monetary policy. Finally, the two political dummy variables have no significant effect on fiscal policy.

All in all, the results confirm that the Bundesbank is independent according to Rogoff's definition. Nonetheless, the Bundesbank seems to have been monetizing the budget deficit somewhat. However, monetizing the budget deficit does not necessarily make the Bundesbank dependent. Alesina and Tabellini (1987) showed that if the social welfare function includes stabilizing the budget deficit then an independent conservative central banker in Rogoff's sense would monetize the budget deficit to some degree but less than the government would. Finally, a structural change (Chow) test applied to separate estimations of the two time periods before and after the change in government in 1982 does not detect a structural change in the Bundesbank's reaction function. The null-hypothesis of no structural change can only

---

[63] Alesina et.al.. used the growth rate of M1 which the Bundesbank never controlled. Compared to central bank money, M1 behaves quite differently and has no stable demand function. See also Trehan (1988). Their finding that the Bundesbank supported the electoral cycle could be distorted by the selection of an inappropriate policy instrument.

be rejected for the fiscal reaction function.[64] In other words, only the fiscal authority but not the Bundesbank was really affected by the change in government.

5.   CONCLUSION: A COMPARISON

The aim of the conclusion is to compare the performance of the target variables of monetary policy under the different policy regimes. Theory predicts that if the policymaker is capable of making a commitment the policy outcome will be first best. On the other hand, if the policymaker is not able to make a commitment a second best outcome can still be achieved through central bank independence.

Table 10

Monetary Policy Regimes

Period	Degree of central bank independence	Policy regime	Commit-ment
1880-1913	Officially dependent Practically independent	Classical Gold Standard	Yes
1925-1932	Officially and practically independent (foreign control until 1930)	Gold exchange standard	Mixed
1950-1973	Officially and practically independent	Bretton Woods system	Mixed
1974-1989	Officially and practically independent	Floating exchange rates	No

Table 10 describes the degree of central bank independence and the monetary policy regime in operation for each time period. The pre-war period was dominated by the gold standard rule. In the inter-war period, monetary policy was independent from the government committed to the reestablished gold standard. Nevertheless, the inter-war period can at the most be characterized as a mixed commitment regime since the Reichsbank's commitment was partly offset by the government's inability to restore its credibility and commit itself to the gold standard.

In the Bretton Woods period, central bank independence characterized the legal and practical status of the monetary authority. However, as seen in section 4, the commitment of monetary policy to the Bretton Woods regime was mixed. The floating exchange rate period, on the other hand, is a clear example of independent and conservative central banking.

---

[64] The F-statistic for no structural change for the monetary reaction function is $F(7,46)=1.26$ and for the fiscal reaction function $F(6,46)=2.14$.

Given the mixed nature of the policy regimes in the inter-war and Bretton Woods period as well as other external factors influencing those periods (depression, reconstruction boom) it seems best to limit the comparison to the Classical Gold Standard period and the floating exchange rate period.

Table 11 exhibits the figures for inflation, output growth, per capita output growth, money growth, money velocity growth, and the debt-GNP ratio for the four periods described in table 10. Inflation and output growth embody the target variables of both monetary and fiscal policy. Money growth and to some extent money velocity are the policy variables of monetary policy. The debt/GNP ratio characterizes the fiscal policy variable. A first examination seems to suggest that the Bretton Woods period did best combining the highest output growth with moderate inflation. By contrast, the inter-war period appears to be the worst, having the lowest and most unstable output growth as well as a massive deflation. However, as pointed out before, the performances in these two periods were distorted by other factors and are not ideal measures to compare the different policy regimes. A first examination of the inflation and output growth performance during the Classical Gold Standard and the floating exchange rate periods does not provide clear results. In terms of average inflation and output growth the Classical Gold Standard period was clearly the better of the two. Yet, per capita output growth was stronger in the floating exchange rate regime. Moreover, in terms of inflation and output growth stability the floating exchange rate period outperformed the Classical Gold Standard period.

In section 1 it had been shown that in terms of a specific social welfare function (quadratic loss function of inflation and output growth) the commitment regime is first best. This social welfare function can be used to compare the performances of the Classical Gold Standard regime and the floating exchange rate regime.

Table 11

Comparison of Target and Policy Variables[66]

Period	Target variables			Monetary policy variable		Fiscal policy variable
	Inflation	Output growth	Per capita output growth	Money growth	Velocity growth	Debt-GNP ratio
1880-1913	0.9 (5.7) up	2.9 (8.1) flat	1.7 (8.1) flat	5.7 (23.4) flat	-1.9 (37.8) flat	53.0 (32.8) up
1925-1932	-0.8 (36.9) up	1.2 (92.6) down	0.6 (89.4) down	1.4 (102.3) down	-1.0 (83.3) flat	28.4 (113.4) up
1950-1973	2.4 (7.7) up	6.8 (19.6) down	5.1 (10.8) down	14.7 (39.4) down	-5.5 (47.0) up	18.5 (4.2) flat
1974-1989	3.5 (4.1) down	2.1 (3.6) down	2.2 (3.7) flat	6.2 (19.1) down	-0.5 (30.2) up	34.0 (55.2) up

For a data description see the appendix. Variances are in parentheses underneath each average. The direction of the trend in each period is indicated below the variances. See also figures 1 to 6.

$$(5.1) \quad y_i = \bar{y}_i + (\pi_i - \pi_i^e) - \varepsilon_i, \; i = CGS, FER$$

$$(5.2) \quad L_i = E[(\pi_i - \pi_i^*)^2 + \lambda_i (y_i - k_i)^2]$$

According to equation 5.1, the natural rate of output growth in the two periods[67] can be set equal to the average rates of output growth in table 11. Minimizing equation 5.2 for both regimes subject to equation 5.1 gives the following inflation and output growth functions.

---

[66] Annual averages

[67] CGS stands for Classical Gold Standard period and FER for floating exchange rate period.

$$(5.3) \quad \pi_{CGS} = \pi^*_{CGS} + \frac{\lambda_{CGS}}{1+\lambda_{CGS}}\varepsilon_{CGS}$$

$$(5.4) \quad \pi_{FER} = \pi^*_{FER} + \mu_{FER}k_{FER} + \frac{\mu_{FER}}{1+\mu_{FER}}\varepsilon_{FER}$$

$$(5.5) \quad y_{CGS} = \bar{y}_{CGS} - \frac{1}{1+\lambda_{CGS}}\varepsilon_{CGS}$$

$$(5.6) \quad y_{FER} = \bar{y}_{FER} - \frac{1}{1+\mu_{FER}}\varepsilon_{FER}$$

Using equations 5.3 to 5.6 equation 5.2 can be rewritten for both periods as follows:

$$(5.7) \quad L_{CGS} = var(\pi_{CGS}) + \lambda_{CGS}(\bar{y}_{CGS}-k_{CGS})^2 + \lambda_{CGS}var(y_{CGS})$$

$$(5.8) \quad L_{FER} = var(\pi_{FER}) + \mu^2_{FER}k^2_{FER} + \lambda_{FER}(\bar{y}_{FER}-k_{FER})^2 + \lambda_{FER}var(y_{FER})$$

Assuming that the weight parameters in the social welfare functions were identical in both periods and furthermore assuming that the difference between natural and desired output growth were equal in both periods, the difference between equations 5.7 and 5.8 is as follows:

$$(5.9) \quad L_{CGS} - L_{FER} = var(\pi_{CGS}) - var(\pi_{FER}) - \mu^2_{FER}k^2_{FER} + \lambda(var(y_{CGS})-var(y_{FER}))$$

Equation 5.9 still contains two unknown parameters, the second power of the inflation bias ($\mu_{FER}{}^2k_{FER}{}^2$) and the weight parameter λ. The value of the second power of the inflation bias can be determined assuming that the Bundesbank allowed for approximately 2% inflation.[68] Then, given that the average inflation was 3.5%, the inflation bias would be 1.5% It is probably impossible to quantify the weight parameter, but the theoretical model implies that under otherwise identical

---

[68] The Bundesbank indicated in its annual reports when setting the annual monetary growth target that it considered approximately 2% annual inflation unavoidable. See Bundesbank annual reports since 1975.

circumstances the loss under commitment should always be smaller than the loss under discretion with central bank independence as long as λ is bigger than zero. Yet, inserting the variances of inflation and output growth from table 2 into equation 5.9 shows that for any λ bigger than 0.16 the loss under floating exchange rates with central bank independence was smaller than under the Classical Gold Standard.[69] Since a λ larger than 0.16 seems not unreasonable for Germany[70] in either period, equation 5.9 implies that social welfare under the floating exchange rate regime with central bank independence was higher than under the Classical Gold Standard.

However, the procedure has not controlled for different output shocks (ε). Yet, different variances of ε can distort the analysis significantly. Deriving the variances for output growth from equations 5.5 and 5.6 and assuming that variances of the output shocks are identical implies that the variance of output growth under discretion with central bank independence must be greater than the variance of output growth under commitment.[71] However, table 11 shows that the output growth variance under the Classical Gold Standard was twice as large as under the floating exchange rate regime. In other words, it must be concluded that the variance of the output shock under the Classical Gold Standard was much greater, distorting the results of the comparative analysis. Bordo (1992) finds that the variance of supply shocks (ε) was 1.7 times larger in the Classical Gold Standard period compared to the floating exchange rate period.[72]

A second distortion could come from the initial assumption that the public was equally inflation averse in both periods. One could easily argue that because of two dramatic inflation periods the German public was more inflation averse in the post-war period. As a result, the previous comparison would be biased in favor of the post-war period.

---

[69] $L_{CGS} - L_{FER} = 5.7 - 4.1 - 2.3 + \lambda(8.1 - 3.7)$.

[70] λ=0 implies that society would tolerate 0.4 percentage inflation above target in exchange for a 1 percentage point increase in output growth above the natural rate of output growth.

[71] $\frac{1}{(1+\lambda)^2}\sigma^2 < \frac{1}{(1+\mu)^2}\sigma^2, \lambda>\mu>0$

[72] See Bordo (1992), table 4.

Appendix
Data Sources

Table 1: d_t: Reichsbank discount rate (monthly average, sa), NBER 13, 15. d_t^{UK}: U.K. discount rate (monthly average, sa), Bank of England, NBER 13, 13.

Table 2:   Same as table 1 but annual averages.

Table 3: p_t: Log of cost of living index (quarterly average, sa), Institut für Konjunkturforschung, Konjunkturstatistisches Handbuch 1936, Berlin, 1935, p.107.

y_t: Log of real net national product (quarterly average, sa), the annual real NNP (Walther Hoffmann, Das Wachstum der deutschen Wirtschaft seit Mitte des 19. Jahrhunderts, 1965, pp.827/8) was benchmarked using the quarterly index of production in manufacturing (Institut für Konjunkturforschung, Konjunkturstatistisches Handbuch 1936, Berlin, 1935, p.52).

w_t: Log of hourly wage index (quarterly average, sa), the index has been constructed by dividing the total wage sums by total hours worked. The total wage sum was obtained from Konjunkturstatistisches Handbuch 1936, Institut für Konjunkturforschung, Berlin, 1935, p.95. Total Hours worked are the product of total employment and average hours per employee. Total employment is an update of the employment data of the Konjunkturstatistisches Handbuch 1936, p.12, and has kindly been provided by Albrecht Ritschl. Average hours per employee is an update from average hours per employee in industry from 'Beschäftigung, Arbeitszeit und Arbeitereinkommen in der deutschen Industrie', Statistisches Reichsamt, Sonderbeilage zu 'Wirtschaft und Statistik', 1935, Nr.13.

Table 4:   Same data as table 3 excluding y_t.

Table 5:   Same data as table 3 plus m_t: Log of currency in circulation (quarterly average, sa), Institut für Konjunkturforschung, Konjunkturstatistisches Handbuch 1936, Berlin, 1935, p.130.

Table 7: m_t: Log of central bank money (quarterly average, sa), Deutsche Bundesbank, Statistische Beihefte zu den Monatsberichten der Deutschen Bundesbank, Reihe 4, table 35.

y_t: Log of real GNP (quarterly, sa), ibid, table 1

i_t: Nominal short run interest rate (quarterly average, sa), day-to-day rate, Deutsche Bundesbank monthly report, table V.6

p_t: Log of cost of living index (quarterly average, sa), ibid, table VIII.7

$\bar{e}_t$: Log of DM/\$ fixed exchange rate (quarterly average), ibid, table IX.9

p_t^*: Log of US consumer price index (quarterly average, sa), Citibase

bp_t: Real balance of payments (quarterly, sa), Deutsche Bundesbank monthly report, table IX.1

Table 8:   Same as table 7.

Table 9:   Same data sources as table 7 plus

D_t: Total government (Federal, States, and Local) budget deficit (quarterly, sa), Deutsche Bundesbank monthly report, table VII.2

Table 11 and figures 1 to 6:

Consumer price index: 1880-1979, Sommariva and Tullio (1987) pp.231-234. 1980-1989, Deutsche Bundesbank, Monthly Reports.

Real GNP: 1880-1979, Sommariva and Tullio (1987) pp.226-229. 1980-1989, Deutsche Bundesbank, Monthly Reports.

Population: 1880-1979, Sommariva and Tullio (1987) pp.234-238. 1980-1989, International Financial Statistics Yearbook 1990.

M2: 1880-1913, Bordo (1986), "Financial Crises, Banking Crises, Stockmarket Crashes and the Money Supply: Some International Evidence" in F. Capie and G. Wood eds., Financial Crisis and the World Banking System, 1924-1933, Bordo and Jonung (1987), 1950-1989, Deutsche Bundesbank Monthly Reports.

Public Debt (Federal, Regional, and Local): Deutsche Bundesbank (1976): Deutsches Geld und Bankwesen in Zahlen 1876-1975, Tables 1.01 and 1.02.

REFERENCES

Alesina, Alberto. 1988. Macroeconomics and Politics. In *NBER Macroeconomics Annual*, edited by S. Fischer. MIT Press.

Alesina, Alberto. 1989. Politics and Business Cycles in Industrial Democracies. *Economic Policy*.

Alesina, Alberto and Guido Tabellini. 1987. Rules and Discretion with Noncoordinated Monetary and Fiscal Policies. *Economic Inquiry*, 25.

Alesina, Alberto and Lawrence H. Summers. 1991. Central Bank Independence and Macroeconomic Performance: Some Comparative Evidence. Unpublished.

Alesina, Alberto, Cohen, G.D., and N. Roubini. 1991. Macroeconomic Policy and Elections in OECD Democracies. *NBER Research Working Paper No.* 3830.

Alesina, Alberto and Grilli Vittorio. 1991. The European Central Bank: Reshaping Monetary Politics in Europe. Prepared for CEPR/IMF Conference on 'The Creation of a Central Bank'.

Bade, Robin and Michael Parkin. 1985. Central bank Laws and Monetary Policy. Unpublished.

Balderston, Theodore. 1971. The German Business Cycle in the 1920's: A Comment. *Economic History Review*, 30.

Balderston, Theodore. 1982. The Origins of Economic Instability in Germany, 1924-30: Market Forces versus Economic Policy. *Vierteljahresschrift fur Sozial - und Wirtschaftsgeschichte*, 69.

Balderston, Theodore. 1983. The Beginning of the Depression in Germany, 1927-30: Investment and the Capital Market. *Economic History Review*, 36.

Barro, Robert L. and David B. Gordon. 1983a. A Positive Theory of Monetary Policy in a Natural Rate Model. *Journal of Political Economy*, 91.

Barro, Robert L. and David B. Gordon. 1983b. Rules, Discretion and Reputation in a Model of Monetary Policy. *Journal of Monetary Economics*, 12.1.

Bendixen, Friedrich. 1919/20. Die Inflation als Rettungsmittel. *Bank-Archiv*, 19.

Bente, Hermann. 1926. Die Deutsche Währungspolitik von 1914 bis 1924. *Weltwirtschaftliches Archiv*, 23.

Bloomfield, Arthur I. 1959. *Monetary Policy under the International Gold Standard, 1880-1914*. Federal Reserve Bank Of New York.

Bloomfield, Arthur I. 1963. Short Term Capital Movements under the Pre-1914 Gold Standard. *Princeton Studies in International Finance*, 11.

Bopp, Karl R. 1954. Die Tätigkeit der Reichsbank von 1876-1914. *Weltwirtschaftliches Archiv*, 72.

Borchardt, Knut. 1976. Währung und Wirtschaft. In *Deutsche Bundesbank (ed.): Wahrung und Wirtschaft in Deutschland, 1876-1975*. Fritz Knapp Verlag.

Borchardt, Knut. 1979. Zwangslagen und Handlungsspielräume in der großen Wirtschaftskrise der frühen dreißiger Jahre. *Jahrbuch der Bayrischen Akademie der Wissenschaften*.

Borchardt, Knut. 1980. *Wirtschaftliche Ursachen des Scheiterns der Weimarer Republik; in Erdmann, K.D. and Schulze, H. (eds.): Weimar, Selbstpreisgabe einer Demokratie*. Eine Bilanz heute. Düsseldorf.

Borchardt, Knut. 1990. A Decade of Debate about Brünings's Economic Policy. In *Economic Crisis and Political Collapse: The Weimar Republic 1924-1933*, edited by Jürgen von Baron von. Berg.

Bordo, Michael D. and Finn E. Kydland. 1992. The Gold Standard as a 'Rule'. *Federal Reserve Bank of Cleveland Working Paper No. 9205*, March.

Bordo Michael D. 1993. The Bretton Woods International Monetary System: An Historical Overview. In *A Retrospective on the Bretton Woods System: Lessons for International Monetary Reform*, edited by Michael Bordo and Barry Eichengreen. University of Chicago Press.

Bordo, Michael D. 1992. The Gold Standard, Bretton Woods and other Monetary Regimes: An Historical Appraisal. Paper presented at Federal Reserve Bank of St. Louis Annual Policy Conference. October.

Bradley, Michael D. & Potter, Susan M. 1986. The State of the Federal Budget and the State of the Economy: Further Evidence. *Economic Inquiry*, 24.

Burdekin, Richard C.K. and Leroy O. Laney. 1988. Fiscal Policy Making and Central Bank Institutional Constraint. *Kyklos*, vol. 41.

Caesar, Rolf. 1980. Die Unabhängigkeit der Notenbanken im Demokratischen Staat: Argumente und Gegenargumente. *Zeitschrift für Politik*, vol. 25.

Cukierman, A., Webb, S.B., and B. Neyapti. 1991. The Measurement of Central Bank Independence and its Effects on Policy Outcomes. Unpublished.

De Kock, Gabriel and Victorio Grilli. 1989. Endogenous Exchange Rate Regime Switches. *NBER Working Paper No. 3066*, August.

Demopoulos, George D., Katsimbris, George M., and Stephen M. Miller. Monetary Policy and Central Bank Financing of Government Budget Deficits: A Cross-Country Comparison. *European Economic Review*, 31.

Deutsche Bundesbank. 1976. *Deutsches Geld - und Bankenwesen in Zahlen, 1876 - 1975*. Verlag Fritz Knapp, Frankfurt/M.

Deutsche Bundesbank. 1989. The Deutsche Bundesbank. Its Monetary Policy Instruments and Functions. *Deutsche Bundesbank Special Series No.7*.

Deutsche Bundesbank. *Annual Reports*, Various Issues.

Die Finanzen des Deutschen Reiches in den Rechnungsjahren 1914-1918: Denkschrift der Reichsregierung vom 12. März 1919. *Finanz-Archiv*, 36.

Eichengreen, Barry. 1992. The Gold Standard since Alec Ford. In *Britain in the International Economy 1870-1939*, edited by S.N. Broadberry and N.F.R. Crafts. Cambridge University Press.

Emminger, Otmar. 1967. Practical Aspects of the Problem of Balance of Payments Adjustment; *Journal of Political Economy*, 75.

Emminger, Otmar. 1976. Deutsche Geld - Währungspolitik im Spannungsfeld zwischen innerem un äußerem Gleichgewicht. In *Währung und Wirtschaft in Deutschland 1876-1975*, edited by Deutsche Bundesbank. Frankfurt/M.

Engle, Robert F. and C.W.J. Granger. 1987. Co-Integration and Error Correction: Representation, Estimation, and Testing. *Econometrica*, 55.2.

Engle, Robert F. and Byung Sam Yoo. 1987. Forecasting and Testing in Co-Integration Systems. *Journal of Econometrics*, 35.

Flink, Salomon. 1929. *The Reichsbank and Economic Germany*. New York.

Fratianni, Michele, Hagen, Jürgen von, and Christopher Waller. 1991. From EMS to EMU. Unpublished. Indiana University.

Friedman, Milton. 1962. Should there be an Independent Central Bank? In *In Search for a Monetary Constitution*, edited by Leland Yeager. Harvard University Press.

Friedrich, Karl. 1923/24. Vom alten zum neuen Bankgesetz. *Bank-Archiv*, 23.

Giovannini, Alberto. 1986. 'Rules of the Game' during the International Gold Standard: England and Germany. *Journal of International Money and Finance*, 5.

Giovannini, Alberto. 1993. Bretton Woods and its Precursors: Rules versus discretion in the History of International Monetary Regimes. In *A Retrospective on the Bretton Woods System: Lessons for International Monetary Reform*, edited by Michael Bordo and Barry Eichengreen. University of Chicago Press.

Goodman, John B. 1989. Monetary Politics in France, Italy, and Germany: 1973-85. In *The Political Economy of European Integration, States, Markets, and Institutions*, edited by Guerrigi and Padsan. Harvester Wheatsheaf, New York.

Goodman, John B. 1910. *Das Geld*. Berlin.

Goodman, John B. 1915. *Deutschlands Volkswohlstand 1888-1913*. 6th edition, Berlin.

Hetzel, Robert L. 1990. Central Banks' Independence in Historical Perspective: A Review Essay. *Journal of Monetary Economics*, 25.

Hoffmann, Walther. 1965. *Das Wachstum der Deutschen Wirtschaft seit Mitte des 19. Jahrhunderts*. Springer Verlag.

Holtfrerich, Carl Ludwig. 1982. Alternativen zu Brünings Wirtschaftspolitik in der Weltwirtschaftskrise. *Historische Zeitschrift*, 235.

Holtfrerich, Carl Ludwig. 1984. Zu hohe Löhne in der Weimarer Republik? Bemerkungen zur Borchardt-These. *Geschichte und Gesellschaft*, 10.

Holtfrerich, Carl Ludwig. 1986. *The German Inflation, 1914-1923*. Walter de Gruyter.

Holtfrerich, Carl Ludwig. 1986. *The German Inflation, 1914-1923: Causes and Effects in International Perspective*. Walter de Gruyter.

Holtfrerich, Carl Ludwig. 1988a. Relations between Monetary Authorities and Governmental Institutions: The Case of Germany from the 19th Century to the Present. In *Central Banks' Independence in Historical Perspective*, edited by Gianni Toniolo. Walter de Gruyter.

Holtfrerich, Carl Ludwig. 1988b. The Monetary Unification in 19th-Century Germany: Relevance and Lessons for Europe Today. In *A European Central Bank? Perspectives on Monetary Unification after ten Years of the EMS*, edited by Marcello De Cecco & Alberto Giovannini. Cambridge University Press.

James, Harold. 1983. Gab es eine Alternative zur Wirtschaftspolitik Brünings? *Vierteljahrschrift für Sozial - und Wirtschaftsgeschichte*, 70.4.

James, Harold. 1986. *The German Slump: Politics and Economics*. Clarendon Press, Oxford.

320 Varieties of Monetary Reforms

Johnson, David R. and Pierre L. Siklos. 1992. Empirical Evidence on the Independence of Central Banks. Unpublished. Wilfred Laurier University.

Keynes, John Maynard. 1973. An Economic Analysis of Unemployment. In *The Collected Writings of John Maynard Keynes*, edited by Donald Moggridge. Vol.13.

Kindelberger, C. 1976. Germany's Persistent Balance of Payments Disequilibrium Revisited. *Banca Nazionale del Lavoro Quarterly Review*, 29.

King, Banaian, Leroy O. Laney and Thomas D. Willett. 1986. Central Bank Independence: An International Comparison. In *Central Bankers, Bureaucratic Incentives, and Monetary Policy*, edited by Mark Toma and Eugenia Toma. Kluwer Academic Publishers.

Kruedener, Jürgen Baron von. 1990. Could Brüning's Policy of Deflation Have Been Successful? In *Economic Crisis and Political Collapse: The Weimar Republic 1924-1933*, edited by Jürgen Baron von Kruedener. Berg.

Lumm, Karl von. 1909. *Die Stellung der Notenbanken in der heutigen Volkswirtschaft*. Berlin.

Lumm, Karl von. 1912. Diskontpolitik. *Bankarchiv*, 11.

Marston, Richard C. 1993. Interest Differentials under Bretton Woods and the Post-Bretton Woods Float: The Effects of Capital Controls and Exchange Rate Risk. In *A Retrospective on the Bretton Woods System: Lessons for International Monetary Reform*, edited by Michael Bordo and Barry Eichengreen. University of Chicago Press.

Masciandaro, Donato and Guido Tabellini. 1988. Monetary Regimes and Fiscal Deficits: A Comparative Analysis. In *Monetary Policy in Pacific Basin Countries*, edited by Hang-Sheng Chong. Kluwer, Boston.

McGouldrick, Paul. 1984. Operations of the German Reichsbank and the Rules of the Game, 1879-1913. In *A Retrospective on the Classical Gold Standard, 1821-1931*, edited by Michael D. Bordo and Anna J. Schwartz. The University of Chicago Press.

McKinnon, Ronald. 1993. International Money in Historical Perspective. *Journal of Economic Literature*. 31.

Mosbacher, Wolfgang. 1974. Reichsbank und Bank von England im Gold Standard vor 1914. *Archiv Sammlung bankgeschichtlicher Aufsätze*, 4.

Müller, Helmut. 1973. *Die Zentralbank - eine Nabenregierung: Reichsbankpräsident Hjalmar Schachtals Politiker der Weimarer Republik*. Westdeutscher Verlag Opladen.

Neumann, Manfred M. 1990a. Precommitment to Stability by Central Bank Independence. *Working Paper Universität Bonn*.

Neumann, Manfred M. 1990b. Central Bank Independence as a Prerequisite of Price Stability. Prepared for 'Economics of European Monetary Union'.

Nordhaus, W. 1975. The Political Business Cycle. *Review of Economic Studies*, 42.

Northrop, Mildred Benedict. 1938. *Control Policies of the Reichsbank, 1924-1933*. New York.

Obstfeld, Maurice. 1993. The Adjustment Mechanism. In *A Retrospective on the Bretton Woods System: Lessons for International Monetary Reform*, edited by Michael D. Bordo and Barry Eichengreen. University of Chicago Press.

Plenge, Johann. 1913. *Von der Diskontpolitik zur Herrschaft über den Geldmarkt*. Berlin.

Presson, Torsten and Guido Tabellini. 1990. *Macroeconomic Policy, Credibility and Politics*. Harwood Academic Publishers.

Prion, Willi. 1919. *Inflation und Geldentwertung: Finanzielle Maßnahmen zum Abbau der Preise. Gutachten erstattet dem Finanzministerium*. Berlin.

Reichsbank. 1911. The Reichsbank, 1876 - 1900. *National Monetary Commission*, vol. X.

Reichsbank. 1912. *Die Reichsbank, 1876 - 1910*. Berlin.

Reichsbank. 1925. *Die Reichsbank, 1901 - 1925*. Berlin.

Reichsbank. *Verwaltungsberichte, 1880 - 1913*. Berlin.

Reichsbank. 1940. *Von der Königlichen Bank zur Deutschen Reichsbank: 175 Jahre Deutscher Notenbankgeschichte*. Berlin.

Roesler, Konrad. 1967. *Die Finanzpolitik des Deutschen Reiches im Ersten Weltkrieg*. Berlin.

Rogoff, Kenneth. 1985. The Optimal Degree of Commitment to an Intermediate Monetary Target. *Quarterly Journal of Economics*, C4.

Schacht, Hjalmar. 1931. *The End of Reparations*. New York.

Schlesinger, Helmut and Horst Bockelmann. 1973. Monetary Policy in the Federal Republic of Germany. In *Monetary Policy in Twelve Countries*, edited by The Federal Reserve Bank of Boston. Boston.

Seeger, Manfred. 1968. *Die Politik der Reichsbank von 1876-1914 im Lichte der Spielregeln der Goldwährung*. Dunker & Humblot, Berlin.

Sommariva, Andrea and Giuseppe Tullio. 1987. *German Macroeconomic History, 1880-1979*. St. Martin's Press.

Stock, James, H. 1987. Asymptotic Properties of Least Squares Estimators of Cointegrating Vectors. *Econometrica*, 55.5.

Trehan, Bharat. 1988. The Practice of Monetary Targeting: A Case Study of the West German Experience. *Federal Reserve Bank of San Francisco Economic Review*.

U.S. Congress. 1952. Monetary Policy and the Management of Public Debt, Report of the Subcommittee on the General Credit and Debt Management of the Joint Committee on the Economic Report, 82nd Congress, 2nd Session.

U.S. National Monetary Commission. 1911. German Banking Inquiry of 1908. vol. 13.

Vergleichende Notenbankstatistik. 1925. *Organisation und Geschäftsverkehr Europäischer Notenbanken, 1876 - 1913*. Berlin.

Webb, Steven B. 1989. *Hyperinflation and Stabilization in Weimar Germany*. Oxford University Press.

Wunderlich, H. 1929. *Aufwertung; Handwörterbuch der Staatswissenschaften*. Ergänzungsband.

CHAPTER 12

THE ORIGINS OF THE MONETARY UNION IN THE UNITED STATES[1]

Arthur J. Rolnick
Bruce D. Smith
Warren E. Weber

I. INTRODUCTION

Monetary unions, areas in which a single, uniform money is used or exchange rates are fixed, have been the subject of much debate in recent years. The formation of at least one monetary union is being discussed in Europe, and the dissolution of another is being considered in the former Soviet Union. Yet, despite the recent debates, the gains to be had from a monetary union are still at best vaguely articulated, and the problems of maintaining and enforcing a monetary union seem to be similarly vaguely stated. While theoretical analyses and empirical explorations using recent data can shed some light on these issues, examination of historical experiences with different monetary systems is also illuminating. In this paper we examine the historical experience of the United States during the colonial, Revolutionary, and Confederation periods.

Although it may seem odd to think of the United States as having had to create a monetary union, it did not have one during its formative years. Each colony or state had the power to—and many did—issue their own paper currencies. These currencies were fiat monies, monies which are irredeemable and intrinsically useless, and circulated against specie and each other at market determined exchange rates. This system had been in place in some form since 1690.

In 1787, the Constitution fundamentally changed the monetary system in the United States. State issue of fiat monies was prohibited and, it can be argued, an

---

[1] Rolnick, Federal Reserve Bank of Minneapolis; Smith, Federal Reserve Bank of Minneapolis and Cornell University; and Weber, Federal Reserve Bank of Minneapolis. We wish to thank Ed Green, Jeffrey Rogers Hummel, Preston Miller, Steve Russell, Pierre Siklos, Dick Sylla, Dick Todd, and especially Neil Wallace for their comments on an earlier draft of this paper. The views expressed herein are those of the authors and not necessarily those of the Federal Reserve Bank of Minneapolis or the Federal Reserve System.

attempt was made to establish a monetary union. Here we examine why such a change in the monetary system was made. We argue that monetary unification was viewed as being desirable because it was a method of resolving problems created by costly exchange rate variability and as necessary because it eliminated a problem with seigniorage.

Our argument proceeds as follows. First, we show that exchange rate variability was an important feature of the monetary environment of the United States prior to 1787. Further, we show that this variability was viewed as being costly. Since these costs could have been avoided simply by fixing exchange rates between the currency issues of the different states, we proceed to explain why state currency issues were prohibited. We argue that simply fixing exchange rates between different state currencies would not have been enough, for it would have left a problem with seigniorage. In particular, it would have left any state with the power to levy an inflation tax on the other members of the monetary union. Historical experience prior to 1787 had established that this power would be used by at least some states and its use would be detrimental to monetary union. The elimination of state powers of money creation addressed what we call the seigniorage incentive problem.

Our analysis is based on a particular approach to thinking about multiple fiat monies. It considers different fiat monies to be intrinsically perfect substitutes.[2] This approach has two important implications that lead to our views about the monetary changes made in the Constitution. The first is that exchange rate variability is unnecessary in the sense that it has social costs that can be avoided. The second is that a seigniorage incentive problem is necessarily present in any system with multiple fiat monies.

An alternative approach to multiple fiat monies treats different monies as limited substitutes (possibly for transactions reasons). In this approach, there are well-defined demand functions for different moneys. As a result, exchange rate fluctuations would likely be caused by changes in economic fundamentals like preferences, technologies, and government policies. We argue that this approach does not successfully explain the United States experience and cannot explain why the Constitution prohibited states from issuing their own fiat monies.

---

[2] Different fiat monies are intrinsically perfect substitutes because, by definition, they have no intrinsic value. Any piece of paper can be used in exchange as well as any other piece of paper. Of course if governments impose legal restrictions favoring the use of one kind of money over another, the monies will cease to be perfect substitutions. (See Wallace 1983 for a discussion.) This situation is inconsistent with a uniform currency. During the period we examine, there were several attempts by governments to impose legal restrictions limiting the substitutability of different colonial/state fiat monies. We argue below that these were reflections of the seigniorage incentive problem that arises with multiple fiat currencies.

Thus, one of the findings of our study is that viewing multiple monies as limited substitutes is less useful than viewing them as perfect substitutes. We think that this result does not only apply to the historical analysis of the United States but to the analysis of modern day monetary unions as well.

2.   MULTIPLE CURRENCIES AND EXCHANGE RATE FLUCTUATIONS

In this section we set the historical stage for our discussion by describing monetary arrangements during the colonial, Revolutionary, and Confederation periods.[3] We document that the fiat monies issued by the various colonies and states fluctuated in value against specie and each other. In the next section, we document some of the problems that this exchange rate variability created.

2.1   The Colonial Period

In 1690 Massachusetts issued the first colonial irredeemable paper currency. It was used to pay troops when tax revenue was insufficient. Eventually each of the 13 colonies issued fiat money called bills of credit.[4]

The colonies issued bills of credit in two general ways. One was to create a "loan office," print money, and lend it at interest. While this money was not redeemable in specie, most enabling legislation for such emissions required currency issues to be retired as loans were repaid: in some colonies these provisions were more and in some colonies less strictly adhered to. The interest on loans was used to fund general expenditures. In colonies with well-run loan offices, interest income often financed all peacetime expenditures, and taxes were only levied in wartime.

The other way of issuing bills of credit was simply to print it and use it in payment for government expenditures. In all colonies enabling legislation for this type of currency issue also included provisions for future taxes to be used to retire the currency. Again, some colonies actually levied such taxes and engaged in this

---

[3]   Also see Sylla (1982) for an overview of some of the issues we discuss.

[4] Prior to the creation of paper money, the colonies had made use of externally minted specie. However, each colony (although it minted no specie of its own) defined a colonial unit of account. This unit was measured in pounds, shillings, and pence of the colony in question, and each colony defined its unit of account to be a certain quantity of Spanish milled dollars. Thus a pound in Pennsylvania meant something different than a pound in South Carolina; throughout we will use the term pound to apply to the colony in question.

currency retirement, and some did not. Colonies that followed this practice, or retired currency issued on loan, had currencies that maintained a relatively stable value. However, some colonies were lax in either collecting taxes involved in currency retirement, or diverted these revenues to other uses. For such colonies seigniorage income was an important source of revenue. In colonies that continually relied on seigniorage, there was typically currency depreciation.[5] As we will see, these colonies also created problems for their neighbors.

When a colony issued fiat money it was issued in the colony's unit of account. The result was that payments to the colony made in fiat money of a certain face value were equivalent to whatever amount of specie was implied by the legal unit of account. However, this valuation did not fix an exchange rate in either of two senses: colonies did not enforce this exchange rate in private transactions[6], and the colonies did not exchange their bills of credit for specie at this rate (as a fixed exchange rate regime would require).

In practice the fiat money of different colonies circulated against specie, and against each other at market determined rates. Extensive data on the behavior of the exchange rates between London and the individual colonies have been collected by McCusker (1978). For instance, (despite having the same unit of account) Pennsylvania and Delaware currencies exchanged against each other at a variable rate, with Delaware currency at discount which "regularly ranged between 5 and 10 percent" (McCusker 1978, p. 182). Similarly, Virginia and Massachusetts' currency prices varied. For example, in 1761 Virginia currency appreciated 14.4 percent against Massachusetts' currency and then depreciated 6.4 percent and 9.7 percent in 1762 and 1763, respectively (McCusker 1977, pp. 142, 211). In general, the McCusker data implies variable exchange rates among all the colonial currencies.

2.2   The Revolutionary War Years

During the Revolutionary War years, there was an even greater variety of fiat monies than there was during the colonial period. As is generally well known, the newly established federal government relied heavily on fiat money and the seigniorage income that resulted. In addition, many states continued the practice of issuing fiat money. According to Nevins (1927, p. 481), all told "the specie value of

---

[5]   For a discussion of different colonial experiences see Ferguson (1953), Ernst (1973), Brock (1975), McCusker (1978), Smith (1985a,b, 1988), Wicker (1985), or Perkins (1992). Smith (1985a,b) provides an explanation for how temporary monetization of deficits was consistent with stable currency values.

[6]   In fact some colonial laws prohibited the legal valuation from being enforced in preference to the market rate of exchange.

the currency issued by the States during the Revolution was estimated by Jefferson in 1786 at $36,000,000, or just as much as the specie value of the Continental (federal) currency." And, while systematic time series data on exchange rates is lacking, it is clear that exchange rates fluctuated among these various monies.

a)   State Currency Issues

The states issued their own irredeemable currencies during the Revolution, and as in the colonial period, the depreciation of these currencies were not uniform. Some state currencies depreciated greatly. For instance, "South Carolina's paper by the final year of fighting was almost worthless, and it became necessary for Governor Rutledge . . . to suspend the laws making it a legal tender" (Nevins 1927, p. 488). In 1781 Virginia exchanged newly issued loan certificates with a face value of $1 for $1,000 of its previously issued currency. In 1781 North Carolina rated $200 of paper currency to $1 specie; in 1782 this rating was revised to 800 to 1. The depreciation of Maryland's currency seems modest by comparison: Maryland redeemed its earliest paper money issues at the rate of 40 to 1 (Nevins 1927, p. 486).

Some other state currencies held their value much better. Pennsylvania is an example. In March 1780 Pennsylvania issued "£100,000 upon the security of lands in Philadelphia and of Province Island, all belonging to the State-the security causing the bills to be called 'island money'" (Nevins 1927, p. 489).[7] A year later another £500,000 was issued. Between 1780 and 1783 this currency exchanged at anywhere from 1.25 to 1 to 5 to 1 in terms of specie (Bezanson 1951, Appendix, Table 4). It was thus one of the least depreciated paper issues of the Revolution.

The states also issued circulating certificates of various sorts in addition to their explicit issues of fiat money. North Carolina, for instance, issued five different kinds of certificate debt over the period 1778–1782, with a nominal value in excess of $40,000,000. Some of these certificates bore a fixed nominal interest rate, some bore interest and were indexed to the value of specie, and some bore no interest. Some also had a special status in certain kinds of payments to the state, while others did not. The result was that the relative values of different types of certificates varied (see Morrill 1969, for a more complete discussion). In addition, the states issued loan certificates, which were analogous to federal loan certificates which we describe below.

---

[7]   It bears emphasis that the legal valuation of pounds in the different states varied considerably. In Georgia a Spanish dollar was valued at 5 shillings, in New England and Virginia at 6 shillings, in New York and North Carolina at 8 shillings, in South Carolina at 32½ shillings, and elsewhere at 7½ shillings. See Nevins (1927), p. 481.

b)   Federal Currency Issues

When the Revolutionary War began, the federal government had no power
to tax. It was forced to rely on loans, requisitions from state governments and
currency issues to meet its revenue needs. However, loans provided little income, and
the legality of the state governments was often poorly established. Even when their
legality was established, the states had little in the way of a tax collection apparatus
in place. Thus, states' own revenue collections were not large and they were reluctant
to pass what they did collect on to the Continental Congress. As a result, the federal
government had to rely mostly on irredeemable paper money (the so-called
Continentals) and other forms of closely related debt to finance its expenditures.
Indeed, from 1775 through 1779, money creation accounted for 82 percent of the
federal government's income (Ferguson 1961, pp. 43–44).

The proliferation of Continentals that permitted this seigniorage revenue to
be raised is well known, as is their depreciation. The Continental Congress issued
over $226,000,000 of Continentals between June 1775 and the end of 1779, after
which it ceased all issues[8]. Just as in the colonial period, people felt that an
important component of imparting value to the currency was to make it acceptable
for tax payments at a fixed rate in terms of specie. Since the Continental Congress
had no powers of taxation, it requested that the states make Continentals acceptable
for taxes. Although the legislation that authorized the first issue of Continentals
provided for them to be retired with taxes collected from the states, such legislation
did not accompany later issues. Further, state retirements of Continentals through
taxation were very limited.

The depreciation of the Continentals was severe. In January 1777, $1.25
Continental was required to purchase $1.00 in specie. By January 1781, $100
Continental was required to obtain $1.00 in specie. Because of this depreciation,
Continental issues ceased late in 1779, and, according to Ferguson (1961), the
Continental ceased to circulate as a currency by the spring of 1781.

In addition to the Continentals, Congress financed its expenditures by selling
loan certificates. These paid interest and were issued in minimum denominations of
$200. Loan certificates sold at face value for Continentals, and like Continentals they
were not redeemable for specie. By 1781 about $60,000,000 had been "subscribed."
Not all subscriptions were voluntary, however, since loan certificates were sometimes
paid out directly for supplies (Ferguson 1961, pp. 53–55). Loan certificates also held
their value better than Continentals, as one might expect from the fact that they were

---

[8] This figure is from Ferguson (1961). It is an estimate; slightly different figures
can be found cited by other authors.

issued in relatively large minimum denominations[9]. Because loan certificates were a superior store of value to Continentals, they came to be used as "a kind of mercantile currency" (Ferguson 1961, p. 40). Thus the federal government was simultaneously issuing multiple currencies, which did not depreciate at the same rate.

Another type of federal government certificate, which had been in use since 1776, were drafts drawn on various departments of the government. Certificates "were issued by all the departments in lieu of money . . . ." At first merely handwritten notes, they later became printed forms. "From the beginning they were connected with impressment" (Ferguson 1961, p. 57), so they were exchanged (involuntarily) for supplies. Ferguson (1961, p. 63) estimates that "the certificates issued by federal officers must have approximated, in nominal amount, the entire sum of Continental currency." The certificates were irredeemable, bore no interest, and were issued in fixed nominal amounts. They apparently tended to be of even less value than Continentals (Ferguson 1961, p. 65n), although Nevins (1927, p. 505) asserts that "it was often difficult, in practice, to distinguish between the certificates and paper money . . . ." And, in fact, the certificates did serve certain functions of money, since they were accepted by some states for taxes after February 1780. The Continental Congress began accepting them from the states in payment of certain requisitions after March 1780.

The last wartime issues of the federal government occurred in 1782 when Congress decided to convert "unliquidated" public debts into a "liquidated" public debt. To this end it appointed federal commissioners to inspect claims against the federal government. "The commissioners verified claims and revalued them in specie if they were stated in terms of depreciated currency. For balances due they issued 'final settlement certificates' amounting to over $3,700,000" (Ferguson 1961, p. 179).[10] Final settlement certificates, though, were also used in government payments. For instance, about $11,000,000 (in specie value) of final settlement certificates were issued in troop payments.

2.3   Confederation

Relative to the colonial period there were additional complications with the monetary system under Confederation. The first came from the array of liabilities the country inherited from the Revolution—some state and some federal. The retirement of this inherited debt was a problem that interacted with and compounded other monetary problems. In addition, much of this debt circulated, adding to the

---

[9] See, for instance, Bryant and Wallace (1984).

[10] The latter refers to specie value.

uncertainty regarding the value of various circulating liabilities.

The second complication arose from new monies that circulated along with the old. Under the Articles of Confederation, from 1783 to 1789, states, like their forerunners, were allowed to issue their own irredeemable paper money. And to a large extent, certain states reestablished the monetary arrangements that they had employed in the colonial period.[11] The Federal government was also permitted to issue money and did so to help finance its debt service. (Fiat money also played a significant role in permitting some states to service their debts.)

The third complication stemmed from a major deflation. After the massive inflation of the Revolution, prices in Pennsylvania had returned to the levels of 1771–73 by 1786 (Bezanson 1951, p. 174). This deflation prompted agitation for money issues to which some states responded and some did not.

a)   State Currency Issues

The combination of a large inherited Revolutionary War debt and a major deflation posed a significant problem for the states. The real value of the claims against them was large and rising, and the problems of debt service and retirement were severe. Further, in 1782 the Continental Congress stopped the payment of interest on all federal loan certificates. Many states assumed the responsibility for paying the interest on these certificates held by their own residents.

Some states (Massachusetts being the most prominent example) sought to raise the required revenue entirely through direct taxation. The result was high tax rates, and an eventual tax rebellion (Shay's rebellion).

Other states attempted to use the power of money creation to address the situation. Such payments were made with irredeemable state-issued liabilities. For instance, Pennsylvania gave public creditors "certificates of interest," and made these certificates receivable for state tax payments. According to Ferguson (1961, p. 222), Pennsylvania "created in the process a kind of state money." New Jersey also issued "revenue money" to its public creditors, and other states would have done so in the absence of other federal action, which we describe below.

These currency issues added to those already in existence from the Revolution. Thus, by early 1785 it was estimated that Pennsylvania had more than

---

[11]   See, for example, Schweitzer (1989) or Ferguson (1961, p. 244), who argues that during Confederation "the various states were reenacting their particular experience with paper money in colonial times."

£160,000 in circulation.[12] In March 1785, Pennsylvania authorized an emission of an additional £100,000 "to pay interest on all public securities held by citizens of the state . . ." (Ferguson 1961, p. 229). Taxes and revenues from the sales of public lands were pledged to retire these issues[13]. Thus Pennsylvania sought to finance debt service by the temporary creation of money. In addition, the state created a loan office along colonial lines, emitting £50,000 for this purpose. All Pennsylvania currency issues were made receivable at face value for all payments to the state.

"From May 1781 . . . until 1790, state paper, which at times depreciated mildly, again became the medium in daily use" in Pennsylvania (Bezanson 1951, p. 326). According to Bezanson (Appendix, Table 4), the ratio of Pennsylvania state currency values to specie fluctuated between 1.05 and 1.12 in 1786, between 1.10 and 1.75 in 1787, between 1.43 and 1.56 in 1788, and between 1.13 and 1.43 in 1789. Thus, while Pennsylvania currency held its value relatively well by the standards of the time, holders of its currency were subject to considerable exchange rate risk.

In 1786 New Jersey supplemented the "revenue money" it had issued to pay interest on inherited debt by emitting £100,000 through a loan office. To promote the acceptance of the currency, New Jersey implemented a set of taxes to be used to retire it, a law making it legal tender for public and private debts, and penalties for discriminating between it and specie in transactions.

According to Ferguson (1961, p. 244), "New Jersey's legal tender bills were fairly steady [in value], although they passed outside the state at a slowly increasing discount." In particular, New Jersey's paper currency had a more stable value internally than it did in either New York city or Philadelphia — a fact which led to political tension between New Jersey and its neighbors. "New Jersey's tender provisions could not be enforced in the neighboring states, and consequently depreciation began in both Philadelphia and New York . . . . Before long, the depreciation in the neighboring states affected the Jersey currency's value at home" (Kaminski 1972, pp. 119–20). Nor was this depreciation uniform. Within its own borders, "in nonspeculative ventures," (Kaminski 1972, p. 124) New Jersey currency went at a discount against specie of between 7 and 15 percent. As early as May 1787 it was at a 12 to 18 percent discount in New York, however. The analogous discount in Philadelphia at the same date was 11 to 20 percent. In 1788 New Jersey currency was discounted by only 7 percent in New York, but by 33 percent in Philadelphia. By 1789, the discount was 33 percent in both New York and Philadelphia. (See

---

[12] Recall that the term "pound" did not mean the same thing in different states. We use the term "pound" to refer to the currency of the state in question. See Footnote 4 for the legal meaning of the term "pound" as used in the different states.

[13] And, in fact, 87,000 pounds had been retired via these means by September 1788 (Nevins 1927), p. 522).

Kaminski 1972, p. 125.)

New York also issued fiat money in 1786 which held its value relatively well, but nevertheless appeared to experience some depreciation. In that year New York issued £50,000 for the purpose of paying the interest on outstanding debt (that is, it was engaged in a form of currency finance), and in addition issued another £150,000 through a loan office. The money

> was made a legal tender for private debt only in the case of suits . . . . By the end of the year even the opponents of the paper issue had to admit that the credit of the bills was good. They fluctuated in value, and at times were at a discount of as much as 10 percent, but they remained a valid circulating medium. In midsummer of 1787 it was boasted that they were 'universally received upon a par with gold or silver' . . . . (Nevins 1927, p. 528. See also Kaminski 1972, pp. 155, 158.)

South Carolina may have had the most stable currency during this period. South Carolina had exchanged its own state debt for federal debt held by its own citizens, so that during Confederation virtually all debt held in South Carolina was state debt. The interest on this debt was paid by state issues of "special indents". Ferguson (1961, p. 233) estimates that "the actual emission of indents varied from $273,000 to a $535,000 annually." (See Higgins 1969 for annual emissions.)[14] These certificates were redeemed out of tax revenue. In addition, £100,000 was issued through a loan office emission in 1786. "The paper held its value. Such was its success that in 1789, when specie dollars were pouring into Charlestown it was preferred as being more convenient to use" (Nevins 1927, pp. 526–27).

The fiat monies of Pennsylvania, New Jersey, New York, and South Carolina fluctuated in value relative to specie, and hence fluctuated in value relative to each other. In the cases of New York and South Carolina in particular these fluctuations relative to specie appear to have been relatively small. This was not the case for the currencies of Rhode Island and North Carolina, which experienced more sustained and dramatic depreciation.

In 1786 Rhode Island issued £100,000 through a loan office. After some initial depreciation, the state passed measures imposing penalties for discriminating in transactions between specie and the state currency, which was also made a legal tender for private debts. Provisions were established which "enabled any debtor to discharge his debt by depositing the required sum with the county judge, who should

---

[14] "The South Carolina pound has been stated in terms of dollars at the rate of $4.286 to £1, which the legislature adopted in 1783" (Ferguson 1961, p. 233).

give notice of the fact in the press" (Nevins 1927, p. 229). Thus creditors were prevented from avoiding payment in Rhode Island currency via the expedient of simply avoiding their debtors.

Rhode Island's currency depreciated rapidly. According to Ferguson (1961, p. 243) it circulated at one-tenth of its face value by 1788, and to Nevins (1927, p. 540) at one-twelfth of its face value by 1789. Finally, "in the autumn of 1789, the Legislature repealed the law making the bills a legal tender at par, and fixed the value at which it should be received by creditors, in satisfaction of awards in lawsuits, at one-fifteenth the value of specie" (Nevins 1927, pp. 540–41). Thus, not only did Rhode Island currency depreciate markedly relative to specie, but also relative to the currencies of the other states as well.

In North Carolina, the certificates issued during the Revolution were accepted for property tax payments through 1786. Different kinds of certificates had varying legal valuations for tax payments, so that even the state did not treat its liabilities as having a uniform value. In addition, in 1787, 1788, and 1789 property tax acts levied two distinct types of taxes; one to be paid in currency or specie, and the other to be paid in certificates. The objective of levying a tax payable only in certificates was to encourage them to circulate (Morrill 1969, p. 42).

To supplement the certificates (and partly to replace them), North Carolina issued another currency. In 1783, £100,000 pounds was issued; and in 1785, another £100,000 was issued. The money was a legal tender for all public and private debts. "All confiscated [Tory] property was to be set aside exclusively as a fund to redeem the new currency . . . . [However] the 1783 Assembly failed to establish procedures by which the confiscated property was to be sold to redeem the currency, and . . . later Assemblies blocked such enabling legislation" (Morrill 1969, p. 59). And, in fact, by 1789 only £21,848 had been retired (Morrill 1969, p. 93).

The currency issued by North Carolina quickly "depreciated to an average of about 25 percent off specie in the purchase of commodities and then stabilized at about 12.5 percent to 15 percent off nominal value when exchanged for hard money" (Morrill 1969, p. 70). This depreciation was largely complete by late in 1783, "after which time the paper's value remained practically steady for two years" (Morrill 1969, p. 71). However, by the end of 1785, the state's currency "slipped from about 25 percent off nominal value to perhaps 35 percent off par, while in exchange for specie the currency declined from about 15 percent off par to about 25 percent off nominal value." (Morrill 1969, p. 75.) By 1786, the paper was about 33 percent below specie, and was 40 percent below by 1787. In 1789, it reached 50 percent of nominal value, where it remained well into the next decade.[15] (Morrill 1969, pp. 87–92.)

The only other state that issued fiat money was Georgia. There £30,000 was issued in 1786. According to Kaminski (1972), this went at a one-third discount by 1789. The other states remained "hard money states," despite substantial political agitation for fiat money in some cases.

b)   Federal Currency Issues

It has already been noted that in 1782 the federal government stopped paying interest on federal loan certificates. In 1784 interest payments on these certificates were resumed by the use of the following system. Certificates of interest, or

> indents were printed by the [federal] treasury and deposited with
> the loan offices in each state, who turned them over to the local
> authority. The states were supposed to issue interest due on public
> securities . . . . Congress had the notion that indents would flow
> freely across state borders and be taken indiscriminately by all
> states for taxes. Since they were printed in small denominations,
> ranging from one to twenty dollars, they would provide a national
> circulating medium (Ferguson 1961, p. 224).

During the years 1786 to 1789 between $703,000 and $1,364,000 of indents were outstanding.

The indent system, which was in place throughout the Confederation period, was meant to be a simultaneous solution of two problems: it constituted a means for financing debt service via a kind of money creation, and it was intended to provide a uniform medium for interstate transactions.[16] This indicates some interest in the problem of creating a uniform currency on the part of Congress. However, Congress could not force the states to accept indents in a uniform way for tax payments, and in fact the value of indents varied from state to state depending, in part, on how they were received by any state in payments. According to Ferguson (1961, p. 228), indents ultimately passed at between one-eighth and one-fourth of their face value,

---

[15] The state's currency continued to circulate for some time after the ratification of the Constitution. The Constitution prohibited the issue of new state currency, but did not require the retirement of old state currency issues.

[16] For further evidence that indents circulated see Bolles (1884, pp.324, 326).

depending on location.[17]

3.   THE COSTS OF EXCHANGE RATE VARIABILITY

During its formative years, the United States experienced two problems which the framers of the Constitution in 1787 attempted to overcome. The first of these was a proliferation of fiat monies accompanied by a great deal of exchange rate variability. We now present some examples of how such variability increased the cost of trade.

3.1   Example 1: Virginia 1755-64

Colonial monetary affairs were subject to British oversight. Over time the monetary relations between Britain and the colonies became an increasing source of frictions. Such frictions came to a head between Britain and Virginia between 1755 and 1764. The result was the Currency Act of 1764, which forbade the colonies to make their own currency a legal tender for public or private debts.[18]

Virginia was the last colony to issue fiat money. When it first issued bills of credit in 1755, the colony was desperately short of specie. (See Ernst 1973 and Brock 1975.) Colonists who borrowed from English merchants, which was a widespread practice, had incurred sterling denominated debts. These debts were routinely (and of necessity) repaid in local currency, which was in fact a legal tender.

---

[17]   In addition to these instruments, specie coined abroad was in general circulation. How important specie was as a component of the money supply is a confused topic. For instance, Nevins (1927, pp. 516–17) asserts a general scarcity of specie in the United States from 1782 or 1783 into 1785. On the other hand, Massey (19??, p. 65) says "it has been estimated that some $10 million in coins of all types moved into circulation in 1782 and 1783." He then claims specie exports were large between 1783 and 1785, after which "coins began to return to circulation." In any event, specie was present, and its value too was uncertain. Clipping of coins was a common practice, and "all coin passed by weight and not by face value . . . . The United States Government in 1782 actually had Timothy Pickering clip a quantity of French guineas which had come over as a loan . . . . If the Government paid them out as they were, the first takers would clip them and reap a snug profit . . ." (Nevins 1927, p. 569). The inefficiencies in exchange of using coins that had to pass by weight are, of course, apparent.

[18]   More specifically, the colonies not covered by the Currency Act of 1751, which applied to New England.

But, of course, the rate of exchange between Virginia currency and sterling was subject to some fluctuations.[19]

Given the legal tender status of Virginia's currency, British creditors could not avoid repayment in this form. However, British creditors objected strenuously to being subjected to exchange rate risk. In 1758, British merchants petitioned the crown demanding "absolute protection against any fluctuations in the rate of exchange. Such risks were to be born by the Virginians alone" (Ernst 1973, p. 52). Thus the allocation of exchange rate risk became a subject of heated political discussion.

In response to British pressure, Virginia law was amended in 1755 "to allow courts of record to settle all executions for sterling debts in local currency—paper as well as coin—at a 'just' rate of exchange. A just rate was taken to be the actual rate at the time of court judgment" (Ernst 1973, p. 54). This became the common legal practice.

However, even this was viewed as inadequate protection against exchange rate variation by British creditors. Virginia law allowed an exchange rate to be set at the time of legal settlement, but British merchants desired protection against exchange rate variation between the time of settlement and the time of payment. British merchants wanted the option of consenting "to accept paper money in amounts they deemed necessary for the purchase of sterling bills of exchange to the original and full value of sterling debts" (Ernst 1973, p. 52).

This was unacceptable to Virginia. In addition to forcing Virginians to bear all exchange rate risk in exchange with Britain, it would give British merchants bargaining power over Virginians who had only local currency as a means of payment.[20] Thus an impasse was reached, leading to the Currency Act of 1764. This act prevented the colonies from making their own currencies a legal tender in public or private payments.

The issue of who was to bear exchange rate risk in the colonial period became a major bone of political contention between Britain and the colonies. Of

---

[19] These fluctuations, in Virginia's case, were hardly dramatic. See McCusker (1978) or Smith (1985a).

[20] If Virginians had been forced to bear all exchange rate risk, one can ask what the "incidence" of this "tax" might have been. In particular, goods prices and/or interest rates might have adjusted to compensate them (partially) for bearing this risk. Whatever its incidence, however, any departure from optimal risk sharing represents a source of inefficiency. Moreover, British creditors were apparently willing to bear whatever price adjustments resulted in order to shed their exposure to exchange rate risk.

course the same issue was present between the colonies themselves, but here the colonies had little freedom of independent action. One method for improving matters would have been to create (or to attempt to create) a uniform North American currency. Such a proposal was in fact made by Benjamin Franklin in 1765, and a similar proposal had been made Britain in 1763. Indeed, the Stamp Act was originally intended to raise funds to support a uniform North American currency. Thus, even at this early date, interest in creating a uniform currency manifested itself on both sides of the Atlantic. But some time was to elapse before this actually occurred.

3.2   Example 2: Confederation

During the Revolution, and continuing into the period of Confederation, interstate commerce was of growing importance.[21] This fact suggests the desirability of a medium of exchange to be used in interstate transactions. One possibility was specie. However, its usefulness for this purpose was reduced by the fact that it seems often to have passed by weight. Another possibility would have been indents; as we have seen, this was intended by Congress. However, the value of indents was not uniform across states. A third possibility was to make use of the various state currencies in interstate transactions. That this did, in fact, occur is indicated by the observation that Pennsylvania currency circulated in "Maryland, central Virginia, and the Ohio Valley; and North Carolina currency [circulated] in western Virginia and Kentucky" (Schweitzer 1989, p. 315). Nevertheless, the use of the state currencies in interstate transactions (as well as at home) was plagued by exchange rate uncertainty.

Consider the problems with Pennsylvania's currency, a currency which maintained its value far better than that of some other states. According to Bezanson (1951, p. 326), "in the spring of 1789 James Cox explained 'the very fluctuating state that our paper money has always been in, makes it difficult to ascertain the value of it at different periods.'" An illustration of the perceived costs of this exchange rate variability is the fact that the Pennsylvania assembly refused to be paid in Pennsylvania currency, which was a legal tender for public, but not private, debts (Kaminski 1972, p. 70).

An even more dramatic illustration is offered by the attitude of the Bank of North America toward Pennsylvania currency. The Bank of North America, chartered in 1781, had successfully circulated its bank notes for several years. In an effort to dissuade the state from issuing fiat money, the Bank announced that it would refuse to accept Pennsylvania currency (at any discount) in transactions. Not only did this not dissuade the state, it led to a revocation of the Bank's charter by Pennsylvania. In an effort to regain its charter, the Bank yielded and offered to receive state currency on deposit, "provided these paper transactions were kept 'entirely distinct and separate' from the specie accounts" (Kaminski 1972, p. 64). This the Bank did,

---

[21] For some quantification of the importance of interstate trade see Bjork (1963).

keeping accounts in Pennsylvania currency completely distinct from specie accounts, even though the state's currency did not initially depreciate. The Bank actually did receive a substantial quantity of state currency, and the keeping of separate accounts led to a "considerable extra expense to the Bank" (Kaminski 1972, p. 67). Apparently this was a cost the Bank was willing to absorb in order to avoid exchange rate risk. (Recall that Pennsylvania currency fluctuated in value, rather than depreciating uniformly.)

New Jersey faced a similar problem with its currency. Nevins (1927) makes the point that four systems of legal valuation of specie were in place among the different states and then argues that

> . . . these difficulties were accentuated by the total unreliability of the paper currencies. It was hard for even well-informed citizens to understand what value to attach to a handful of bills, and the tables of exchange between states would have filled a fat volume . . . . A man could not be sure that what was sound money in one county would pass when he crossed an imaginary line, nor that if his bills did pass, he would not be charged a ruinous discount (pp. 569–70).

Some of the costs this exchange rate uncertainty imposed are illustrated by the problems that New Jersey's Governor Livingston had in making transactions out of state:

> [The Governor, who] naturally did much business in New York city, found it so impossible to use Jersey money "at the unconscionable discount which your brokers and merchants exact" that he collected what New York money was due him and saved it to employ across the Hudson (Nevins 1927, p. 569).

Even in South Carolina, whose currency had a fairly stable value, exchange rate fluctuations between different kinds of circulating liabilities imposed costs. In Higgins' (1969, p. 127) description

> All financial transactions were difficult and unstable when there was little specie and the value of the various monetary substitutes was either unknown or unpredictable. The Revolutionary bonds, and the interest certificates which came from the South Carolina treasury annually, served as a circulating medium, but they were limited in use. Although the notes could be transferred by endorsement, negotiations were difficult as the value of a certificate and the amount of any given transaction were not identical.

4.   THE SEIGNIORAGE INCENTIVE PROBLEM

The second problem that the United States faced, and that the Constitution's framers attempted to address, was a seigniorage incentive problem. This problem is that — when possible — governments will attempt to collect seigniorage from citizens outside their jurisdiction, and thereby redistribute revenue to their own citizens.[22] With this power being exercised, neighboring states (colonies) have an incentive to retaliate, however. One possible form of retaliation is to impose legal restrictions limiting the use of the offending state's currency or promoting the use of the "domestic money." But such restrictions undermine the uniformity of the currency, potentially lead to exchange rate variability, and cause a welfare loss due to the implied restrictions on interstate trade.

This situation arose in New England during the colonial period. The problem reemerged under Confederation. We now discuss these two episodes.

4.1   Colonial New England

By 1710 all of the New England colonies had issued their own currencies. The respective currencies easily crossed colonial borders. Even though there was no government attempt to fix exchange rates officially or to enforce or sanction the practice, "the bills of the several New England colonies customarily, although not always, passed current in all the rest at a uniform value" (Brock 1975, p. 35). In other words, the exchange rates among the currencies of these colonies were constant at a rate of one-to-one. This constancy of exchange rates implies, in turn, the potential for any one colony to levy the inflation tax on its neighbors. Countries with money stocks growing faster than the average can collect seigniorage from residents of countries with money stocks growing less rapidly than average under such an exchange rate regime.

This potential did not go unexploited in New England. Here Rhode Island was the culprit: "the fact that Rhode Island bills circulated widely in other colonies permitted her to levy tribute on her neighbors" (Brock 1975, p. 39). Between 1710 and 1744 the New England money supply grew at any average rate of almost 8 percent per year; over the same period the supply of Rhode Island bills of credit grew at an average rate of almost 14.5 percent per year. Most of this increase went into circulation in other colonies: "it was estimated that as many as five-sixths of the Rhode Island bills were absorbed by Massachusetts" (Brock 1975, p. 41). By 1744, 43 percent of the New England money supply had been issued by Rhode Island, which had only about 10 percent of New England's population.

---

[22] For other discussions of the seigniorage incentive problem in monetary unions see Casella and Feinstein (1989) and Zarazaga (1991).

Given the high rate of inflationary taxation levied by Rhode Island on its neighbors, it is not surprising that constant exchange rates did not persist (although it may be a testament to the costs of exchange rate uncertainty that they lasted as long as they did). In 1749 Governor Hutchinson of Massachusetts proposed the retirement of the colony's own paper currency, after which "no person should receive or pay within the province bills of credit of any of the other governments of New England."[23] In 1749 Massachusetts passed a law prohibiting the circulation of other New England currencies within its border, with a fine of 50 pounds for a violation.

Connecticut took similar action to prohibit the circulation of Rhode Island currency. In February 1747 (or 1748, the date is unclear), citizens of Norwich, Connecticut petitioned the colonial assembly, "The Rhode Islanders have the Last Fall Sapped our Interest by buying up wth Their pernicious bills our best provisions . . . [,] and are now out buying up our Cows & best Stock [,] what They can with Those same pernicious bills." (quoted by Brock, p. 314). Merchants in New Haven noted the same effect, "that the colony of Rhode Island by the present Large unequal proportion of outstanding bills are Enabled Annually to buy off A great part of the product of this Colony the Labour of an Industrious people, to the no Small Detriment of the Inhabitants of this colony" (quoted by Brock, p. 314f).

In May 1752 the Connecticut assembly did prohibit the circulation of Rhode Island bills emitted after 1750. Thus, the monetary union that had been (unintentionally) achieved in New England had broken down.

4.2   Confederation

The seigniorage incentive problem is not limited to regimes in which exchange rates are constant or fixed. It recurred during the Confederation period when some states attempted to collect seigniorage from their neighbors by issuing irredeemable paper money accompanied by legal-tender laws. Again, the neighboring states retaliated by imposing legal restrictions that prohibited the use of the "foreign money" within their borders. "The [resulting] want of a uniform currency created financial and commercial difficulties that were prolific of ill-feeling among citizens of the different states" (Nevins 1927, p. 568).

One attempt to extract seigniorage income in this way occurred in New England, and again the primary culprit was Rhode Island. It was the only one of the New England states to create a fiat money, and its currency depreciated rapidly. In opposing Rhode Island's currency emission, some of the merchants of Newport and Providence argued that "a paper money law . . . would ruin Rhode Island's commerce with other states, which would not accept payment for their goods in rag money" (Nevins 1927, p. 228). Not only did Rhode Island nonetheless emit a currency; it

---

[23]   Quoted by Brock (1975), pp. 249–50.

made it impossible for creditors to its citizens to insist on payment in any other form. The result was a legal retaliation by Massachusetts and Connecticut, who "passed laws enabling their citizens to pay all debts owed to people of a paper-tender state in just the same manner as the latter paid their debts to the citizens of Massachusetts and Connecticut. That is, Rhode Island creditors were virtually outlawed in the neighboring states . . ." (Nevins 1927, p. 571). Thus credit transactions between citizens of Rhode Island and citizens of Connecticut or Massachusetts were impaired due to Rhode Island's attempt to force the use of its currency in debt payments.

The seigniorage incentive problem also recurred in North Carolina. There some merchants who were within-state creditors might have been expected to oppose the creation of a depreciating currency which was legal tender for private debts. However, a "factor that qualified the [negative] attitude of some merchants [to the state's currency] was that while they were creditors to many persons, they themselves were debtors to other merchants of the state and, more often, to mercantile interests outside North Carolina. A number of North Carolina merchants, in fact, came to dare their out-of-state creditors to sue for recovery in the postwar fiat currency" (Morrill 1969, pp. 64–65). And indeed, so eager was North Carolina to force circulation of its currency by making it a legal tender for private debts "that judges would not allow the nominal value of the currency to be altered even with the consent of the debtor and creditor involved in the case . . ." (Morrill 1969, p. 86). Similarly, "with Virginia merchants particularly in mind, legislators at the 1786 Assembly introduced a bill that would have made it a misdemeanor to demand specie payment for merchandise, to refuse to accept paper money in payment, or to accept paper money at less than nominal value" (Morrill 1969, p. 89).

The problems this would create were, of course, anticipated by opponents of legal-tender currency. Some such opponents predicted "that the lack of confidence in the currency and in the government of the state would further decrease the flow of commerce into the ports of North Carolina" (Morrill 1969, p. 80). And, indeed, neighboring states took some retaliatory action. "When Georgia sold her confiscated property, the Legislature ordered that no currency of other states be accepted" (Nevins 1927, p. 570). This action was viewed in North Carolina as particularly aimed at it. However, Virginia, and South Carolina merchants were also refusing to accept North Carolina currency. This limited the ability of North Carolina to levy an inflation tax on residents of Virginia, which had no currency of its own, or South Carolina, which had a currency with a stable value.

These episodes represent another illustration of the seigniorage incentive problem. Even though for both North Carolina and Rhode Island the exchange rate between their currencies and specie varied, seigniorage was still an issue. Both states forced residents of neighboring states to accept their currencies in payment of debts at unfavorable rates of exchange. To the extent they were successful, this redistributed resources to their own citizens and also enhanced their ability to levy inflationary taxation on other states.

5.   A SOLUTION TO THE SEIGNIORAGE PROBLEM

In this section we explore the extent to which Article I, Section 10 of the United States' Constitution can be interpreted as an attempt to solve the exchange rate variability and seigniorage incentive problems. This article states:

> No State shall . . . coin money; emit bills of credit; make anything
> but gold or silver a tender in payment of debts; pass any bill of
> attainder, ex post facto law, or law impairing the obligation of
> contracts . . . .

In particular, we focus on the provision of this section which seems to form a monetary union by eliminating the possibility of states issuing their own individual currencies.

There are two mutually exclusive perspectives that one could use to understand how this provision in the Constitution solved these problems. These perspectives differ in their views of the degree of substitutability between the different currencies in use.

The first perspective assumes that currency substitution is quite limited; different currencies are viewed as imperfect substitutes for transactions purposes. According to this view, there are well defined demand functions with the usual properties for different currencies. Moreover, exchange rate fluctuations — under this view — would likely be the result of fluctuations in the economic fundamentals — preferences, endowments, technologies, and government policies — that determine currency demands and supplies.

This perspective does not help us understand the Constitutional prohibition of state currency issues, however. First, it does not necessarily explain why the Constitution would have contained any provisions that attempted to limit exchange rate variability. In particular, it is unclear that this view implies that it is desirable to eliminate the exchange rate variability that arises due to variability in fundamentals. For instance, Lucas (1982) displays an economy where fundamental exchange rate fluctuations are fully consistent with Pareto optimality.

Second, and more important, even granting that this view could explain why eliminating exchange rate variability was desirable, it does not explain why the prohibition of state currency issues was necessary in order to do so. This perspective would imply that exchange rate variability could have been eliminated simply by requiring the states to fix their exchange rates against a common currency (say a federal currency, or alternatively, sterling). Moreover, to the extent that the individual states were "small," this arrangement would have solved the seigniorage incentive problem because it would have eliminated any state discretion with respect to raising seigniorage revenue. Indeed state money supplies would have been fully determined by the necessity of maintaining the fixed exchange rate. Thus, simply fixing exchange rates would have eliminated both the exchange rate variability and the seigniorage incentive problems.

Finally, it is not clear that this viewpoint can confront basic observations from the period under consideration. For instance, it is not at all apparent how imperfect substitutability between currencies can be reconciled with the constancy of New England exchange rates before 1750.

The alternative perspective is that different fiat monies are intrinsically perfect substitutes. Such a viewpoint motivates the work by Kareken and Wallace (1981) and King-Wallace-Weber (1992). Kareken and Wallace (KW) display a model in which agents choose among currencies solely on the basis of their real returns. In such a model, KW show that exchange rates among fiat monies are indeterminate in the sense that any unchanging exchange rate between two currencies is consistent with a perfect foresight equilibrium. (Notice that this explains the experience of colonial New England.) When the exchange rate between two currencies does not change, they will have the same rates of return, and agents will be indifferent as to which of the currencies they hold.[24] King-Wallace-Weber (KWW) modify the KW analysis to allow for uncertainty. In the KWW economy, agents choose among currencies based on their rate of return distributions. They show that exchange rate indeterminacy extends to a large class of random processes for exchange rates, where the randomness is nonfundamental.[25]

Such "sunspot" fluctuations in exchange rates are unnecessary in the sense that the social costs they impose could be eliminated with fixed exchange rates or a uniform currency. KWW demonstrate that when there is not complete participation in markets for hedging exchange rate risk, the randomness in exchange rates is costly because it carries over to real wealth and consumption. Because this exchange rate risk is unrelated to preferences, technologies, or government policies and can be eliminated, it represents an unnecessary social cost. It is always possible to find lump sum taxes and transfers that will support an equilibrium with constant exchange rates,

[24] There is an issue as to whether the exchange rate indeterminacy result of Kareken-Wallace applies when one or more of the currencies is to be retired. It certainly applies if currency is only retired "asymptotically," which is not an implausible description of the events we have described. It is also possible to produce methods of retirement which deliver an indeterminacy result even if the currency is retired in finite time.

[25] See also Shell (1977), Azariadis (1981), and Cass and Shell (1983) for a discussion of the related notion of a sunspot equilibrium.

consumption, and real wealth. When at least some agents are risk averse, this equilibrium will be Pareto superior to the equilibrium with fluctuating exchange rates.

According to this perspective, requiring the states to fix their exchange rates against a common currency would have eliminated exchange rate variability but it would not have eliminated the seigniorage incentive problem. Kareken and Wallace show that, with perfectly substitutable currencies, a fixed exchange rate regime places no particular restrictions on the rate of growth of any state's money supply. By implication, then, no restrictions are placed on the ability of an individual state to raise seigniorage revenue.

The KW result implies that if the countries in a monetary union have the individual ability to issue money, then they also have the ability to use money creation to collect seigniorage from residents of other countries. In an equilibrium with unchanging exchange rates between monies, countries with money stocks growing faster than the average will collect seigniorage from residents of countries with money stocks growing less rapidly than the average. If this ability is exercised, then those countries bearing the tax may choose to retaliate in any one of several ways. They could increase their own rate of money creation as a way of "collecting back" seigniorage income. The result might be high inflation, diluting the benefits of a monetary union. Or, alternatively, controls on the use of "foreign" currency might be imposed to limit its use, and thereby to limit how much seigniorage revenue other countries can raise at the expense of the domestic country. Such controls, however, work against a monetary union; they reduce the substitutability of currencies, but substitutability is the essence of a monetary union.

Thus, a fixed exchange rate regime may be difficult to maintain unless institutional arrangements are made to mitigate the seigniorage incentive problem. Prohibiting individual entities within the union from issuing money, as the United States did in its constitution, is one such arrangement.

6.   OTHER EXPLANATIONS FOR THE PROHIBITION OF STATE FIAT MONIES

The formative years of the United States help illustrate why a monetary union is desirable, yet difficult to maintain. Exchange rate variability was significant and costly during these years. But the experience with different colonies and states trying to export inflation and tax their neighbors suggests why a monetary union could not have been maintained simply by requiring the states to fix exchange rates.

Our position is that the newly formed country's desire to create a lasting monetary union was at least partly responsible for the constitutional prohibition on the power of states to issue currency (bills of credit). Moreover, the prohibition on state currency issues would seem — at least superficially — to have resolved seigniorage incentive problems by eliminating altogether the power of the states to generate seigniorage. We are not the first to try to explain the willingness of states to give up the power to issue money. Nevertheless, we feel other explanations are either unconvincing or cannot stand on their own. In this section we briefly review and critique other explanations that have been proposed for the Constitutional prohibition of state currency issues.

One popular explanation for the prohibition of state currency issues is the memory of the depreciation of the Continental. According to this view, the losses that many incurred were still deeply ingrained in people's memories and people were simply opposed to the creation of state currencies, which had always been of the inconvertible paper variety. This view appears explicitly in Calomiris (1988), but is certainly implicit or explicit in a variety of other literature.

We think there are reasons to doubt that this is a complete explanation for the Constitutional prohibition of state currencies. First, this explanation suggests that the federal government should have been prohibited from issuing bills of credit. But this prohibition, while considered, was not enacted. Second, the Confederation period witnessed deflations as large as the wartime inflation in states that had issued fiat money (for instance, Pennsylvania). Third, if this explanation accounted for opposition to state currencies, how and why did seven states issue inconvertible paper monies during Confederation? And fourth, this explanation does not account for why the Federalist Papers (p. 226) refers only to "the loss which America has sustained *since the peace* [our emphasis] from the pestilent effects of paper money; . . ." that is, there is no reference to problems that arose during the Revolution.

A second explanation of the Constitutional prohibition of state-issued bills of credit has been offered by Nevins (1927) and Schweitzer (1989a). They have argued that a combination of state issues of currency and legal tender laws were disruptive of (particularly interstate) commerce. Under this view, it is suggested that some states (colonies) issued currency, which they allowed to depreciate, and passed laws preventing creditors in other states from extracting payment in any other form from within-state debtors. To the extent that this practice was followed, it would have acted as a tax on various kinds of interstate commerce accomplished via credit extension. Of course what enforced the use of depreciated state currency issues were legal tender laws passed by the states, causing Schweitzer (1989a, p. 320) to conclude that "it was the damage of legal tender laws to interstate relations, rather than . . . the memory of the Continental, that resulted in a prohibition of state paper money."

Indeed, we have seen that Rhode Island and North Carolina in particular issued fiat money, which depreciated, and made it a legal tender for private debts. This certainly was attended by some retaliation by other states, and was disruptive of interstate commerce. Thus Nevins (1927, p. 569) could argue that "the worst state disputes connected with currency arose from the enactment of measures impairing the obligation of contracts . . . . They were the making of depreciated paper a legal tender for debts . . . ." Similarly, Schweitzer (1989a, p. 318) could assert that "many believed that tender laws were increasingly causing friction between states," and could (p. 319) quote Madison to the effect that fiat money "is producing the same warfare and retaliation among the states as were produced by the state regulations of commerce."

While we believe that this explanation helps explain why states agreed to give up the power to emit bills of credit, we do not think it is a complete explanation. In particular, if interference with private contracts was the problem, the Constitution could have simply prohibited (as it did) the states from making anything but gold and silver a legal tender for private debts. This was in fact recognized at the Constitutional Convention, as it was a point raised by Madison in debate (Elliot's Debates, p. 445).

7.   CONCLUSION

In conclusion, we believe there are obvious gains from having a monetary union.[26] However, a monetary union in which fiat money can be issued at the discretion of the individual members gives rise to an incentive problem: members of the union can gain seigniorage income at the expense of other members. The only way to address this problem is either to find an acceptable way to share seigniorage among the members or to prevent members from issuing currency. The United States chose to take this latter approach when in 1787 it adopted a constitution that prohibited states from issuing their own currency.

The United States' attempt at creating a monetary union raises an obvious question that we do not address in this paper: Did the actions taken by the United States in 1787 result in a monetary union in the sense that exchange rates were constant among the various monies circulating in the country? In the sequel to this paper we argue that the answer is no. Unresolved seigniorage incentive problems plus a loophole in the system regarding bank creation and regulation prevented the United States from achieving a monetary union at least until the late 1800s. In the sequel, we also identify the mechanisms by which monetary union was finally achieved.

---

[26] We do not mean to imply, however, that every "country" should become part of a global monetary union, even if institutional arrangements can be found to mitigate the seigniorage problem. The reasons countries may not find it in their interest to be part of the same monetary union are suggested by Canzoneri and Rogers (1990). In their analysis a fixed exchange rate regime is optimal only if agents in the countries belonging to it have roughly similar preferences for collecting revenue through seigniorage. Seigniorage preferences may differ due to different preferences for government spending or different abilities to collect revenue from sources other than money creation.

REFERENCES

Azariadis, Costas. 1981. Self-fulfilling prophecies. *Journal of Economic Theory* 25 (December): 380–96.

Behrens, Kathyryn L. 1923. *Paper Money in Maryland: 1727–1789.* Johns Hopkins University Studies in Historical and Political Science, Series 41, No. 1.

Bezanson, Anne. 1951. *Prices and inflation during the American Revolution: Pennsylvania, 1770–1790.* Philadelphia: University of Pennsylvania Press.

Bjork, Gordon C. 1963. *Stagnation and growth in the American economy, 1784–1792.* Ph.D. Thesis: University of Washington.

Bolles, Albert. 1884. *The financial history of the United States, from 1774 to 1789,* vol. 1, 4th edition. New York: D. Appleton and Co. (reprinted in 1969 by Augustus M. Kelley).

Brock, Leslie V. 1975. *The currency of the American colonies, 1700–1764: A study in colonial finance and imperial relations.* New York: Arno Press.

Bryant, John, and Wallace, Neil. 1984. A price discrimination analysis of monetary policy. *Review of Economic Studies* 51 (April): 279–88.

Calomiris, Charles W. 1988. Institutional failure, monetary scarcity, and the depreciation of the continental. *Journal of Economic History* 48 (March): 47–68.

Canzoneri, Matthew B., and Rogers, Carol Ann. 1990. Is the European community an optimal currency area? Optimal taxation versus the cost of multiple currencies. *American Economic Review* 80 (June): 419–33.

Cass, David, and Shell, Karl. 1983. Do sunspots matter? *Journal of Political Economy* 91 (April): 193–227.

Casella, Alessandra, and Feinstein, Jonathan. 1989. Management of a common currency. In *A European central bank? Perspectives on monetary unification after ten years of the EMS,* ed. Marcello de Cecco and Alberto Giovanni, pp. 131–56. Cambridge: Cambridge University Press.

Commission of the European Communities. 1990. *One market, one money: An evaluation of the potential benefits and costs of forming an economic and monetary union.* Luxembourg: Office for Official Publications for the European Communities.

Ernst, Joseph A. 1973. *Money and politics in America: 1755–1775.* Chapel Hill: University of North Carolina Press.

Feldstein, Martin. 1992. Europe's monetary union: The case against EMU. *The Economist* 324 (June 13): 19–22.

Ferguson, E. James. 1953. Currency finance: An interpretation of colonial monetary practices. *William and Mary Quarterly,* 3rd series, 10: 153–80.

Ferguson, E. James. 1961. *The power of the purse: A history of American public finance, 1776–1790.* Chapel Hill: University of North Carolina Press.

Hamilton, Alexander; Madison, James; and Jay, John. 1787. *The Federalist papers* (reprinted 1982). New York: Bantam.

Higgins, W. Robert. 1969. *A financial history of the American Revolution in South Carolina.* Ph.D. dissertation: Duke University.

Kaminski, John Paul. 1972. *Paper politics: The northern state loan offices during Confederation*. Ph.D. dissertation: University of Wisconsin.

Kareken, John, and Wallace, Neil. 1981. On the indeterminacy of equilibrium exchange rates. *Quarterly Journal of Economics* 96 (May): 207–22.

King, Robert G.; Wallace, Neil; and Weber, Warren E. 1992. Nonfundamental uncertainty and exchange rates. *Journal of International Economics* 32 (February): 83–108.

Lucas, Robert E., Jr. 1982. Interest rates and currency prices in a two-country world. *Journal of Monetary Economics* (November): 335–60.

Morrill, James R. 1969. *The practice and politics of fiat finance: North Carolina in the Confederation, 1783–1789*. Chapel Hill: University of North Carolina Press.

McCusker, John J. 1978. *Money and exchange in Europe and America, 1600–1775: A handbook*. Chapel Hill: University of North Carolina Press.

Nevins, Alan. 1927. *The American states during and after the Revolution, 1775–1789*. New York: Macmillan.

Perkins, Edwin J. 1992. *Continuities and innovations: American public finance and financial services, 1700–1815*. Manuscript: University of Southern California.

Schweitzer, Mary M. 1989a. State-issued currency and the ratification of the U.S. Constitution. *Journal of Economic History* 49 (June): 311–22.

Schweitzer, Mary M. 1989b. A new look at economic causes of the Constitution: Monetary and trade policy in Maryland, Pennsylvania, and Virginia. *The Social Science Journal* 26: 15–26.

Shell, Karl. 1977. *Monnaie et Allocation Intertemporelle*. CNRS Seminaire d'econometric de Roy-Malinvaud. Manuscript.

Smith, Bruce D. 1985a. American colonial monetary regimes: The failure of the quantity theory and some evidence in favor of an alternate view. *Canadian Journal of Economics* 18 (August): 531–65.

Smith, Bruce D. 1985b. Some colonial evidence on two theories of money: Maryland and the Carolinas. *Journal of Political Economy* 93 (December): 1178–211.

Smith, Bruce D. 1988. The relationship between money and prices: Some historical evidence reconsidered. *Federal Reserve Bank of Minneapolis Quarterly Review* 12 (Summer): 18–32.

Sylla, Richard. 1982. Monetary innovation and crises in American economic history. In *Crises in the economic and financial structure*, ed. Paul Wachtel, pp. 23–40. Lexington, Mass.: Lexington Books.

United States. Constitutional Convention. 1787. *Jonathan Elliot's debates in the several state conventions on the adoption of the Federal Constitution as recommended by the General Convention at Philadelphia in 1787*, vol III. Richmond, VA: James River Press.

Wallace, Neil. 1983. A legal restrictions theory of the demand for "money" and the role of monetary policy. *Federal Reserve Bank of Minneapolis Quarterly Review* 8 (Winter): 15–24.

Wicker, Elmus. 1985. Colonial monetary standards contrasted: Evidence from the seven years' war. *Journal of Economic History* 45 (December): 869–84.

Zarazaga, Carlos E. 1991. Hyperinflations and moral hazard in the appropriation of seignorage. Manuscript. University of Minnesota.

CHAPTER 13

ON THE COYNE-RASMINSKY DIRECTIVE AND RESPONSIBILITY FOR MONETARY POLICY IN CANADA[1]

Thomas K. Rymes

PROLOGUE

A commonplace is that central banks should be made more independent of democratic political processes. A variant of this major theme is that central bankers should have autonomy over monetary policy, such autonomy being restricted ultimately, of course, to preserve democratic control, by the device of <u>directives</u> issued by their political masters. I investigate here the Canadian variant, the Coyne-Rasminsky Directive. The Directive, though said to be originally designed to strengthen democratic control over the Bank of Canada, has had the opposite effect. It is not just an instrument to enhance the autonomy of the Bank of Canada, it is in fact a device to enhance the autocracy of the Bank, an outcome which is the general product of the attempt to replace discretion with rules in the conduct of monetary policy in a modern democratic state.

1.   INTRODUCTION

In the early 1960s, Canada witnessed a dramatic controversy over the constitutional position of the Bank of Canada and the monetary policy of the second Governor of the Bank, Mr. James Coyne. Prior to the mid-1950s, the constitutional position of the Bank of Canada was seemingly clear. While the Bank of Canada was responsible for the day-to-day implementation of policy, responsibility for monetary policy rested with the Minister of Finance and the Government, ultimately, of course, responsible to Parliament and to the Canadian electorate.[2] Though there were no

---

[1] I am indebted to Professors Steve Ferris, Jack Galbraith, Scott Gordon, Pierre Siklos and anonymous referees for comments on an earlier draft. I am alone responsible for the arguments now widely deemed today to be incorrect.

[2] Neufeld writes "The Bank was originally thought of as being subject only to the ultimate supremacy of parliament, but the idea developed, in fairly distinct stages, that the Bank not only should be subject to the government of the day but should be,

formal procedures set out in the Bank of Canada Act by which the Government could ensure that its view as to the appropriate monetary policy would prevail in any fundamental disagreement between the Bank and the Minister, it was understood that, in the event of such a disagreement, the management of the Bank, i.e., the Governor and Deputy-Governors, would implement the policy desired by the Government or "...that any government sufficiently displeased with the Bank or its management could bring about a change in management" (Royal Commission (1964, p.540). Mr. Graham Towers, first Governor of the Bank, appearing before the House Committee on Banking and Commerce 1954, during the decennial revision of the Bank Act, argued that (The Porter Commission, 714) "...parliament has placed squarely on the shoulders of the directors and management of the Bank of Canada the responsibility for monetary policy", that "...the central bank should be either a pure department of government and known to the public as such, or it should have independent responsibility", **but went immediately on to say** "...sovereign power...always lies with the administration which commands a majority in Parliament". Appearing before the Committee on 15 May 1956, Mr. Coyne said "If there were any dispute between the governor and the board of directors, provision is made [in the Bank of Canada Act?] for it to be referred to the Minister of Finance and he submits the matter to the governor in council, who has the power to decide it."(748) and while that it is not the same as saying that the Government must have the final say, he went on to state, on 22 May, that both he and Mr. Towers would agree that "...if the government of the day were sufficiently displeased with the bank or the management of the bank, they could put in motion steps which would bring about a change in the management.

At some stage in that process, if the government were so determined as to make a real issue of it, a public issue presumably, the governor would have to resign".

While the preamble to the Bank of Canada states that

"... it is desirable to establish a central bank in Canada to regulate credit and currency in the best interests of the economic life of the nation, to control and protect the external value of the national monetary unit and to mitigate by its influence fluctuations in the general level of production, trade, prices and employment, so far as may be possible within the scope of monetary action, and generally to promote the economic and financial welfare of the Dominion..."

and the business and powers of the Bank laid out in the Act give the Bank the instruments to try to achieve such objectives, nowhere in the Act is there an explicit statement about the Bank's responsibility for monetary policy, and, its responsibility

---

in fact, the instrument for implementing the policy of that government." Neufeld (1958, p.4).

compared with that of the Minister of Finance and the Government,   because **monetary policy is not defined in the Act.**

The Governor of the Bank of Canada, appointed by the Board of Directors of the Bank, is really a government appointment since the Directors's choice must be approved by the Governor in Council. Unlike (say) the Deputy Minister of Finance, appointed at pleasure, the Governor's and Deputy Governor's appointments are on good behaviour. An appointment on good behaviour is terminable either by resignation, death, agreement or possibly by a joint address before both Houses of Parliament.

In the mid-1950s, the Minister of Finance, confronted with political heat associated with increases in the Bank Rate, argued the Government of Canada was not responsible for monetary policy, rather it was the responsibility of the Bank and ultimately Parliament.[3] A consequence was that the Governor was immediately thrown into the maelstrom of the political arena. More importantly, the Bank of Canada was now considered to be much more responsible, or at very least, jointly (with, if not in fact independent of, Government through the Minister of Finance) for monetary policy.

The Government, desiring a change in policy, but trapped by its own rhetoric that the Bank of Canada was responsible for monetary policy or at least had significant joint responsibility for monetary policy, proceeded not by amending the Bank of Canada Act, not by pressuring the Governor to resign because of a disagreement about policy and thereby reaffirming that the Government had the responsibility for monetary policy, but rather by initiating a bill to declare vacant the position of the Governor of the Bank[4].

---

[3] The various political events and statements leading up to this change in the understanding of the position of the Bank of Canada are outlined in Gordon (1961, 1961a). See also "The status and organization of the Bank of Canada", Chapter 26 of The Porter Commission. Professor Gordon notes that Prime Minister St. Laurent's remarks to the House (cf., *HOUSE OF COMMONS DEBATES*, 1956, 7351), suggesting that the Bank of Canada's monetary policy was even beyond, subject to amendment of the Bank of Canada Act, the purview of Parliament, can be interpreted as an historical aberration. See Neufeld, (1958).

[4] The legislation passed the House and then was considered by Senate. (That the Governor had behaved improperly was a charge anyone familiar with the incorruptible James Coyne knew to be completely fantastic!) The Governor stated before the senators that if they would not accept the bill he would resign, with his reputation intact. The Senate directed the bill back to the House, the Governor resigned and the unprecedented drama on Parliament Hill associated with the Coyne Controversy came to an end.

Once the dust had settled, the third Governor, Louis Rasminsky, issued a statement that the Bank was normally responsible for monetary policy and, in the event of a disagreement between the Governor and the Government about monetary policy, the Minister of Finance would issue a Directive, indicating the type of policy the Government wished the Bank to follow. Should the Governor not wish to follow such a policy, the Governor, it was understood, would resign. Mr. Coyne earlier suggested the Directive device to the Government.[5]

Mr. Rasminsky, in his statement 1 August 1961, said

"I believe that it is essential that the responsibilities in relation to monetary policy should be clarified in the public mind and in the legislation. I do not suggest a precise formula but have in mind two basic principles to be established: (1) in the ordinary course of events, **the Bank has the responsibility for monetary policy**, and (2) if the Government disapproves of the monetary policy being carried out by the Bank it has the right and the responsibility to direct the Bank as to the policy which the Bank is to carry out." (*Bank of Canada Annual Report*, 1961, p.3, my emphasis)

The Minister of Finance, the Honourable Donald Fleming, released a simultaneous statement allowing that "The views expressed by the Governor of the Bank of Canada in his statement today regarding the relationships between the monetary and fiscal authorities are in harmony with those of the Government and were known to the Government prior to his appointment". [6]

The Coyne-Rasminsky Directive represents a fundamental shift in the constitutional position of the Bank of Canada. Not only was it necessary for the Minister of Finance, in the event of a disagreement between the Governor and the Minister, to supply a Directive, outlining the required change in policy but that, though admittedly only in the ordinary [sic] course of events, **the Bank has the responsibility for monetary policy**. Earlier, though characterized by ambiguity, it would appear to have been established that the Government was responsible for monetary policy, the Bank for its implementation. Admittedly, day-to-day

---

[5]   See "Statement by James E. Coyne Regarding a Bill Declaring the Position of Governor of the Bank of Canada to be Vacant: Before the Senate Committee on Banking and Commerce" in Neufeld (1965).

[6] Bank of Canada *Annual Report 1961*, 5 As Professor Gordon noted, Mr. Fleming, while in opposition had insisted that the Government was responsible for monetary policy but changed his mind when he became Minister. He was not, then, in a position, particularly following the Coyne affair, to disallow the Bank's claim to be normally responsible for monetary policy.

implementation of that policy implies second-order responsibility for policy and should such day-to-day events entail no shift nor basic reconsideration of monetary policy, one could argue, as did Towers, Coyne and Rasminsky, that in that limited sense the Bank had responsibility for not merely the techniques and implementation of policy but also for the policy itself. Gone now, however, was the understanding that monetary policy was the responsibility of the Government, it had become normally the responsibility of the Governor, subject to the Coyne-Rasminsky Directive, and only ultimately that of the Government.

One would have thought that, given the Coyne Controversy, a Government would have clearly stated that monetary policy was its responsibility and that, if a Governor disagreed with that policy and was unable in conscience to implement the Government's monetary policy, that Governor must resign. A Governor could be obliged to make known to the community the reasons for a resignation and the Government could be able to reply. Instead, the Government's approved a statement by the new Governor that monetary policy was normally the responsibility of Bank of Canada and that if the Government disapproved of the Bank's policy, then an elected politician, a member of the Government, the Minister of Finance, **would be required** to direct the Governor, a bureaucrat, appointed on good behaviour, as to the course of monetary policy desired by the electorate as represented democratically by the Government. Passing strange!

Extraordinarily, the Coyne-Rasminsky Directive received the blessing of the *PORTER COMMISSION* and it became part of the Bank of Canada Act in the 1967 Revision[7]. Section 14 says

> **14** (1) The Minister and the Governor shall consult regularly on monetary policy and on its relation to general economic policy.
>
> (2) If, notwithstanding the consultations provided for in subsection (1), there should emerge a difference of opinion between the Minister and the Bank concerning the monetary policy to be followed, the Minister may, after consultation with the Governor and with the approval of the Governor in Council, give to the Governor a written directive concerning monetary policy, in specific terms and applicable for a specified period and the Bank shall comply with such directive.

---

[7] In the submission of the Bank of Canada to the Porter Commission, there was no discussion of the responsibility for monetary policy nor of the Coyne-Rasminsky Directive, save that the August 1961 statement by Mr. Rasminsky is repeated as an appendix, not to the section of the submission on 'The constitution and functions of the Bank of Canada' but rather to the section on **"The role of monetary policy'**. My emphasis.

(3) A directive given under this section shall be published forthwith
in the **Canada Gazette** and shall be laid before Parliament within
fifteen days after the giving thereof, or, if Parliament is not sitting,
on any of the first fifteen days next thereafter that Parliament is
sitting. [8]

The Bank of Canada has expressed the view that the Directive, though one
has never been issued in Canada, makes it clear that the Government has the ultimate
say in monetary policy. Should the disagreement between the Governor and the
Minister reach such a point where the Minister published the Directive, the Governor,
if unable to accept the direction of monetary policy desired by the Minister and set
out in the Directive, would resign.[9]

2.   THE COYNE-RASMINSKY DIRECTIVE AND THE THEORY OF MONETARY POLICY

The basic idea behind the Directive is the need to preserve autonomy for the
Bank of Canada, autonomy, that is, not in the day-to-day implementation of monetary
policy about which there has not been dispute (though there could be), but rather the
preservation of autonomy with respect to the conception and formation of monetary
policy.

---

[8] Bank of Canada Act, *Revised Statutes of Canada*, 1967. No changes in this
section were made in the 1980 revision of the Act.

[9] In a limited sense, there is no advance on the constitutional position of the Bank
of Canada taken to be the case before the Coyne Controversy. In the event of an
issued Directive, the Governor, if unable to agree with the policy proposed by the
Government, would resign. That was the understanding in the 1950s before the
Directive was created but a clear difference is that earlier the disagreement would not
necessarily come to light before the resignation of the Governor occurred. With the
Directive idea in force, the disagreement leading to the resignation of the Governor
might be made public. Indeed, the Directive requires such publicity. With a Directive
published, the Governor need not resign and might follow the dictates of the
Directive. Then it would be difficult to see why the Directive would be published in
the first place. Again, a Governor could be in disagreement with the policy suggested
by the Minister and resign even without a Directive being issued. No where in the
pre- or post-Directive regimes is there legislation indicating that and when the
Governor **must** resign. If a Directive was issued and the Governor refused to change
monetary policy in the indicated direction, i.e., refused to comply with the Directive
and refused to resign, then again the joint address procedure would have to be
initiated. It is in this limited sense that no advance has occurred.

Autonomy of the central bank is deemed necessary because without it the conduct of monetary policy would result in taxation by inflation as the Government would pursue a mix of taxes which had the least political cost, and the inflation tax as Keynes argued (Keynes (1973)) is a tax for which the general public finds difficult to understand and nearly impossible to avoid. Modern public finance (Lucas (1986)) argues, however, that the inflation tax, since it amounts largely to a tax on intermediate inputs, is an inefficient tax and should not be imposed. More fundamentally, Monetary Authorities, under the influence it is said of a later Keynes, will try to reduce unemployment rates below those which are 'natural' and will engage in time-inconsistent policies. If expansionary monetary policy can temporarily reduce the 'natural' unemployment rate,[10] then it will be undertaken. Everyone will eventually, if not logically immediately, expect it to be undertaken. The expectational equilibrium is that there will not be any permanent reduction in the rate of unemployment but only a steady positive rate of inflation. If a positive rate of inflation imposes Paretian inefficiencies something is lost.[11] Indeed, the fundamental argument, which follows from new classical economic and time-inconsistency theories, is that discretionary monetary policy can only do harm!

What can prevent such fruitless and costly inflationary expansions of the money supply engineered by a Minister of Finance confronted with an electorate still stupidly in the grips of Keynesian fallacies that money has 'real' effects in the short and long run? Three possibilities exist. First the Government could get rid of central

---

[10] Barro and Gordon (1983). The private sector is prepared to make nominal pre-commitments laying themselves open to the opportunistic behaviour of the central bank. Of course, the private sector would soon learn to index its nominal commitments which then means that the central bank has no incentive to inflate. In a Keynesian full-employment equilibrium where short-period expectations are correct, it is impossible for the central bank to fool people in the short period or to take advantages of any imperfections or externalities said to be associated with the labour market. Any central bank expansion would only result in higher prices. A central bank knows that if it does try to fool the people they know that the central bank is so behaving, then the inflationary equilibrium will not stand because both the people and the central bank know that everyone would be better off in a non-inflationary equilibrium. People and central bankers, with short-period expectations being confirmed, cannot cheat on each other, the central bank precommits and the problem of time inconsistency vanishes. See Goodhart (1989) and the extensive discussion in Fischer (1990).

[11] Some argue that the costs of inflation are high. See Selody (1990) and Howitt (1990).   No costs of inflation could be higher than Feldstein's infinite cost. See Feldstein (1979).

banks and therefore eliminate the possibility of policy-induced inflations.[12] To prevent Monetary Authorities from generating Pareto-inferior allocations by behaving opportunistically, choose not to have them! It is interesting that central bankers who argue that they need defense through autonomy against the ignorant public and their political leaders and the problem of time-inconsistency (Crow (1993)) never suggest that the threat to monetary stability defined as price stability comes from the mere existence of central banks. Second, one could impose a rule, even a conditional rule, on the Bank of Canada that fiat high powered money, i.e., Bank of Canada notes and net settlement balances of the direct clearers such as major banks with it, should be constrained to grow at some rate consistent with overall price stability and the Bank should be charged to follow such a rule and not a policy of discretionary monetary policy. Third, the Government could mandate the Bank of Canada to pursue price stability and price stability only.[13]

---

[12] In monetary economics today there is an ultimate argument dealing with the need for independence of Monetary Authorities from the evils of democracy. Get rid of central banks and monetary authorities altogether! I do not deal here with this wing of New Classical Monetary Economics. See, however, Smith (1990), Selgin (1988), Glasner (1989) and Dowd (1989).

[13] This is not the place to record the debate about such a proposed revision to the mandate of the Bank of Canada. The majority of the economists who testified before the Sub-committee on the [mandate of the] Bank of Canada of the Standing Committee on Finance in the Fall of 1991 argued that it would be unwise to restrict so narrowly the mandate of the Bank of Canada because the state of economic theory does not offer support for the one monetary theory on which the revised mandate would rest. The Governor of the Bank, who supported the Government's restriction of the Banks's mandate, does not seem to understand the point being made by the economists testifying before the Committee, namely that the set of economic theories receiving support from a wide spectrum of economists does not support the idea of a narrow mandate restricted to one economic theory. See Mr. Crow's speech before the Canadian Economics Association in June 1992, "What is to be done with the Bank of Canada[? sic]. It is interesting to note that a former Governor, when asked a related question, argued that ".. it would be a mistake to incorporate into the legislation any specific instruction to the central bank to focus its policies and its attention exclusively on the achievement of any single objective." Evidence (1964, p.13). One can illustrate the point about changing fashions in economic theory by considering an argument in Professor Gordon's pamphlet. He was critical of Governor Coyne when he wrote (32) "The Governor apparently wishes to put unemployment policy outside the sphere of monetary policy altogether.". A few years ago in economics, that statement, with which the present governor would agree, would be taken not as a criticism of the Governor but as the highest praise. Now, the tide is turning again. See Howitt (1991, 1990).

The Coyne-Rasminsky Directive can be regarded as a variant of the idea of removing the dangers of short run discretionary policies being followed if the Bank of Canada, through the Minister of Finance, was subject to the vagaries and whims of the democratic political processes, biased as they are supposed to be toward inflation. The reason for autonomy for the Bank then is to blunt the inflationary excesses of the democratic electorate. As the Porter Commission, citing the submission of the Bank's first Governor, said (541) "The main reason...for conferring some measure of autonomy on the central bank has been the historical tendency of government of all forms to develop the habit of inflating the currency". Indeed, as Mr. Coyne argued, that was the basic reason for the Governor to be appointed on good behaviour (Neufeld (1965), p. 333-4).

The fundamental reason then for past and current recommendations for an independent central bank, and the Directive as an identifiable part of the institutional forms which enhance the central bank's independence, is the fear that a democratic electorate will 'debase the coinage'. If monetary policy is in the hands of democratically elected governments there will be a tendency for those electorates to act in discretionary ways to enhance their welfare when in fact it would be better, in a world of uncertain knowledge, if the electorate constrained itself to follow rules with respect to the conduct of monetary policy.

This is an old and fundamental argument. Keynes was greatly influenced by the Cambridge philosopher G. E. Moore who argued, in his *PRINCIPIA ETHICA*, that good, an undefinable primitive, was best exemplified by the contemplation of beauty and the love of friends. Should more than contemplation be required, then moral acts consisting of enhancing the possibility of good would be necessary. When knowledge was insufficient to judge where enhancement was probable, conventions or rules might come into play. Insufficiency of human knowledge led to situations in which rule-utilitarianism would be preferred to act-utilitarianism (Rowe (1989)). The early Keynes reacted critically and argued that conventions were rational and modifiable acts in the face of uncertain and vague knowledge. He later apparently modified (Keynes (1972)) his position and recognized the role conventions or rules may have in minimizing the damage which could result from human caprice in an uncertain world.[14] Yet the conventions were never to be slavishly followed and were certainly never a substitute for rational discourse and action based on that discourse. All modern arguments in monetary economics about the need for Monetary Authorities to follow rules for the conduct of monetary policy, such as fixing the rate of growth of the money supply or pursuing price stability and price stability only are part of the

---

[14] For discussion of the extent to which Keynes did, in fact, change his early position and embraced rules, see O'Donnell (1989) and Bateman (1991). For an interpretation of Keynes's monetary theory suggesting he was vitally interested in conventions which preserve monetary stability, which certainly was his concern in his **TRACT**, see Meltzer (1988) and Littleboy (1990).

attack on the possibility of an enlightened electorate, through debate and discussion, arriving at rational and time-consistent decisions for the conduct of discretionary monetary policy.

The Coyne-Rasminsky Directive is a (albeit small) part of the *REASON OF RULES* (Brennan and Buchanan (1985)) and is subject to the same questions and criticisms which Keynes directed against rules, namely that rules and conventions may be followed when definite knowledge is insufficient to permit one to act in a discretionary way but must always be subject to amendment and critical scrutiny. As definite knowledge always changes and yesterdays's conventions come to be replaced by today's knowledge, no rule with respect to the conduct of economic affairs should be enshrined in the constitution because no unchanging conventions of any kind should be enshrined there.

Game theoretic analysis which concludes central banks acquire credibility by adhering steadfastly to rules (so that it is unprofitable for the public to behave strategically) neglect completely the fact that knowledge and understanding undermine rules and those with the greatest credibility are those open to the need to change their minds (See also Gordon (1976)). What should be enshrined in any constitution is the need to keep the system open to discretion and the requirement that a free electorate should engage in the search for the knowledge which permits rational discretionary acts. The defense against human caprice in economic affairs is not rules determining monetary policy nor the conduct of policy by rote but constant discussion, debate and examination of the knowledge and conventions and definite knowledge used to enlighten and conduct economic affairs.

At the mundane and institutionally detailed level of the Coyne-Rasminsky Directive, it is a device to insulate monetary policy as much as possible from the vagaries and capriciousness of democratic political processes and more importantly the possibility that discretionary acts will make us all worse off compared with rules. The Directive throws up costs in front of the Minister of Finance, the Government and the electorate, that is, constrains them, in seeking to exercise their responsibilities for the execution of rational economic policy. It seeks to reduce the responsibility for rational economic policy by making it costly to exercise that responsibility in a discretionary way.

3.   AUTONOMY OR AUTOCRACY?

As a specific part of the general position that central banks should be as independent as possible from control of democratic parliamentary institutions, the Coyne-Rasminsky Directive had two objectives .

Ministers of Finance had denied their responsibility for monetary policy and therefore had put themselves in a situation where the only way in which a Government could rid itself of a Governor, appointed on good behaviour, would possibly be by a joint address which ends up constituting an ugly attack on the person rather than an effective criticism of the policy. Once the Ministers disavowed the doctrine that the responsibility for monetary policy rested with the Government and not with the Bank, then it was difficult for the Government to obtain the resignation of the Governor on the grounds of disagreement about policy. If one argues that it is Parliament and not the Government which is responsible for monetary policy then it is Parliament which must call for the Governor to resign.

The Coyne-Rasminsky Directive can be interpreted as a device by which the Governors are protected from the personal attack involved in the joint address proceedings.

On the wider scale of rules versus discretion, the Directive is seen much more fundamentally as one of many institutional devices designed to strengthen the independence and autonomy of the Bank. Monetary policy is now jointly shared by the Governor of the Bank and the Minister of Finance, even though it is understood that the Minister has the final word. Non-execution of a Directive implies that the Government agrees with the monetary policy of the Bank. In the past it was understood that the final responsibility for monetary policy rested with the Government and in that sense the Directive adds nothing to our understanding and interpretation of the constitutional relations between the Bank and the Government. It was also earlier understood that in the event of a disagreement the Governor would resign. The Directive implies that not only is a disagreement brought out into the public, with consequences for the capital markets, exchange rates and the general state of business confidence, but it also implies that, within the context of such disagreements , it is the Minister of Finance who must present detailed criticisms of the policy not of an elected official but of an official appointed on good behaviour, yet responsible for a policy with widespread economic, political and social implications. The Directive does not require the Bank, given that there is a recognized disagreement between the Bank and the Minister, to present a detailed defense of its policies to the Minister, rather the onus is on the Minister and basically on the electorate to defend its criticism of the policy of an autocrat. The Directive has therefore strengthened the independence of the Bank of Canada in a manner inconsistent with the idea of a responsible democratic electorate.

Writing before the advent of the Coyne-Rasminsky Directive, Professor Gordon said (Gordon, 1961, 13)

> "When we consider the Bank of Canada as an agency of government we are dealing not with an institution that has been given some modicum of independence from ministerial control, but with one that enjoys perhaps the largest degree of independence with which a state institution may be endowed in a democratic

society."

With the Directive that degree of independence has been enhanced.

Why? Is the independence of the Bank consistent with a democratic state? The theory of public choice would predict that, in their self-interest, central bankers would seek to make their operations obscure so that accountability for them would be difficult (See, for example, Acheson and Chant (1973)). Yet the Coyne-Rasminsky Directive seems to make the accountability clear in the sense that the Governor must be accountable to the Minister rather than Parliament as a whole. Yet the Directive has had the de facto effect of increasing the responsibility of the Bank for monetary policy and, while it has made the Bank more accountable, in any dispute it is the elected Minister who must account to the Bank for the Government criticisms directed against it. That component of public choice theory seems not to shed much light on the problem.[15]

A wider public choice perspective, however, may be more in accord with the Coyne-Rasminsky Directive. To Professor Gordon Tullock (Tullock (1987)), democratic government is a rare and unstable means with which people are prepared to arrange collectively their lives. Self interest would seem to dictate autocracy would be more commonly observed. Central bankers may increase their welfare by

---

[15] The public choice argument, that bureaucrats will try to make accountability complex, has difficulty rationalizing the fact that the Bank of Canada has supported the Government of Canada's proposals that the Bank be accountable for the one goal of price stability and price stability only. Even given the fact that the Bank is now producing its own CPI, certainly such a mandate is clearer than the mandate as laid out in the preamble to the existing Bank of Canada Act. The willingness of the Bank of Canada to improve its measured accountability is nonetheless a difficulty for the position that bureaucrats in their self interest will try to obscure how to measure what they do. Professor Chant has admitted that the bureaucratic theory of central bank behaviour "... is somewhat wrong or maybe very wrong...". See Minutes of Proceedings and Evidence of the sub-Committee on the **BANK OF CANADA** of the Standing Committee of Finance, Issue No. 7, 19 December 1991, 20. I think Professor Chant may be overly harsh on his own analysis. It is possible to argue that a goal, which is less costly to attain and for which accountability offers fewer difficulties, may be better for a central banker as bureaucrat to embrace than one with more substance though more generally stated and more difficult to achieve. Sir Humphrey of **Yes Minister** fame would no doubt appreciate being charged with a responsibility which the theory he advances behind it claims he may be able to achieve rather than to embrace responsibility for outcomes which the same theory assures him he cannot achieve. As well, the economic theory of measurement would suggest that the easier or less costly one can measure something the less substance it may have.

increasing their independence of the democratic political processes and may contemplate institutional forms increasing their strength as autocrats. Professor Tullock admits the theory of autocracy is in a primitive state. He states that (190-1) "...the feeling that democracy is not the true equilibrium state, can be taken as an argument simply for guarding it more carefully in hopes that if we guard it carefully we can keep it or at least keep it a lot longer." If it predicts such institutional mechanisms as the Coyne-Rasminsky Directive, it would be a good thing if the preamble of the Bank of Canada Act were revised to state clearly that monetary policy is the responsibility of the Minister of Finance and the Government and ultimately through them to Parliament and a democratic electorate and that the Governor of the Bank of Canada is not jointly responsible for monetary policy but is responsible only for the implementation of that policy. It would a small part of the process of returning the responsibility for monetary policy to the Canadian democratic electorate if the Coyne-Rasminsky Directive, which may enhance the autocratic nature of the position of the Governor of the Bank of Canada, were removed from the Bank of Canada Act.

The Oxford English Dictionary defines autonomy and autocracy in similar ways, the former being the right of self government, occasionally applying to administrative structures and the latter entailing absolutism, with the self-sustained powers of states being equated to autonomy.

In attempting to measure the independence of central banks, Professor Cukierman (Cukierman (1992)) unwittingly measures the autocracy of central banks. While he provides a number of indices about which there would not be much debate, such as the extent to which the central bank is limited in making advances to the government, indicators such as the length of appointment and dismissal procedures are considered. The longer the term and <u>no</u> procedures for dismissal are taken as positive indicators of independence and autonomy. Governors appointed for life with the democratically elected government having no power of dismissal over them would no doubt be independent and autonomous but they would also be better described as dynastic autocrats.

4.   EPILOGUE

Keynes, aware of the dangers of the "presuppositions of Harvey Road", was nevertheless committed to the consideration of all possible policies, including such apparently time-inconsistent ones as a capital levy. He argued (**TRACT**, 56-7) that "...nothing can preserve the integrity of contract between individuals, except a discretionary authority in the State to revise what has become intolerable" and went on to argue that when

> '...we enter the realm of State action, **everything** is to be considered and weighed on its merits. Changes in death duties,

income tax, land tenure, licensing, game laws, church, establishment, feudal rights, slavery, and so on through all ages, have received the same denunciations from the absolutists of contract, who are the real parents of revolution".

Would those who argue for autonomy and autocracy for central banks have the same commitment to freedom as did Keynes!

REFERENCES

Acheson, Keith and John F. Chant, "Bureaucratic theory and the choice of central bank goals", *Journal of Money, Credit and Banking*, V, May 1973, 637-655.

Barro, Robert and David Gordon, "A positive theory of monetary policy in a natural rate model", *Journal of Political Economy*, 1983, 589-610.

Bateman Bradley W. and John B. Davis, *Keynes and Philosophy: Essays on the Origin of Keynes's Thought*, (Aldershot: Elgar, 1991).

Bateman, Bradley W., "The rules of the road: Keynes's theoretical rationale for public policy", in Bradley W. Bateman and John B. Davis *Keynes Philosophy: Essays on the Origins of Keynes's Thought* (Aldershot: Elgar, 1991).

Brennan, Greffrey and James M. Buchanan, *The Reason of Rules: Constitutional Political Economy* (Cambridge: Cambridge University Press, 1985).

Crow, John W., "Monetary policy, and the responsibilities and accountability of central banks", the Gerhard de Kock Memorial Lecture, University of Pretoria, South Africa, 10 February 1993.

Cukierman, Alex, *Central Bank Strategy, Credibility and Independence: Theory and Evidence* (Cambridge, Mass.: MIT Press, 1992).

Dowd, Kevin, *The State and the Monetary System* (Oxford: Philip Alan, 1989).

Evidence of the Governor Before the The Royal Commission on Banking and Finance (Ottawa: Bank of Canada, 1964).

Feldstein, M., "The welfare cost of permanent inflation and optimal short run economic policy", *Journal of Political Economy*, LXXXVI, August 1979, 745-768.

Fischer, S., "Rules versus discretion in monetary policy", in B.M. Friedman and F.H. Hahn (eds.), *Handbook of Monetary Economics*, II (Amsterdam: Elsevier Science Publishers, 1990).

Glasner, David, *Free Banking and Monetary Theory* (Cambridge: Cambridge University Press, 1989).

Goodhart, C., *Money, Ionformation and Uncertainty* (Cambridge, Mass.: The MIT Press, second edition 1989).

Gordon, H. Scott, "The Economists versus The Bank of Canada (Toronto: The Ryerson Press, 1961) "The Bank of Canada in a system of responsible government", *Canadian Journal of Economics and Political Science*, XXVII, February 1961a, 1-22.

Gordon, H. Scott, "The new contractarians", *Journal of Political Economy*, LXXXIV, June 1976, 573-590.

Howitt, P. W., "A skeptic's guide to Canadian monetary policy", C. D. Howe Commentary, 25, December 1990, 1-16.

Howitt, Peter, "Zero inflation as a long-term target for monetary policy, in Richard G. Lipsey (ed.), *Zero Inflation: The Goal of Price Stability* (Toronto: C.D. Howe, 1990).

Howitt, Peter, "Keynesian policy analysis, rational expectations, and the Bank of Canada", in Thomas K. Rymes (eds.), *Welfare, Property Rights and Economic Policy: Essays and Tributes in Honour of H. Scott Gordon* (Ottawa: Carleton University Press, 1991).

Keynes, J. M., A Tract on Monetary Reform, IV, *The Collected Writings of John Maynard Keynes* (London: MacMillan, 1973).

Keynes, J. M., "My early beliefs", *Essays in Biography Collected Writings of John Maynard Keynes*, X (London: Macmillan, 1972).

Littleboy, Bruce, *On Interpreting Keynes: A Study in Reconciliation* (London: Routledge, 1990).

Lipsey, Richard, *Zero Inflation: The goal of price stability* (Toronto: C. D. Howe, 1990).

Lucas, Robert Jr. "Principles of Fiscal and Monetary Policy", *Journal of Monetary Economics*, XVII, January 1986, 117-34.

Meltzer, Allan H., *Keynes's Monetary Theory: A different interpretation* (Cambridge: Cambridge University Press, 1988).

Neufeld, E. P., *Money and Banking in Canada* (Toronto: McClelland and Stewart Ltd. for the   Carleton Library, 1965).

Neufeld, E. P., *Bank of Canada Operations and Policy* (Toronto: University of Toronto Press, 1958).

O'Donnell, R. M., "Keynes: Philosophy, Economics and Politics. *The philosophical foundations of Keynes's thought and their influence on his economics and politics*"(London: Macmillan, 1989).

Rowe, Nicholas, *Rules and Institutions* (Hemel Hempstead: Philip Allan, 1989).

Royal Commission on Banking and Finance [The Porter Commission] (Ottawa: Queen's Printer, 1964).

Selgin, George A., *The Theory of Free Banking: Money Supply Under Competitive Note Issue* (Totowa, N. J. : Roman and Littlefield, 1988)

Selody, Jack, "The goal of price stability: A review of the issues", *Bank of Canada Technical Report 54* (Ottawa: Bank of Canada, 1990).

Smith, Vera C., *The Rationale of Central Banking and the Free Banking Alternative* (Indianapolis: Liberty Press, 1990)

Tullock, Gordon, *Autocracy* (Boston: Kluwer Academic Publishers, 1987).

CHAPTER 14

CRIPPLED MONETARY POLICY IN TRANSFORMING ECONOMIES: WHY CENTRAL BANK INDEPENDENCE DOES NOT RESTORE CONTROL[1]

István Ábel
John P. Bonin
Pierre L. Siklos

1.   INTRODUCTION

With privatization programs stalled in many of the transforming countries, the importance of creating a flexible and effective capital market in the earlier stages of the transition is gaining recognition. Brainard (1991) asserts that a reasonably well-functioning capital market is a necessary condition for privatization to occur on a large scale.[2] According to Brainard, although all proposals for reforming financial institutions in transforming countries begin with increasing the financial discipline on companies they miss the essential point and thus fail to produce the desired result. For him, the crux of the issue is balance sheet losses. He recommends "sanitizing" company balance sheets using one or some combination of bankruptcy, rehabilitation, and privatization.

Calvo and Frenkel (1991) call for financial markets with the breadth and depth to provide the information necessary to distinguish "good" from "bad" companies, a condition also required for Brainard's proposal to proceed. However, as these authors argue, financial markets in the transforming countries are not

[1] We acknowledge gratefully the support provided by the **National Council for Soviet and East European Research Fund** (grant number 807-07), the WLU Academic Development Fund, a WLU Preparation Grant, and the Social Sciences and Humanities Research Council of Canada (grant number 410-93-1409).

[2] Note we do not say pre-condition. There is certainly considerable controversy about whether privitization should precede the development of capital markets. At the very least, these should be viewed as joint products though governments in the formerly centrally planned economies have opted to put off completing the privitization process.

developed enough to provide this sorting outcome. Firm-specific risks that would be diversifiable in well-functioning capital markets remain because of inter-enterprise linkages. Overall macroeconomic and political uncertainty add to non-diversifiable risk.

Moreover, the vestiges of credit allocation procedures from the old central planning system hinder the institutional development required to support the fledgling capital markets. The separation of monetary and fiscal instruments and the decoupling of the central bank from commercial loan activities are both necessary (but not sufficient) conditions for allocating credit effectively and controlling the overall liquidity in the system.

Hungary is considered to be the transforming country that has made the greatest strides to date in restoring central bank independence and developing its capital market. But the Hungarian example is not yet a success story as the legacies of the past still weigh heavily. Since all of the transforming countries are struggling with the problem of creating capital markets, an understanding of the Hungarian experience to date will provide insight into what may be reasonable expectations for the speed with which flexible capital markets can be created during the transition.

Without meaningful progress toward developing efficient financial intermediation early in the transition, the transformation will quickly run out of gas. Not only will privatization be impeded but, as we will argue in this paper, a major tool of macroeconomic stabilization, monetary policy, will be blunted. Since credibility is such an important currency for the reform designers, the lessons (harsh though they may be) must be heeded.

In the next two sections, we provide a detailed account of the organizational and institutional changes in Hungary throughout the eighties. To highlight the legacies of the past, we develop the notion of segmented monetary circuits and the preeminence of fiscal policy. We also consider in detail the banking reform in which independent commercial banks were spun off from the old monobank structure. In section four, we argue that these banks have yet to be weaned from the state and we evaluate their financial health. In section five, we examine the effect on monetary policy of both disintermediation through the extension of inter-enterprise trade credit and the development of the T-Bill market. The concluding section draws several lessons for the transforming countries from the Hungarian experience to date.

2.   THE BUILDING BLOCKS: A BRIEF FINANCIAL HISTORY FROM 1968 TO 1987

In the traditional centrally planned economy (CPE), financial planning was designed to play a subservient role to physical planning. Monetary policy appears to have been completely passive. Quantitative instruments were used to allocate credit based on the sectoral capacity-expansion directives contained in the five-year plan. Inter-enterprise transactions were settled on the books of the commercial department of the state bank. Liquidity was required only to pay workers in cash in accordance with an enterprise's planned wage bill. Separate state banks existed to grant credits for financing construction projects and foreign transactions that had been authorized by the plan. In essence, the state bank was a subsidiary financing wing of the state planning commission.

The New Economic Mechanism (NEM) in Hungary represented the first attempt to create a modified CPE in 1968. These reforms dismantled the annual physical planning apparatus and abolished compulsory plan targets on enterprises. However, capital markets were not allowed to function as resource allocators. As Kornai (1986) has documented, fiscal taxes and subsidies were used to redistribute profits in the manufacturing sector during this period. Fiscal interference prevented profit from signalling resource movements under NEM and the central allocation of investment was retained. NEM was not designed with the creation of capital markets in mind. Tardos (1988) claims that, although commodity markets were established, feedbacks from commodity markets to factor markets and relationships between factor markets were non-existent. Consequently, we seek a clear understanding of how the monetary sector actually worked in that period to understand more fully Hungary's legacies.

To model the financial arrangements under NEM, Ábel and Székely (1992) divide monetary flows into three circuits, household, enterprise and government.[3] The total money stock is defined conventionally so that the compulsory reserve funds of the enterprises (used by the government to confiscate profits) and the clearing accounts of the fiscal budget (a discretionary instrument of fiscal policy and not part of the monetary system) are excluded. On the other hand, savings notes (a government bond that acts like a savings deposit) held by the households are included in broad money (M2). The household money circuit consists of currency, demand deposits, time and savings deposits held by the households. The enterprise money circuit is defined as liquid enterprise bank deposits (with the exception of the compulsory reserve fund deposits referred to above). Flows in the government money circuit are equated with the fiscal deficit which is monetized directly by the national bank.

Using quarterly data for the period 1974-1986, Ábel and Székely find that the household money and the enterprise money circuits are separate in the sense that no causal relationship between these two circuits in either direction is detected by Granger causality tests. However, the authors find strong causality running from the government money circuit to enterprise money and weak causality from government

---

[3]   Lane (1992) is, however, successful in modelling money demand in Poland using a variant of a cash-in-advance model.

money to household money. Consequently, they conclude that fiscal deficits significantly influence the money flows in the other two circuits while the household and business sectors are not connected by financial flows. In essence, monetized fiscal deficits provided the required overall liquidity to the economy.

Institutionally, households and enterprises were separated by the division of banking activity along functional lines. The four major banks in order of size (value of assets) were the National Bank of Hungary, the National Savings Bank, the National Bank for Development and Construction, and the National Bank for Foreign Trade. The National Bank of Hungary, a state monobank exclusively for enterprises, was responsible for all commercial banking activities. The National Savings Bank maintained a monopoly over household accounts collecting deposits and issuing housing mortgages at government-controlled subsidized rates. Intermediation between household deposits and commercial credit was blocked institutionally by the functional separation in the banking sector. As a result, maturity conversion and financial intermediation occurred through the fiscal budget.

Segmentation in capital markets is a pervasive legacy as the history of the reintroduction of bonds in Hungary attests.[4] Beginning in 1983, enterprise bonds were issued but to other enterprises only. These bonds were expected to be an instrument for redistributing liquidity within the business sector. Restrictions were lifted in 1986 so that companies could issue a second category of bonds for purchase by households only. The household sector, starved for a new financial instrument, proved to be a fertile ground. Until the end of 1987, the bond market grew rapidly as spreads were about 3% above rates paid on time deposits, the only other interest-earning financial asset available to households. Furthermore, bonds issued to households were fully guaranteed by the government, interest income was not taxed, and excess demand fueled a secondary market that insured liquidity.

The bond market collapsed in 1988 with the onslaught of higher rates of inflation, an end to government guarantees on household bonds and the appearance of a new and preferable instrument (T-Bills; see section V below). Volume in the market fell back to 1984 levels but the removal of special treatment for household issuances paved the way for integration of the market. In 1988, 70% of the bond issuances had no restriction on the purchaser (Székely, 1990). The fledgling bond market, by moving away from segmented offerings, was beginning to assume its rightful place in a true capital market.

---

[4] Székely (1990) provides details of the growth and ultimate collapse of this market.

3.   THE END OF CENTRAL PLANNING: FINANCIAL REFORMS
       SINCE 1987

Banking reform began in 1987 in Hungary with the establishment of a two-tier banking system headed by an independent central bank, the Hungarian National Bank (HNB). Hungary was the first of the former CPE to introduce such reforms to its financial system. In the first stage, activities previously under the control of the HNB had to be spun off into several large banks.

The credit sections of the former state monopoly bank were spun-off into three new commercial banks, the Hungarian Credit Bank (HCB), the National Commercial and Credit Bank (NCCB) and the Budapest Bank (BB). Two other commercial bank charters were granted; joint venture banks and other financial institutions existed.[5] At the time, the National Savings Bank (Országos Takarék Pénztár or OTP) retained its virtual monopoly over household accounts. Furthermore, competition for commercial accounts was not permitted initially. Companies were required to do business with the bank to which they were assigned (in essence, the officers whom they had previously done business with). The portfolios of the newly-created banks and the previous working relationships between bank officers and company clients were inherited legacies of past policies.

From their formation, the three major commercial banks faced little competition. As Székely (1990) reports, they accounted for 87% of deposits and 76% of gross assets of all financial institutions dealing with the companies. Table 1 records the financial situations of HCB, NCCB and BB for 1990 along with three joint venture banks, Inter-Europa Bank, Citibank-Budapest, and Creditanstalt. As the first two columns indicate, the Hungarian banks are much larger than the joint venture banks. Ranked according to total assets in 1990, the National Savings Bank (1), the State Development Bank (2), and the State Foreign Trade Bank (4) would fill out the other top six places. The largest bank with foreign participation had assets of HUF43.4 billion in 1990. The Creditanstalt bank was a newly formed bank in 1990 with just slightly less assets than Citibank-Budapest.

For the three Hungarian commercial banks, pre-tax profit to asset margins range from 5% for BB to 3.6% for HCB. Citibank-Budapest earned the highest such rate 8.0%. Referring to the situation immediately following the reform, Székely (1990) cites "very high pre-tax profits-to-assets (3.2% to 3.8%)" as evidence of a lack of competitiveness. The more recent data indicates that, by this measure, competitiveness has not improved since deregulation. A further comparison of the usual profitability measures, return on assets (ROA) and return on equity (ROE) in the final two columns of Table 1, with U.S. banks corroborates the high profitability of banking in Hungary.

---

[5] For details, see Székely (1990).

By way of comparison, the average ROA for U.S. banks in 1990 was about one-half on one percent (0.5%) and the average ROE was 7.9%.[6] For large U.S. banks having assets in excess of $1 billion (about 75 billion forints), ROA was 0.4% and ROE was 6.9%. For the Hungarian commercial banks, ROA (column 5) is more than four times the U.S. average and more than five times the average for large banks. To compare ROE (column 4), adjustments should be made for inflation. In Hungary, the CPI index increased by 28.19% in 1990 while the same index increased by 5.4% in the U.S.. Therefore, the inflation-adjusted average return on equity in the U.S. was 2.5% for all banks and 1.5% for large banks. From the table, equivalent measures for Hungarian commercial banks range from 9.94% to 18.34%. The joint-venture banks in the table exhibit inflation-adjusted returns from - 1.98% for Creditanstalt to 64.41% for Citibank-Budapest. Relative to U.S. banks then, Hungarian commercial banks are very profitable and, with the exception of the upstart Creditanstalt, joint venture banks are even more profitable.

During the eighties, the Hungarians began to lay the cornerstones for a vibrant financial sector. Commercial banks extending credit according to economic criteria, an integrated and active bond market for company and government issues, and a nascent equity market[7] are the three pillars upon which the fledgling capital market of the nineties must depend for its strength. Indeed, the new Banking Act of 1991 stipulates that domestic financial institutions adhere to the Basel capital adequacy standards by January 1, 1993, which means that financial institutions must achieve a weighted risk-asset reserve ratio of 8%.[8] Nevertheless, the organizational and institutional changes of the eighties were insufficient to anchor the pillars. In the next two sections, we argue that the dual legacies of separation (fragmentation) in capital markets and the weakness of monetary policy still loom heavy on Hungary's transition to a market economy.

---

[6] All figures for U.S. banks are from Goudreau and King (1991).

[7] We have not discussed the development of the Budapest Stock Exchange (BSE) due to space considerations. A fledgling stock exchange with reasonably detailed regulatory legislation is operating in Hungary. According to a recent estimate by Barrons, the BSE handles a volume of transactions equal to about one-fifth of the volume on the Columbian stock exchange. Obviously it does not satisfy the breadth and depth conditions of Calvo and Frenkel.

[8] See article 23 of the New Banking Act in Hungary. Article 98 of the same Act provides exemptions to the Basel rules on a case by case basis but only until December 31, 1994. For details of the Basel agreement on capital adequacy standards, see Siklos(1993).

4.   THE BANKS AS SHAKY PILLARS OF REFORM

Given the financial building blocks that are currently in place in Hungary, what is still missing for meaningful progress toward the creation of a true capital market? To understand the ability of the Hungarian commercial banks to take on the appropriate tasks of credit allocation, we consider three questions. Are the banks weaned from the state (i.e., are they truly independent)? Are they undercapitalized? How substantial is the problem of inherited non-performing loans?[9] Taking first the issue of independence from the state, Table 2 records the direct ownership claim of the state in each of the Hungarian banks and exhibits a striking difference in the dividend policies of the Hungarian commercial banks and the joint-venture banks. While the latter pay no dividends, about one-third of after-tax profit is returned to the owners of the Hungarian banks.

Table 1
Financial Situation of Selected Banks in Hungary, 1990

Name	Assets Ft BN (1)	Ranking by value of assets (2)	Equity as % of Assets (3)	After Tax Profit as % of Equity (4)	After Tax Profit as % of Assets (5)
Hungarian Credit Bank	256.3	3	5.42	39.91	2.18
National Commercial and Credit Bank	191.5	5	6.57	38.15	2.51
Budapest Bank	103.4	6	6.38	46.53	2.96
Inter-Europa Bank	25.0	9	11.2	46.06	5.16
Citibank	15.3	14	6.53	92.60	6.03
Creditanstalt	15.3	15	9.15	26.21	2.39

Source: Pénzügykutató Rt., Heti Világgazdaság and Figyelő (various issues)

As column 3 indicates, the state has a direct ownership claim of between 35% to 50% in the three Hungarian commercial banks. The remaining ownership claims are held

---

[9] Unlike Czechoslovakia, Hungary did not set up a Consolidation Bank where bad loans, also called "permanent loans", of state enterprises were spun off as a device to permit new commercial banks to begin operations with clean balance sheets. See Duchatczek and Schubert(1992), and Aghlevi, Borensztein and van der Willigen (1992).

by state-owned companies and thus indirectly by the state. Consequently, the three Hungarian commercial banks are still owned by the state.

As an immediate consequence of this ownership and the dividend policy of the banks, the government budget receives revenues in addition to taxes from the Hungarian banks. Taking account of direct ownership revenues only, the three commercial banks contributed about HUF2 billion in dividend payments to fiscal revenues in 1990. In addition, these banks paid over HUF8.8 billion in profit tax to the state. The total flow from gross profits of the major commercial banks to the fiscal budget was HUF10.87 billion in 1990 or about 1.7% of fiscal receipts. A major factor in the decline of the fiscal budget deficit from HUF54 billion in 1989 to HUF1.4 billion in 1990 was a substantial increase from HUF21.3 billion (1989) to HUF48.6 billion (1990) in profit-tax and dividend revenues from financial institutions. This category accounted for 7.6% of fiscal receipts in 1990 providing another indicator of the profitability of the financial sector. Consequently, we answer the first question with an emphatic "No" and record the substantial financial support provided by the Hungarian commercial banks to their parent state.

As a benchmark for evaluating the capitalization of the Hungarian banks, we use the target of 8% for equity to assets specified in the BIS Basel Guidelines for Prudential Regulations. As Table 1 indicates, all three of the Hungarian banks fall short of this figure since equity as a percentage of assets is 5.42% for HCB, 6.38 for BB, and 6.57% for NCCB. The new banking law in Hungary aims to achieve the BIS target in five years. Interestingly, Citibank-Budapest also falls short of the 8% recommendation. For further comparison, the average equity to asset ratio is 9.96% for all U.S. banks but only 5.7% for large U.S. banks. For two of the three Hungarian banks, the equity to asset ratio exceeds the average for large U.S. banks. Consequently, the answer to the question posed is a firm "Yes," Hungarian banks (like some of their American counterparts) are undercapitalized.

Calvo and Frenkel(1991) argue that the balance sheets of banks must be "cleaned-up" without excessive fiscal budgetary costs. To evaluate the feasibility of this suggestion, we examine the magnitude of the required clean-up. In 1987, an estimated 70 to 80 billion forints of loans in the three Hungarian banks were considered to be risky. Reserves held against risky loans totaled less than HUF10 billion. Auditors (Price Waterhouse, Arthur Anderson, Ernst Young Bonitas) of the banks balance sheets in 1989 estimated that reserves of between HUF40 and HUF50 billion should be held against risky loans if Western standards were applied. By the fall of 1990, a total of HUF36.5 billion loans in the portfolios of the three Hungarian commercial banks were actually non-performing amounting to 6.62% of total gross assets. As Table 2 indicates, non-performing loans as a percentage of equity ranged from 160.9% for BB to 77.8% for NCCB.

Table 2

Non-performing Loans of Selected Banks in Hungary, 1990

Name	Non-performing Loans as % of Equity (1)	Dividends as % of After Tax Profit (2)	State Owned Share in % (3)	Foreign Share in % (4)
Hungarian Credit Bank	115.1	35.6	49.3	0.0
National Commercial and Credit Bank	77.8	38.5	34.9	0.0
Budapest Bank	160.9	31.4	41.7	0.0
Inter-Europa Bank	n.a.	0.0	0.0	22.5
Citibank	n.a.	0.0	0.0	80.0
Creditanstalt	n.a.	0.0	0.0	75.0

Source: Pénzügykutató Rt., Heti Világgazdaság and Figyelő (various issues)

For the sake of comparison sake, non-current commercial loans as a percent of total commercial and industrial loans in U.S. banks stood at 4.75% in September 1991.[10] Using the average equity to asset ratio of 9.96% and a loan-to-asset ratio of 75%, non-current loans as a percent of equity would average about 35% for all U.S. banks. The highest rate by region recorded for non-current commercial loans in the U.S. in September 1991 is 5.89% in the Northeast. Using the equity/asset ratio for big banks of 5.7%, non-current loans as a percent of equity for large Northeastern banks would average about 77.6%. Taking again the worst regional case in the U.S., the percent of non-current real estate loans is 8.39 in the Northeast. Using the large bank equity-to-asset ratio, the resulting percentage on equity would be 110.3%. If the definition of non-current loans in the U.S. is similar to that of non-performing loans in Hungary, the Hungarian commercial banks look again like troubled large U.S. banks.

How much of the non-performing loan problem is due to the inherited portfolios of the three banks? When the banks were created non-performing loans in value and as a percent of the portfolio were respectively, HUF5 billion and 3% for

---

[10] The source for this information is the FDIC Quarterly Banking Profile - Third Quarter 1991. Non-current loans are defined as loans that are past due 90 days or more or in non-accrual status.

HCB, HUF2.5 billion and 2% for NCCB, and HUF1.9 billion and 2% for BB. This total of HUF9.4 billion was augmented by HUF4.7 billion of loans to coal mines with government guarantees by BB after 1987. Consequently, of the total of HUF36.5 billion of non-performing loans in the fall of 1990, only HUF14.1 were on the books or pending in 1987. The increase in non-performing loans totaled HUF22.4 billion for the three banks by 1990. Deteriorating economic conditions in the intervening years most likely turned some existing loans into non-performing ones. However, the combination of high profit margins affording discretionary behavior and "old-boy" linkages between loan officers and "clients" of long-standing also resulted in "business as usual" for many of the less-efficient companies. Some of the non-performing loans were probably new loans in which good money was chasing after bad money. Presently, commercial customers are no longer tied to an individual bank so that the potential for competition over clients exists. However, the balance sheets of the banks continue to be an impediment to their functioning as true commercial banks and to the prospects for privatization.

Calvo and Frenkel (1991) argue that cleaning up the balance sheets of banks must be accomplished without excessive fiscal budgetary costs and without incentive problems. The policy options considered in the literature amount to either debt forgiveness or debt for debt swaps. Socializing the debt by swapping government debt in the form of T-Bills for bad debt (non-performing loans) is favored by Brainard (1991) as the solution for cleaning up bank balance sheets. This would have the advantage of providing a fresh flow of real capital due to the spread of T-Bill rates over inflation. Obviously, the moral hazard problem must be faced if either of these two policies are adopted.

Our analysis of Hungarian banks suggests a third policy alternative for cleaning up the banks' balance sheets that may meet, more closely, the criteria set out by Calvo and Frenkel(1991). Deposit the taxes and dividends paid to the state into a reserve fund to be held against non-performing loans. The combined tax and dividend flows in 1990 amounted to about 30% of the accumulated value of non-performing loans on the books of the three commercial banks at that time. If current flows were maintained and the value of non-performing loans were not increased, such a fund would accrue a sum equal in value to the total accumulation of outstanding non-performing loans in slightly more than three years. To discourage the practice of making additional bad loans, the state could assess a penalty on any new loans that become non-performing and place these monies in the reserve fund as well.

In 1990, the cost to the fiscal budget of such a scheme would have amounted to 1.7% of receipts in 1990. Furthermore, the reserve fund could be held in government securities so that the final outcome would be equivalent to a debt for debt swap and serve to recapitalize the banks. The only difference would be the gradual accumulation of current taxes paid on profit and current dividends. Thus, the balance sheet changes are made over a period of time reducing the impact on the fiscal budget in any one year and the moral hazard problem of appearing to reward banks that make bad loans is avoided. In addition, the penalty clause would encourage banks to examine carefully the creditworthiness of new borrowers. At a time when equity margins need rebuilding and non-performing loans need to be covered, the Hungarian commercial banks can ill afford to continue to support financially the fiscal budget. Our modest proposal stems this flow and uses the proceeds to begin to build a stronger financial base for the banks so that they may assume their proper role in the capital market.

5.   MONETARY POLICY AND CENTRAL BANK INDEPENDENCE: THE LEGACY

5.1   The New Hungarian National Bank

The HNB was made independent of government in the sense that it was no longer committed to finance deficits automatically as before under central planning. Moreover, the central bank is now endowed with the goal of protecting the internal and external value of the domestic currency (the forint). Nevertheless, the Act governing the operations of the HNB stipulates that it can finance up to 3% of government revenues (Balassa (1992), pp.62-3). Finally, and most importantly, it is expected that the HNB will asssist the central government in accomplishing its national economic objectives. Taken together these basic rules are not significantly different from those of many western industrialized countries. But, unlike the countries the HNB statutes are modelled after, the Hungarian central bank oversees a banking system that is saddled with some of the legacies of the past at the same time as it promotes a full range of government financial instruments in order to assist in the development of a modern capital market. As argued below, this leads to a fundamental conflict in monetary policy and produces a situation whereby the HNB may be legally independent but is not economically independent of government.[11]

5.2   Disintermediation and the Birth of T-Bills

As a legacy of the old system, persistent shortages of materials led good and bad companies alike to maintain high levels of material inventories. However, the market for short-term financing was severely segmented in Hungary. Less than 50% of the companies used short-term bank credit and the ones that did tended to be inefficient loss-making companies. As Table 3 indicates, inter-enterprise trade credit was an important source of short term credit during the early eighties.[12] From 1982

---

[11] The distinction between economic and legal independence was suggested by Grilli, Masciandro, and Tabellini (1990). See also Johnson and Siklos (this volume).

[12] See Ábel and Siklos(1992) for a fuller description of the impact of trade credit on Hungarian monetary policy in the transition period.

to 1987, changes in trade credit are mirrored in changes in the fiscal deficit as a percent of GDP. When fiscal liquidity was tightened, trade credit increased. As a consequence, good and bad companies were linked together by increasing (and, most likely, involuntary) extensions of inter-enterprise credit at the beginning of the eighties.[13]

Table 3
Inter-enterprise Trade Credit

Year	Inter-enterprise Trade Credit as % of Company Balances in Liquid Deposit Accounts	Inter-enterprise Trade Credit as % of Short Term Credit
1982	27.3	14.0
1983	72.3	29.5
1984	75.1	29.1
1985	40.2	19.0
1986	17.5	7.6
1987	16.1	7.6
1988	65.4	27.7
1989	88.8	34.6

Source: Pénzügykutató Rt. (Heti Világgazdaság, December 22, 1990, p.88.)

The extension of inter-enterprise trade credit rose dramatically in the late eighties. When the HNB attempted to tighten monetary policy and restrict credit in 1988 and 1989, the credit queue lengthened as companies turned to trade credit. In such a situation, what may appear to be restrictive monetary policy by the usual aggregate measures (e.g. rate of growth of M2) is counterbalanced by (involuntary) inter-enterprise credit extension. The growing use of inter-enterprise trade credit for short-term financing in Hungary places a serious obstacle in the path of authorities wishing to use monetary policy as a stabilization instrument during the transition.

---

[13] In 1986, Hungary adopted a modern bankruptcy law. From its inception until 1990, only ten requests for initiation of bankruptcy proceedings were submitted by creditors in Hungary. Mitchell (1991) provides several explanations for such creditor passivity. Inter-enterprise credit linkages between good and bad companies provide a further rational for the relatively few bankruptcies. The financial repercussions of one bankruptcy will reverberate throughout the economy and, most likely, bring down good companies with bad ones.

The bond market was also altered significantly in the late eighties by the introduction of a new instrument, the treasury bill (T-Bill), in 1988. The T-Bill gained immediate popularity in <u>household</u> portfolios because of its liquidity and competitive rates (more return at less risk).[14] The Ministry of Finance arranged separate issues having low face value designed especially for households. In investors' portfolios, good bonds (T-Bills) drove out bad ones (company bonds) leading to the collapse of the commercial bond market (as we already noted in a previous section). The existence of these short-term government securities is important for monetary policy as it affords the possibility of open market operations. The direct participation by households in this market differentiates it from the T-Bill market in the U.S. for example.

The difficulty, however, is that T-Bills are, by their nature, short-term instruments while the emerging private sector is starved for long-term financing. The resulting mismatch, exacerbated by contining expectations of high inflation, further restricts the effectiveness of monetary policy. Moreover, the imposition of relatively high reserve requirements (16% of deposits on a daily basis) while the rest of the industrialized world is removing such requirements (see Siklos (1993)), as well as the essentially default risk-free government financial instruments, mean that the already shaky banking sector will attempt to clean up its balance sheet by skewing its portfolio toward holding T-Bills in particular and will shy away from commercial lending.[15] This raises the spectre of future bail-outs of commercial concerns by the HNB under government pressure, a possibility not excluded from the current legislation governing the HNB. Therefore, while legal independence may have been granted to the central bank, it is far from having secured economic independence from the government.

6.   CONCLUSION: LESSONS FROM HUNGARY'S QUEST

Organizational change and new legislation, though necessary conditions for a meaningful transformation, are not sufficient. The legacies of the past system must be recognized and the impediments they present to forward motion must be identified. At the various stages of the transition, policies must deal realistically with these initial conditions. Segmentation in capital markets and credit linkages between companies are legacies found in all the transforming countries. The call to "clean up" the balance sheets of banks and companies is valid. However, the policy chosen must recognize the implications of doing so in the existing environment. In a fledgling segmented

---

[14]   Székely (1990) provides details about the T-Bill market.

[15]   This situation is further hindered by the new Banking Act's stipulation that in making loans banks follow the Basel banking supervision committee's guidelines. Such a requirement effectvely excludes much commercial activity at the present time.

capital market where the liquidity position of companies is linked by the predominance of trade credit, bankruptcies can quickly snowball through the system so that even well-meaning legislation designed to begin this process is likely to be insufficient to induce meaningful change.

The financial legacies of the old system result in a few large undercapitalized commercial banks, currently earning high profit margins but saddled with non-performing loans against which they are not holding sufficient reserves. The government retains significant direct and indirect (through the state-owned companies' shares) ownership in these banks. To the extent that the banks pay out a significant portion of after-tax profit to shareholders in addition to paying a tax on profits to the state, the banks remain an important source of revenue for the fiscal budget. To clean up the banks' balance sheets, we propose a reversal of this flow to build up the equity of the commercial banks. The taxes and dividends due to the state should be used to purchase T-Bills to cover non-performing loans. Replacing bad debt with T-Bills in the portfolios of the commercial banks has the added advantage of laying strong foundations for open market operations and effective monetary policy.

The de jure separation of monetary and fiscal policy is also necessary but not sufficient to secure the desired results. If the fiscal authorities respond to the pressure to maintain jobs by continuing to bail out inefficient companies, tight monetary policy will be countervailed. To the extent that the household sector holds T-Bills, open market operations have a significant direct effect on household liquidity. However, if the banking system is segmented so that the vast majority of household deposits are held in the national savings bank, monetary policy will have a weakened impact on the deposits of the commercial banks. Thus, monetary policy may be a crippled instrument of stabilization during the transition.

REFERENCES

Ábel, I., and P.L. Siklos, " Constraints on Enterprise Liquidity and Its Impact on the Monetary Sector in Former Centrally Planned Economies", *Comparative Economic Studies* (December 1992, forthcoming).

Ábel I. and I. Székely, "Monetary Policy and Separated Monetary Circuits in a Modified CPE (The Case of Hungary)", *Acta Oeconomica*, 44(3-4, 1992): 393-428.

Aghlevi, B.B., E. Borensztein, and T. van der Willigen, " Stabilization and Structural Reform in Czechoslovakia: An Assessment of the First Stage of the Reform", IMF working paper 92/2, January 1992.

Balassa, A., "The Transformation and Deevelopment of the Hungarian Banking System", in D.M. Kemme and A. Rudka (Eds.), Monetary and Banking reform in Postcommunist Economies" (New York: Institute for East-West Security Studies, 1992), pp. 6-42.

Blanchard, O., R. Dornbusch, P. Krugman, R. Layard, and L. Summers, " Reform in Eastern Europe and the Soviet Union", *UN-Wider Report*, 1990.

Brainard L. "Strategies for Economic Transformation in Central and Eastern Europe: Role of Financial Market Reform", in Blommestein, H. and M. Marrese (eds.) Transformation of *Planned Economies: Property Rights Reform and Macroeconomic Stability*, Paris: OECD, 1991, pp. 95-104.

Calvo, G. A. and J. A. Frenkel, "Obstacles to Transforming Centrally-Planned Economies: The Role of Capital Markets", NBER Working Paper No. 3776, 1991.

Duchatczek, W. and A. Schubert, "Monetary Policy Issues in Selected East European Economies", SUERF Papers on Monetary and Financial Systems no. 11, Tilburg, 1992.

Goudreau, R.E., and B.F. King, "Profitability: Hampered Again by Large Banks' Loan Problems", *Economic Review, Federal Bank of Atlanta*, Volume 76, Number 4 (July/August) 1991, pp. 39-54.

Grilli, V., d. Masciandro, and G. Tabellini, "Political and Monetary Institutions and Public Financial Policies in the Industrial Countries", *Economic Policy*, 13: 342-392.

Johnson, D. R., and P.L. Siklos, " Political Effects on Central Bank Behaviour: Some International Evidence", this volume.

Kornai J., "The Hungarian Reform Process: Visions, Hopes, and Reality", *Journal of Economic Literature*, December 1986, pp. 1687-1737.

Lane, T. D., Household Demand for Money in Poland: Theory and Evidence", IMF working paper 92/6, January 1992.

Mitchell, J., "The Link Between Financial Institutions and Bankruptcy: Implications for Reform" paper presented at *Moving to a Market Economy*, Jerome Levy Economics Institute, October 1991.

Siklos, P. L., *Money, Banking, and Financial Markets: Canada in the Global Environment*, (Scarborough, Ont: McGraw-Hill Ryerson Ltd., 1993).

Székely I., "The Reform of the Hungarian Financial System", *European Economy*, No. 43. March 1990, pp. 107-124.

Tardos, M., "How to Create Markets in Eastern Europe: The Hungarian Case", in Brada J. C., E. A. Hewett and T. A. Wolf (eds) *Economic Adjustment and Reform in Eastern Europe and the Soviet Union, Essays in Honor of Franklyn D. Holzman*, Durham: Duke University Press, 1988, pp.259-284.

Abel, I. 367-82
Adenauer, K. (Chancellor) 247
Alesina, A. 98, 130, 132, 171, 190, 244, 303
Argentina 46, 72, 73, 82, 91-2, 101
Australia 139
Austral plan 83, 86, 92
Austria 8, 145, 179n
Autoregressive conditional heteroskedasticity (ARCH) 4n, 54n, 54-5, 221
Autoregressive Moving Average (ARMA) 301ff

Bade, R. 99, 132, 171, 192, 303n
Banaian, K. 8, 178n, 304n
Bank of Canada 351ff
Barro, R.J. 97, 159, 240, 357n
Beck, N. 131, 193-218, 265
Belgium 107, 176
Bonin, J.P. 367-82
Bordo, M.D. 3n, 4, 140n, 280-321
Brazil 71, 72, 88
Bretton Woods 4, 99, 140-41, 213, 235, 269, 287
Bundesbank 12, 170, 192, 204, 208, 219-45, 247-77
Bundesrat 248ff
Bundestag 247ff
Burdekin, R.C.K. 8n, 8, 45-72, 61n, 130, 170, 184, 293

Calvo, G. 156, 356, 364, 365, 366
Canada 4, 12, 21, 28, 98, 111, 137, 340
Canzoneri, M. 159, 346n
Capie, F.H. 95-131, 100, 130, 173
Central Bank Independence 6-12, 96, 135-7, 159, 195-96, 239-42, 271-74, 351-33, 360ff
Chile 88-9, 101
Cointegration 294ff
Continentals 323ff
Continental Congress 324ff

Convergence 5
Convertibility 102, 213, 283, 295
Coyne, J. 351ff
Coyne-Rasminsky directive 349, 356-60
Credibility 7-8, 45-6, 75, 275
Crow, J. 358
Cruzado plan 72, 90, 92
Cukierman, A. 8, 73-94, 83n, 101, 132, 171, 358
Currency Unions 12-16
Czechoslovakia 373n

Davidson, L.S. 7n
Dollarization 72
Dornbusch, R. 2n, 4, 6

Eichengreen, B. 3, 25, 197n
Erhard, L. 257
Error correction 221, 298ff
Eschweiler, B. 280-321
European Central Bank (ECB) 132, 165-91, 237, 268-270
European Community (EC) 25, 196, 271
European Monetary System (EMS) 4, 27, 37, 44, 72, 84, 135, 139, 178, 240
European Monetary Union 12-16, 184, 205, 215
Exchange Rate 27
    fluctuations 303-10
    pegging 45-72
    real 27
    regimes 3-6
    rules 82-4
Exchange Volatility 4, 328-32
Exchange Rate Mechanism (ERM) 5, 44, 52

Federal Open Market Committee (FOMC) 202
Federal Reserve 178, 186, 187
France 30, 35-6, 102

Frankel, J. 4
Fratianni, M. 7n, 51, 131, 165-91, 167, 265

Germany 8, 14, 27, 35-6, 59, 101, 140, 146, 173, 190, 194, 214-45, 247-77
German unification 223-39, 273
German political system 253-56, 267-71
Giovannini, A. 4n, 51, 280
Gold standard 71, 101, 279, 283-90
Gordon, D.B. 97, 160, 240, 357n
Grilli, V. 8, 160, 195, 283n, 303n, 377n

Havrilesky, T. 196-7
Hendry, D.F. 223
Hibbs, D. 192, 246
Hochreiter, E. 135n
Holtfrerich, C.-L. 13, 290, 295n
H-spread 102-10
Huang, H. 165-91
Hungary 367-82

Inflation 11, 100, 103-10, 142, 193
Inflation tax 101
Italy 5, 27, 56, 107, 141, 204
Inter-enterprise trade credit 374
Israel 74

Japan 4, 29, 100, 146, 176, 191
Johnson, D.R. 133-63, 183n, 299, 377n

Keynes, J.M. 351, 353, 354
Kiguel, M.A. 72, 73-94
Kohl, H. (Chancellor) 255
Kydland, F.E. 98, 158, 241, 279, 298

Laney, L. 8n, 178n, 172, 298, 304n
Laviatan, N. 11, 73-94
Lohmann, S. 11, 76n, 247-277
Lucas, R.E. 169, 336, 351

Maastrich Treaty 2, 5, 165, 178, 184n, 267-68
Masciandaro, D. 8, 135n, 172, 194, 303n, 377n
Masson, P.R. 23-43
Maxfield, S. 248
McKinnon, R.I. 28
Meltzer, A.H. 171, 356n
Mexico 46, 73
Mills, T.C. 95-131, 112, 132
Mitchell, B.R. 100
Monetary Reforms 1-3
Mundell, R. 3, 24

National Bank of Hungary 367ff
Netherlands 56, 60, 147, 176
New Economic Mechanism (NEM) 371ff
New England (colonial times) 333-34
New Zealand 11, 31, 100, 113, 133, 179n, 180, 189, 194
Nordaus, W.D. 131, 159, 190, 244
Norway, 151

Optimal Currency Areas 23-43
Organization for Economic Cooperation and Development (OECD) 141, 190

Parkin, M. 99, 132, 171, 192, 303n
Peru 86-7
Pöhl, K.O. 235, 256
Political business cycles 7n, 130, 171, 189-91, 243-44
Prescott, E.C. 98, 158, 240, 298
Privatization 361
Purchasing Power Parity (PPP) 293

Rasminsky, L. 351ff
Rational Expectations 46
Reaction functions 134, 136-7, 283ff
Reichsbank 283-98
Rogoff, K. 243, 260, 268, 278, 300
Rolnick, A.J. 323-49
Rymes, T.K. 351-66

Seigniorage 277-8, 464, 488-98
Siklos, P.L. 1-21, 133-63, 183n, 190,
    300, 367-82
Smith, B.D. 323-349
Soviet Union (former) 323
Strom, K. 143
Sweden 108, 146
Switzerland 8, 145n, 178, 197

Tabellini, G. 8, 135n, 179n, 193,
    241, 303n, 304, 377n
Taylor, M.P. 23-43
Tietmeyer, H. 235
Time inconsistency 11, 99, 160, 240-
    42, 352

Unemployment 11, 141
United Kingdom 5, 32, 56, 102, 146,
    249
Unit root 224ff, 298
United States 4, 13, 24, 29, 100, 101,
    191, 250
United States monetary union 323-49

Végh, C.A. 2n, 6
Vector autoregression (VAR) 139
Velocity of circulation 224
Virginia 335-37
Volcker, P. 4, 6
von Hagen, J. 7n, 52, 138, 167, 171,
    196n, 219-45, 265

Wallace, N. 324n
Waller, C. 167, 196n, 241, 245
Walsh, C. 243
Weber, W.E. 343-99
Weimar Republic 290
Westbrook, J.R. 45-72, 61n
Willett, T.D. 8, 35n, 45-72, 61n, 130,
    132, 179n, 194, 304n
Wohar, M. 7n
Wood, G.E. 95-131, 100, 132, 173
Woolley, J. 11, 203n